The Global Eighteenth Century

THE JOHNS HOPKINS UNIVERSITY PRESS

The Global Eighteenth Century

Edited by Felicity A. Nussbaum

The Johns Hopkins University Press
Baltimore and London

The Johns Hopkins University Press
2715 North Charles Street
Baltimore, Maryland 21218-4363
www.press.jhu.edu

Library of Congress Cataloging-in-Publication Data

The global eighteenth century / edited by Felicity A. Nussbaum.
    p.   cm.
Includes bibliographical references and index.
    ISBN 0-8018-6865-3 (alk. paper)
    1. Imperialism—History—18th century.   2. Europe—Colonies—
History—18th century.   3. Slavery.   I. Nussbaum, Felicity.
    D292 .G56   2003
    909.7—dc21   2002012550

A catalog record for this book is available from the British Library.

For John

Contents

Illustrations

Acknowledgments

This collection was inspired by a yearlong series of conferences sponsored by the Seventeenth- and Eighteenth-Century Studies Center and the William Andrews Clark Memorial Library. Peter Reill, Director of Clark/UCLA Center, offered enthusiastic support from the beginning for the seminars on "The Global Eighteenth Century." He has provided guidance and encouragement at every turn. Among the Clark conferences in the series was "Crossings: Racial and Sexual Intermixture," which I happily co-chaired with Sara Melzer. Bruce Whiteman, librarian of the Clark Library, helpfully brought the resources of the library to bear on the topic, including his mounting an exhibit called "The Margins of the World: The Seventeenth- and Eighteenth-Century View." The superb staff of the Clark/UCLA Center—especially Nancy Connolly, Marina Romani, Kathy Sanchez, Candis Snoddy, and Elizabeth Spellman—has been unfailingly patient and knowledgeable.

I particularly appreciate the stimulating suggestions that Ali Behdad, Laura Brown, Harriet Guest, Jean Howard, and William B. Warner contributed after reading portions of the typescript. Many other colleagues willingly offered their advice and loyal friendship, including Donna Guy, Carole Fabricant, Lynn Hunt, Margaret Jacob, and Alice Wexler. Readers solicited by the Johns Hopkins University Press have helped me to shape the book and clarify my arguments.

My only regret is that all of the excellent talks given in the seminars could not be included in this volume. I gratefully acknowledge my colleagues at the University of California at Los Angeles in the English Department and beyond, who are a constant source of challenge and support, especially Joseph Bristow, Helen Deutsch, Jayne Lewis, Françoise Lionnet, Anne Mellor, Max Novak, and Jenny Sharpe. Thomas Wortham, chair of the department of English, granted release time and research support for work on this project, and I value his friendship and skillful leadership. My graduate assistants Carol Wald, Chris Loar, Anne Sheehan, and Johanna Schwartz made the editing process move along more easily; Linda Holmes and Juan Tan provided good-humored computer guidance.

An earlier version of Vincent Carretta's chapter appeared as "Olaudah Equiano or Gustavus Vassa? New Light on an Eighteenth-Century Question of Identity" in *Slavery and Abolition* 20, no. 3 (1999): 96–105 by permission of Frank Cass Publishers. Laura Brown's chapter is reprinted from her *Fables of Modernity: Literature and Culture in the English Eighteenth Century* (Cornell University Press, 2001), and Anna Neill's chapter is reprinted from her book *British Discovery Literature and the Rise of Global Commerce* (Palgrave, 2002), both with the permission of the publishers.

As always, my writing has meaning for me within the sustaining context of my family near and far, especially my children, Marc and Nicole Wilett. Their *joie de vivre* delights me, and they enhance my life beyond measure. My parents, Janet and Leo Nussbaum, are a constant source of inspiration and pleasure, as are my siblings Margaret Cooley and Lu Nussbaum and their families. Most especially I thank John Agnew, who from the first generously shared his formidable knowledge and understanding of things local and global, and who has more recently become my cherished fellow traveler.

The Global Eighteenth Century

Felicity A. Nussbaum

Though contemporary scholars generally accept the idea of a *long* eighteenth century, we have only begun to formulate methods of inquiry that are especially applicable to a *widened* eighteenth century. The chapters in this volume aim to contribute to something we might call "critical global studies." They resituate eighteenth-century studies within a spatially and conceptually expanded paradigm, though inevitably Europe remains central to such discussions. The authors analyze the European encounter with other populations throughout the world and offer ways to think critically about the imperative of that imperial project. At the same time, they query the boundaries of national histories and literatures that have limited our understandings to reconsider sexual and racial intermingling, religious encounters, the exchange of goods and diseases, indigenous knowledge, and the real and imagined mapping of the earth's domain. The point of gathering these essays, and of broadening scholarly perspectives beyond Europe, is not so much to write a new, grander narrative of a wider eighteenth-century world as to spark more nuanced accounts of the relations among freshly juxtaposed regions, disciplines, and methodologies. Interpreting the eighteenth century in this global way is a matter of scale, scope, and perspective rather than an attempt to replicate Enlightenment's universalism.

These chapters in an evolving field also add a crucial historical element to the concept of the global. During much of the eighteenth century, the European vision of the world was characterized as constituting distinct quadrants of the world. Its four corners were of course fictitious, an act of the colonial imagination, as were many of the conventional assumptions about them, though by the eighteenth century it was well recognized that the globe could be circumnavigated. These "corners" of the earth were frequently represented iconographically as female figures in ornamental frescoes that decorated the four corners of a drawing room or bedroom (e.g., Charles LeBrun's paintings in the rooms at Versailles or Tiepolo's frescoes in Würzburg), or as naked, veiled, or feathered figures in the cartouches of eighteenth-century maps. In a characteristic figuration America was represented as barebreasted, with a feathered headdress, carrying arrows and a bow; Asia bore incense and was veiled against a backdrop of desert and camel, or the harem; Africa, naked except for an elephant headdress, sat on a lion, and was flanked by a cornucopia signifying its natural riches; and Europe was represented as a muse surrounded by arts and letters as well as the signs of military victory. In compendious "coffee table" books such as George Henry Millar's *New and Universal System of Geography: Being a Complete Modern History and Description of the Whole World* (1782), these traditional female images were supplemented by pictures of the measuring instruments of trade, commerce, and the new sciences. By the later eighteenth century, Millar's book and others like it claimed to formulate a comprehensive worldwide knowledge. As Mary Louise Pratt suggests, "travel writing and enlightenment natural history catalyzed each other to produce a Eurocentered form of global or . . . 'planetary' consciousness."[1] The scopic nature of that knowledge, given the contending iconographic representations employed, was itself problematic since it was inevitably linked to an Enlightenment impulse to master and classify the objects of its scrutiny. The contributors to this volume contest this sort of global consciousness.

Defining the global as "universal" implies a belief in unchanging truths and tenets and in a stable human nature that is consistent across time and culture. Such a way of regarding the world elides differences between Hindus and Iroquois, or Chinese and Arabs, to claim the fraternity of the human race.[2] In this volume the "global" means focusing on the particular (though not the provincial) more than the universal, and paying attention to "the *movement* of ideas across borders and over time," as geographers David Livingstone and Charles W. J. Withers characterize the Enlightenment.[3] The global includes, then, tracing worldwide crossings—the circuits of commerce, cargo, and peoples as they actually occurred in the past, and as they are represented then and now. The global applies here to the world itself, to the actual territory of the earth, rather than to the virtual circuitry of identities, images, commodities, and information common to contemporary globalization. In fact, contemporary terms that refer to world connections and divisions often offer anachronistic tools for understanding globality's earlier history.[4] For example, the common modern division between West and East, between Renaissance Italy and the Ottoman empire, was not a separation immediately recognizable to people living in the eighteenth century. When scholars attend closely to the maps of earlier periods, as Jerry Brotton has shown, they will find that "the distinction between a Europeanized 'west' and an orientalized 'east' is a retrospective divide which makes little sense when trying to trace the cultural exchanges which came to define the shape of the early modern world."[5] These and other understandings of the eighteenth century and its representation are now appropriately being reassessed. The goal here is not to achieve a prehistory of European modernity but instead a genealogical understanding on a global scope in order to address its homogenizing effects and its specific manifestations in particular geographical locales.

The term *global* may easily be confused with *globalization,* itself an ambiguous term; and while I do wish to invoke aspects of recent developments in the burgeoning field of globalization studies, I mean to suggest that their application to the eighteenth century may require a rather different approach. "Critical global studies" goes beyond received notions in its attempt to problematize ahistorical discussions of globalization, to contextualize contemporary debates about globalism, and thus to provide genealogical clues to our current understandings. In particular, a historically located critical global studies questions a narrative that leads inexorably from the eighteenth century to modernity and its conjunctions with globalization, a story of progress or disintegration—and instead reassesses the problematic nature of that heritage. Our reading of the Enlightenment allows us to see in part that globalization, though not uniformly objectionable, is less an overcoming of Enlightenment's tyrannies than its troubling fulfillment.

Humanists and social scientists continue to engage in vigorous debates about where and when the global—and now globalization—began, and the extent to which those occasions coincide with the inaugural moments of modernity or postmodernity. The result is a fertile, complex, and confusing variety of positions, and eighteenth-century studies has something substantial to contribute to these debates. Global systems—if we confine the term to mean principally close and active economic and cultural linkages across the world rather than virtual networks of instantaneous communication and trade—is thoroughly embedded in history, beginning perhaps as early as 1492, though even that early date would seem to be "symptomatic of a North American form of historical interpolation."[6] For example, such limited understandings obfuscate the way that much of the globe continues to live within social formations characterized by orality, myth, and mystery rather than linearity and progress. Whether one construes these ways of knowing as premodern—residual aspects of earlier times—or as thoroughly implicated within the modern has been subject to stimulating debate.

In fact, the very category of modernity in non-European countries is often arguably significantly different from Western concepts of it. Janet Abu-Lughod and others have contended that global networks (including political interdependencies, systems of credit and debt, as well as groups capable of eluding state regulations in pursuit of capital) existed as early as the thirteenth century, and that these reticulations were not European in origin.[7] World systems theory has afforded a more recent, if still limited, way of regarding the earth and its oceans as intensely dependent upon one another. This system, according to Immanuel Wallerstein, is primarily a European world economy that is bolstered by other connections.[8] Yet the defining elements of early globalization such as state sovereignty, nation-based citizenship, and economic institutions were not fully congealed even in Europe in the eighteenth century.[9] Although eighteenth-century global relations were beginning to be organized in these ways, it was not until the late twentieth century that contemporary information technology brought a radical transformation from previous forms of communication.

If *global* is not to be understood in a conventional way, then neither is it the same as *globalization*—a term often applied to our fast-paced economy, which is propelled by corporate interests that transcend national boundaries, conducted through technology networks, and characterized by its elusive nature. Globalization offers both an extension of the global and a rupture from it. Within a contemporary globalized economy, the core of every region's economy is closely linked, deeply dependent, and unevenly empowered in a world market that was emergent in the eighteenth century but not yet dominant and pervasive.[10] Economic and technological effects of globalization intermingle with ancient traditions to reach into the most remote regions of the world. For example, in the caves and mountains of Afghanistan, a sophisticated venture capitalist and his wide-reaching network employed at once traditional practices of monetary exchange and modern multinational banking techniques in order to disrupt global economic networks. Such activities are a reminder that we may at the very least need new methods of analysis to understand the future of globalization.

Critical to deciding its history—that is, when did globalization occur?—is determining whether the establishment of the current hierarchies of world power coincided with the Enlightenment—and if not, where and when modernity begins. Several conflicting paradigms emerge. Many contend that modernity is inextricably associated with European colonialism and its attempt to spread concepts of civilization, progress, and technology.[11] Walter Mignolo, believing that modernity and coloniality are "two sides of the same coin," argues convincingly that the pernicious aspects of modernity date from as early as the fifteenth-century Spanish and Portuguese empires in the Americas. The Enlightenment, then, was "the second phase of modernity" rather than the historical moment of its origins, and Europe is displaced as the world center that perceives itself to be at the core but is actually "not an *independent,* autopoetic, self-referential system."[12] I suggest, then, along with other recent thinkers, that a particular formation of modernity, continuous with but not identical to later modernity (like the early modern global, akin to later forms but still distinct from contemporary globalization) is located in the earlier period.[13] Critical global studies helps us to understand that the unmodified term "globalization"—like "modernity"—is inadequate in reflecting its many historical meanings, and imprecise in conveying the complexities of varied social, economic, and cultural conditions in their specific geographical locations.

For others who argue that modernity is inextricably linked to the later eighteenth century's nascent colonialism, industrialism, and the nation-state rather than to earlier centuries, modernity would seem to give birth to a new kind of global society to which the eighteenth century was inexorably leading. Edward Said's influential and controversial study *Orientalism* contends that the West's construction of an exotic, inscrutable, and mystical East formed modern global divisions, and that it corresponded with the emergence of colonialism. Similarly Ranajit Guha believes that the Enlightenment ushered in modernity at the same time that England began to dominate India and that, like colonization, decolonization occurs within the modern condition.[14] In these renderings of modernity, Europe's curiosity about the larger world erupted because of commercial and imperial self-interest. These and other narratives may give scholars pause to ask how critical global studies can avoid becoming complicit with the nefarious aspects of globalization while also resisting a thoroughgoing condemnation of its more attractive effects. Globalization, with its instant communication, computer simulation, encrypted video games, and quick replay, facilitates networks of violence as well as economic exploitation. Yet in spite of its many destructive consequences, globalization may actually empower the previously disempowered, especially if the political, economic, cultural, and subjective are examined as distinct categories of analyses. The rapid distribution of information, increased speed of transit, and access to the world's goods may sometimes seem salutary, while other effects prove unmistakably deleterious, such as increasingly unequal relations of power that encourage multinational worldwide assembly lines or designate entire continents as irrelevant to the world's economy. Critical global studies, reflecting that "progress" is not universally advantageous at all times and around the world, makes clear that the concept of modernity involves highly contested origins and meanings; it does not reject modernity's terms but rather makes them a question worthy of ongoing investigation.

In short, while some critics have argued that the eighteenth century inaugurates the first stage of modernity, others find that its advancement to increased industrialization and colonialism is more characteristic of a second or third stage. In any of these narratives, then, is globalization emergent in the earliest world systems, or is its arrival contemporaneous with eighteenth-century modernity or even with a later postmodernity? There is a great deal at stake in the answers to these questions. In particular, postmodern thinkers, Marxist theorists, and, more recently, feminists and historians of race, have significantly complicated our understanding of the genealogy of human difference. For some, belief in a continuous process over many centuries is necessary in order to justify seeking the prehistory of current globalization. For others, the radical difference of contemporary globalization instead closely parallels postmodernity's fracturing of history.

Manuel Castells, for example, finds that globalization entails a sharp break from an industrial revolution that had earlier transformed mid-eighteenth-century Europe. In a new globalized economy, he writes, "The core activities of production, consumption, and circulation, as well as their components (capital, labor, raw materials, management information, technology markets) are organized on a global scale, either directly or through a network of linkages between economic agents. It is informational *and* global because, under the new historical conditions [pertaining in the late twentieth century], productivity is generated through and competition is played out in a global network of interaction."[15] Similarly, Arjun Appadurai more exactly associates postmodernity with a well-defined fissure between modernity and the current practices of globalization.[16] What especially distinguishes globalization from earlier technological models, then, is the increased tempo of the transfer of information and the rapid networking between agents and countries.[17] The languid pace at which letters and goods reached their intended recipients after having been carried on eighteenth-century ships crossing the Atlantic or the Pacific cannot compare to the speed of today's electronic global communications transmitted in nanoseconds, or of the express delivery of goods. Current technologies and worldwide markets produce an undeniable difference from the past, characterized by signs of postmodernity, yet its continuum with an imperial project gives pause to those who would argue for a radical break. From postmodern critical discourses we have learned how interwoven are the culturally contingent histories of human differences; at the same time, postmodern epistemologies (or lack of them) are finally inadequate to theorizing agency, formulating a political agenda, or negotiating the reciprocal relation between representation and the material world in regard to globalization's effects.

There are, then, multiple recoverable prehistories of globalization, but recent manifestations of globalization split as well from those various pasts to take uncharted paths. Globalization, I am arguing, is the end result of a long historical process (the prehistory of which we can seek in the eighteenth century and earlier) and also, in its most current form, a rupture from that process characterized by unprecedented acceleration of visible, invisible, and virtual worldwide entanglements. Critical global studies seeks globalization's investment in the past to isolate antecedents of contemporary global-ization, but it also recognizes the discontinuity from that past in its virtual nature, its radical augmentation of the speed of connection, and its particular form of late capi-tal. Critical global studies is not so much a continuous prehistory as it is an uneven ge-nealogy, complicated by rupture, of our current understandings of interdependencies on a global scale.

The belief that colonialism engenders modernity has complicated immensely any claim that indigenous, non-European modernities can be authentic, autonomous, or radi-cally distinct. Neither can we assume a simple equation between modernity and colo-nialism because modernity in non-European countries may occur in different con-figurations across the globe and at distinctly different historical moments (for example, the Americas were colonized centuries before India and the South Pacific). Critical global studies clearly shares some of the perspectives of postcolonial studies and the new imperial studies. Imperial studies in the past have centered on European empires to question how Europe imagines itself in relation to its potential subjects and objects of conquest. The new imperial history reexamines the impulse that propelled England, France, Spain, and Holland to gain territory and to urge their cultural assumptions onto large portions of the known world.[18] These colonial projects, though imitative, were not all the same. The Portuguese, for example, started out with a design to capture In-dia that soon dissipated, while the British and Dutch began as pirates and explorers who ultimately legitimated their activities. The new historiography in its most recent man-ifestations attempts to explicate the production of colonial difference and actively seeks to interrupt its reproduction. While incorporating new understandings on a worldwide scale, it also more subtly analyzes the distinctions between various national imperial trajectories, and the complex interrelations between colonizer and colonized. "Modern imperialism," contends Edward Said, "was so global and all-encompassing that virtu-ally nothing escaped it," and he shows in his study of canonical literary works within a framework of colonialism that even Jane Austen's provincial world required "overseas sustenance."[19] Yet imperial studies may fail to give sufficient attention to the local, or to unconquered or uncolonized areas. To confine one's understanding to imperial history may commit a disservice to local epistemologies worldwide.

While the methodologies and goals of critical global studies are generally compati-ble with the impulses of the new imperial history, they aim to be differently inflected and more encompassing. As we have noted, national perspectives often limit the modes of inquiry. Though one could make a case that imperial projects thoroughly infused the metropole and the periphery even as their impact was veiled or obfuscated, in the eigh-teenth century vast areas and groups of people were relatively untouched by empire. In addition, the focus of an historically specific critical global studies is to afford greater attention to non-European areas, to indigenous peoples and knowledges, to diasporic mobility, and to the social, economic, and ideological investments of colonialism on a worldwide scale. Subaltern or peasant peoples have often simply been written out of history and assumed to lack the political and intellectual maturity consonant with European notions of modernity. In addition, though European empires certainly had extraordinary reach, large parts of the globe remained unknown or unsettled and, in the case of oceans or uninhabitable areas, impossible to claim. Imperial eighteenth-century histories often fail to consider that Russia, China, the Levant, or the Maghreb might better be construed under a rubric other than the colonial because Europe did not rule them during that century. Within extranational and extraimperial territories, native populations may have resisted or somehow escaped the reaches of empire in the eighteenth century. To imply that empire embraced the entire world in the eighteenth century veers perilously close to replicating the assumptions of Millar's *Universal History* or similar mappings and measurements that encouraged Europeans to assume that they understood human nature everywhere and always, and that they could know a culture without having seen it. Though the differences from the new imperial studies are largely matters of degree, these are among the several factors that distinguish critical global studies from it.

If information flows and transnational networks do not seem to pertain to the eighteenth century, the increased mobility of commodities and ideas, the unprecedented expansion of global trade, improved navigational techniques, and cultural and racial mixing are of course very germane. To the period's well-known diasporas of the black Atlantic (Caribbean, British, African, and American) might be added histories of empires other than the European—Ottoman, Mughal, and Qing. For example, David Brion Davis and others have argued convincingly that "the origins of African slavery in the New World cannot be understood without some knowledge of the millennium of warfare between Christians and Muslims that took place in the Mediterranean and Atlantic and the piracy and kidnapping that went along with it."[20] In other words, the Arab world and its rather different history of enslavement need to be factored into the global picture. Furthermore, the terms by which we understand colonization are being reevaluated through closer scrutiny of the histories of the colonized themselves. Histories of colonialism look distinctly different if interpreted from the non-European perspective of the Americas, India, China, Japan, Oceania, or the Arab world. Colonial powers would not as a matter of course fold the history of, say, India into the narrative of their own pasts, while Indian historians would be more likely to incorporate the story of British imperialism as critical to the story. Britain's active implementation of global designs may in fact precede the Battle of Plassey (1757) rather than being that country's passive response to an alleged native disorder. The colonial presence in India has been found to have been aggressive even before that critical date, and imperial England may have been responding less to the collapse of the Mughal empire than to a powerful new indigenous order.[21]

In a similar vein, critical global studies attends to indigenous and native ways of knowing in order to question, or at least to complicate, Europe's assumed superiority in defining what counts as learning. Most Western textbook surveys translate other civilizations into examples of themselves or of a primordial past in an effort to make the strange less troubling, but other systems of belief, even while inchoate and perhaps contested from within, may well represent at least equally valid ways of representing the world.[22] Subjugated, silenced, or disqualified knowledge, less saturated by Enlightenment's premises—is often represented as irrational, natural, and primitive, and its relationship to objects, ancestors, the land, and the spirit world are determined to be ancient and superstitious.[23] In this regard Manuel Castells asks, "Why did a culture [China] and a kingdom that had been the technological leader of the world for thousands of years suddenly become technologically stagnant precisely at the moment when Europe embarked on the age of discoveries, and then on the industrial revolution?"[24] Certainly classical economic theorists such as Adam Smith in his *Wealth of Nations* (1776) made claims for a viable world economy that would produce its own modes of regulation. Yet there are also places deserving of study within a global eighteenth century where little or no commercial circulation existed. The new global studies seeks to juxtapose these alternative paradigms of indigenous traditions and other non-European civilizations with more familiar models of understanding in order to tell stories from the less visible interiors of the world.

It may never be possible fully to escape Eurocentrism, given the current organization of knowledge, even when critiquing its premises. Disciplinary boundaries, as many critics have shown, arose at the same historical moment as eighteenth-century brands of nationalism, modernity, and colonialism. Not only have various regions of the world been examined largely in isolation from each other, with European nation-based studies dominating, but also when educated in the richer regions scholars from non-Western and non-Northern regions may not find it possible or advantageous to incorporate indigenous knowledge. Across today's globalized world the uneven development of resources, as Appadurai attests, sets up "a fragmented and uneven distribution of just those resources for learning, teaching, and cultural criticism that are most vital for the formation of democratic research communities ... That is, globalization resists the possibility of just these forms of collaboration that might make it easier to understand or criticise."[25] Another symptom of current intellectual fragmentation is that the history and culture of eighteenth-century Japan, New Zealand, or Peru are often allocated to language programs, area studies programs, or subfields in history departments. Consequently, drawing connections among these areas of analysis in specific historical periods has succeeded only occasionally or intermittently. Yet significant aspects of globalization such as greater global mobility or access to texts and documents via the worldwide web may paradoxically improve opportunities for intellectual interchange across the world and grant greater voice to the previously disenfranchised.

In short, the particular category of space or place extends beyond nation to subject the very object of study to new scrutiny. Other temporal linkages among the subaltern and the enslaved might be drawn if our intellectual forays are no longer limited by nationalist histories, literatures, and their interests. We may also begin remapping the connective tissues of resistance circulating among distant venues throughout the globe. Connecting southern American slave culture to Indian mutiny in the mid-1800s, and psychic panic to political action, Homi Bhabha argues that local rebel agency spread speedily to unlikely and unexpected places.[26] Instead of imagining the globe in terms of centers and peripheries we might turn to diasporic areas of cultural mixture such as the Maghreb, "a geohistorical location that is constructed as a crossing instead of as a grounding (e.g., the nation) . . . between Orient, Occident, and Africa" of Turks, Christians, and Jews, of Moors, Arabs, Bedouins, Berbers, and Kabyles,[27] or we may organize intellectual investigation around bodies of water rather than land masses. To take a case in point, the very idea of dividing land masses into continents is a perception that dates only from the European eighteenth century. Because continents were simply considered to be continuous geographical areas, traveler Richard Hakluyt in 1599 could call the West Indies a continent, and English novelist Eliza Haywood similarly described Sumatra in 1745. The idea of the seven continents as we know them is a recent construct.

As we develop conceptual frameworks distinct from national history, we may freshly appreciate the ways that the local, regional, and the global are imbricated within one another. This concept of the "glocal" (a term coined to inspire "a careful rereading of the means of articulation" between two geographical coordinates) simultaneously makes legible the larger and smaller scales.[28] In this configuration, neither the local nor the global is the superior term. Lisbet Koerner has recently shown, for example, that Carl Linnaeus, among the most relentless of classifiers and collectors, linked natural history with his Swedish province to articulate an abortive "local modernity" that aimed to retain a self-sufficient and self-contained regional insularity without forfeiting economic growth.[29] New attention will hopefully be focused on empires other than European ones, on nonimperial territory, on indigenous knowledge, and on histories recounted from a different nexus. At its best critical global studies tacks back and forth between and among various territorial levels to examine the ways in which the local, regional, national, transnational, and global are mutually implicated while remaining reflective about its methodologies, humbled by its ignorance, and attuned to its investments.

Early modern critical global studies seeks then to recognize the problems that the asymmetric distribution of resources presents to worldwide analysis, and it attempts to revamp the disciplinary boundaries that impede alternative forms of historical knowledge. Recent studies usefully and intelligently complicate the picture of a unilinear process from Europe outwards. The work of imagining larger, reciprocal knowledge has already begun in the writings of scholars such as Srinivas Aravamudan, Richard Grove, Harriet Guest, Jonathan Lamb, Nigel Leask, David Porter, and many others, including the authors whose writing is included in this collection, and many others who contributed so significantly to the seminars that sparked this volume.[30] Though I do not have space here to review the important historically and geographically specific work now underway, scholars have begun to conceptualize new ways to think about cultural convergences and reciprocal enculturation.

Closely aligned with these kinds of studies, *The Global Eighteenth Century* is historically specific, employs innovative methodologies, and asks transnational and transcultural questions about human and social difference. More specifically historical than much postcolonial work, which tends to focus on contemporary issues, this volume includes theoretically informed approaches but locates its objects of interest in the past as they are understood in the present moment. It extends the insights of other approaches in several ways: (1) it looks beyond the European empire and its reaches to other perspectives to question the validity of metropole-periphery studies; (2) it assumes that European knowledge, often nation-based, is itself local in origin; (3) it employs thoroughly transdisciplinary methods of inquiry, calling into question the terms by which disciplines, founded at a time coincident with a European modernity, define their objects of study; (4) it articulates in a reflexive way its own paradigms and horizons; and (5) it pursues a genealogy of the global in articulation with "modernity" and "postmodernity." The essays in this collection aim toward these ambitious goals but only begin to point toward their achievement. Ideally, the volume will encourage refinement of these approaches as well as challenges to them.

None of the heuristic categories into which the chapters are divided is completely distinct from the others, and their topics and themes overlap. The first set of essays on "Mappings" explores both speculative and actual representations of the eighteenth-century world. The long eighteenth century saw the movement from imagined geography to a new reliance on the developing art and science of cartography, and to a more transparent and replicable view of the world. Yet how, Glyndwr Williams asks, were indigenous maps indicative of perhaps more bona fide ways of representing the world than those readily available to the European world? Williams contends that the knowledge displayed in the line drawings of Tupaia, a Polynesian navigator who joined the first Pacific voyage on the ship *Endeavour,* made him an equal participant rather than a subordinate on Captain Cook's voyages. Possessing an uncanny sense of navigational direction and a superior understanding of the islands, Tupaia apparently sketched eight watercolor drawings (previously attributed to Joseph Banks) to guide the voyagers. In making the case for these drawings, Williams transforms our understanding of early maritime history and of the knowledge indigenous to Oceania.

Often an anachronistic and circumscribed view distorts our understanding of the global past. The Dutch were the great geographers and natural historians of the early modern period, and Dryden's play *Amboyna* (1673), set on an island in Southeast Asia, contrasts a tyrannical Dutch power to the pacific English who had greater pertinence half a century earlier. In his essay on this colonial representation, Benjamin Schmidt addresses Michel Foucault's question: "What shape did knowledge take as it became increasingly *disengaged* from power?" Schmidt wonders about the seemingly anomalous rise of Dutch global mappings—dazzling globes, stunning maps, fine atlases, and expert prints—as their empire waned. The essay shows that the Dutch strategically represented and marketed the world as exotic, specifically for the purpose of forwarding the interests of the Dutch Republic. In their remapping of eclectic curiosities, they actually increased the numbers of what persuasively could be termed commodities and objects of desire.

Turning to another area of the globe, Philip Morgan explores the Caribbean's role as the first region of the New World to feel the full force of European colonial development. The Caribbean islands are best viewed, this essay maintains, as an integral part of an increasingly cohesive, unitary pan-Atlantic world. He regards the Caribbean and its islands, the first planetary colonies in world history, as multiple ports inhabited by an extraordinarily heterogeneous population. Transoceanic passages, he shows, ought to be envisaged as connecting routes rather than as barriers to communication, trade, and migration, even though they exposed travelers to disease and to natural disaster.

Robert Batchelor also describes a mutual process of encounter and exchange, this time between eighteenth-century China and Britain. The process moves beyond acculturation to create "new patterns of circuitry and new ways of imagining the social." He emphasizes the concept of *sharawadgi* (beauty without apparent order, which comes neither from China nor Europe) in the Chinese house at Stowe to argue that ideas about Chinese nobility evoke a transcultural model that defies a notion of a fixed East and West. Batchelor's discussion of an aesthetically satisfying mélange of discrete artifacts or images without apparent order connects with Benjamin Schmidt's description of

Dutch maps and *Wunderhammer* collectibles to suggest the viability of the arbitrary exotic as a larger global concept.

Offering a related example of the development of planetary consciousness, Matthew Edney probes the materiality of maps to demonstrate the way that humans literally bend and shape them for use in order to comprehend large and distant places. In his essay on the imperial mappings of India, he shows that, as reference works, maps functioned as substitutes for actual knowledge and as purveyors of European authority and rationality. Faith in such panotopical maps, he shows, was misplaced and even delusional.

Another kind of simulacrum was the eighteenth-century theater, which itself became an atlas of England's imperial world. Accessories (such as the parasol, perhaps an analogue to the Englishman's umbrella) employed in dramas serve as emblems of global difference. Joseph Roach draws an intriguing connection between stage presentations of the globe and its actual mapping and atlases published and illustrated by John Ogilby. Part of actor Thomas Betterton's assortment of travel books, they may have inspired his elaborate ethnographic costuming and scenery. Also looking to metaphor, Laura Brown scrutinizes the poetry of empire in the eighteenth century. Surveying the fluid energies in oceanic and commercial metaphors as emblems of Britain's cultural superiority, she finds that Thomas Gray, William Cowper, and Alexander Pope composed poems obsessed with formidable expansion rather than serenity and observation. Their sense of the water's vastness projects a compelling moral system that would seem to authorize the extension of a national destiny across the globe. Oceans may serve equally as the means to transport slaves and goods or as the dumping ground for wastage, but the Augustan poets perceive bodies of water as enticing avenues to imperialist ventures. This essay, like all of the essays in Part 1, re-interprets the spaces between real and imagined geography to think anew about the relations of regions to the globe.

In Part 2, "Crossings," the essays seek to investigate how sexual and cultural intermixtures—or the regulations forbidding them—had lasting effects on constructions of race, nation, and identity when these notions were in the very process of formation. What factors figure in the attitudes that the new citizen of the world adopts toward sexuality and its commodification across the globe? The essays grouped together here consider whether the eighteenth century may have witnessed previously unrecognized sexual identities, and what effects those relations might have on literature, the visual arts, and history. Exploring ideas of racialization, hybridity, and purity, these essays focus on the different "crossings" among the various populations both from the perspective of the European colonizers and of the colonized. On the one hand, regions of the world were driven to interweave their populations with those of other territories for economic and political reasons. On the other hand, despite this hybridized reality, colonizing nations sought to create the illusion of uniformity by promoting fictions of a singular national identity.

To date, limited attention has been focused on the gendered nature of globalization theory. The expansion of women's history into the global realm makes a very significant difference in Indian colonial historiography, as Betty Joseph makes clear. Using original archival research from the records of the East India Company, she revises the familiar trope of the confined or secluded woman—a subaltern allegedly incapable of being an historical agent—to examine the gender trouble that the Rani of Burdwan caused. In exposing the Rani's ability to manipulate colonial power as a native elite *and* as a protected subject, Joseph's essay reexamines earlier assumptions made by subaltern critics to articulate a special kind of resistance to colonialist powers. Linda Colley also expands and corrects postcolonial ideas about Orientalism to find that figuring the Barbary Coast as despotic or sensual is finally unhelpful. She contends instead that Orientalism preexists the late eighteenth century, extends beyond Islamic societies, and is an insufficient measure of colonialist and imperial ideologies. The narrative of a captive Englishwoman in North Africa, Elizabeth Marsh's tale of resistance to conversion marks an important shift from British fear of bodily and geographical penetration toward a more aggressive colonialist attitude typical at midcentury and after.

Kate Teltscher and Beth Fowkes Tobin both delve into questions of cultural translation. Teltscher characterizes the "inconsistencies, silences, and elision" posed in a friendly cultural exchange between a Scot, George Bogle, and the Tibetan Lama, whose first-person point of view is not known. Warren Hastings, Governor General of India, appointed him to set up a trade route, but Bogle, drawing from Scottish Enlightenment thought to interpret his newfound Shangri-La, accommodates Tibet and Bhutan to a nostalgic primitivism reminiscent of the Highlands. Like Swift's Gulliver, who believes himself to be a Houyhnhnm, Bogle fancies himself Tibetan in order to deliver a critical history of Europe to the reigning monarch. In nearby Bengal, on the other hand, Tobin describes the emergent nabobs—examples of the convergence of Indian and European—who derive from the English landed gentry and aristocracy and export the genre of the garden conversation piece into a new context. The essay explains the popularity and significance of the genre, especially Johann Zoffany's portraiture, to India's colonial elite. Finding both generic parody and repetition in which the English attempt to show themselves visually as equivalent to dynastic landowning families, Tobin also studies the Indian servants who appear in the pictures.

Kay Dian Kriz finds that the highly fashionable, refined, and polite society portrayed in these East Indian conversation pieces is largely absent from depictions of the West Indies, suggesting a way in which colonial territories distinctly differ in their representations. When European colonizers traversed the Atlantic to the New World, they mixed with the native populations and impersonated them. Some colonizers massacred or enslaved them; others engaged in exchange and conversion, actively encouraging interracial marriage for various ends. When the traders forced Africans into the New World as slaves, this further complicated the racial mixtures that would result. In her richly illustrated chapter Kriz analyzes images of the mixed-race West Indian women who dominate Brunias's genre paintings to propose that ethnographic representation was surprisingly flexible. She argues that Brunias uses the mulattresses to figure the West Indies as a potentially refined commercial space, based upon widely accepted social theory that evaluated societies based upon their treatment of women. Peter Hulme also focuses on ethnogenesis, the creation of new mixed populations in the racial crucible of the New World. The last war against the indigenous population of the Caribbean took place in 1795–96 on the island of St. Vincent and ended with the removal of most of that population to Central America, where they survive as the Garifuna or Black Caribs. Drawing from new French sources, Hulme rewrites that chapter in colonial history (one previously constructed by the British victors) that tells of the Yellow Caribs gradually overwhelmed by the Black Caribs, a new group of Caribs and escaped African slaves.

Nicholas Rogers maintains that the Caribbean world provided little space for interracial or intercultural alliances on board ships. He considers the ugly contest between West Indian and colonizing authorities resulting from the attempt to muster manpower for warships. Segregation and racism undermined British naval efforts to man sufficiently its fleets; for instance, it tended to recruit prisoners of war rather than skilled black seamen, whether slaves or free men. Countering other recent historians, Rogers maintains that the predatory nature of maritime war and the sheer struggle for survival among the marginal and exploited did not promote an international fraternity of the dispossessed. Also carefully combing ship records, Vincent Carretta argues that Olaudah Equiano may have been born a slave in the Carolinas rather than a free man in West Africa, thus significantly calling into question the authenticity of his account of eighteenth-century Africa. Equiano's *Interesting Narrative* (1789), enormously influential in the abolition struggle, may then be dismissed as fiction, or it may be analyzed instead for its powerful strategy of covertly manipulating the colonial powers in order to transform the lives of future slaves. This essay, like the other essays in this section, reconsiders the categories of separation by color and geography in order to reshape the global eighteenth century.

In the final part of the collection, the focus turns even more directly upon eighteenth-century islands to consider anew the territories themselves, as well as the figurative concepts they evoke. Islands have often been described as idealized, if peripheral, locations for colonization and settlement, including especially the various Caribbean islands and those of the Pacific (such as Tahiti, Fiji, Bali, New Zealand, and Australia). Islands are often regarded in relation, for example, to the continents or countries nearest to them in the cases—for example, of Cuba and the Americas, of Madagascar and Africa, of Sicily and Italy, or of Sri Lanka and India. Islands may also be seen in relation to their island groupings as in the case of Indonesia or the Canary Islands. Islands frequently become "spatio-temporal" reference points for other geographical locations, and the islands themselves may consequently be obscured from view.[31] More recent conceptualizations of islands have suggested that their relationship to the ocean that surrounds them, as in the case of Oceania "the sea of islands," is most appropriate to understanding "islandness."[32] Islands may be imagined as exotic retreats and as authentic utopian paradises. Yet other islands (such as Alcatraz, Ireland, the Falklands, the Hebrides, or Corsica) were in fact sites of dissension and war rather than primitive or picturesque tropics.[33]

Those seeking adventure and fortune viewed eighteenth-century islands as locations for colonization and settlement but also as distant places where undesirables might safely be resettled. Islands too could breed terror and mystery, as in the case of Daniel Defoe's very popular *Robinson Crusoe* (1719). This section reexamines islands throughout the eighteenth-century world as economic and cultural bridges to the continents— as places for crossings and departures, trading and exploitation, contagion and healing—and antithetically as places where populations developed local expertise rooted in specific histories independent of colonizers who wished to extract indigenous knowledge.

Showing the importance of placing sexuality within a global fabric, Neil Rennie describes the Point Venus scene of public copulation in Tahiti (14 May 1769) as symbolic of European expectations of South Seas sexuality. Comparing voyagers' conflicting accounts, he shows that Sir John Hawkesworth, for example, turns the scene into a religious rite of sexual love, while Joseph Banks focuses on the shamefulness of the spectacle. The allegedly irresistible beckoning of the South Seas women and their public display of sexuality also becomes an alibi for the adventurers' commercial ventures and an "explanation" for the *Bounty* mutiny, and its traces still persist in the imagery of twentieth-century tourism.

Similarly raising important issues of revision, Rod Edmond introduces the concept of "reencounter" to describe the way eighteenth-century travelers revisited Tahiti, Tonga, and New Zealand and dealt with the cumulative effects of their earlier visits. With special attention to Cook's second voyage, Forster's *Journal,* and Forster's *Observations,* Edmond examines the shifting interpretations of disease (scurvy, venereal disease, and yaws) and its visible residue over time. Scrutinizing native bodies for the disfiguring marks of signs of infection, the damage of previous visits, the journal writers feared that they were spreading disease along with trade. These islanders' skin, Edmond suggests, was the surface on which cultural contact was written.

Both Carole Fabricant and Jill Casid offer case studies of the ways in which the eighteenth-century utopian imagination was ideologically complicit in the most brutal dystopic practices of the day—specifically slavery and empire building—while retaining its potential for a more progressive vision. Drawing connections among England, Ischia (off the coast of Naples), Aquidneck, and the Bermuda Islands, Fabricant demonstrates the abortive effect of the collision between Berkeley's romantic idealism in the Bermuda Project—his plan to found an ideal community—and his adherence to an evangelical racialism. His promotion of tar-water as an unlikely remedy for disease nevertheless registers as a project that reveals the more exactly racial implications of the utopian imagination as it is nurtured by watery surroundings.

Arguing that fiction helps to realize the concept of empire by veiling violence in the plantation economy, Jill Casid writes about introducing alien plants to foreign soil as agricultural conquest and the sowing of European seed in the fictive and real island gardens of Defoe, Rousseau, and Saint-Pierre. She focuses on the Isle of France (now Mauritius) as an ideal state as represented in Bernardin de Saint-Pierre's *Paul et Virginie* (1789). Characters themselves take on the traits of plants, their corpses serving to fertilize and ultimately reproduce the empire in the guise of a harmonious global garden. Arousing grief at its loss, empire thus achieves a physical embodiment in the colonial landscape of the island into which these alien transplants, at once corpses and seeds, are interred.

Anna Neill, too, brings an important focus to the affective structures of global colonization and trade. Famous sea captains such as James Cook and William Bligh attempted to incorporate "moral sentiment into commercial imperialism" through their manner of shipboard governance. Drawing on Adam Smith's theories of sympathy, she shows that the most astute captains affected high standards of character in order to arbitrate between native peoples and seamen, and that the voyagers propelled their expeditions through affecting an impartial and distant stance. Neill's essay implicitly raises the question of whether these technologies of sympathy might have arisen at the same time as global commerce. Finally, again drawing attention to the importance of colonial repetition and reencounter, Greg Dening concludes the volume with a historical and personal reflection upon circumnavigation and, in particular, the replica of James Cook's vessel *Endeavour* and *Hokule'a,* the Polynesian voyaging canoe now sailing the Pacific. In the performance of history in the present, Dening gracefully yokes the global eighteenth century to urgent contemporary issues in Oceania and elsewhere, as well as to the history of the social sciences. Reliving the moments of maritime voyages in the best of all possible global worlds, he argues, affords the opportunity to connect an indigenous past with an indigenous present. Neither past nor present enables a simple or uninterrupted narrative that easily lays claim to coherent tradition or a unified modernity.

This collection is meant to be an introduction to the concept of a global eighteenth century. The essays are often transdisciplinary in origin, and readers may be hard-pressed to identify the disciplinary affiliation of individual authors when judging them in the context of their essays. Among the contributors are six historians, two art historians, a geographer, an anthropologist, and a dozen literary scholars whose countries of origin include Australia, New Zealand, India, the United Kingdom, Canada, and the United States. Many of the essays are admittedly Eurocentric and, more specifically, Anglocentric. Each of these chapters attempts, however, to make a problem of that Eurocentrism. They confront the ways in which European knowledge is itself a situated knowledge, neither universal nor objective, and the ways that indigenous systems of belief are not inherently inadequate or naive.

As with any inaugural volume, *The Global Eighteenth Century* cannot hope to exhaust the possibilities or even to offer a representative sampling, which would focus in turn on Africa, Asia, the Americas, and the Pacific. Though many areas of the globe are discussed (including oceans and islands, diasporas, and places of crossing), "coverage" is not the intention. Suggestive rather than comprehensive or encyclopedic in terms of place, strategies, and approaches, the purpose of this volume is to expand the scale of eighteenth-century studies and to point toward new directions for a historically based global studies in remarking on the mutual exchange of ideas and goods between indigenous populations and Europe, on the skillful manipulation of a European readership by a former slave, on the contrast between Carib notions of skin pigmentation and those of the colonizers, or more generally on the nature of cultural contact as transmutation and exchange as well as violence and erasure. Interested in multiple empires and their limits, a historically specific critical global studies is wary of globalization but attentive to its effects, cognizant of the problematic posed by the modern and its relation to the postmodern, open to indigenous wisdom, alert to potential Eurocentrism, and actively engaged in reconfiguring the territories of knowledge. It is my hope that these essays will foster intellectual debate among students and scholars who may not ordinarily encounter each other's ideas as we continue to forge a broader, sharper, and more collaborative understanding of the eighteenth century.

Part I / Mappings

CHAPTER ONE

Mapping an Exotic World

The Global Project of Dutch Geography, circa 1700

Benjamin Schmidt

Geographic Maneuvers

For a brief moment in the spring of 1673—on or about the advent, one might retrospectively say, of the "long" eighteenth century—a small Moluccan island suddenly occupied the center of London's theatrical world. In that year, John Dryden's *Amboyna* "succeeded on the Stage" (as the playwright himself averred) by conveying English audiences to a steamy East Indian archipelago and thrusting before them, front and center, a "tragedy" of strikingly global dimensions.[1] Exotic drama, of course, was hardly new to Restoration London: Dryden's own *Indian Queen* (1664) and *Indian Emperour* (1665) had played to enthusiastic crowds only a few years earlier. Yet *Amboyna* brought the tropics to the Thames perhaps more sensationally and certainly more forcefully than its competitors. More so than other performances of its day, it embraced a plainly geographic orientation to go along with its pugnaciously political agenda—which speaks to both the image of the exotic world and the ironies of its representation at the dawn of the global eighteenth century.

Amboyna gets to geography in a curious if also confrontational way. Politics and place are brought sharply together in a drama forged in the heat of battle—composed, that is, against the backdrop of a veritable world war between the English crown and the Dutch Republic, a conflict somewhat unassumingly known as the Third Anglo-Dutch War. For Dryden and his fellow Britons, the third war was the charm, in that England finally succeeded in cutting the upstart republic down to size: Charles II's Royal Navy at last overwhelmed the formidable fleet of the Netherlands; significant portions of the Dutch countryside, after enduring months of plunder, fell to the marauding troops of Charles's sometime ally, Louis XIV. Yet this war, like the previous two, also extended overseas: to America, where England claimed possession of the colony that would henceforth be called New York; to Africa, where Admiral Holmes assaulted Dutch forts along the Gold Coast; and to Asia, where British ships habitually harassed enemy trade. Dryden wished to make this internationalism central to his play, and he set his drama in Southeast Asia, on the spice island of Amboina, where a tropical tale with an unabashedly polemical twist unfolds. *Amboyna* presents a story of high intrigue and low villainy, in which the Dutch act the part of monstrous colonials, raping the island's natives and then blaming the English traders, who happen also to be stationed there, for their crimes. In the process, the play pushes every baroque button imaginable—sex, violence, torture, treachery—to persuade its audience that the Dutch, unlike the English, are despicable tyrants and unfit to govern abroad. To articulate this idea concretely and early in the action, the playwright adopts a conspicuously and *graphically* geographic metaphor: "No Map shews Holland truer than our Play," declares Dryden in his prologue, meaning thereby to introduce his audience to the character—the essence—of what the play will later term "the Dutch race."[2]

Why the geographic maneuver? In Dryden's mapping metaphor there are a number of ironies of which late-seventeenth-century viewers and readers were sure to take note. First, it was precisely the Dutch—as Dryden well knew and elsewhere acknowledges—who were the preeminent mapmakers of Europe; Holland itself was the source of the sumptuous atlases of Joan Blaeu, Johannes Janssonius, and Frederick de Wit, which showed England, along with the rest of Europe, the shape of the late-seventeenth-century world.[3] Blaeu's authoritative *Atlas maior* had debuted just a few years before Dryden's play; and lavish, hand-colored, folio editions were by now available in London's finest shops. By the 1670s, moreover, the Dutch had emerged as the reigning geographers: of Europe in general and of England in particular, which imported Dutch maps, Dutch charts, and Dutch geographies in ever growing numbers. This goes for plainly "Dutch" products and for ostensibly English ones as well. Thus, the pride of British mapmaking, John Seller's *English Pilot,* was produced "from old worn Dutch plates," as Samuel Pepys reproachfully put it.[4] Meanwhile, the so-called royal geographer of the realm took the person of John Ogilby, a former-dancer-turned-printer whose major contributions to geographic studies were nothing more than English translations of Dutch-composed texts—works printed with Ogilby's name on the cover—

though under the direction of the entrepreneuring Amsterdam publisher Jacob van Meurs. The Dutch, more generally, produced the leading accounts of Asia, Africa, and America, and made them widely available in English, French, and Latin. It was from these Dutch sources, in fact, that Dryden and his audience (and, for that matter, readers across Europe) derived much of their information about the world. The despised autocrats of Amboina, it turns out, happened also to be the reigning authorities on Amboinese geography.

A second irony has to do with the timing of this well-after-the-fact "Map" of Holland. Dryden's drama was based on an actual colonial event that had taken place much earlier in the century—in February 1623, precisely half a century prior to the play. Yet the Dutch by this time no longer constituted the rising, menacing, colonial power they once had been. The rapid expansion of the earlier half of the seventeenth century, when the original Amboina scandal had taken place, had lately given way to a recession of trade and a contraction of territory for the republic overseas, and the notion of the Dutch as lords of an expanding global empire made little sense by the 1670s. In Africa, what few possessions the Dutch West India Company might once have claimed were now regularly besieged by the English Royal African Company. In America, the short-lived colony of Dutch Brazil had returned to Portugal by 1654, and the ill-fated settlement of New Netherland had been forfeited to the duke of York only ten years later. In the very year of *Amboyna*'s production, the Dutch West India Company was busy drawing up papers of bankruptcy. A once mighty colonial power, the Dutch Republic was now fading into the background of the European imperial world. Still active in parts of the East Indies, perhaps, elsewhere it was giving way in the great colonial contests of the later seventeenth and eighteenth centuries. Dryden, the audience could not help but note, had launched his polemical broadside against a ship already sinking.

The two ironies of Dryden's mapping metaphor are subtly related. By the later decades of the seventeenth century (and this goes for the early eighteenth century, as well), the Dutch were fast becoming the leading geographers of Europe—prolific authors of literary and cartographic texts, producers of tropical paintings and colorful prints, promoters of exotic rarities and imported *naturalia*—while at the same time assuming a less active role in the theater of European expansion. Or, put another way, the Republic was becoming less and less engaged in conquering the world as it became more and more vested in describing it. Two linked ironies make three central questions: Why would the Dutch role as geographers of Europe expand at the very moment that their role in the expansion of Europe contracted? How, furthermore, did the Dutch describe a world that they had a diminished stake in possessing? And—to frame the issue in starkly Foucauldian terms—what shape did knowledge take as it became increasingly disengaged from power?[5]

This essay explores the production of geography in the Netherlands and its impressive dissemination and consumption throughout Europe circa 1700. As the global eighteenth century got underway, a remarkable profusion of geographic materials issued from the Dutch Republic—an explosion of books, maps, prints, paintings, curiosities, and other objects pertaining to the representation of the non-European world—effectively mapping for the rest of Europe the shape of the expanding globe. Yet both the intense production and the avid consumption of Dutch geography should give pause to students of culture and empire. For geography in early modern (no less than late modern) Europe was a highly interested, generally contested, and idiosyncratically "national" endeavor not easily transplanted abroad. Dryden designed a most malevolent "Map" of Holland's character for propaganda purposes, plain and simple, and one hardly imagines the play performed outside of England. The Dutch, too, engaged in their share of cartographic conflict and geographic fashioning, originally at the expense of their longtime nemesis, Spain, and later taking aim at the English and French. Yet this habit of tactical—call it "local"—geography appears to change by the final decades of the seventeenth century, at which time the Dutch appear also to recede from the battleground of global empire. Indeed, what is most striking about this later corpus of Dutch geography is, first, how broadly accessible, attractive, and appealing it is (this, to be sure, from a European perspective); and second, how strikingly unpolemical, apolitical, and disinterested it seems—at least relative to earlier patterns of Dutch geography and, for that matter, competing European traditions of geography. By the later seventeenth century, the Dutch had learned to make "maps" that appealed to Dryden's audience—and far beyond.

This chapter probes the very foundations of the global eighteenth century by examining the production of European images of the world circa 1700 and by considering the forms and purposes of those images at this critical moment of history. After briefly reviewing the patterns and traditions of geography in the Netherlands, it outlines the extraordinary expansion of geography in the Dutch Republic in the decades surrounding 1700, and then explores some of the methods and meanings of these sources. By way of conclusion, I wish to propose a very specific Dutch strategy of representing the world at this time, a broadly appealing mode of mimetic engagement that may be termed—to pose the issue as provocatively as possible—*exoticism*.

Making Maps and Other Geographies

Some background: The miracle of Holland, as the phenomenal political, economic, and social expansion of the Northern Netherlands was dubbed even by contemporaries, occurred largely over the first two thirds of the seventeenth century. It is less essential to detail here the astonishing growth of Dutch resources and power—military and diplomatic, commercial and demographic, literary and artistic—than it is to emphasize the timing of the Dutch Republic's meteoric rise from the late sixteenth century and underscore its exceptionally wide-reaching economic and cultural attainments by the middle of the seventeenth century. More pertinent to the subject of geography is the republic's expansion overseas, which likewise took off spectacularly in the earlier seventeenth century, only to level off or regress thereafter. Trade to Asia began around 1600, with significant conquests (largely at the expense of Portugal) through the middle of the century. After that, though, the Dutch East India Company (Verenigde Oost-indische Compagnie, or VOC) gave ground to the English and French; and, if the VOC still turned a profit, it did so increasingly as middleman in inter-Asian trade rather than as master of pan-Asian domains. The story of the Dutch in America presents a still starker model of rise and fall, with conquests in Brazil (again at Portugal's expense) and settlement in New Netherland taking place in the 1620s through 1640s. These gains, however, were followed by the catastrophic loss of Brazil in 1654 and of New Netherland in 1664. The Dutch Atlantic slave trade may have followed a slightly different pattern than other American commerce, in that contracts for slaves increased in the second half of the seventeenth century when the Republic could deliver cargoes for their former Iberian enemies. Yet this traffic was relatively marginal compared to the slaving activities of the English, French, and Portuguese; in Africa more generally, Dutch colonial reversals date from the 1660s and 1670s, when Dutch trading forts fell to superior French and English forces. By the final third of the century, in all events, the Dutch filled the role, in the West no less than the East, of middlemen. Much as they moved colonial goods, they had a minimal stake in colonies per se.[6]

The world according to the Dutch had a lot to do with those events that coincided with its articulation of geography, since the Dutch world view took shape as the Dutch *became* Dutch—as the Netherlands waged its epic struggle against Habsburg Spain, the searing Eighty Years' War that culminated in the Republic's foundation in 1648. Geography played a crucial role in this campaign, though it played a very particular role—by which is meant a provincial and idiosyncratic role—in expressing a new Dutch identity to match the new Dutch state. Over the course of the revolt, that is, cultural geographers in the Netherlands fashioned a version of the globe that suited the struggles of the Republic. This applies less for Asia and Africa, in which the Dutch initially showed less interest, than for America, whose "discovery" and conquest coincided (more or less) with the Dutch revolt. America was the site of Spanish "tyrannies," which the Dutch pronounced to be parallel to tyrannies committed in the Netherlands. The Indians were construed as allies, fellow sufferers of colonial oppression and brothers-in-arms in the war against Habsburg universal monarchy. "Colonialism" itself took on an Old World no less than New World meaning: the duke of Alba's subjection of Dutch rebels was habitually juxtaposed with the Habsburg subjection of Indian comrades. This comparison, of course, was an exaggeration, but it was an exaggeration that worked and one that encouraged copious descriptions of "cruelties" in America, the "destruction of the Indies," and the tragedy of the *Conquista*—all of which were related to events back in the Netherlands. (It was in this period—the 1570s through 1620s—that the Dutch produced scores of editions of Bartolomé de Las Casas's catalogue of atrocities, *The Mirror of Spanish Tyrannies in the West Indies,* sometimes slyly published with a pendant volume, *The Mirror of Spanish Tyrannies in the Netherlands.*) Dutch geography, in this way, was every bit as polemical in the early seventeenth century as Dryden's play a half century later. Indeed, it is yet another of the cheeky ironies of the latter that Dryden dared to compare the Dutch behavior in Amboina to that of Spain in the Netherlands: "D'Alva, whom you / Condemn for cruelty did ne're the like; / He knew the original Villany was in your Blood," offers the poet, opportunistically, in 1673. By this time, though, the Dutch had long abandoned the rally cry of "Spanish tyranny in America," since they had long ended their war against Spain, both at home and abroad.[7]

Timing here is crucial. The project of geography for the Dutch in the earlier years of the century was implicated in the project of "nation-ness" (to adopt Benedict Anderson's term, more appropriate for the early modern period than "nationalism").[8] Once the precarious moment of foundation had passed, however, such meaningful representations of the world lost their purpose. By the later decades of the century, the Dutch abandoned the topos of "Spanish tyranny in America," quit their publication of Las Casas and other polemical tracts, and generally reoriented their geography away from their distinctly provincial image of America. Yet they did not abandon the project of geography altogether. Quite the contrary, they began to produce in these years more works, in more forms, than ever before. The sparkling maps, dazzling globes, and exceptionally well-regarded atlases produced in the Netherlands were coveted across the continent. Dutch-made prints, tropical paintings, and rare curiosa were traded among European princes, merchants, and scholars; while Dutch natural histories, protoethnographies, and accomplished geographies, in multiple editions and translations, became the standards throughout Europe. In presenting these materials, moreover, the Dutch adopted a distinct strategy of exoticism in order to market a version of the world that, rather than remaining peculiarly Netherlandic, was rendered more widely attractive to the whole of Europe. No longer as invested in the race to colonialize, the Dutch could afford to step aside and operate the concession stand, as it were, of European expansion, offering images of the world to those fast entering the competition.

The materials produced by the Dutch are unusually bountiful and strikingly beautiful. They are notably broad-ranging as well, both in their impressive attention to the vast baroque world and in their remarkable span of genres, media, and objects enlisted to represent that world. They comprise, most basically, "traditional," printed geographies which, in the humanist mode gave broad outline to the cosmos. These include such massive, learned compilations as Philipp Clüver's (Cluverius's) *Introductionis in universam geographiam,* which appeared in a staggering sixty-seven editions by 1725; Bernardus Varenius's authoritative *Geographia generalis;* and the omnibus works of Georg Horn (Hornius)—"social" studies on the empires of the world, the origins of the races, the nature of the polities, and so forth—forty editions of which were printed in the final third of the century. Slightly less global in their focus, regional geographies took the form of fabulous folio works, which were sometimes called "atlases" and were always chock-full of foldout maps, engravings, and the like: Johan Nieuhof on China (which Ogilby sold as the *Atlas Chinensis,* sometimes with a companion *Atlas Japonensis* that was likewise done from a Dutch original); Olfert Dapper's lavish volumes on Asia and Africa; Arnold Montanus' best-selling (and thrice translated) *America;* Nicholas Witsen on Muscovy and "Tartary"; Engelbert Kaempfer's nonpareil *Japan;* and the magnificent, five-volume *Oud en Nieuw Oost-Indiën* (Old and New East Indies) by the Dutch dominee Francois Valentijn. Exotic travel narratives, a more peripatetic genre, likewise streamed off Dutch presses at a torrential pace: over fifty editions of Willem Bontekoe's adventures in the Indian Ocean; Ogier Busbecq's much-cited account of life among the Ottomans; and Cornelis de Bruyn's journeys from the Near to Far East. And there are also impressive travel anthologies: sprawling, multivolume collections, including Joost Hartgers's "Voyages" and Isaac Commelin's "Travels" (which formed the basis of Renneville's and Churchill's likewise gargantuan collections, in French and English, respectively); and the twenty-eight-volume geography series of Pieter van der Aa, which served as the standard reference work for half a century. A final category that falls under the rubric of literary text is the Dutch "books of wonders"— a genre approximating printed *Wunderkammer*—which jumbled together the multiple marvels, mores, and curiosities of the world; arranged these with happy disregard for context or place; and then packaged them with such come-on titles as "The Great Cabinet of Curiosities," "The Wonder-Filled World," or, more prosaically, "The Warehouse of Wonders."[9]

Most of these works included maps, an indication that the Republic by this time had become the unrivaled capital of cartography. To be sure, the Dutch had excelled in mapmaking for much of the seventeenth century. Yet it was only in the second half of the century, *after* the fall of the Republic's American colonies and setbacks in Asia and Africa, that the stupendous "grand" atlases of Blaeu, Janssonius, and de Wit appeared in deluxe editions and in most major languages. Add to this category the water-worlds produced by the ateliers of Colom, Donker, and van Keulen—stunning sea atlases that, if always fairly decorative, had lately become even more so by the inclusion of hand-colored cartouches, elaborate vignettes, and baroque marginalia brimming with "ethnographic" detail—and it becomes apparent how thoroughly the Dutch dominated the field. They were, in short, the mapmakers of Europe. This applies, moreover, to a remarkably wide range of products and consumers, for the Dutch cartographic industry served both ends of the market. It churned out cheap sheet maps, topical news reports, and copious city views for the less affluent buyer; while also manufacturing premiere globes, watercolor topographies, and opulent wall maps—such as Blaeu's stupendous, three-meter wide *mappa mundi* (a copy of which reached the court of the shogun in Edo) and his brilliant map of Brazil, decorated with extensive "local" scenery engraved by the artist Frans Post (fig. 1.1).[10]

Post's name is associated chiefly with a whole other class of images—tropical landscapes—that rightfully belong to the field of geography. The Dutch invented and then abundantly produced the tropical landscape, a new genre that developed in the final half of the seventeenth century—not, that is, in the Golden Age of Dutch painting, when landscapes were dedicated almost exclusively to domestic, or perhaps Italian,

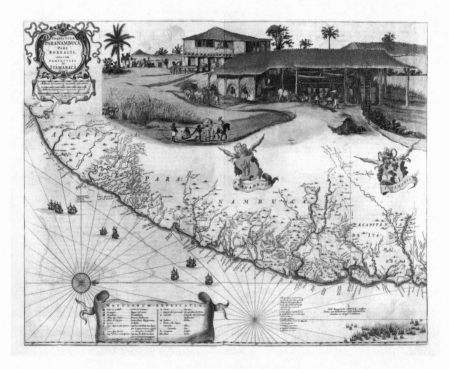

Figure 1.1. Joan Blaeu and Frans Post, "Praefecturae Paranambucae," in Blaeu, *Atlas maior* (Amsterdam, 1662). Courtesy of the John Carter Brown Library, Brown University.

Figure 1.2. Frans Post, *View of the Franciscan Cloister of Igaraçu* (71 × 101 cm). Courtesy of the Historisches Museum, Frankfurt am Main.

scenes. Now, however, the expanding colonial world could be viewed on canvas in bright and vivid color (fig. 1.2). Post himself concentrated on Brazilian scenes and pastoral settings, his lush foregrounds overflowing with the rich *naturalia* of the tropics. Other regions attracted other painters. Dirk Valkenburg cornered the market on Suriname; Andries Beeckman covered the East Indies; Reinier "Seaman" Nooms portrayed northern Africa; and Gerard van Edema applied his brush to that urban jungle lately known as New York, which he painted almost exclusively for English patrons. Dutch artists also undertook various still lifes of foreign flora, fauna, and indigenous peoples. And the places, races, and products of the Indies, East and West, might be further collapsed into a single canvas—as in Jacob van Campen's *Triumph, with Treasures of the Indies* (fig. 1.3), in which the central basket is Congolese, the vase is Ming (draped with tropical, mostly East Indian shells), and the scarlet macaw is Brazilian. All of these images, finally, could be recycled in tapestries—the Gobelins series for Louis XIV being among the most famous example—or in earthenware or other decorative arts, produced largely in Delft though sold throughout the continent.[11]

The objects shown in the paintings and decorative arts were sorted out more meticulously in natural histories, of which the Dutch produced, once again, the most impressive samples. European scholars turned to Willem Piso's *Historiae naturalis Brasi-*

Figure 1.3. Jacob van Campen, *Triumph, with Treasures of the Indies* (380 × 205 cm). Courtesy of the Paleis Huis den Bosch, Royal Collections, The Hague.

liae for tropical crustaceans and edentates, they consulted twelve thick volumes by Hendrik van Reede tot Drakestein on the natural wonders of Malabar, and they relied on Jan Commelin for comprehensive data on Asian flora—perhaps even visiting the renowned *Amsterdam hortus,* where Commelin grew his plants. More specialized, though no less spectacular, works include Georg Rumpf's (Rumphius's) monumental meditation on Moluccan shells, *D'Amboinsche rariteitkamer* (The Amboinese Curiosity Cabinet), and the breathtaking *Metamorphosis insectorum Surinamensium* by Maria Sibylla Merian, which showed the insects of Suriname crawling among those plants they called home. (Both texts appeared during what David Freedberg has so felicitously called the Netherlands' "*decennium mirabilius*" of exotic natural history, 1695–1705.)[12] Actual specimens could be handled or even purchased from Dutch *Kunst-* and *Wunderkammern,* which swelled in number during these years. Shells were the best preserved and therefore most popular items, though a wide variety of *naturalia, artificialia,* and hybrid items bridging the two categories—finely painted shells, artfully crafted fossils, ingeniously worked coral—could be had from Dutch dealers. Finally, paintings of collectibles also sold briskly: still lifes of rare flowers, exotic shells, or other imports from the Indies; or paintings of the very cabinets themselves—sometimes real though often imagined—like the fabulous renditions of connoisseurs' cabinets from the hand of Jan van Kessel (fig. 1.4).[13]

The commerce in collectibles (and in geography more generally) highlights the impressive migration of these products, and it is important to stress just how far and wide Dutch geography dispersed and how influential the Dutch version of the world consequently became. Though not all of these sources can be readily traced, certain patterns of patronage can be reconstructed, especially as they pertain to Europe's most prominent consumers. German, French, and English aristocrats, among others, avidly collected Dutch tropical landscapes, for example. Louis XIV acquired a spectacular trove of Americana in 1679, including twenty-seven canvases by Frans Post. Maps and globes also circulated in the finest studies and drawing rooms of Europe. Queen Christina of Sweden assembled a collection of stunning cartographic watercolors, the so-called Vingboons atlas, illustrating nearly every port of interest in the non-European world. Peter the Great came to Amsterdam to buy, among other things, every *Wunderkammer* he could lay his hands on, following in the steps of Grand Duke Cosimo III de' Medici, who had raided Dutch collections only a few years earlier. Less is known about consumption at less elevated levels because fewer traces remain, though it is apparent that Dutch prints and sheet maps scattered widely and that their images were recycled aggressively across the continent. The circulation of published geographies makes a still deeper impression. Printers in Paris and London—Ogilby being a prime example—poached, pirated, and otherwise published Dutch texts, and sources originating in Hol-

Figure 1.4. Jan van Kessel, *Americque* (1666) (48.5 × 67.5 cm). Courtesy of the Bayerische Staats-gemäldesammlungen, Alte Pinakothek Munich.

land spread from Stockholm to Naples and from Dublin to Dresden. Readers of German, Latin, English, French, Swedish, and Spanish all had access, in one form or another, to the bounty of Dutch geography. Consumers of books and prints, maps and paintings, rarities, and other mimetic forms of the world as imagined circa 1700—the dawn, that is, of the global eighteenth century—could avail themselves of the flood of products that streamed so impressively from the Dutch Republic.

Mapping an Exotic World

Why the universal attraction of Dutch geography? How (to frame the issue from the perspective of the producer) did these materials win such a wide following? Consider the fantasy cabinet of Jan van Kessel, which purports to portray a collector's ideal—and thus the allure of this brand of geography (see figure 1.4). Whatever the panel's many charms, one is hard pressed to identify a single theme, or a signal object, that draws the viewer into this undeniably compelling collection. On the contrary, one is struck by the abundance and variety of stuff and by the shapeless bric-a-brac quality of its arrangement. The painting is labeled *Americque,* though it would seem to lack a tightly focused

American theme. One of a number of Indians sits in the foreground, though she is coupled with a dark-skinned African clad in feathers. To the woman's left stands a cherubic Indian boy, also decked in feathers and armed with an iconic bow and arrows; yet at her feet kneels another child—naked and less fair than the "Indian"—who plays with a set of Javanese gamelan gongs. The woman dancing through the door, meanwhile, wears *East* Indian costume, and to the right is a depiction of a Hindu suttee. Numerous other visual devices, in much the same manner, point to the subtle blending of races and the nonchalant bleeding of regions that occur throughout the panel. Next to the Javanese drummer boy struts an African crowned crane whose curving neck guides the viewer's eye toward a perched macaw and a toucan—two birds closely associated with Brazil. Between these glamorously tropical fowl, a whiskered opossum heads toward a sturdy anteater—we are, once again, in the landscape of America—yet the framed (and framing) insects and butterflies (top and bottom right) derive from both Old and New World habitats. The background statuary bracketing the open door features Tapuya Indians (modeled closely on drawings by the Dutch painter Albert Eckhout), while the niches on the right display a pair of Brahmins. Between these stone figures, in the corner, rests a suit of Japanese armor whose sword points plainly toward a Brazilian agouti and a centrally placed armadillo—the latter belonging to the standard allegorical representation of America, as codified earlier in the century in Cesare Ripa's *Iconologia*.[14] In place of specificity—the strategy that had characterized Dutch geography at the height of its struggle against Spain, when images of America resolutely stressed the theme of Habsburg tyranny abroad—the panel conveys a remarkable sense of indeterminacy. Rather than the New World per se (let alone a Dutch New World), one gets an almost haphazard assembly of exotica from around the globe. Objects are in disarray and, in a crucial sense, decentered. Why title the work "America" at all, if it comprises so much more of the generically non-European world?

This sort of indeterminacy characterizes many of the sources emanating from the Republic circa 1700. There is a mix-and-match quality to Dutch geography of this period that stands in sharp contrast to the more sharply focused view propagated earlier in the century. When Johannes de Laet, a director of the Dutch West India Company, published Willem Piso's natural history of Brazil in 1648, he made clear in his prefatory materials the vital place of the Dutch in America—where they still retained, after all, important colonies. A number of years later (by which time those colonies had been lost), the work was reissued by an Amsterdam publisher with the patriotic preface excised, replaced by a poem in praise of wonders. A study of nature in the East Indies had also been added, along with a wholly new frontispiece that casually blends a heraldic Brazilian figure with a vaguely Persian one.[15] The same process also transformed a chronicle of the Brazilian travels of Johan Nieuhof, which originally lauded the Republic's rise in the West. When they later appeared in print in 1682, however, Western adventures merged with Eastern tales (Nieuhof's visit to China and Persia), the frontispiece once again inviting the reader to join in a more dizzying spin of the globe. The text itself does present two separate sets of travels in the order they took place, yet the illustration program is less fussy. Facing a description of Jewish merchants in Brazil is an otherwise incongruous engraving of a Malay couple, intoxicated with tobacco (a subtle allusion to international commerce?). An image of a Malabar snake charmer turns up in a section on indigenous Brazilians allied with the Dutch, leaving readers to ponder the relation between New World Indians and Old World enchanters, and the far-fetched correlation of the two (fig. 1.5).[16]

Relative to earlier models, then, the new geography promoted a freshly decontextualized, vertiginously decentered world. It offered sundry bric-a-brac—*admirabilia mundi,* as one writer put it—intended for a vast and cluttered mental cabinet of curiosities. Dutch sources of this period expressly do not develop the sort of polemical themes of the earlier literature, choosing instead to highlight the collectively admired, if indistinctly located, rarities of the world. One best-selling author states his strategy as purposeful discursiveness. He confesses to offering no more than quick "morsels" of exotica, since variety, surely, was the spice of geographic life. Spain's colonial record, so central for his predecessors, is briefly considered and mildly commended, even, for the manner in which God had been delivered to the tropics. For another writer, Simon de Vries, Spain's greatest imperial sin was its lack of *curiosity* in its colonies—an appalling lapse for this author of tens of thousands of pages of "curious observations" of the Indies. Rarity is de rigueur in de Vries's *Great Cabinet of Curiosities;* the reader is invited to rummage through the strangeness, otherness, and oddities of the world. This volume amounts to a two-thousand-page descriptive tour de force that skims nimbly over events and habits, objects and creatures, scattered across the globe. Wampum in New York and wantonness in Brazil, dragons in India and drachmas in Attica, cabalism of the Jews and matrimony of the Lapps: all are deposited into a single "warehouse of wonders" (the title of another de Vries vehicle) from which readers could pick and choose the curiosa of their choice.[17]

These volumes' marvelous eclecticism, stunning breadth, and formidable vastness suggest a whole new order of geography. The Dutch had repackaged the world and transformed it into gargantuan, sprawling compendia of "curiosities." Like the exuberantly cluttered foregrounds of Frans Post's tropical landscapes, they teemed with lush description and dense detail of the late baroque world. Rather than restricting attention to Dutch deeds and Dutch settlements, they explored with encyclopedic interest *all* of the savage creatures, unusual inhabitants, and unknown landscapes of the globe. Rather than following the familiar tropes of earlier Dutch narratives, these works cele-

Figure 1.5. Willem vander Gouwen, "Malabar Snake Charmer" in Johan Nieuhof, *Gedenk-weerdige Brasiliaense zee- en lantreize* (Amsterdam, 1682). Engraving. Courtesy of the Universiteitsbibliotheek Amsterdam.

brated precisely the unfamiliar and indeterminate "strangeness" of the Indies. Dutch geography tolerated—encouraged even—variety. It cultivated chaos, and it reveled in randomness. Most importantly, it declined to play to a specific audience or perspective; it did not promote a particular place or purpose; it targeted no contested region or ri-

Figure 1.6. Title page illustration (signed "A. Streip") in Petrus Nylandt, *Het schouw-toneel der aertsche schepselen* (Amsterdam, 1672). Courtesy of the Universiteitsbibliotheek Amsterdam.

val. It pursued, rather, what one magnificent tome of Asiana pronounced the "pleasures" of the exotic: *Amoenitates exoticae.*[18]

Along with the metaphor of the warehouse and commerce, the cabinet and collecting, Dutch geography also adopted the metaphor of the theater and stage—as in Petrus Nylandt's *Schouw-toneel der aertsche schepselen* (Theater of the World's Creatures, 1672), a printed performance of global marvels that spanned everything from the feathered American turkey to the turbaned Ottoman Turk—both shown on its splendidly jumbled title page (fig. 1.6).[19] Nylandt's theatrical conceit allows this essay to conclude where it began—with Dryden's *Amboyna,* a work that overlaps exactly, yet contrasts tellingly, with that of Nylandt. Both texts, in a sense, are works of geography; both offer a vision of the world and their audience's place within it. Yet, in contrast to Dryden's "Map" of Dutch deceit and hotly drawn sketch of Amboina, Nylandt presents a more temperate view of the globe. He emphasizes the pleasure of wonder and the diversity of culture in a rich and plentiful world; his broad-ranging tour of the extra-European universe deliberately strips that world of all geopolitical specificity. Nylandt purges his "theater" of polemics; he makes no mention of colonial contests; he favors delight over didacticism. Or rather, Nylandt's message, like that of so many other practitioners of Dutch geography, eschews the pugnacious and political in favor of a generically appealing version of the globe that seemed to sell. Nylandt made the world palatable to all by offending none—in Europe, at least.

The global dramas staged by Nylandt and his contemporaries—the immense stock of geography, cartography, natural history, tropical painting, and travel literature produced in the Dutch Republic—was indeed an "embarrassment of riches." Yet they were riches meant to be moved from the shop, atelier, and merchant ship to the shelf, study, and *Kunstkammer* of consumers across Europe. To do so, the Dutch created an image—pursued a marketing strategy, as it were—that presented the increasingly contested globe as a decontextualized, decentered repository of bountiful curiosities and compelling collectibles. Less and less involved themselves in colonizing overseas, the Dutch could now afford to present a neutral, widely agreeable, perhaps even bland image of the world. Rather than the local and provincial, they now strove for the global and universal—at least, it merits reiterating, from the colonial European perspective—in projecting a world of alluring, enticing, spectacular richness. By the opening of the global eighteenth century, that world had become simply exotic.

CHAPTER TWO

Tupaia

Polynesian Warrior, Navigator, High Priest—and Artist

Glyndwr Williams

The significance of the role of Tupaia, the learned Polynesian high priest who joined the *Endeavour* on Captain James Cook's first Pacific voyage, has long been recognized— both in terms of his practical usefulness to the expedition, and in the wider context of early European-Polynesian contacts. In outline at least the story of Tupaia is fairly clear.[1] Born in about 1725 in Raiatea into a family noted for its skills in navigation, Tupaia became a high priest of the cult of Oro (the principal god of the Society Islands) and adviser to the ruling family until invasion drove him from the island. In about 1760 he arrived at Tahiti, where he formed an alliance with an ambitious woman chief, Purea. At the time of Captain Samuel Wallis's sighting of Tahiti and four-week stay there in 1767—the first by any European—"Queen Oberea" (Wallis's term) and Tupaia seemed in control of the island.

When Cook reached Tahiti in 1769, civil war had tilted the balance of power away from Purea, and Tupaia had lost influence. This may explain why toward the end of the *Endeavour*'s stay, Tupaia was among those islanders who volunteered to join the ship and leave their homeland, perhaps forever. Cook turned down most of these requests, but rather against his own inclination he was persuaded by Joseph Banks, the young (and soon to be famous) naturalist on board the *Endeavour*, to take Tupaia on board together with his young boy servant, Taiata. Cook rationalized the decision in his journal: "This man had been with us the most part of the time we had been upon the Island which gave us an oppertunity to know some thing of him: we found him to be a very intelligent person and to know more of the Geography of the Islands situated in these seas, their produce and the religion laws and customs of the inhabitants than any one we had met with."[2] Banks added: "What makes him more than any thing else desireable is his experience in the navigation of these people and knowledge of the Islands in these seas; he has told us the names of above 70, the most of which he has himself been at." Then he lapsed into a rather unpleasant analogy: "I do not know why I may not keep him as a curiosity, as well as some of my neighbours do lions and tygers at a larger expence than he will probably ever put me to."[3] The master of the *Endeavour*, Robert Monkhouse, who had been at Tahiti with Wallis, added to the general chorus of praise: "Tobia [*sic*] during our acquaintanceship with him has appear'd always to be infinitely superiour in every Respect to any other Indian we have met with."[4]

Tupaia more than fulfilled expectations. In the months that followed he acted as guide, interpreter, and mediator in the Society Islands and then along the coast of New Zealand. In New Zealand Tupaia was of greatest service to the expedition, for his ability to converse with the Maori took the heat out of several tense confrontations, as well as convincing Cook that the Society Islanders and New Zealanders had "one Origin or Source."[5] At Queen Charlotte Sound, Cook noted, "Tupaia always accompanies us in every excursion we make and proves of infinate service."[6] Together with Taiata he was also making "great progress with the English tongue," the astronomer Charles Green being their teacher. There is a passage in Banks that seems to show that he and Tupaia were able to converse in at least rudimentary English. The passage has a wider interest as it describes one of Tupaia's efforts to pacify potentially hostile Maori at Hauraki Gulf on North Island. "They answered him in their usual cant 'come ashore only and we will kill you all.' Well, said Tupia, but while we are at sea you have no manner of Business with us, the Sea is our property as much as yours. Such reasoning from an Indian who had not the smallest hint from any of us surprizd me much."[7] And sometime before the end of 1769, Tupaia drew the celebrated chart of the Pacific islands that, whatever problems of interpretation it poses, has generally been accepted, as Johann Reinhold Forster put it, "as a monument of the ingenuity and geographical knowledge of the people in the Society Isles, and of Tupaya in particular."[8] The end of the story is a sad one. During the *Endeavour*'s northward run along the east coast of Australia, Tupaia suffered from scurvy. Although he recovered by eating fish he caught for himself at the Endeavour River, he was ill again on the voyage to Batavia—so much so that when the coast of Java was sighted, Cook's first action was to send a boat ashore to try to get fruit for Tupaia. During the stay at Batavia, Tupaia and Taiata were among the several fatalities from malaria among the ship's company. The boy died first, followed three days later by Tupaia, who refused all medical help and, in the words of the expedition's artist, Sydney Parkinson, "gave himself up to grief; regretting, in the highest degree, that he had left his own country."[9]

In eighteen months Tupaia had made a remarkable contribution to the *Endeavour* voyage. What stands out in the comments of his shipboard companions is the self-confidence he showed in a variety of different situations: demonstrating to an appalled ship's company the best way to cook a dog, piloting the *Endeavour* into safe anchorage, discussing religious customs with Maori elders, and laying down rules of behavior when parties landed from the ship. This last was demonstrated within a few days of Tupaia's arrival on board when the *Endeavour* reached Huahine. Cook described what followed in words that leave no doubt as to Tupaia's dominant role:

> I went a Shore, accompanied by Mr Banks, Dr Solander and Dr Munkhouse, Tupia, the King of the Island and some other of the Natives who had been on board since the morning. The moment we landed Tupia striped himself as low as his waist and disired Mr Munkhouse to do the same, he then sat down before a great number of the natives that were collected together in a large Shade or house, the rest of us by his own desire standing behind; he then began a long speach or prayer which lasted near a 1/4 of an hour and in the Course of this speach presented to the people two handkerchiefs, a black silk neckcloth, some beads and two very small bunches of feathers, these things he had before provided for this purpose, at the same time two Chiefs spoke on the other side in answer to Tupia as I suppose on behalf of the people and presented us with some young Plantain Plants and two small bunches of feathers. These were by Tupia order'd to be carried on board the Ship.[10]

When this self-confidence extended to matters of navigation, piloting, and ship-handling it did not always endear Tupaia to Cook and his officers, men who had presumably expected a more deferential attitude, an eagerness to learn rather than to instruct. It was at once impressive, and rather mortifying, that regardless of distance Tupaia could point to Tahiti—even during his last days at Batavia many thousand miles away.[11] If a narrative of Cook's second voyage is to be believed, Tupaia was "by no means beloved by the Endeavour's crew, being looked upon as proud and austere, extorting homage, which the sailors who thought themselves degraded by bending to an Indian, were very unwilling to pay." Taiata, by contrast, "was the darling of the ship's company."[12] On that voyage, Cook told the story of how Tupaia, "when he heard that the king of England had a numerous offspring, declared he thought himself much greater, because he belonged to the arreoys" (*arioi*, a prestigious subchiefly group or cult that practiced infanticide and much else).[13] As far as we can tell from scanty evidence, the members of the ship's company who were closest to Tupaia were Joseph Banks, Sydney Parkinson, and Charles Green; it is significant, perhaps, that none of them were navy men. In a rather sour note at the time of Tupaia's death, Cook admitted that he was "a Shrewd, Sensible, Ingenious Man," but went on to say that he was also "proud and obstinate which often made his situation on board both disagreeable to himself and those about him."[14] There is an echo of this characterization in one of J. C. Beaglehole's footnotes in which he wrote, "One suspects Tupaia of a certain intellectual arrogance," not a charge Beaglehole leveled at many among the Pacific peoples Cook encountered. The accusation that Tupaia was "proud" was a more damning comment than it might seem at first glance when one remembers Cook's early years in John Walker's Quaker household. A hint of the forcefulness of Tupaia's personality comes from Banks, who wrote as the *Endeavour* left the Society Islands, "we again Launchd out into the Ocean in search of what chance and Tupia might direct us to."[15]

References in Banks's journal show that Tupaia carried a musket when he went ashore with Cook and the others—an unusual concession—and in one skirmish shot and wounded two Maori warriors.[16] In appearance he must have been a formidable figure, scarred by wounds from earlier wars including "one made by a spear of his countrey headed with the bone of a stingrays tail which has peircd quite through his body, entering at back and coming out just under his breast."[17] He was, according to Banks, about forty-five years old.[18] In general terms Cook left readers of his journal in no doubt about Tupaia's importance. In March 1770 as the *Endeavour* left New Zealand waters, Cook mused about the prospect of further discovery voyages and wrote: "should it be thought proper to send a ship out upon this service while *Tupia* lieves and he to come out in her, in that case she would have a prodigious advantage over every ship that have been upon discoveries in those seas before."[19] It was this consideration, as well as common humanity, that prompted Cook to do his utmost to keep Tupaia in good health as the long months on shipboard took their toll of the two Polynesians. He was an altogether more impressive figure than his fellow Raiatean, Mai, the "Omai" of Cook's second voyage who cut so dashing a figure in London society in the mid-1770s. How Tupaia would have fared if he had survived to reach England is impossible to tell; in the event, it was the young and callow Omai who became the archetypal Polynesian of the European imagination.

To Tupaia's acknowledged range of skills one must now add yet another talent, hitherto unsuspected. Among the Joseph Banks collection of papers from the *Endeavour* voyage in the British Library is a set of eight watercolor drawings by an unknown hand. In their magnificent work, *The Art of Captain Cook's Voyages,* Rüdiger Joppien and Bernard Smith placed this set as being by the "Artist of the Chief Mourner"—a reference to the subject of one of the drawings—and concluded that the artist was probably Joseph Banks. The circumstantial evidence is strong. At a ceremony at Tahiti, Banks saw and described the dress worn by the Chief Mourner, "most Fantastical tho' not un-

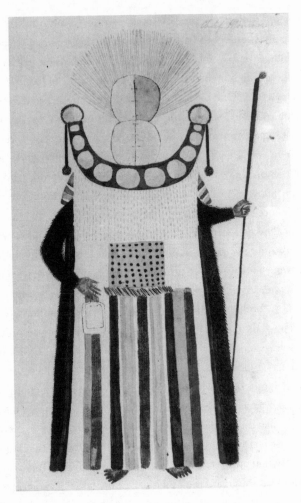

Figure 2.1. The Chief Mourner (watercolor). By permission of the British Library.

becoming," and referred to a drawing of it (fig. 2.1). One of the unknown artist's drawings of a Tahitian scene carefully delineated pandanus, breadfruit, banana and coconut
trees, and the taro plant, showing much the sort of botanical knowledge that Banks possessed (fig. 2.2). Finally, the best-known of the drawings shows a Maori and Englishman
exchanging a crayfish and taro cloth, probably at Tolaga Bay (Uawa) or the Bay of
Plenty, though speculation that Banks himself is portrayed runs up against the problem that the Englishman seems to be wearing the uniform of a naval officer (fig. 2.3).
Although Joppien and Smith were careful to point out that their identification was tentative, the unknown artist's use of watercolors again points to his being an influential
member of the ship's company—perhaps Banks—since the supply of watercolor pig-

ment was limited and otherwise used only in natural history drawings by Parkinson and Spöring.[20]

There the matter rested until 1997 when Harold Carter, doyen of Banks scholars, re-examined transcripts of some Banks letters he had made twenty-five years earlier. Among them was a letter dated 12 December 1812 referring to a legal wrangle over the timing of a farm sale. "Such a conduct," Banks wrote of the offending party, "I have never heard of in all Nations the delivery and the Payment is done at the same moment Tupia the Indian who came with me from Otaheite Learned to draw in a way not Quite unintelligible The genius for Caricature which all wild people Possess Led him to Caricature me and he drew me with a nail in my hand delivering it to an Indian who sold me a Lobster but with my other hand I had a firm fist on the Lobster determind not to Quit the nail till I had Livery and Seizin of the article purchasd."[21] Despite the error concerning the item Banks remembered holding in his hand (a piece of bark cloth or tapa, not a nail), the passage clearly refers to the drawing of the exchange between a Maori and Englishman either at Tolaga Bay (Uawa) or the Bay of Plenty (see fig. 2.3). The drawing, together with the others in the set, was still in Banks's possession and remained so until after his death. What is striking about Banks's note is not only the ev-

Figure 2.2. A Tahitian scene (watercolor). By permission of the British Library.

Figure 2.3. A Maori bartering with an English naval officer (watercolor). By permission of the British Library.

idence it provides of the retentiveness of his memory forty-three years after the event but also the casual way in which Banks recalls the drawing of the barter scene simply to make a point about the normal procedure in commercial transactions. It was as though there was nothing remarkable about either the drawing or the artist. Banks's journal entry for 1 November 1769 at the Bay of Plenty may refer to this scene because Tupaia was also there: "7 [canoes] soon came up with us and after some conversation with Tupia began to sell Muscles and lobsters of which they had great plenty. In the beginning they dealt fair but soon began to cheat, taking what we gave them without making any return."[22]

If, as Banks's evidence shows, Tupaia drew the barter scene, then he was almost certainly responsible for the other drawings attributed to the "Artist of the Chief Mourner" (see figs. 2.1, 2.2, 2.4–2.6). In contrast to the crude nature of much of the artwork, parts of the drawings show some delicacy of touch—the feathers on the Chief Mourner's cloak, the buttons on the Englishman's jacket, the fine detail of trees and plants in the Tahitian scene (though the perspective between boats and land has defeated the artist). In the drawings that include figures, the fingers and toes are poorly drawn, with little indication of joints or (in the case of toes) of different lengths. The eyes are shown as jet black spots, staring straight out of the drawing even when the face is in profile. This is the distinguishing feature in the drawing of the Aborigines that otherwise might appear to be by a different hand (see fig. 2.4). It has been suggested that the emphasis given to the eyes by Tupaia has a particular significance.[23] A central part of the cult of Oro involved a ceremony of human sacrifice in which the eye of the dead man was presented to the chief, who ate it, or at least pretended to eat it.[24] Cook witnessed such a ceremony on his last visit to Tahiti in 1777, when the chief, Tu, was presented with the eye taken from a human sacrifice. When James Morrison, one of the *Bounty* mutineers, saw human sacrifice in 1791 at an inauguration rite of the young Pomare II, "I enquired the Cause of the Eye being offered, and was thus informed. The King is the Head of the People for which reason the Head is sacred; the Eye being the most valuable part is the fittest to be offered."[25]

To consider the implications of the identification of Tupaia as the previously unknown artist on the *Endeavour* raises a whole series of questions. To begin with the query that a skeptic might put, is it conceivable that Tupaia, coming from a nonliterate society that did not include naturalistic drawing or painting among its arts, could within weeks of the arrival of the *Endeavour*, be drawing figures, places, and scenes? This

Figure 2.4. Australian Aborigines fishing from bark canoes (watercolor). Courtesy of the British Library.

Figure 2.5. A Dancing Girl (watercolor). By permission of the British Library.

form of realistic if naïve representation would seem to have little in common with the intricate and repetitive designs used in the processes of tattooing or staining bark cloth, or indeed with the carved wooden figures, some human or partly so, that were positioned in *marae* or at the bows of the great war canoes. What links there might be can be gathered from James Marra's account of Tahiti written on Cook's second voyage: "Their painting appears to be in a rude state, and chiefly confined to the figures represented on their bodies, and the ornaments on their vessels of navigation. The figures represented on their bodies are generally those of birds and fishes, sometimes after nature, and sometimes the creatures of the artist's fancy; but whatever is represented, the outline is traced with astonishing exactness. This act is solely confined to the priest-hood."[26]

Before Banks's evidence about the paintings came to light, some scholars doubted whether Tupaia actually drew the chart attributed to him. G. S. Parsonson, for example, has asserted that "a non-literate man was fundamentally incapable of projecting his geographical knowledge on a piece of flat paper."[27] On the other hand, we have Cook's firm statement that the chart was "Drawn by Tupaia's own hands."[28] Even more significant as far as the eight drawings are concerned is a later, little-noticed comment by Cook during his second voyage. In the middle of a long journal entry about the tactics used with war canoes in Tahiti, Cook mentioned that during the *Endeavour* voyage Tupaia had "made a drawing of one of these Vessels."[29] Marra's account of the second voyage paid tribute to Tupaia as "a man of real genius, a priest of the first order, and an excellent artist," though his description of the arts of Tahiti seems to indicate that when the writer referred to "painting" he had tattooing in mind.[30]

Tupaia's achievement is the more noteworthy in that the drawings seem to have been made from life. There is little evidence that Tupaia was copying drawings made by Parkinson or others on board the ship—a simpler and more imitative process than drawing from life—though he must have observed his fellow artists with some care. One can never be certain how much material has disappeared, but among the large number of drawings and paintings from Cook's first voyage only the drawings by Parkinson of Raiatean dancing girls might be regarded as providing possible models for

Figure 2.6. Tahitian musicians (watercolor). By permission of the British Library.

Tupaia's representation. There are also drawings by Parkinson and Spöring of the Chief Mourner, but they show significant differences from Tupaia's painting (the wand held in a different hand, for example).[31]

Inspection of the originals suggests a steady hand at work; there are no obvious corrections or paint smears. A point of interest is that some of them show that the outline of the figure was done in pencil. This is clearest in the drawing of the dancing girl (fig. 2.5), where in the original the legs are faintly visible through the skirt. One of the two penciled drawings of the *marae* has outer lines drawn with a ruler or other straight surface,[32] while in the Tahitian scene some of the small figures in the boat are left in pencil. Is it possible then that Tupaia had help with the drawing, if not the painting, of his pictures? The obvious candidate for such assistance, as well as for supplying the all-important watercolors, is Sydney Parkinson, but there is no reference in his journal (a posthumous publication) to such help, or indeed any reference to Tupaia engaged in drawing or painting. This indifference is a feature of the other journals. Tupaia's drawings were of enough interest to be brought home and carefully kept by Banks, but evidently *not* of enough interest to be mentioned by him in his journal. By contrast, Archibald Menzies, naturalist on George Vancouver's *Discovery* in 1791–95, wrote at some length in his journal about the artistic efforts of "Towereroo" (Kualelo), a youth from the Hawaiian island of Molokai who was on board. He had been taken to England in 1789 in a trading vessel on which Menzies was surgeon, and was now being returned home. Vancouver wrote brusquely of Towereroo's eighteen-month stay in England that he had lived "in great obscurity, and did not seem in the least to have benefited by his residence in this country." Menzies told a rather different story. Although attempts to teach Towereroo to read had failed, "in writing he had made greater progress, that is, he soon acquired a habit of copying whatever was placed before him with great exactness in the same manner he would do a drawing or a picture; indeed to the art of Drawing in general he appeard most partial, & would no doubt in a short time make great proficiency with the aid of a little instruction, but in this uncultivated state of his mind he seemd fondest of those rude pictures called Caricatures & frequently amused himself in taking off even his friends in imitation of these pieces."[33]

The lack of interest on the *Endeavour* in Tupaia's efforts to sketch and paint is the more puzzling because toward the end of the stay in Tahiti, Banks entered in his journal that Tupaia went ashore carrying "a miniature portrait of mine to show his friends," while on Raiatea Banks described how he took Parkinson to a *heiva* so that he could sketch the dancing girls. Neither of these events would seem to be as worthy of record as the sight of Tupaia putting brush to paper. Other lacunae are also puzzling. Given the mark that Tupaia made on the voyage, it seems odd that although Parkinson drew the young servant, Taiata, as far as we know he did not draw his master. Perhaps too much should not be made of this: no portraits seem to have been made of any of the leading figures on Tahiti on this voyage. Even so, the lack of interest in Tupaia as a subject is surprising given his conspicuous role on the voyage and the length of time he spent on the *Endeavour.*

Let us return to Tupaia the artist. If we accept that he was working from life and not from another's drawings or in retrospect, then his paintings (or at least those that survive, and what proportion they might be of the whole we cannot tell) were done at quite lengthy intervals. The scenes from the Society Islands would have been sketched between June and August 1769; the New Zealand barter scene in October or November; and the drawing of the Aborigines fishing during the *Endeavour's* enforced seven-week stay at Endeavour River between June and August 1770. Out of Tupaia's known eight drawings, six represent peoples and scenes close to home; but two depict a European, a Maori, and Aborigines, all in their different ways unfamiliar as far as Tupaia was concerned. Can we read into Tupaia's change of subject matter an increased confidence in his own skills, or a growing interest in the novel and the unknown? The small number of drawings under consideration would seem to warn against such generalizations, but they make an interesting contrast with the subjects of Parkinson's drawings. As artist with Banks on the expedition, his main task was precisely to record that which was exotic and strange—especially flora and fauna—in order to convey to a public at home where the *Endeavour* had been and what its crew had seen.

In assessing the wider significance of Tupaia the artist, it is worth remembering that: "Ways of seeing may often reflect relationships of power . . . To shoot or poison the local people and appropriate their land is to exercise one kind of power. To measure their heads, cover their loins, record their tongues, sketch their faces, or film their ceremonies is to exercise quite another kind of power, milder, subtler, often benign in its intentions, yet possessed none the less of its own significance, implying a relationship of subject to object, observer to observed."[34]

Tupaia had in a sense reversed the usual order of things. By the time he recorded the New Zealand exchange, he was drawing not simply figures or buildings but behavior and attitudes. As Banks remembered all those years later, Tupaia drew a crucial moment in the contact between Maori and European, and the sketch over the years has achieved emblematic significance, though the unquestioning assumption has always been that it was drawn by an Englishman. That it was drawn by a Polynesian from the Society Islands has significant ramifications. Tupaia decided what to draw; he was as much in control of the situation as he was during the landing at Huahine. Once again he had not conformed to his expected role—helpful but deferential—which is presumably why Cook thought him "proud and obstinate," too often involved in "disagreeable" situations. What lay behind Cook's words we can only guess. I think that David Turnbull goes too far in suggesting that Tupaia "had, in effect, been the expedition leader through-out the voyage from Tahiti around New Zealand and up the Australian coast,"[35] but it is quite likely that Tupaia was not above questioning the captain's decisions and thus implicitly challenging his authority. This was the cardinal sin, we might remember, that led to trouble between Cook and that other knowledgeable but troublesome supernumerary, Johann Reinhold Forster, on the second voyage. It may or may not be significant that on his second voyage Cook refused to carry any Polynesians back to England and that it was Captain Tobias Furneaux on the *Adventure* who took Mai on board. The uncertainty about Tupaia's status on the *Endeavour* is a reminder of how much is lacking in our knowledge about shipboard relationships on the discovery vessels. However detailed the official logs and journals, they mainly dealt with the externals of the voyages.

There is no doubt that the New Zealand leg of the *Endeavour*'s voyage saw an enhancement of Tupaia's status. In trying to explain Maori religious beliefs, Banks wrote that their account of creation was much like Tupaia's, and he went on: "he however seemed to be much better vers'd in such legends than any of them, for whenever he began to preach as we calld it he was sure of a numerous audience who attended with most profound silence to his doctrines."[36] On Cook's second voyage, the first question asked of the crews when they landed in New Zealand was where Tupaia was.[37] At Tolaga Bay what George Forster described as "a kind of dirge-like melancholy song" was performed in his memory.[38] In Tahiti, few showed any interest in Tupaia or his fate, but at Raiatea and Huahine there were inquiries and expressions of sorrow (and at Raiatea the Forsters were shown a great *marae* that they thought might be named after him).[39] In New Zealand even Maori not encountered on the first voyage inquired about Tupaia, a puzzle Cook tried to explain: "It may be ask'd, that if these people had never seen the Endeavour or any of her crew, how they became acquainted with the Name of Tupia . . . to this it may be answered that the Name of Tupia was at that time so popular among them that it would be no wonder if at this time it is known over great part of *New Zealand*, the name of Tupia may be as familiar to those who never saw him as to those who did."[40] In 1777, when Cook called at Queen Charlotte Sound on his third voyage, he found that the *Endeavour* was remembered as Tupaia's ship.[41]

Memories of Tupaia lingered. In 1835 the trader Joel Polack visited Cook's Tolaga Bay and talked to Te Kani, the grandson of the high chief who had controlled the area at the time of the *Endeavour*'s visit. He was told that "Tupaia was a great favourite with our fathers, so much so, that to gratify him, several children who were born in the village, during his sojourn among us, were named after him." Polack was shown blue beads left by Cook and was then taken to the cave where Tupaia had often rested during the day. On the walls were charcoal drawings of a variety of subjects, and "Above our reach, and evidently faded by time, was the representation of a ship and some boats, which were unanimously pointed out to me, as the productions of [Tupaia]."[42] Whether this precise attribution was correct or not is perhaps less important than the evidence the episode provides of Maori memories of Tupaia, both as a leading figure in momentous events and as a recorder of them. Here was a man who until his final illness seemed, on the surface at least, to move between two worlds with some ease.

CHAPTER THREE

The Caribbean Islands in Atlantic Context, circa 1500–1800

Philip D. Morgan

The Caribbean was the first region of the New World to feel the brunt of European colonial development. Although the Antilles produced the first black republic and second independent nation of the Americas, colonialism lasted longer in the Caribbean than in most regions of the world. "No part of the so-called Third World," declares Sidney W. Mintz, "was hammered so thoroughly or at such length into a colonial amalgam of European design." The most dramatic aspect of this battering was the virtual extirpation of the indigenous population, whose destruction occurred earlier and more completely in this region than anywhere else in the Americas. Moreover, the Caribbean has the dubious distinction of being the first region in the Americas to be introduced to slavery, sugarcane, and the plantation system. Nowhere was the influence of this unholy trinity more systematically and intensely felt: the region received more slaves over a longer period of time, produced more sugar, and developed the most regimented plantation system of any in the Americas. Arguably, then, the Caribbean was the focal point of overseas European expansion in the early modern world. By 1700, for example, Barbados was an economic powerhouse, "the Hong Kong of the pre-industrial era," probably exporting more product relative to its size and population than any previous society. With pardonable exaggeration, Abbé Raynal noted of the mid-eighteenth-century Caribbean that "the labors of the colonists settled in these long-scorned islands are the sole basis of the African trade, extend the fisheries and cultivation of North America, provide advantageous outlets for the manufactures of Asia, double perhaps triple the activity of the whole of Europe. They can be regarded as the principal cause of the rapid movement which stirs the Universe."[1]

The region's importance is matched only by its complexity. The Caribbean contains thousands of islands, which have been organized into about fifty major societies. The islands are dotted along an arc about 4,000 kilometers in length, and range in area from pocket-size Saba to mighty Cuba. Diversity in size and terrain is matched by the variety of human occupation. Scores of separate Native American societies existed in the region on the eve of European contact and continued to exist for some time thereafter. After 1492, settlers from Spain, France, Britain, the Netherlands, Sweden, and Denmark occupied various islands—often almost in hailing distance of one another—sometimes dwelling on the same islands at the same time, and sometimes sequentially as many islands changed hands. Joining these diverse Europeans and their enforced intimacy were Africans coerced to migrate from literally hundreds of states and stateless societies. Even a few Chinese arrived in Trinidad in the early nineteenth century, harbingers of a much larger Asian migration later in the same century. Together, these varied ethnic and racial groups created one of the most heterogeneous social mosaics anywhere. The Caribbean region "has been one of the truly great arenas for interpenetration of African, European, American, and Asian traditions."[2]

So how should this diverse, complex, vital region be represented? The most venerable tradition is the imperial approach. Commendably broad in scope, the imperial perspective in practice narrowed to a description of the formal structure of imperial governments. Imperial historians generally studied institutions, not people, and they usually concentrated on the affairs of a single imperial power. As empires crumbled and Caribbean nations gained their independence, a nationalist perspective supplanted the imperial tradition. Individual islands found their own historians, and the local gained precedence over the regional. Indigenous scholars began writing from the inside rather than from the outside. Unfortunately, the nationalist perspective often narrowed the focus and tended toward provincialism.[3]

In the imperial and nationalist schools, analysis of the Caribbean region has often taken the form of oversimplifying paired polarities—Arawak versus Carib, colonizer versus colonized, buccaneer versus settler, planter versus peasant, absentee versus resident, master versus slave, settlement versus exploitation colony. In anthropology, Peter Wilson's fascinating book *Crab Antics*, an exploration of the organization of social life on the Colombian island of Providencia and more generally of anglophone Antillean islands, argued that two counterposed value systems—"respectability," which had its roots in the colonizing society, and "reputation," which was indigenous to the colony—

governed social relations and behavior. In his analysis of Caribbean traditions of elo-
quence, Roger Abrahams distinguished between good talkers and good arguers, between "talking sweet" and "talking broad." The Caribbean experience seems to lend
itself to stark dichotomies and dualities, but the mechanistic juxtaposition of opposites
seems unlikely to capture fully the region's extraordinarily rich and complex mosaic of
peoples, traditions, and customs.[4]

What is needed is an approach that attends to the full complexity of life in the
Caribbean and that puts the region in its full Atlantic context. This chapter aims to illustrate the advantages of a wide angle of vision, a broad transoceanic framework, when
viewing the Caribbean. It explores three topics—Native Americans, the environment,
and slavery. Too often, the Caribbean is lovingly explored in all its particularity. It is, of
course, necessary to sharpen the focus, to examine regions and locales in depth, to embrace specificity. At the same time, it is also vital to place local developments within
large-scale orbits and trace the networks and interconnections linking seemingly dis-
parate borderlands. It is best to view the Caribbean as part of Atlantic history, a single,
complex unit of analysis. This large-scale vision means opting for a dynamic diasporic
approach, attending to flows, dispersals, and mixtures of people, goods, plants, and
much else. Thus a moving camera, a microscope, but, above all, a telescope will be required.

The story of Native American life in the Caribbean is gradually becoming more complex. In protohistoric and historic time, the standard story now goes, three main Indian
peoples and cultures, together with accompanying subcultures—not the simplified duality of Arawaks and Caribs of even older accounts—inhabited the Caribbean. By far
the most important were the Classic Taino who lived on Hispaniola and Puerto Rico,
probably with outposts in eastern Cuba, the Turks and Caicos Islands, and St. Croix.
Socially, Classic Taino culture exhibited a class system; familially, it was matrilineal,
tracing descent through mothers, and avunculocal, with husbands residing in the villages of their uncles; and politically, it was organized hierarchically into chiefdoms. Important villages contained ceremonial plazas and ball courts, about eighty of which have
been discovered on Puerto Rico alone. Religion was of vital importance, for there were
priests, temples, and cave shrines. Alongside the Classic Taino were two subcultures: a
western branch encompassing Jamaica, central Cuba, and the Bahamas, and an eastern
branch extending through most of the Virgin and Leeward Islands. These two subgroups spoke essentially the same language as the Classic Taino, but were less populous,
had no regional chiefdoms, and apparently lacked ball courts.

Two other distinct cultures, the orthodox story now posits, existed on either side of
the Tainos. To the west were a remnant of Archaic Age Indians, sometimes referred to

as Ciboneys but more accurately as Guanahatabeys, who were still present in western Cuba when the Spanish arrived. Apparently, they lived in mobile bands, sometimes inhabiting caves and relying on hunting, fishing, and gathering for subsistence. They lacked both pottery and agriculture. To the southeast were the Island-Caribs who, in most accounts, were recent invaders from the Central American mainland. They adopted the so-called Igneri language, an Arawakan language of the island peoples they supposedly conquered; Island-Carib men also spoke among themselves a pidgin language, which was basically Cariban in vocabulary and which they probably used to trade with their neighbors on the mainland. Island-Carib men lived apart from their wives in separate houses, emphasized warfare and trade, and elected temporary war chiefs.[5]

This coherent narrative has been constructed from what are literally shards of evidence, and it is possible to look at the same pottery fragments and offer alternative, though not as yet equally coherent, views. For example, questions have been raised about the ascription *Taino*. The term is not a reference to a language or ethnic group but rather derives from the adjective meaning good or noble and was used by the natives to explain to the Spaniard how they could be differentiated from other Indians. For this reason, some scholars prefer the term *Island Arawak,* in recognition of the many linguistic and cultural traits that the island and mainland Arawaks shared, although such advocates have to recognize that Island Arawaks and mainland Arawaks differed significantly in both language and culture. Questions have also been raised about the description of the people of western Cuba as Archaic Indians. Archaeologists may have relied too uncritically on flawed early Spanish accounts of a savage people living in caves. Perhaps the Guanahatabeys were not a survival of Archaic hunter-gatherers but rather a local variant of Tainos.[6]

One way to resolve some of these questions is with more refined investigations of mainland-island links, broadening the unit of inquiry to examine patterns of filiation and derivation. For instance, Archaic Age skulls are long, narrow, and wide, and Ceramic Age skulls are broad and low (Tainos flattened their foreheads by binding hard objects against them in childhood). Skeletal and dental analyses have the potential to trace biological ancestry and locate the original homes of migrants. Further linguistic analysis of the lexicon and morphology of the Arawakan language family—which has already shown a close relationship between Taino, Igneri, and Arawak—may reveal other linkages. Surveys of petroglyphs are uncovering close connections and some significant differences between mainland and islands. Computer simulation models are helping to determine the most likely maritime movements of people in the Caribbean region, and mainland-island connections from the origins of the ball court to actual contact across sea passages promise to reveal much about island life. Links between mainland and island are important in the historic period, too. Tituba of Salem was not an African, as she is sometimes portrayed, but rather an Indian, probably captured from South America, enslaved by pirates, and taken to Barbados. There she may have worked on the estate of a Thompson family, where a documented "Tattuba" has been discovered. It is also possible that she was from Florida because the term Spanish Indian, which is how she was described, often referred to Indians captured from the missions there and sold north. Tituba then was a Native American from either the Caribbean or the circum-Caribbean.[7]

Important as these investigations promise to be, no issue is more controversial than the standard Manichean division of Caribbean Indians into good and bad, Taino and Island-Carib, peaceful agriculturalists and fierce warriors. Irving Rouse, the dean of Caribbean prehistory, still holds to this view, asserting in his most recent book that Island-Caribs "ate bits of the flesh of opposing warriors in order to acquire the latter's prowess." The theory that the Caribs were late invaders is usually based on a number of factors: the Taino told the Spanish that they faced raids from a fierce group of Indians, some of whom were said to be Caribs (or a word that approximated that term); the Spanish were anxious to label aggressive Indians as Caribs or cannibals because they were then candidates for slavery; the presence of Cariban speakers in Venezuela suggested that it was the original home and language of the Carib invaders. In fact, the Island-Caribs spoke primarily an Arawakan language; thus, there is no compelling linguistic evidence that Island-Caribs identified themselves with the mainland Cariban-speaking Kalina. It is also inaccurate to depict the Caribs as moving only in a northward and westward direction. They raided southward, particularly on the eastern coast of the mainland, where their deadliest enemies, the Lokono, were located. This orientation further suggests that they were well established in the Lesser Antilles before they began pushing outward.[8]

In short, Island-Carib culture may have been primarily a local development within the islands but with noticeable infusions from the mainland, with which the Island-Caribs were in regular contact. Alternatively, as Rouse maintains, the Island-Caribs were true invaders from the mainland who conquered the local Igneri population but then assimilated with them. Whichever hypothesis proves to be true, there seems little doubt that the earlier simplified dichotomy between Taino and Island-Carib must be jettisoned, even if one does not go so far as to argue that Taino and Island-Carib were one and the same or that Caribs were essentially a European invention. Certainly, Island-Caribs and Tainos had much in common. The bow and arrow was not exclusively an Island-Carib weapon but rather existed among the Taino, and both groups used noxious gases—throwing pepper into pots with live coals—as an offensive means of war. The Island-Caribs worshiped personal deities like those of the Taino. The Tainos acquired power by keeping the bones of their ancestors in their houses; reports of Island-Carib cannibalism often resulted from little more than the same practice. Both groups coopted *zemis* or personal spirits resident in ancestors, friends or enemies: in pre-Columbian Puerto Rico, for example, the ancestors of Tainos made pendants by drilling human teeth. Overall, the mythologies of the two groups were similar.[9]

A rescaling of perspective to encompass mainland and island promises, then, to illumine the most local, provincial developments in Indian life, as well as the larger regional history. In fact, the world of Caribbean Indians should encourage us to think of the sea as a bridge rather than a barrier, for their history was in many ways the story of the sea. Caribbean Indians were adept fishermen, employing a variety of fishing techniques. A staple of their diet was the green turtle, which has been likened to the bison of the American plains: it was abundant, quite easy to cull, and a good source of protein. The Indians' canoes, which could carry from 50 to 150 people, drew praise for their functional design and elegance. Most important of all, Caribbean Indians tended to interact more closely with their neighbors across sea passages than with the residents of their own islands. Distinct cultural areas have been found to encompass adjoining halves of neighboring islands. Ocean passages facilitated interaction among a seafaring people, while island landmasses often acted as barriers. The Indians' world was in many ways oriented more toward the sea than to the land. Thus, their world was joined not sundered by the sea. Why should it have been any different for the invaders?[10]

The rapid obliteration of a large Indian population is but one of a number of severe traumas of global significance that shaped the early Caribbean; another is the enormous environmental degradation that has occurred on the islands. Much of the indigenous fauna has either disappeared entirely or become greatly depleted, largely through the European colonizers' actions and the aggressive animals (such as the African green monkey and the rat) they introduced. "More faunal species," notes David Watts, "have become extinct in the West Indies within the last century than in any other part of the world except Antarctica." Spanish colonization led to an "explosive growth" of secondary vegetation and a major destruction of vegetation and soils through the trampling and grazing of domesticated animals, but the real ecological maelstrom to hit the islands was sugar cultivation. Barbados was the first Caribbean island to experience fully the commercial sugar revolution, and in just twenty years almost all of its tropical rain forest had disappeared. By the late seventeenth century, the island's open landscape was filled with the sound of turning windmill sails rather than birdsong. Exhausted soils, eroded landforms, and the spread of many alien plant species, particularly shrub weeds, replaced the lush, native vegetation. The sugar industry undoubtedly "supported the densest concentrations of rural population in the Americas," an indication of the press of numbers on resources. Planters inscribed their attitude toward space on island landscapes; they emphasized geometric order, precisely defined plantation boundaries, and demarcated fields by straight lines. They had surveyors provide lovingly detailed estate maps, which were always more highly developed in the sugar colonies than in any other part of the New World.[11]

A broader frame of reference in which to understand Caribbean environmental degradation is the global study of island ecologies. For example, biologists have coined the term *island syndrome* to describe the process of rapid species extinction. From the early modern era onward, the Caribbean has lost more bird species than the whole of the American continent. Similarly, more mammals have become extinct in the region than throughout Africa, Asia, and Europe combined. Island species are more readily extinguished than their mainland counterparts because of population size and fluctuation. Islands support fewer species than mainlands, and small islands generally contain fewer species than big islands. Furthermore, all populations fluctuate in size from year to year, and small populations are more likely to fluctuate to zero. With less margin of security, a small island population is vulnerable to various forms of human persecution and natural catastrophe. The Caribbean region is particularly precarious environmentally because of its unpredictability, being especially prone to earthquakes, volcanic eruptions, hurricanes, and droughts.[12]

Another Caribbean vulnerability was its disease environment. Because the region could host a range of tropical diseases and because it was such a hub of trade, its microbiotic traffic was particularly intense. The Caribbean was a notably lethal crossroads of contagion, where the velocity of infection was swift. The first known New World pandemic of smallpox began in Hispaniola in December 1518 and moved westward to Cuba and the Central American mainland the following year before reaching Mexico in 1520. When forced migrants from Africa arrived in great numbers, they brought with them new, more virulent strains of disease. Despite some of their immunities to yellow fever and malaria, about a third of Africans exposed to a new disease environment and thrust into the sugar fields typically died off within their first year or so in the islands. The Caribbean was a fearsome charnel house for Europeans. Garrison mortality averaged about 20 percent annually, but the worst casualties were among the unseasoned expeditionary forces. About three-quarters of various European armies sent to the Caribbean were killed off in a matter of months of arriving in the region. Spain's ability to hang onto its Caribbean islands owed much to its disease-experienced troops and to the other invaders' lack of immunities. Approximately 60,000–70,000 Europeans lost their lives in trying to put down the slave rebellion in St. Domingue in the 1790s and early 1800s. Almost all of these men died from disease. The British decision to create the so-called West India Regiments, essentially an Africanization of its army, was a response to the region's lethality.[13]

In addition to the human toll exacted by Caribbean diseases, a particularly distressing feature of the region's ecological vulnerability is its ability to host—along with other island regions—many of the world's most exotic life forms, whether plants or animals. Islands are havens and breeding grounds for anomalies. Jamaica, for example, has an unusually big anguid lizard; Cuba had a giant flightless owl, now extinct. Islands are, in David Quammen's words, "natural laboratories of extravagant evolutionary experimentation." The potential for speedy divergent evolution in small populations explains why so many prodigious or diminutive species exist on detached and remote islands.[14]

Under ordinary circumstances, the species lost from an island during a given span of time are roughly equal in number to the species gained by the same island over the same period. Some remarkable immigrations to various Caribbean islands are known to have occurred. Coconut palms achieved widespread dispersal because the coconut is such a seaworthy seed. The European and African newcomers introduced vast numbers of new plants and animals—some 500 or so African weeds into Jamaica, for instance; trees such as the ackee, coffee, tamarind, bissy, and baobab, or vegetables such as yams, millet, plantains, and pigeon peas; animals such as the guinea fowl, camels, and long-haired sheep also came from Africa. Mango, jackfruit, citruses, and, of course, sugarcane were brought from Asia; horses from North America; cattle and donkeys from the Azores and Canaries; breadfruit, taro, and the Otaheite apple from the Pacific. The flip side of environmental degradation, therefore, is a remarkable infusion and efflorescence of new plants, trees, and animals.[15]

Although few regions of the world were more exclusively committed to a single economic activity than was the Caribbean, and although some islands might seem to have been little more than one vast sugar plantation (albeit divided into plural estates), it is a mistake to ignore the alternative economic structures that paralleled or serviced the plantation. Major secondary crops such as coffee, cotton, indigo, cacao, and pimento dominated parts of some islands; provisioning estates and livestock ranches were important satellites of sugar plantations and often outnumbered them. Minor staples and activities such as ginger, arrowroot, and aloe cultivation, and fishing and salt raking were commonplace on many islands. Urban places were also impressive—the proportion of the population living in towns was at least 20 percent in most Spanish and Dutch islands, and 10 percent in most French and British territories. Higher percentages of island populations lived in urban places than did people in North America.[16]

In part because of the networks urban places fostered, environmental degradation was not just allowed to happen in the Caribbean. The region's planters and imperial officials often tried to offset the enormous costs of the environmental revolution in which they participated. Planters engaged in many areas of agricultural innovation, including the use of mill trash as a fuel in order to minimize further deforestation, manuring to restore soil fertility, and the widespread practice of cane holing to minimize erosion. As Richard Grove has shown, colonies often pioneered conservationist policies; colonial expansion promoted the rapid diffusion of new scientific ideas between colonies, and between the metropole and colony. The isolated oceanic island directly stimulated the emergence of a critical view of European behavior, and its peculiar flora sowed the seeds for concepts of rarity and fears of extinction. Tropical islands became the location for some of the earliest experiments in systematic forest conservation, water-pollution control, and fisheries protection. As early as 1764 programs of forest protection, systems of forest reserves, were quickly being put into effect on newly acquired British territories in the Caribbean. The colonial botanical garden as developed, for example, on St. Vincent (founded in 1765 and the first in the Americas) formed the basis for a new kind of learning, information collecting, and networking in the tropical environment. The proximity of Caribbean islands inspired emulation. Alexander Anderson, keeper of the St. Vincent Botanic Garden, followed innovations most particularly on the Spanish colony of Trinidad and the Dutch colonies of Demerara and Essequibo. Despite the distance from metropolitan authority, science was innovative on the colonial periphery, and the colonies had a significant impact on the history of environmentalism. Caribbean environmental thinking can be best understood, as in much else, by exploring the interconnections between scientists and protoscientists in various Atlantic outposts.[17]

Just as the Atlantic Ocean knitted together an empire of science, so it generated an empire of labor. While undoubtedly inelastic, inefficient, and segmented, an Atlantic labor market that functioned as one vast unit arose in the early modern era. The cornerstone of this ramshackle but unitary system was, of course, slavery. No "British West Indian colony," Barbara Solow emphasizes, "ever founded a successful society on the basis of free white labor." Before 1800, for every European more than six Africans crossed the Atlantic to the Caribbean. Because the institutions of the slave trade were common to the Atlantic community, an Atlantic perspective is the only way to understand fully what was the largest intercontinental migration then known to the world.[18]

    The most exciting feature of a recently created database on the transatlantic slave trade is the new light cast on links between particular African and American ports. The data set has evidence from 27,233 transatlantic voyages, drawn from every major European slaving power between 1527 and 1866. Information is now available on about two-thirds of all the ships that made a transatlantic slave voyage. More is now known about the forced migration of Africans than the voluntary migration of Europeans in the early modern era. Approximately 5 million Africans were carried to the Caribbean over the three and a half centuries of the slave trade—just under a half of the total brought to the Americas. About two of these five million arrived in the half-century from 1760 to 1810.[19]

More important than some modest revisions of the timing and overall numbers of Caribbean immigrants is the ability to trace connections between particular African regions of departure and Caribbean destinations. Some of these connections were remarkably close. Thus, half the Africans leaving the Senegambian region went to St. Domingue, and two out of three Africans leaving the Bight of Biafra went to the British Caribbean. Barbados and the Danish islands drew disproportionately on the Gold Coast. But, of all the receiving regions in the Americas, the Caribbean received the greatest mix of African peoples. No single part of Africa, for example, supplied more than about 30 percent of arrivals to either Cuba, Barbados, Martinique, Guadeloupe, or the Danish islands.[20]

Over time, furthermore, any Caribbean destination drew on different provenance zones that generally became more diverse. Consider Barbados. In the third quarter of the seventeenth century, three-quarters of the slaves brought to the island came from just two African regions: the Bight of Biafra (supplying 48%) and the Bight of Benin (28%). By the last quarter of the eighteenth century, the two leading African regional suppliers provided only about a half of the island's slaves, and the dominant supplier was now West-Central Africa (37%), a region that provided no slaves to the island a century earlier. The pattern of arrivals to Jamaica was similar; an initial dominance by one or two regions gave way to growing heterogeneity over the course of the eighteenth century. A dynamic diasporic approach indicates how readily slaves were drawn from a changing and generally more diverse series of African coastal regions over time.[21]

The demographic structure of the slave trade also meant that different combinations of people arrived on different islands. The enduring impact of any migration on either the receiving or donor societies depends on the age and sex structure, as much as on the size and regional origin, of that migration. Although long-distance migrations are most typically dominated by young men, variations occurred. When compared to the trade in indentured servants or convicts, the slave trade comprised a surprisingly large number of women and children. The proportion of adult women also varied quite markedly, both between African regions of embarkation and American regions of arrival. The ratio of male to female slaves leaving Africa varied from about 70:30 in West-Central Africa to about 55:45 at the Bight of Biafra. Early Barbados and Jamaica received almost equal numbers of African women and men, whereas, much later, Cuba received two and three times more men than women. St. Domingue, the most dynamic market in the second half of the eighteenth century, generally absorbed more males and fewer children than other French Caribbean colonies.[22]

Once in the Caribbean, about one in ten Africans moved from one island to another or to the mainland. Roughly a quarter of the Africans who arrived in Jamaica were then shipped to Spanish islands. A much smaller but not insignificant number of Africans who came into Barbados ended up on other islands. Among the French islands, Guadeloupe was notable for receiving most of its Africans from other places—most often Martinique—rather than directly from the continent. The French Windward islands as a whole drew slaves from Dutch and English islands as well as from Africa. Curaçao was a major entrepôt in the Dutch trade. Indeed, perhaps 85 percent of the slaves arriving in the Dutch Caribbean were quickly reembarked for ports on the Spanish Main.[23]

In addition, major internal trades existed within islands. In Cuba, for example, almost all the arrivals moved through Havana and western ports into the sugar heartland. Planters indiscriminately bought Africans who perforce intermingled on plantations. Jamaican planters generally bought just a few Africans at a time, and they bought whatever slaves they could get, from wherever slaves originated. Most Africans who went to Jamaica arrived in Kingston, and the common experience for the majority of slaves was to be separated from their shipmates on sale. Because a vigorous retail trade in slaves flourished alongside the wholesale trade, most Africans in Jamaica, as on other Caribbean islands, experienced flux and frequent separation from friends, family, and country people.[24]

Aggregate, sequential, and structural analyses emphasize that the Caribbean, seen in its full Atlantic context, received a remarkable mixture of peoples from Africa. This finding runs counter to some recent scholarship, which argues for homogeneity in the Middle Passage. Some historians see slave ships drawing their entire cargoes from uniform catchment areas. John Thornton, for instance, states that "An entire ship might be filled, not just with people possessing the same culture, but with people who grew up together." Once in the Americas, he continues, "Most of the slaves on any sizable estate were probably from only a few national groupings." Therefore, "Most slaves would have no shortage of people from their own nation with whom to communicate." For Thornton, particular African national groups tended to dominate particular slave societies in the Americas.[25]

Contrary to this viewpoint, heterogeneity is the story of the slave trade to the Caribbean, and it facilitated and encouraged the borrowing, adaptation, modification, and invention of cultural forms that was such a feature of Caribbean slave life. The three African songs heard in late-seventeenth-century Jamaica by Hans Sloane revealed evidence of interchange and experimentation among them, even though each was given an ethnic label. Similarly, although the Dahomean or Ewe-Fon influence in Haitian

voodoo is paramount, reflected in the major deities and most of the African vocabulary of this New World religion (and consistent with the predominance of the Bight of
Benin as the source of Africans to St. Domingue in the first quarter of the eighteenth
century when sugar cultivation took off in the colony), other African sources, most notably from West Central Africa, were important. A joining together of different African
cultures occurred in this New World religious form. The same was true of Cuban Santeria. Cuba drew its Africans from a wide array of coastal regions; its African influx was
fairly short-lived, lasting about eighty years (from 1790 to 1867), and the African arrivals
comprised many children (38%) and few women (less than 30%). All of these developments should have undermined the ability of Cuban slaves to maintain regional African
cultures, but one of the major components of Cuban Santeria was a traditional African
religion, the *orisha* (spirit) worship as practiced by the Yoruba. The Yoruba were an important group of arrivals in Cuba, particularly in the mid–nineteenth century. Perhaps
more important is how the heterogeneous Yoruba subgroups of Africa became Lucumis
in Cuba. People sold by the Yoruba became Lucumi: people of Allada and the Ibo were
incorporated within the so-called Lucumi nation. Furthermore, while Lucumi culture
had a Yoruba focus, it incorporated traits from far afield. Some Lucumi words and
phrases are not Yoruba in origin, and seem to be Ewe or Fon in derivation. The story of
Cuban Santeria is therefore one of New World blending and of ethnogenesis.[26]

Bringing an Atlantic frame of reference to bear on Caribbean developments—whether
the subject is Indians, the environment, or slavery—broadens perspectives and illuminates the provincial. Local events can no longer be understood in local terms only. It is
difficult to think of a more appropriate place for a pan-Atlantic, panglobal approach
than the Caribbean, since it was such a hub of this emerging Atlantic world. The
Caribbean islands represented the first major outposts of a global imperium, and the
first transoceanic sphere of European power was the Caribbean Sea. In Eric Hobsbawm's words, these islands were "a curious terrestrial space-station from which the
fragments of various races, torn from the worlds of their ancestors and aware both of
their origins and of the impossibility of returning to them, can watch the remainder of
the world with unaccustomed detachment."[27]

As Hobsbawm implies, the early Caribbean was precociously modern. A region now
considered backward and marginal was then a pioneer of modernity and central to the
Atlantic world: there developed the largest private enterprises of the day. The factory
and the field were joined, and a sugar revolution occurred—the only revolution named
after a commodity. Managers developed highly time-conscious and draconian work
regimes; capitalism's first real commodities were produced. In that modern place, people ate imported foods, and a significant reshuffling and redefinition of gender-based

roles occurred. People came there from far afield, bringing few kinfolk or possessions with them, having to refashion languages from more than one source, and having to forge cultures from mangled traditions. Caribbean peoples learned to embrace variety and difference. They also learned a measure of social detachment that came from being subject to rapid, radical, uncontrolled change.[28]

These raw outpost societies were, then, the first of a kind. Yes, the Caribbean was a periphery—a diminished, regressive world. Caribbean islands were, according to some scholars, "monstrous distortion[s] of human society" and "disastrous social failures." V. S. Naipaul declares that the "history of the islands can never be satisfactorily told . . . History is built around achievement and creation; and nothing was created in the West Indies." Caribbean territories have no "internal reverences," he continues; they were "manufactured societies, labour camps" where "nothing was generated locally." Even allowing for the nightmarish quality of much of the Caribbean experience, the region was also a forward line, a generative front, a creative frontier, a gathering place of broken pieces. In language, music, foodways, architecture, and much else, survival, adaptation, resilience, and vibrancy describe Caribbean life. The vitality of the cultural fusions— evident in the scores of languages, rich architectural styles, and the flowering of religious exoticism—is best summarized as creolization, which refers to anything or any person of the Old World born or developed in the New. What typifies creolization, as Sidney Mintz has noted, is not just the fragmentation of culture or its destruction but rather the creation and construction of culture out of violent and disjunct pasts.[29]

CHAPTER FOUR

Bringing India to Hand

Mapping an Empire, Denying Space

Matthew H. Edney

Eighteenth-century Europe's understanding of the world was fueled by the maps that were central to a variety of geographical, historical, and political discourses. More than direct statements of geographical fact, maps provided their readers with an understanding of those extensive spatial organizations and structures that no one individual could ever hope to experience directly. Drawing on three centuries of geographical representations and the experiences of thousands of people, maps were synoptic devices. Both mapmakers and map readers were well aware of the problems inherent to the construction of the map image, problems that unavoidably detracted from a map's coherence and comprehensiveness. Even so, they read maps as "God-like views" of the world, to use a common twentieth-century phrase. Numerous commentators have observed that maps allow their readers to comprehend a wide extent of geographical space without having to expend actual energy in traversing that space. As one geographical pedagogue wrote shortly after 1700, "by this Science [of Geography], the Divine, Merchant, Soldier and Traveller, may (without danger of those apparent Hazards they are like to fall under) take a particular View of those vast and pleasant Countries they have Occasion to visit or mention in their several Vocations."[1]

Map reading entails an act of spatial denial. In bringing a distant place to hand, the map reader ignores the realities of geographical space. Huge expanses of space—even

the entire globe—become readily understood and comprehended. Once comprehended, those spaces become fair game for control and exploitation as *territory,* regardless of the practicalities of actual control or exploitation. The purpose of this essay
is to highlight some of the ideological underpinnings of such cartographic acts of spatial denial in the particular context of the British East India Company's mapping of
South Asia and the configuration of "India" in the eighteenth century. (While I refer to
"India" and to "the British" as convenient labels, these idealized categories did of course
undergo profound changes during the 1700s.)

The role of maps in providing images of distant places is evident in the case of the
first map to frame the modern conception of "India." On returning to Britain in 1778,
James Rennell, the East India Company's first surveyor general of Bengal, set himself
up as a commercial publisher of maps and geographical books with a distinctly imperial flavor. One of the first maps that he published for the London market, in December 1782, was a two-sheet map, simply entitled *Hindoostan* (fig. 4.1). Rennell characterized this map as a repository of geographical facts which might be readily consulted in
the same manner as one might consult an encyclopedia or other reference work. It
would, he wrote, "explain the local circumstances of our political connections, and the
marches of our Armies" in India.[2] There was certainly a demand in London for such
geographical information in the early 1780s: The company was embroiled in a struggle
for control of South Asia, in competition with the Maratha confederacy, Mysore, and
the still powerful Mughal empire; in London, the company's rapidly developing territorial ambitions were the subject of intense debates in both Parliament and the coffee-
houses, debates that would lead to the company's reorganization under the 1784 India
Act. Rennell accordingly published the map for the general British "public," which is to
say the white, educated, mostly male, mostly wealthy, genteel, and overwhelmingly urban portion of society who participated in "public print discourse."[3]

At the same time, however, Rennell hinted at a less episodic and more pervasive role
for his map in London's public print discourse. He suggested that his map would be
"highly interesting to every person whose imagination has been struck by the splendor
of our victories, or whose attention is rouzed by the present critical state of our affairs"
in India. Overtly, this comment referred to Rennell's own promotion of a British empire out of the ruins of the Mughal empire. He explicated this imperialist desire in the
map's remarkable title cartouche with its iconography of Britannia taking the Indian
polities under her protection and of the military power that enforced that "protection,"
all beneath an imperial Roman wreath—an icon of glorious conquest and territorial
power—made not from the divinely hallucinogenic laurel but from the opium poppy.[4]

The crucial point for this essay, however, is that Rennell indicated that his map not
only might be *used* as a political instrument of knowledge and persuasion, but also it

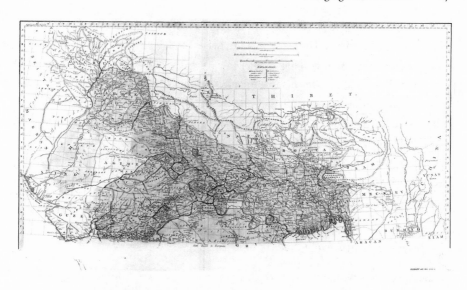

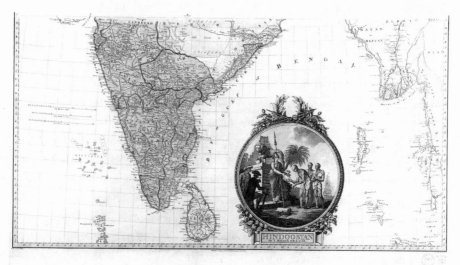

Figure 4.1. James Rennell, *Hindoostan* (London, 1782). A copper-engraved map in two sheets at 1:4,377,600. Courtesy of the Geography and Map Division, Library of Congress.

might be *read* in lieu of the land of South Asia itself. By reading his map, Rennell suggested, a Briton would be able to see and comprehend the geographical essence of "Hindoostan"/India. Indeed, of the fifty copies of the map purchased by the company, only twenty were allocated for the use of senior British officials in South Asia, whereas thirty were distributed among the company's directors in London, most of whom had never been to India.[5]

Rennell came close to pointing out the discursive role of geographical maps in bringing distant places to hand. His maps of South Asia—both his *Hindoostan* (1782) and his twice-as-large *New Map of Hindoostan* (1788)—gave their readers a spatial image with which to refer to "India." They made the place both concrete and real to the participants in the private, parliamentary, and public discussions of the company's tangled affairs in South Asia. Rennell's maps were in fact the first to frame the region that we today call India, unlike earlier maps of either the circumscribed limits of the Mughal empire or the whole sweep of the Indies, encompassing Asia from the Indus to China.[6] Rennell's maps constructed India to be the locus of British imperial ambitions for all educated Britons, whether or not they had been to India.

Some Cartographic Caveats

Before discussing the ways in which eighteenth-century Europeans construed the meaning and significance of the maps they used to envision and conceptualize the world, we must first clearly delimit this essay's scope. We need to be clear about the precise kinds of maps under discussion. The British made many different kinds of maps during their centuries-long engagement with South Asia. Most of them were generated after the intensification of that engagement in the early nineteenth century, but even before 1800, the British employed several different cartographic modes in India.[7] Sea *charts* and harbor *plans* were, for example, made and read by mariners for the purposes of navigation. *Surveys* were made of the routes taken by army columns; the resultant schematic linear diagrams were collected by a variety of military officers and were also used for strategic planning. Nor should we forget the many different *plans* and *views* taken of fortifications and towns. Although they were all as much spatial conceptions as they were functional instruments, these spatial images remain beyond the scope of this presentation for two reasons. First, they did not possess the same geometrical structure as geographical, regional *maps;* their epistemological claims to represent geographical truth were accordingly somewhat different. Second, they had a restricted circulation among mariners and company officials and did not circulate in public. That is, they did not contribute to the repeated presentation to the public of the cartographic image of India. That role was fulfilled by printing geographical maps.

We should distinguish between two kinds of geographical maps. The leading surveyors in Madras, Bombay, and Calcutta all made large maps of India, which were housed and, in some cases, permanently displayed in the council chambers of senior British administrators. Copies were made of many of these maps; these in turn were sent to the company's directors in London, and several seem to have been hung on the walls of their offices. For example, one very large map of India, at least six feet on a side (and probably larger), which had been made in 1809 by Charles Reynolds, surveyor general of Bombay, was hung up in London by the directors "in a room appropriated for that purpose"; the map no longer survives.[8] Indeed, several large maps in the company's archives show signs of having been damaged by being hung up. Before they tore themselves apart under their own weight or were permanently obscured by smoke and soot, these wall maps would have served to bring India to hand for the directors and their secretaries. However, they would not have been seen by anyone outside of the company's inner circles.

The regional maps that made India seem more concrete to Britain's literate social and professional elites were all printed.[9] They circulated in the marketplace in historical and political tracts, in monthly periodicals, in general atlases, in children's geographical textbooks, and as separate publications. They also occurred in a number of more ephemeral forms, such as on playing cards and screens. Large wall maps, such as Rennell's *Hindoostan*, were produced in several possible formats: they might have been assembled and hung on walls; they might have been dissected and mounted onto cloth so that they could be folded and easily carried around; or they might have been left unassembled, perhaps bound into special atlases. Wall maps seem to have been hung in a variety of essentially public, masculine places: in schoolrooms and council chambers, in the halls and reception rooms of houses, in coffee houses, and even in barber shops. Maps in books and atlases had a similarly wide, but nonetheless highly gendered, distribution. Some women did, however, receive a geographical education. It was, perhaps, rare for the daughters of wealthier families to be taught geography in the early eighteenth century, but the practice seems to have been quite common by 1800. In the 1770s, for example, geography could be described as "a Study both entertaining and useful to Ladies as well as to Gentlemen . . . The *Fair Sex* may intermingle these Amusements with the operations of the Needle and the knowledge of a domestic life"; some girls learned geography by embroidering cartographic samplers.[10] Once out of the nursery, however, most women would have encountered maps far less frequently than did their brothers and husbands, who participated more fully in the liberal public sphere and its geographical discourses.

It must be emphasized that outside the realm of public print discourse, few Britons would have seen maps of India. Maps were too expensive to be included in cheap printed literature. At best, the cheaper textbooks might have included a map of the world and perhaps maps of each continent. Such maps showed India only in broad outline and with little detail. For the illiterate or semiliterate mass of Britain's population in the eighteenth century—tied to the land and to the burgeoning industries—India probably remained an unspecific and mythic place, the distant and exotic source of expensive cottons, of soldiers' tales, and of the fabulous wealth of a few fortunate "nabobs."

Dominating the Material Map

Exploring the dissemination of printed regional maps in the public sphere reminds us of their materiality. Maps are not abstract entities. They are artifacts, physical things that are made. They can be picked up and carried around. They can be rolled up and folded, tucked into pockets or bound into books; they can be torn or burned; they can be discarded. Most significantly, when reading maps, we physically situate ourselves with respect to them. We do so in the same manner in which we situate ourselves with respect to books: we adopt a commanding position from which to read them. We lean across them; we unfold them; we turn the pages of an atlas. We move larger maps around so as to get a better view of them. We *interrogate* them. Wall maps, some of which might be thought to dominate their readers by their sheer size, do invert the physical relationship between reader and map, but they are still dominated by the reader. With the map fixed to the wall and so stationary, the individual moves about in order to explore the map's surface. (The long-established practice by which rulers impressed their power and territorial sovereignty on their subjects through the display of large wall maps, seen in outline but unreadable in detail, seems to have been curtailed by the formation of more participatory, print-based political discourse in the eighteenth century.) In short, humans dominate maps.

The domination of the map is central to Bruno Latour's understanding of "what is specific" to "modern scientific culture," of what it is that distinguishes the Western investigation and understanding of the world from the investigations and understandings of other peoples. Rejecting the intrinsically racist and ahistorical arguments that posit the development of some newly rational mind in sixteenth-century Europe, Latour looks instead to the practices by which Europeans have investigated the world around them. In doing so, he identifies two hallmarks of "modern science." First, modern science reduces all phenomena to visual representations, or "inscriptions," whether or not the phenomena can themselves be sensed by human vision. (Indigenous peoples, on the other hand, habitually include evidence from the other senses and from internal experiences in their investigations of their worlds.) Second, the inscriptions of modern science are constructed as material objects—such as books, paintings, maps, and records—which are intended to be physically circulated without alteration; in Latour's terminology, they are "immutable mobiles." Able to be moved—the motive power being the protocapitalism that drove Europe's investigations of the world—the inscriptions are readily collected in particular "centers of calculation." Once physically collected, the inscriptions can be compared, discrepancies between them can be identified and perhaps reconciled, and eventually they can be combined into new inscriptions. For the individual privileged to read the assembled inscriptions, "domains which are far apart become literally inches apart; domains which are convoluted and hidden become flat."[11]

Latour thus argues that the sixteenth century's "new interest in 'Truth'" was emphatically not the result of some "new vision" nor of some newly developed "rational mind"; Europeans did not suddenly become a new species of *Homo sapiens* distinct from the indigenous peoples of the rest of the world. Rather, Latour argues, Europeans have kept "the same old vision" and mental faculties but began in the Renaissance to apply them "to new[ly] visible objects that mobilize space and time differently." Finally, for Latour, the act of collecting and comparing many visual representations of the world into one site is an act of domination. "There is nothing you can *dominate*," he writes, "as easily as a flat surface of a few square meters; there is nothing hidden or convoluted, no shadows, no 'double entendre.'"[12] Maps play a key role in Latour's arguments about the differences between European and non-European ways of knowing. For Latour, mapmaking exemplifies the central process of capitalist science, specifically the making of stable, portable inscriptions.[13] (We should note that Latour takes for granted the privileging and empowerment of vision in Western culture; fortunately, a number of critical scholars have problematized sight and observation, bolstering his arguments.)[14]

The physical and intellectual domination of the map was made explicit by James Welsh, a British officer in the company's Bombay army who visited Charles Reynolds in the 1790s, while Reynolds was working on his first map of India. Welsh remembered that "I had the gratification of *crawling over a map* fourteen feet long and ten feet broad; to do which, without injury to a production intended to be presented to the Court of Directors, [Colonel Reynolds] furnished me with silk stockings for hands and feet; and cased in these I moved about at pleasure, stopping at particular spots for information." He ended his reminiscence by noting his incredulity that Reynolds was then engaged in producing a yet larger map that would measure thirty feet by twenty feet. Welsh's tone suggested that he fully expected even this truly huge map to be explored at will—"at pleasure"—by other Britons.[15]

In such ways, maps were material worldviews. More than metaphors, they allowed their readers to view, or to imagine they viewed, the world. For Latour, maps, landscape paintings, and other inscriptions accordingly constituted panopticons, devices with which viewers might examine, comprehend, and control nature in detail, and piece by piece. The inscriptions constitute comprehensible representations of nature; to comprehend an inscription through dominating it is thus to comprehend and dominate nature.[16] Of course, such inscriptions are not panopticons in the same way that Michel Foucault understood Jeremy Bentham's panopticon to be paradigmatic of the technologies of surveillance. Prisoners housed in Bentham's panopticon would be fully aware that they were under surveillance: the fundamental point of discipline is that self-awareness of surveillance would train the prisoner to act in a normal and proper manner, which is to say to discipline themselves. In the case of the cartographic panopticon, the object of the inscription is not aware of being inscribed, nor is it capable of self-correction; the land itself cannot be disciplined. There is, however, a sense in which Latour is correct in talking about maps and other inscriptions as functioning like panopticons, in that their viewers treated them as such. That is, eighteenth-century Europeans approached their maps with something of a delusional attitude.[17]

The Presumed Rationality of Maps

The intellectual domination of the world through maps clearly depended upon the construction of a hard and fast linkage between the map and the world, a linkage that was, of course, an ideological construct. The core principle in this linkage was rehearsed using the same basic three-step argument outlined in the opening chapters of every eighteenth-century geographical textbook. (Many rudimentary, cheaper textbooks consisted solely of this argument.) In the first step, the world is presented as an almost spherical object that can be legitimately modeled as a globe. In the second step, the globe is used to demonstrate the geometry of the earth, defined through the various "imaginary circles" inscribed on the globe's surface: the equator and the parallel circles of latitude; the lines of longitude, beginning with the "first meridian"; the zodiacal circle formed by the plane of the ecliptic cutting through the earth; the two tropics; and the arctic and antarctic circles. (Pamphlets dedicated to outlining the nature and use of globes constituted a substantial literature throughout the 1700s.) The third step of the argument established the geographical map as a projection of those circles from the three-dimensional globe onto the two-dimensional plane. In order to make the link between the globe and the projected map absolutely clear, the map invariably took the form of a world shown in two hemispheres, clearly referencing the world's globular nature (fig. 4.2). (The widespread belief, promulgated by Arno Peters, that European world maps have all been made on the rectangular Mercator projection since 1569 is quite false.)

The implication of this argument was explicated in only rare instances.[18] It was nonetheless clear: the geometrical structure of the geographical map is the same as that of the globe, which is the same as that of the world itself. The globe might be a "better" representation of the world than the map, in the same way that a statue shows an individual "in full Proportions" whereas a portrait shows only the individual's "Lineaments."[19] Yet the geographical map was still understood to be an adequate and efficient representation of the world's essence. Because of their foundation in the graticule of meridians and parallels, even the least detailed and most schematic maps were held to possess a fundamental verisimilitude to the world's spatial structure. It was the geo-

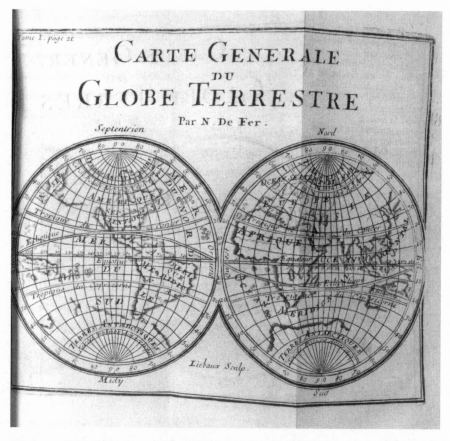

Figure 4.2. Nicolas de Fer, "Carte Generale du Globe Terrestre," in Jacques Robbe, *Méthode pour apprendre facilement la géographie* (Paris, 1748), between 20 and 21. By permission of the Osher Map Library, University of Southern Maine.

graphical map's power to organize space in a truthful manner that underlay the eighteenth-century use of "mapping" as a metaphor for classification and categorization. Natural historians such as Linnaeus or Michael Adanson, celebrated by Foucault as exemplifying Enlightenment "rational" and "systematic" thought, tended to explain their taxonomies and orderings of the world through analogies with mapmaking; similarly, the editors of the great encyclopedias also understood themselves as mapping the terrain of knowledge.[20]

The importance of the graticule—the network of meridians and parallels—to the geographical map was borne out in the process whereby maps were made. A graticule was first constructed, establishing the geometric framework into which geographical information from multiple sources would then be fitted. The information was attached to the framework through a few crucial places whose latitudes and longitudes had been determined by astronomical observation. (Such a mapping process was replicated in introductory geographical texts in which children would copy model maps into pre-printed graticules.) The graticule provided a geometrical framework to which any geographical information could be adapted and fitted: a graticule could be drawn as easily for a county as for the entire world. All that was needed to relate any geographical information—including detailed surveys, marine navigations, and non-European geographies—to the global framework was the definition of the latitude and longitude of just one location. Both French and English officers accordingly sought during the eighteenth century to translate Indian astronomical observations for longitude into the European system in an attempt to appropriate Indian geographies for European geographical knowledge.[21] Once related to the common geometrical foundation, different geographies could be carefully compared and any differences and discrepancies between them reconciled by either mathematical or graphical methods. That is, mapping was understood to be a process of eliciting the truth of nature, and a map to be one selection from the great, cumulative geographical archive.[22]

The fundamental principles and practices of geographical maps were well known to educated Europeans of the eighteenth century. Geography was widely understood as a crucial element of the period's canons of knowledge. Robert Dodsley placed geographical knowledge as the third arena of "polite learning" to be mastered by children, after reading and writing, and arithmetic and geometry, but before history, rhetoric and poetry, logic, ethics, laws, and manners. Whether the child was "born to the Ease of a large Fortune, . . . dedicated to any of the Learned Professions, . . . [or] designed for the Arts of Commerce, or Agriculture," Dodsley opined, "no Studies afford more extensive, more wonderful, or more pleasing Scenes; and therefore there can be no Ideas impressed upon the Soul, which can more conduce to its future Entertainment."[23] Most educated Europeans were probably exposed to the basic geography texts that proliferated in the period; they perhaps had made their own maps as children. So familiar were the principles of map making that some gentlemen made maps as part of their participation in the public sphere. In the context of the British engagement with South Asia, we should cite the example of Robert Orme, East India Company bureaucrat and "nabob," who made several maps of southern India as part of his highly politicized history of the company's activities in South Asia.[24] That is, in the 1700s, geographical mapping was an integral, and perhaps major, part of the life of anyone who claimed any political, historical, or mercantile expertise.

In this environment, maps were widely understood to epitomize European rationality. As such, they were a prominent part of the communal British definition of its "self" vis-à-vis the Indian "other." The depth of that constructed divide is evident, for example, in Adam Smith's history of astronomy. Smith yoked rationality to the other defining characteristics of Britain constructed by public discourse in the eighteenth century: Protestant Christianity, in the form of natural theology, and the liberal state. Polytheism and belief in the supernatural, Smith asserted, were inevitable to the "savage mind" impressed by the force and wonder of nature. Only with the provision of "order and security" under the rule of law would the savage have the opportunity to satisfy his curiosity about the world and so recognize "the chain" that linked together nature's "seemingly disjointed phenomena," which is to say the Christian God.[25]

The distinction between Europeans as liberal, Christian, and rational, and other peoples, notably Indians, as despotic, pagan, and irrational, found expression in European conceptions of how non-Europeans viewed and mapped the world. These opinions would increasingly be in evidence after 1800: British surveyors and administrators in India would argue that an education in geography and surveying would be the most efficient means to dispel Indian "mysticism" and "irrationality"; British evangelicals would further hold that this process of rationalization would inevitably lead Indians to convert to Protestant Christianity.[26] Ultimately, such conceptions would be codified in Jean Piaget's schema for cognitive development, in which the cartographic activities of Westerners are taken as the norm for adult spatial cognition and in which non-Westerners are explicitly identified as functioning at the cognitive level of a five- or six-year-old Western child because of their lack of cartographic activity.[27]

Although European preconceptions of non-European rationality and spatial abilities were expressed less forcefully in the eighteenth century, they were no less pervasive. It seems as though every time a European explorer encountered an indigenous group and asked for geographical information, the European recorded his surprise at the map-making abilities of people who supposedly did not make maps. Always pragmatic, the British in India did employ indigenous sources of geographical information when no other information was available. In the late 1780s, for example, the British resident at Pune, Sir Charles Malet, employed Sudanando, a Brahmin from Cambay, to make a map of Gujarat, which was at the time inaccessible to company officers. Sudanando drew the map in a European style, complete with clearly indicated latitudes and longitudes, but wrote it in Hindi in Devnagri script. Nevertheless, British use of such information was always qualified. Even when the Indian informant was validated as a source of reliable information, corroboration had to be obtained, preferably from British sources. In preparing the second edition of his *New Map of Hindoostan,* James Rennell noted that Malet had called Sudanando "a Bramin of uncommon genius and knowledge"; even so, Rennell still corroborated Sudanando's work by comparing it to the section on Gujarat in Abu'l Fazl's *A'in-i Akbari,* the late-sixteenth-century geographical description of the Mughal Empire.[28]

European public discourse therefore held geographical maps to be inscriptions that bore a direct and essential relationship with the world. Ideologically, the validity of those representations rested on a faith in the rational self defined in opposition to the irrational, non-European other. Viewing maps was accordingly tantamount to viewing the essence of the world. The maps themselves are not constructed from a "God-like view"; rather, map readers attain that "God-like view," that blissful state of spatial denial, through their domination of the map.

Problems with Eighteenth-Century Geographical Ideals

The British faith in their maps of India was therefore delusory. In practice, the veracity of the British mapping of India was seriously undermined by a variety of flaws. British surveyors suffered from innumerable acts of resistance from all levels of Indian society—ranging from covert hostility and minor annoyances to overt violence and obstruction—which affected the British ability to gather information. If such instances reflect localized and contingent flaws in the idealized ability to know the land, then a more systemic flaw was the linguistic divide between the British and their native informants. In addition to persistently limiting the British surveyors, this divide was cartographically manifested in the orthographic confusions and inconsistencies that riddled British maps.

Equally systemic was that the British related to and understood Indian landscapes in ways quite different than did the indigenous people of South Asia's several cultures. Such differences were recognized and mentioned by the British only on the rare occasions when they were jolted out of their comfortable habits of thought. One such instance occurred in 1839 when William Morison, a member of the Supreme Council in Calcutta and himself a former military surveyor, criticized the very large-scale cadastral maps made of each village in northern India because they "might be supposed to represent some part of Europe quite as much as any part of India."[29] Francis Buchanan, the botanist and statistician, identified a telling problem that plagued British maps of Bengal late in the eighteenth century. Rivers in Bengal constantly change course, carving out new channels while old channels deteriorate into stagnant marshes. A cultural dissonance occurred in the naming of these channels: the British, in line with European practice, conceived of a river, bearing one name, as a single "principal channel" traced from an estuary back to a source; the local inhabitants continued to call each old channel by its original name and gave new names to the new channels. The British, Buchanan wrote, were "apt to be enraged" by and were "in general very unwilling to admit of these absurdities," and they insisted on constructing "maps according to their own plan, with the same name following the same river from its more remote source to its mouth." He admitted, however, that such an "improvement" was "attended with considerable inconvenience to those who wish to use the maps on the spot, and often leads them into most troublesome mistakes" and would continue to do so "until it shall have been adopted by the inhabitants of the country." Yet the Bengalis "obstinately" refused to modify their understanding of the landscape. The British nonetheless persisted in their "rational" naming of rivers, correcting their maps as if they were indeed correcting the world. In this, they thought to exercise a control over the world that they did not, in fact, possess.[30]

The British also readily admitted to the presence of significant technical flaws in their cartographic ideal. In particular, the determination of latitude and longitude from astronomical observations was known to suffer from several types of unquantifiable error. The ability to fit the world properly to the paper graticule was thus in doubt. Also, the difficulties of making astronomical observations meant that there were very few places whose positions were fixed with any degree of accuracy and which could be used to provide geometric control for detailed geographical surveys. (In the later 1700s, only Bombay and Madras were reliably fixed in India.) Thus the available control could support only highly general maps that did not show India in as great detail as the interested public perhaps expected; for example, when Rennell published his two-sheet map, *Hindoostan,* he expected to "incur some censure" because "many people who peruse maps" naively expect to find both "a large extent of the country, and all the minute particular[s] of it, on the same map."[31] These technological problems masked the cultural differences between the British and the Indians. When those differences became acute at the very end of the eighteenth century, the British sought a better technology with which to map India, certain that better maps would be true to the landscape and would so eliminate those cultural differences.

The technological panacea was triangulation; the principal such survey in India was the Great Trigonometrical Survey. A complex, mathematically rigorous, laborious, and expensive process, triangulation determines very precisely the locations of a large number of points. In 1817 Colin Mackenzie, the surveyor and Orientalist, frustrated by trying to keep track of thousands of villages by their names, held out the possibility of replacing those names with the villages' geographical coordinates: a truly rational correction of the world.[32] These well-defined points would in turn control the highly detailed topographic surveys. The detailed surveys generated through the intensification of Britain's engagement with India were initially assembled in London into ever larger, multiple-sheet maps. These elephantine maps soon blurred into atlases. In 1822, Aaron Arrowsmith published a sixteen-sheet *Atlas of South India,* which led in turn to the 177-sheet *Atlas of India,* made for the East India Company by Arrowsmith's successors. The basis of these maps in the direct and extensive measurement and observation of the landscape gave them a new claim to truth. As a result, the prosecution of the Great

Trigonometrical Survey served only to intensify British claims for a rational self and an irrational other. Yet the Indian triangulation and *Atlas* were themselves as flawed as the eighteenth-century maps. Technologically, there were as many problems in implementing the triangulations and dependent surveys as there had been with the eighteenth-century reliance on astronomical control. Nor did the better technology override the cultural, linguistic, and political divides that continued to separate the British from the Indians.[33]

Geographical maps served Europeans in the eighteenth century by bringing distant places to hand. The complex ideologies of vision and of mapping gave the act of viewing maps a certainty and authority that denied the actual space of the world. Geographical maps thereby brought the entire potential field of imperial action into Europe's council chambers and coffee houses, there to be discussed, consulted, and controlled. They allowed Europeans to conceptualize the world and to think that they could dominate the world itself. The shift to a new ideal of mapmaking, although rooted in a different epistemology of survey and observation, served only to perpetuate and intensify this panoptical sense of domination after 1800.

CHAPTER FIVE

Concealing the Bounds

Imagining the British Nation through China

Robert Batchelor

The Third Earl of Shaftesbury's unpublished manuscript "Second Characters" (ca. 1713) contains an aesthetic rant against everything Oriental: "'Bad figures: bad minds.' 'Crooked designs: crooked fancies.' 'No designs: no thought.' So Turks, etc. 'No imitation: no poetry.' No arts of this kind: no letters, or at least in a poor degree. So politeness always holds proportion with laws and liberty . . . And where it ceases and tyranny (such as the Eastern monarchies, ancient and modern) prevails, art and 2nd Characters accordingly sink. See Japan! Mogul! China! . . . Show but so much as a vase! til in China taught by use and the Dutch."[1] Shaftesbury writes in response to the vast seventeenth- and eighteenth-century trade in images on porcelains, prints, and screens. This trade drew its vitality from the sophisticated regional trading networks of Chinese merchants and the industrial production of paper and porcelain in Ming and Qing China.[2] Technologies of print in both Europe and China allowed designs for complicated hybrid cultural objects to be shuttled back and forth across the globe during the seventeenth century. The complexities of these exchanges meant that a neoclassical aesthetics of beauty as order required radical redefinitions and innovative defenses of boundaries to survive in a developing commercial society driven by the vanities of consumption. The encounter between Europe and China in the seventeenth century had a profound impact on how national communities such as "Britain" were imagined in the eighteenth century.[3] Nowhere does this process appear more clearly than in attempts by self-styled British patriots of the 1730s to reformulate feelings about beauty and merit by appealing to a Chinese notion of aesthetics as embodied in the garden.

One problem with critical studies of "Orientalisms" has been the reduction of transcultural processes to binary discursive oppositions rooted in inherited ideas about national cultures, imperial economies, and civilizational contrasts. The notion of transculturation suggests a multidirectional, creative process of encounter and exchange that does not result in the absorption of a dominant culture's symbolic elements or cultural practices (acculturation) but instead opens new possibilities for translation and new ways of imagining the social.[4] Concepts such as a national culture or economy developed out of the interactions and exchanges of the seventeenth and eighteenth centuries and only then were disseminated, replicated, and transformed through the mechanisms of print capitalism.

Unquestionably, part of these broader processes involved the Orientalist practices of producing through texts and chinoiserie commodities what scholars often refer to as an image of China, a "domestic representation" or "European hallucination" used for the purpose of demonstrating a lack (the empty space of desire).[5] Since the sixteenth century, encounters with Chinese society have helped to define the nature of modernity for numerous European authors, not only because China developed the technologies of gunpowder, the compass, and printing before Europe but also because its well-organized system of internal commerce and manufacturing maintained urban populations on a scale unknown in European cities (including London) and played a central role in the Asian system of trade.[6] In the seventeenth and eighteenth centuries, an extensive Dutch and Jesuit literature with an eye toward commerce and conversion described China as a populous, urbanized, commercial society with strong institutions devoted to the cultural replication of merit, namely, the examination system and the civil cult of Confucius.[7] According to much of this travel literature, the Chinese had developed the most well-governed, mannered, and stable nation on earth, grounded upon—to use the language of the sinophilic Tory patriot Lord Bolingbroke—an ancient and good "constitution."

Not only did such images of China actively engage with the politics of defining various competing social imaginaries in Europe during the seventeenth and eighteenth centuries but they also emerged out of diverse, complicated, and developing systems of production, distribution, and consumption in both "Europe" and "China." Therefore, such images neither stabilized into a passive and timeless representation of the East nor fit into neat discursive paradigms. To take the case of the print culture in the early eighteenth century, Whig writers like Defoe and Shaftesbury felt that distinguishing England from such global flows of commerce and imagining coherent national circulation patterns required a "disavowal" of this China, and several recent studies focus on the role of nationalist reflection and "commercialist" expansion in forming negative British impressions of China in the eighteenth century.[8] Yet, for other English writers in the 1720s and 1730s, the travel literature of the seventeenth century and the image trade had a much more lasting influence. Old Whigs and post-1688 Tories showed a greater interest in the question of ancient virtue than in modern wealth, and, for many, China was less a commercial competitor than an exemplary model of stability for an emerging commercial society like Britain. The rise in the 1740s of patriotism as a popular movement—which played a central role in imagining Britain as a nation—had deeper connections with the Old Whig and Tory opposition to Robert Walpole that developed during the 1720s and 1730s than with "possessive individualist" radical Whigs like Locke or even "modern Whigs" like Defoe.[9] In the new nation of Britain that emerged territorially in 1707 and politically in 1688, 1714, and 1722, imagining China and Britain was an open-ended and conflict-ridden process rather than a fixed and instituted set of significations that could be employed in simple negative or positive self-reflection.

The most famous text of the opposition patriots, Lord Bolingbroke's *The Idea of a Patriot King* (1739), opens a window onto these complexities. Although the immediate aim of the privately circulated manuscript might appear to be the concrete political goal of making a "patriot king" out of either Frederick Louis, Prince of Wales, or Frederick's son (the future George III), born in June 1738, the essay's strength lies in its attempt to address the fundamental problems faced by the fragmented and struggling opposition to Walpole during the late 1730s. According to Bolingbroke, this question involved not simply organization or ideology but had deep roots in the nature of the social. Walpole had taken the "minds of men," "narrowed [them] to personal regards alone," and "confined [them] to the present moment." "Sentiments," argues Bolingbroke, "are debased from the love of liberty, from zeal for the honour and prosperity of their country." This left the patriot opposition with the problem of how to "reinfuse into the British nation," itself a recent political construct, a new nationalist "British spirit" and how to "reform the morals, and to raise the sentiments of a people."[10] It seemed like an impossible task, especially for one man (king or writer), and Bolingbroke, exiled and stripped of all his rights as a "British subject" except "inheriting," recognized his own rather Quixotic position. The double hollowing out of British subjects and Bolingbroke's own subjectivity left little for even a good prince to "mirror," requiring Bolingbroke to resort to quasi-Platonic and messianic figures for his patriot king.

The task of replenishing the British spirit, reforming morals, and raising sentiments ultimately demanded a fundamental reimagining of the monarchy. Yet, Bolingbroke only had at his disposal "the broken traditions which are come down to us of a few nations." Out of such fragments, he puts forward an argument that "Merit had given rank; but rank was soon kept, and, which is more preposterous, obtained, too, without merit." Bolingbroke then employs the example of China as an exceptional nation that has uniquely preserved the association between merit and rank: "Nobility in China mounts upwards: and he, who has it conferred upon him, enobles his ancestors, not his posterity. A wise institution! and especially among a people in whose minds a great veneration for their forefathers has been always carefully maintained. But in China, as well as in most other countries, royalty has descended, and kingdoms have been reckoned the patrimonies of particular families" (225–26). Legitimized by merit, the Chinese nobility has the interesting ability to rewrite dynastic history, even though Bolingbroke carefully excludes the monarchy from this process. Such a formulation would have interested Bolingbroke on a number of levels, if not as a crypto-Jacobite then at least as a political historian. After 1735, merit in the form of an aristocracy of talent had become Bolingbroke's primary political focus.[11] The Chinese nobility of merit seemed to have the ability to repair "broken traditions" and in particular revitalize the counseling function of the nobility so that proper mirroring for princes could occur.

In an essay that generally reads as if written by a sixteenth-century humanist, the paragraph on China makes the only reference, aside from conventional classical allusions, to the world outside of Europe. Why does Bolingbroke expand his set of rhetorical reference points to include China? Bolingbroke's turn to China could be read as a trope of distance, implying an ironic relationship to humanistic universalism as remote and absent from the British polity. The essay itself begins at "a great distance from the present court," since in March 1738, the Prince's patriot supporters had been publicly banned from St. James by George II. China could be read as an allegory of the spatial distance that provides critical perspective, paralleling the temporal distance of references to Greek, Roman, and Persian antiquity. Yet, while there is a whiff of the utopian in the reference to China and the neo-Platonism of the essay as a whole, Bolingbroke clearly had practical political considerations in mind as well.

The rationalization and reduction of apparent distance through the technologies of print capitalism also defined the parameters of a crucial problem for imagining a community in the 1730s—coordinating ethics and sentiments across national space.[12] For a developing nation like Britain, China as a vast and stable nation based upon a community of print suggested a model for sustaining sentimental unity over distance. As the devolution-minded Scottish patriot Andrew Fletcher argued during 1703 debates in the Edinburgh parliament over the stalled plans for union with England, "If any man say, that the empire of China contains divers kingdoms; and that the care of the Emperor, and his knowledge of particular men cannot extend to all: I answer, the case is the same with us; and it seems as if that wise people designed this constitution [of merit-based councilors] for a remedy to the like inconveniences with those we labor under at this time."[13] Framed in this way, issues of distance arose as elements of an effective model rather than an abstract comparison, open to borrowings and dialogues at the level of the social imaginary rather than a fixed and frozen fantasy appealing to a previously instituted order.

What might it mean to posit that a transcultural model of a Chinese nobility of merit undergirded Bolingbroke's reworking of Harringtonian thought about the coherence of a commonwealth? What might it mean to argue that such revisionary notions resided at the core of the institution of British nationalism in the eighteenth century? Bolingbroke himself would by no means have imagined that a fundamentally different constitution (laws, institutions, customs) could simply be transplanted from China to Britain because of historical and cultural differences. Nor, from the perspective of historical hindsight, would it make any sense to contend that "Chinese culture" as an entity encountered "British culture" as an entity and produced some kind of Anglo-Chinese transcultural fusion. At minimum, such a reductive formulation would conceal the historical processes in Hanoverian Britain and Manchu China that imagined and instituted diverse formations of community. Finally, trade between southern China and Europe and the Americas (mercantile capitalism) did not alone serve as a ground for transculturation, despite commerce's important role in generating an exchange of images between the two regions during this period. It is essential to understand that the circulation of commodities and signs can only partially explain the socially imagined institutions that draw upon their movements. The crux of the problem lies in the fact that a writer like Bolingbroke explicitly wants to develop a structure of sentiments that will work politically and socially to make this highly complex interaction of signs coherent.

Though the concise elegance of Bolingbroke's essay might suggest otherwise, the development of the notion "China" in the early eighteenth century did not grow out of one particular textual tradition or set of historical developments. The particular field of cultural production in which "The Idea of a Patriot King" intervenes helps to explicate how defining "China" was itself a contested and political process. The initial "private" circulation of the essay avoided one of the most characteristic aspects of the age of Walpole, the intense political and economic struggles over newspapers and pamphlets (the "public sphere"). Print became central to the practice of opposition politics during the 1720s and 1730s.[14] Among members of the opposition press, references to China were a popular means of justifying their productions and opposing the corrupt patronage of Walpole. For those writers living on "Grub Street" who wanted access to the spoils of political patronage yet had no desire to abandon the social legacy of aristocratic distinction, Chinese-style merit provided an attractive model and conveniently exotic allegorical space. The great cultural artifacts that could serve as a reference point for much of this feeling were two massive competing English translations of the synthetic account of China by the French Jesuit Jean-Baptiste Du Halde (Paris, 1735), which began publication in 1736 and 1738, respectively. Dedications to political and cultural patrons as well as well-organized advertising campaigns suggest that much was at stake in the success of these multivolume translations. Yet, as the publishing battle for the translation of Du Halde suggests, the press accounts of China in the 1730s had the feel of "Grub Street" writing, often relying upon century-old clichés for self-justification rather than delving into aspects of China that would translate a sense of dynamic interaction. Bolingbroke's use of China as a cliché from the print wars was simultaneously safe and dangerous because of its links to a politics of replication and denunciation, leaving him open to charges of hack journalism familiar to him from his role as a writer for the opposition paper, the *Craftsman.*

As a way of distinguishing their interests from the fray of political and commercial London, the upper echelons of the patriot opposition focused the question of political merit by looking to Chinese gardening traditions. If theater had been the space of affect par excellence in Restoration England, the open and multiple perspectives of the garden came to overshadow the stage in the eighteenth century. Through their gardens the patriots attempted to build "natural" structures through which sentiment could be directed away from entanglements with print and mercantile capitalism toward the construction of an aristocracy of merit. Even James Thompson's masque *Alfred,* which contained the famous song "Rule Brittania," had its first performance in August 1740 in the gardens of the Prince of Wales's lodgings at Cliveden in Buckinghamshire. Although eighteenth-century London commercial gardens like Vauxhall and Ranelagh testify to the diffusion and contestation of such spaces, the semipublic space of landscape gardens surrounding the country house had more profound effects on both aesthetics and politics during the 1730s.

In 1734, the year after Walpole deprived several old Whigs of their military and government commissions for failing to support the Excise Bill, the amateur architect Sir Thomas Robinson wrote that a radically new style of gardening had appeared at the estates of the Prince of Wales, the Earl of Burlington, the Duke of Newcastle, and Lord Cobham: "when finished, it has the appearance of beautiful nature, and without being told, one would imagine art had no part in the finishing, and is, according to what one hears of the Chinese, entirely after their models for works of this nature, where they never plant straight lines or make regular designs."[15] These wealthy aristocratic landowners were formerly loyal Whigs who grew increasingly disillusioned with Walpole by the 1730s.[16] A war hero, Richard Temple, Lord Cobham had been deprived of his military commission due to his vote on the excise. After 1733, Cobham began to politicize his already famous gardens at Stowe, inspired by his role as the central patron of a key patriot opposition circle that included his "cousins"—William Pitt, Richard Grenville, George Lyttelton, and Lord Chesterfield—a group closely linked with the Prince of Wales as well as the circles of Bolingbroke and Alexander Pope. In 1738, as Bolingbroke was writing his essay, Cobham built the first Chinese house on the British Isles at Stowe. By this time, the gardens contained several explicitly patriotic buildings such as the Temple of British Worthies and the Temples of Ancient and Modern Virtue (a ruin with a headless statue of Walpole); others like the Gothic Temple (dedicated to liberty) and the Temple of Friendship (with statues of opposition members) were in the works.[17] Along with the Chinese house, these patriotic temples were situated in a part of the gardens called the Elysian Fields. Designed by Cobham and William Kent, this area departed from the continental style of formal patterns in favor of a "naturalized" landscape with unclear boundaries and carefully dispersed plantings. The Elysian Fields would not only display patriot iconography but also provoke patriotic feelings ranging from love and pride in "Britain" to a sense of liberty and naturalness in relation to social institutions based on imagined customs rather than a rationalized and bureaucratic state.[18]

Back in the 1680s when Cobham's Tory father Sir Richard Temple was using the spoils of a customs post to make initial improvements to Stowe, a more respectable if less prosperous relation, Sir William Temple, initiated a discussion of Chinese gardens in his essay "Upon the Gardens of Epicurus: Of Gardening, in the Year 1685." He argued that the Chinese scorned planting gardens according to an overt geometry of "proportions, symmetries, or uniformities." Instead,

> their greatest reach of imagination is employed in contriving figures, where the beauty shall be great, and strike the eye, but without any order or disposition of parts, that shall be commonly or easily observ'd. And though we have hardly any notion of this sort of beauty, yet they have a particular word to express it; and where they find it hit their eye at first sight, they say the *Sharawadgi* is fine or is admirable, or any such expression of esteem. And whoever observes the work upon the best Indian gowns, or the painting upon their best screens or purcellans, will find their beauty is all of this kind, (that is) without order.[19]

Such ideas possibly came from Temple's experience as an ambassador to Holland in the 1670s, which through its colonial outposts in Indonesia, factory in Nagasaki, and embassies to Beijing had access to Chinese commodities and Qing courtly culture. By translating the word *sharawadgi,* Temple linked the fragmented images of the widespread Dutch and English trades in landscape and garden images on porcelains, prints, and screens from China into a formalized model.

Attempts to root the term *sharawadgi* linguistically and in terms of a precise historical moment of translation have produced inconclusive results.[20] Temple himself left it open, citing the widely varied assortment of Chinese commodities in Europe as a visual authority and hearsay as a linguistic origin rather than offering evidence from a particular source. Temple moves from the Chinese "word" to construct a "notion," a formulation used by John Locke in his 1690 *Essay Concerning Human Understanding* to denote "mixed modes" or "complex ideas," often unique to the particular "fashions, customs, and manners of one nation, making several combinations of ideas familiar and necessary in one, which another people have had never an occasion to make . . . Where there was no such custom, there was no notion of any such actions; no use of such combinations of ideas as were united, and, as it were, tied together, by those terms: and therefore in other countries there were no names for them." For Locke, this explains the historicity of language: "Because change of customs and opinions bringing with it new combinations of ideas . . . new names, to avoid long descriptions, are annexed to them; and so they become new species of complex modes."[21] In the realm of the imaginary during the late seventeenth and early eighteenth centuries, *sharawadgi* became immensely productive as a new "notion" that neither came out of English tradition nor could be traced to any particular text or commodity, word, or thing, instead gathering together a wide variety of transcultural significations out of the long historical encounter between Europe and China.

According to Temple, the aesthetics of *sharawadgi* worked on two separate levels. The essay begins by contrasting two ways of moderating the passions—diverting and subduing. Ideal for diverting affect, gardens produce "the most exquisite delights of sense" because "fruits, flowers, shades, fountains, and the music of birds that frequent such happy places, seem to furnish all the pleasures of the several senses, and, with the greatest, or at least the most natural perfections."[22] Certain rare souls, however, do not require diversion but instead can manage "to subdue, or at least to temper their passions" through moral philosophy. In opposition to the social scramble for distinction, the garden provided the "Tranquillity of Mind" and "Indolence of Body" necessary for the cultivation of moral philosophy. To achieve both of these methods—the popular and the elite—of moderating the passions through gardening was a difficult task, one perfected perhaps only by the Chinese. Temple suggests that he "should hardly advise any of these attempts in the figure of gardens among us; they are adventures of too hard achievement for any common hands; and though there may be more honor if they succeed well, yet there is more dishonor if they fail, and 'tis twenty to one they will; whereas in regular figures, 'tis hard to make any great and remarkable faults."[23] Common hands could only imitate the surface level of grotesque disorder and exotic images (ornamental chinoiserie) seen by common eyes rather than engaging with the Chinese notion of beauty "without apparent order." Only the most civilized people of the seventeenth century, the Chinese, could govern garden aesthetics so as to create a free and ir-regular appearance.

The Chinese could succeed in this kind of advanced gardening technique because of broader cultural institutions that had linked distinction with merit. In the same vol-ume, in an essay entitled "Of Heroic Virtue," Temple lavishly praises the Chinese gov-ernment for being based not on flattery or corruption but on "the force or appearance of merit, or learning, and of virtue." Confucius, a prime example of heroic virtue and "a very extraordinary genius, of mighty learning, admirable virtue, excellent nature, a true patriot of his country, and lover of mankind,"[24] had laid down the tenets for moral virtue in China. For Temple, the "noble composition" of heroic virtue is still aristocratic in character but needs to be supplemented by merit. In China, argues Temple, class does not divide according to "noble and plebeian" but "learned and literate." By shifting cat-egories, Temple directly addresses the desire to shift the basis of aristocracy and the mode of distinction in Europe and in particular England from a standard based purely on heredity toward one that took learning (literacy conceived of culturally as "ancient learning"—classical and customary, not experimental) into account. This system had been developed in an empire with numerous and vast cities engaged in lively commerce. Other than China there was "no country in the known world so full of inhabitants, nor so improved by agriculture, by infinite growth of numerous commodities, by canals of incredible length, conjunctions of rivers, convenience of ways for the transportation of all sorts of goods and commodities from one province to another, so as no country has so great trade, though till very lately they never had any but among themselves."[25] Tem-ple was well aware that for the new post-1688 Britain, already well integrated into the Atlantic and Mediterranean economies and increasingly linked to the commercial sys-tems of Asia and the Baltic through its Dutch and later Hanoverian monarchs, dramatic social, political, and economic changes would be required at home to give a sense of co-herence to the nation.

The Chinese garden had the ability to focus sentiment and imagination within the individual. In the *Spectator* essays entitled "The Pleasures of the Imagination," Joseph Addison recapitulated Temple's argument without crediting him or mentioning the word *sharawadgi*. Shifting attention away from the moment of transcultural creation (*sharawadgi*), Addison focused on the anonymous spectator, in particular the imagi-nation as it relates not simply to mimetic representation or perception but as a source of pleasure. Gardens for Addison worked as an affect structure to produce such feel-ings. In *Spectator* no. 412 (23 June 1712), Addison details the way in which landscape can produce a particular set of feelings—"a spacious horizon is an image of liberty"—and alter moods ("pleasing astonishment," "agreeable surprise"). Beauty "diffuses a secret satisfaction and complacency through the imagination." At the most general level, God has designed nature to provoke emotional effects so that the world functions as a kind of simulacrum: "In short, our souls are at present delightfully lost and bewildered in a pleasing delusion, and we walk about like the enchanted hero of a romance, who sees beautiful castles, woods, and meadows; and at the same time hears the warbling of birds, and the purling of streams; but upon the finishing of some secret spell, the fantastic scene breaks up, and the disconsolate knight finds himself on a barren heath or in a solitary desert" (*Spectator* no. 413, 24 June 1712). Upon this basis, Addison in *Spectator* no. 414 (25 June 1712) posits an intimate link between nature and art. He describes the perfections of Chinese gardens, drawing directly from Temple, as "always conceal[ing] the art by which they direct themselves." "They have a word, it seems, in their language," Addison writes without including the translated term, "by which they express the particular beauty of a plantation that thus strikes the imagination at first sight, without discovering what it is that has so agreeable an effect." The goal of a garden or prospect as Addison explains in *Spectator* no. 417 (28 June 1712) is to awaken a "set of ideas" connected by "a set of traces belonging to them in the brain, bordering very near upon one another." Not only does this allow the activation of the "whole prospect or garden" in the imagination, but also it helps "to open a man's thoughts, and to enlarge his imagination, and will therefore have their influence on all kinds of writing, if the author knows how to make a right use of them." Like the essay, the garden structured sentiment so as to reorganize the chaos of significations in the urban space of London and the various productions of print capitalism that have created confusion at the level of aesthetic percept and political concept.

In the early 1730s, Alexander Pope suggested in his "Moral Epistles" that such artful confusion could actually be a political strategy in the struggle with Walpole. Pope saw the potential for gardening to become a key element of the opposition patriot program as well as a topos for distinguishing poetic writing from the prose of political hacks and literary "dunces." Gardening could answer Bolingbroke's question of how to "reform the morals and raise the sentiments of a people"; he would write the initial manuscript for the *Patriot King* between December 1738 and April 1739 while staying at Pope's famous villa and gardens in Twickenham.

Writing "Of Taste" (1731) to Burlington, the great self-appointed arbiter of Palladianism of the 1720s, Pope explains of gardening,

He gains all points, who pleasingly confounds,
Surprizes, varies, and conceals the Bounds.
Consult the Genius of the Place in all;
That tells the Waters or to rise, or fall,

. . . .

Now breaks, or now directs, th' intending Lines;

Paints as you plant, and, as you work, designs.

Still follow sense, of ev'ry art the soul,

Parts answ'ring parts shall slide into a whole,

Spontaneous beauties all around advance,

Start ev'n from difficulty, strike from chance;

Nature shall join you; time shall make it grow

A work to wonder at—perhaps a Stowe.   (ll. 55–70)

The poem articulates a tension between the derivation of the garden from the particular spirit of the local genius, a classical topos, and from the skilled and active artistry of one who knows how to "pleasingly confound," the concealed strategy of *sharawadgi*. In his "Essay on Man," Pope restates Addison's contention that the apparent natural wildness of the world is a grand piece of God's artifice, "All nature is but art, unknown to thee / All chance, direction, which thou canst not see; / All discord, harmony not understood." The gardener in this sense imitates God, imposing a sentimental structure for the soul from his particular point of privilege and understanding of the passions. The gardener's action thus restores coherence in the same way that "Poet or Patriot rose but to restore / The faith and moral, Nature gave before."

Pope names Stowe as the principal location for the potential development of this program in 1731, and he later writes in the epistle "To Cobham: Of the Knowledge and Characters of Men" (1734) that the "ruling passion" of the owner of Stowe is love of country. From 1734, Cobham begins to fill Stowe's new Elysian Fields with iconography suggesting historical models for Britishness, such as the Temple of British Worthies (1734–35) and the Temple of Ancient Virtue (1736). As in the case of the poetic text, the garden makes it possible to evoke various feelings through allusion. Yet, this proliferation of political signs is also to a certain degree a subtle joke, the multiplication of "Temples" suggesting that the patriotic canon is ultimately just a series of rearrangeable signs and lineage groups, a desacralized text adaptable to the strategies of print capitalism and Walpole's political machine. Finally, at its most complex level, that which "common eyes" would fail to see, the garden works according to the interplay of an emerging aesthetics of *sharawadgi*, based on the writings of Addison and Shaftesbury, who admire the pleasures evoked by nature as well as those of Pope and Temple who plot how to create nature itself. The unstructured appearance of the Elysian Fields, a dramatically reshaped landscape in which Cobham uprooted trees, hills, and even the village of Stowe, conceals a well-planned order. Subtle lines of sight guide the visitor through the garden, calculated to evoke sentiments through juxtapositions, surprises, and vistas. A finite set of variations invite the visitor to play with signification and sentiment while always remaining within the bounds of the garden's broader compositional paradigm. The Elysian Fields thus draw in sentimental affect and mark out distinctions on at least three subjective levels: political and ironic (the active patriot), natural and national (the contemplative spectator), and structural and "concealed" (the nobility of merit that "gains all points").

Situated on a pond on the edge of the Elysian Fields, the more explicit iconography of the Chinese House had a radically ambiguous character. Built around 1738 during the height of the "patriot" circle's activities, and using lacquer screens that were part of a larger gift of Chinese commodities from the Prince of Wales to Lady Cobham, the Chinese house was the first of its kind in Britain and set off a long line of imitations. At one level, the fragile building clearly raises associations with Chinese gardens, the direct inspiration for the aesthetics of the Elysian Fields. Yet, this image of China is compromised by strong hints of effeminate luxury, alluded to by the delicate construction of the house itself, which contrasts radically with the solidity of the adjacent masculine masonry temples of Ancient Virtue and British Worthies. A statue inside the house of "a Chinese lady as if asleep, her hands covered by her gown" suggests feminine passivity and the ephemeral nature of dream-like images. Finally, the chinoiserie designs present a surface of pure visual play. The fanciful paintings by the Venetian artist Francesco Sleter on the outside and images cut from lacquer screens on the inside were conventional enough to be read as a part of the broad field of "Chinese" representations produced in both Europe and China, embracing a transcultural eclecticism of image and passion that "pleasingly confounds." In this role, the Chinese house was too conventional to arouse profound sentiments. As one visitor wrote in 1738, "odd and Pretty enough, but as the form of their [Chinese] Building is so well known from Prints and other Descriptions, there is no Occasion to say more of it." The garden as a whole rather than the particular chinoiserie artifact generates the "delightfull Scenes that . . . entertain the Eye" and affect the sentiments.[26]

In addition to having the first "Chinese" or "naturalized" landscape garden in Britain and the first Chinese house in a garden, Stowe was the first landscape garden to have a series of tourist guidebooks produced about it. While emphasizing the patriotic themes of the garden and explaining historical references to English history, the guidebooks portrayed Anglo-Chinese gardening as a great English cultural invention with a whiff of chinoiserie; the average tourist's "common eyes" presumably would not understand the complex artifice involved. A 1742 poem by the classical scholar Samuel Boyse describes the Chinese house in terms of artificial and exotic chinoiserie as a place "Where all her wild grotesques display'd surprise . . . And mimic glories glitter all around."[27] The numerous guidebooks produced about Stowe from the 1740s onward followed this type of interpretation and became pioneers of the genre. They fail to examine the structure of the garden as a whole in relation to *sharawadgi*, preferring to see the landscape as natural rather than artificial or Chinese. Subsequent improvements on the garden during and after the 1740s would aid this reading by further refining the illusion of a simulacrum of nature. The guidebook worked as the hinge between the worlds of print culture and the garden, comforting unknowing visitors so they would not feel over-whelmed by the confusion, and thus deactivating the complex translations necessary to grapple with transcultural distance (*sharawadgi*—the "Chinese" garden in "Britain") in order to focus on a more limited one (what does it mean to have a "British" eye/I?). In some ways, the guidebook contests the claims of the proprietor of the estate to control its meaning, but as an object for "common hands," the guidebook also accepts the rules of the game, its basic language, and the visitor's role as a consuming rather than an ex-changing or producing subject.

In the late 1740s and especially the 1750s, a homegrown chinoiserie industry began to internalize and make English what had once been thought of as culturally hybrid. Pope's friend William Whitehead wrote in the *World*, on 22 March 1753:

> We may rest secure that our firm faith will never be flaggered by the tenets of Fohi, nor our practice vitiated by the morals of Confucius; at least we may be certain that the present in-novations are by no means adequate to such an effect: for on a moderate computation, not one in a thousand of all the stiles, gates, rails, pales, chairs, temples, chimney-pieces, &c.&c.&c. which are called Chinese, has the lest resemblance to any thing that china ever saw; nor would an English church be a less uncommon sight to a traveling mandarin, than an English pagoda . . . our Chinese ornaments are not only of our own manufacture, like our French silks and our French wines, but, what has seldom been attributed to the En-glish, of our own invention.[28]

In the emerging imagined community and structure of affects known as "Britain," a complicated and subtle opening remained for the translation of things Chinese sep-arate from but related to the process of commodifying rococo chinoiserie. In poems by Gay, Swift, Pope, and others, the person who excessively enjoyed the chinoiserie artifact (allegorized as female, characterized as effeminate) constantly suffered from confusion of sentiments, and to make a fetish of china (as opposed to China) meant allowing a confusion between spatial distance and sociopolitical distance to infect the imagination and corrupt proper judgment. Wallowing in consumption was in many ways radical, a constant and anarchic generation of a general confusion based upon distance (exotics as outsiders) that tended to undermine older aristocratic and patriarchal epistemolo-gies of value and communal identification. Yet, those who had an interest in maintain-ing sociopolitical distance could use such confusion as a marker to enable social dis-tinction based upon merit, the merit of knowing how to attract and focus affect. The second China, the Chinese landscape garden, helped "conceal" such distinction by making garden space appear both natural and national. As the Chinese House at Stowe suggests, these two Chinas overlapped, and to "pleasingly confound" through chinoiserie was ultimately a management strategy developed by the patriot opposition to attract a range of sentiment that could compete with the fiscal power of the Robinocracy. Landscape gardens "founded on noble and liberal principles," remained the epitome of good taste and patriotic merit, as another writer for the *World*, Richard Owen Cambridge, wrote in the 3 April 1755 issue. The new gardening styles of the 1730s and 1740s had turned "private amusement" into a "national good," thus having the direct "political benefit" of teaching by example. "It is the peculiar happiness of this age to see these just and noble ideas brought into practice, regularity banished, prospects opened, the country called in, nature rescued and improved, and art decently concealing herself under her own perfections."[29] Cambridge cites Sir William Temple as a pioneer of this national style and thus has to deal with the paradox of Temple's crediting its invention to the Chinese. Here Cambridge hedges and notes that "Whatever may have been reported, whether truly or falsely, of the Chinese gardens, it is certain that we are the first of the Europeans who have founded this taste" (78) making Britain now a Grand Tour destination and a unique contributor to European culture with its dramatic departure from French, Italian, Dutch, and German aristocratic and absolutist formality. By the mid to late eighteenth century, the touring of Britain's gardens had become de rigeur, so that when Jefferson and Adams were there on diplomatic missions in the 1780s, they felt compelled to tour Stowe, which remained one of the most frequently visited gardens in Britain throughout the eighteenth century.

"Merit" in Bolingbroke's sense of the term gave this strategic and patriotic use of the Chinese landscape garden political and social coherence while "sentiment" gave it power. The invisible hand of the patriot gardener in the countryside could give an appearance of national coherence to the confusion of boundaries created by complex transnational wars, trade patterns, and finance markets so evident in the city of London, limiting the space necessary for comprehension and offering the comfort of sentiment to those who feared an anarchy of the soul in an increasingly global eighteenth century. Constructed around the duality of reading according to merit or sentiment, the double character of patriotism allowed a certain amount of political play.[30] Yet, this dual character also derives from the process of "concealing the bounds," so that as an open-ended affect structure "British" patriotism refers to an aristocracy of talent that can in secret "manage the contrasts," maintain the "constitution" as a social institution, and thus achieve social cohesion and reproduction. Rather than functioning as a patriotic language or national culture, "Britain" in this sense works as a developing praxis of class, one that derives an ever-so-problematic strength and vitality in both conservative and radical senses from the process of transculturation.

CHAPTER SIX

The Global Parasol

Accessorizing the Four Corners of the World

Joseph Roach

John Ogilby (1600–76), the London publisher who pirated his great folio atlases from the Dutch, began his career as a man of the theater. Apprenticed to a dancing master by his improvident parents, he made his way as a professional dancer and actor until he was forced from the stage and into theater management by a crippling injury suffered in a fall during the performance of a Stuart court anti-masque. As an entrepreneur, Ogilby was anything but improvident. Under the assertive but precarious patronage of the Earl of Strafford, he became Master of Revels for Ireland, setting up a theater in St. Werburgh Street, Dublin, in 1637. After a hiatus during the Interregnum, during which he ventured into a publishing career with richly illustrated translations of Homer, Virgil, and Aesop, he reclaimed his office and opened the Smock Alley Theatre, Dublin, in 1662. Smock Alley, which continued its distinguished history into the eighteenth century, was the first playhouse in the English-speaking theater purposely built to house scenes and machines in the Italianate scenographic style.[1]

Moveable scenery painted in perspective was an important innovation on the Restoration stage. It altered the means of representing—and changing—locale. The practitioners of the previous age had boldly named their best-remembered theater "The Globe," imagining that the poet's words, held aloft by the labor of Hercules, would inspire the audience members to work out the decor by themselves: "For 'tis your

thoughts that now must deck our kings" (Shakespeare, *Henry V,* Prologue, l. 28). After
the Restoration, producers localized the names of their theater buildings much more
narrowly, tying them to a street or neighborhood address—Smock Alley, Lincoln's Inn
Fields, Dorset Garden, Drury Lane, and later the Haymarket and Covent Garden—but
inside they illustrated globe-spanning locales on painted canvas vistas shimmering under candle-powered suns and moons. Now, in the twinkling of an eye, machines could
move the wings and change the scene, potentially to any one of the four corners of the
world and back again, affording opportunities for a kind of vicarious tourism, which,
abetted by the proliferation of travel narratives and geographies, emerged long before
the improved safety and affordability of travel made actual tours feasible for large numbers of people.[2]

Enter Ogilby, the impresario-turned-illustrator, "one of the most visually minded
men of his century."[3] His print-world debut as Charles II's royal geographer was well
timed. Unprotected by copyright, the atlases of Olfert Dapper, Johan Nieuhof, and
Arnold Montanus were as vulnerable as unescorted Dutch merchantmen to the depredations of English pirates (see chap. 1 in this volume). From 1669 to 1673, Ogilby issued
seven folio atlases with translated and augmented commentaries, mapping Africa, Asia
(Persia and India), China, Japan, and the Americas, profiling their topographies and
ethnographies and illustrating them with numerous "sculptures and cuts." His credit
line as publisher, which advertises his continuing theatrical role as Master of Revels in
the Kingdom of Ireland as well as his more recent offices as His Majesty's Cosmographer and Geographic Printer, frames the terms that I will be addressing here: the related techniques of representing global human difference in graphic and theatrical media. Mindful of the expanding scope of recent scholarly work on the role of Restoration
and eighteenth-century English drama in Britain's imperial project, including the popular understanding of "exotic" lands,[4] I propose to offer an amplifying annotation based
on the material culture of Restoration stagecraft. The evidence that allows scholars to
reconstruct the stage pictures of this period is admittedly very limited, but a significant
plurality of the extant examples—engravings illustrating the first edition of *The Empress of Morocco* (1673), for instance, and several portraits of exotically costumed actors
and actresses—shares certain key conventions with the atlases. Jointly employing visual tropes that function similarly to figures of speech such as synecdoche and metonymy, the illustrated atlases and the stage performances offered their viewers pioneering
versions of what postcolonial theory has lately termed *ethnoscapes*—landscapes of persons who constitute the shifting world in which modern subjects live and through
which they represent to one another and to themselves their relationships of identity
and difference.[5] To be sure, the early modern ethnoscape appeared with conventions of
representation specific to its own time and quaint to later ones. Self-conscious authen-

ticity of scenery and costume, for instance, was underdeveloped in comparison with late-eighteenth- and nineteenth-century graphic and theatrical travelogues. Most scenes and costumes for day-to-day operations were drawn from stock, and they remained generally conventionalized within contemporary European norms, whatever the country or clime. In the selective use of costume accessories, however, as in the occasional use of an iconic set-piece—the palm tree, the Chinese garden, the turban, the scimitar, the face made up in black, the feathered headdress, and especially the parasol—the Restoration stage decked its (alien) kings in ways that signified their difference. With the goal of illuminating the principles of selection of those featured objects, I also speculate about the meaning of one suggestive but previously neglected piece of evidence bearing on the popularization of ethnographic images in this period: John Ogilby's atlases, along with other travel books from diverse authors, were in the possession of Thomas Betterton, the greatest actor on the Restoration stage and the producer of some of its most opulent scenic extravaganzas.

Betterton played many kinds of roles in a fifty-year career that began with the Restoration and ended with his death in 1710 at the age of seventy-five. Samuel Pepys remarked on his Hamlet in 1661, and Richard Steele reviewed it one last time in 1709, when the septuagenarian was still the only actor that the public would accept in the prince's role, gout and decrepitude notwithstanding. Betterton also played some of the Restoration's greatest roles of alien potentates and heroes, including Solyman the Magnificent twice, in both Sir William Davenant's *The Siege of Rhodes* (1656) and the Earl of Orrery's *Mustapha* (1665). He was famous as Othello and noted as Montezuma in Dryden's *The Indian Emperour; or, The Conquest of Mexico* (1667). Leading the trend (along with Ogilby and Davenant) toward more elaborate scenery and special effects, Betterton journeyed to France at the command of Charles II to study the latest techniques of continental stagecraft. When the Duke's Company opened the technically advanced Dorset Garden Theatre in 1673, the actor-manager was credited with many innovations behind the scenes of the spectacular productions introduced there.[6] Significantly, the only one of those to have been illustrated in a fancy edition was also the most geographically exoticized, Elkanah Settle's *The Empress of Morocco*. The style of its tropical iconography—in one scene the black-faced and bare-limbed "Moors" of the *corps de ballet* gather before a palm tree "about which they dance to several antick instruments"—resembles that of the Ogilby atlases in several particulars.[7] The most eye-catching of these is the conical parasol held aloft by a supernumerary to shade an important on-stage spectator; it was a scene that theatergoers and atlas readers would see repeated. Based on its appearance at each of the four corners of the world in Ogilby's folios and at two of the four on the stage, this lackey-borne umbrella seems to represent an icon in the atlas of cultural difference.

I am featuring the word *atlas* to suggest that the theater offers a revealing glimpse into the processes of mapping, not only in its literal sense of producing a schematization of space on paper but also in its larger cognitive sense of fashioning a world simulacrum. Everyone eventually learns his or her own version of such a mental map. Carried around in memory, it accumulates detail and authority over time. As Henry Fielding's character "Politick" says in *Rape upon Rape* (1730): "Map me no Maps, Sir, my Head is a Map, a Map of the whole world."[8] Everyone brings a mental map with him or her to each encounter with a foreigner (or on each journey as one), and everyone takes away from these experiences a somewhat different map. No two are identical, though different cultures impart distinctive styles of mental mapping. The most assiduous cartographers might regularly check their mental maps against printed ones, but unless an atlas is constantly at hand, they must check every geographical reference they hear against the globe that is spinning continuously only in their imaginations. That global atlas is the product, in various combinations, of study and travel, of exposure to popular culture and world news, of daydreaming and fantasizing, and, I believe, of playreading and theatergoing.

Like the stage, the atlas of the mind is busily populated with costumed performers. In and around the linear depiction of continents and nations there proliferate illustrative images of peoples, including their habitats, their manufactures, and their activities (fig. 6.1). In mental cartography, as in the illustrative cartouches on seventeenth- and eighteenth-century maps, these imaginary peoples and their cultural totems tend to fill in the blank spots: ships and strange fish float on the open oceans; natives pose partially nude or festooned with feathers; natural resources, foodstuffs, weapons, tools, or handicrafts spill out from the apparently inexhaustible cornucopia of authenticating detail, which may or may not be acquired by firsthand experience of the peoples represented. Mental atlases abhor a vacuum. In addition to images and legends, they accommodate behaviors as markers of locality; the weird festive dance, the bizarre culinary flourish, or the mysterious religious rite serve to flesh out spaces as places. These illustrations and mental images fill in the areas that earlier European cartographers marked with the legend "Here be Dragons." By the end of the seventeenth century, the dragons had mostly changed into alien ethnoscapes. They depicted noble savages, primitives, cannibals, and exotic women (on cartouches of Africa, America, and the South Seas), and tyrants, artisans, coolies, and exotic women (on those of Asia). As well as place names and travel tips, their narrative texts recounted alien practices such as widow burning, foot binding, polygamous sex, festive funerals, juridical tortures, mass executions, and occult performances of many kinds.

Such sensational imagery contributes to the normalizing ethnocentrism that not infrequently marks atlases of the mind. Even miniature ethnoscapes of performance show

Figure 6.1. John Ogilby after Arnold Montanus, frontispiece to *America* (1671).

its foreshortening effect, a kind of parallax view of cultural difference. Sir Richard Steele, in the *Tatler* number immediately preceding his poignant eulogy of Thomas Betterton, demonstrates a relatively benign way in which performances located peoples on his mental atlas. In an aside concerning the intercultural conventions of tuning musical instruments, Steele warns of the mistake made by "the Eastern Prince, who, according to the old Story, took *Tuning* for *Playing*." The *Tatler* advises English musicians to tune before the audience comes into the theater and English dancers to muffle their heels with cotton, so "that the Artists in so polite an Age as ours, may not intermix with their Harmony a Custom which so nearly resembles the Stamping Dances of the *West-Indians* or *Hottentots*."[9] Here the East, funneled through the solitary figure of an ignorant potentate, mistakes cacophony for harmony. Such a faux pas is surpassed in comparative infelicity only by the accidental resemblance of European ballet acoustics to the music and dance forms of African peoples. The inhabitants of "so polite an Age as ours" occupy a different time (now) and a place (England) in which sweet harmony will follow swiftly and graciously upon the earnest remonstrances of the tonally well informed. Thus organizing the world according to a geohistorical hierarchy of performance, Steele's head is a map, one on which Asians and Africans make music beyond the pale of fine-tuning.

This kind of mapmaking shares with theatrical representation the ever-useful trope of synecdoche—the part stands in for the whole, the species for the genus, the one for the many: "since a crooked figure may / Attest in little place a million" (Shakespeare, *Henry V,* Prologue, ll. 15–16). Synecdoche shares pride of place in theatrical signification with her sister metonymy, whereby the word for one thing stands in for another of which it is an attribute or with which it is associated, especially when that association occurs through bodily contiguity or propinquity. Physical objects like hand props or articles of dress thus make vivid verbal and visual metonyms, as they do when either *scepter* or *crown,* for example, stands in for the idea of kingship. When a crown arrives onstage as a visual metonym, it substitutes for many of the things its wearer would otherwise have to say and do to introduce himself or herself convincingly to the audience.

On the stage and (cartographic) page at the beginning of the long eighteenth century, the four corners of the world were represented synecdochically or metonymically in the form of selected costumes, sets, properties, and (where racial difference is concerned) makeup—hence the powerful symbolic importance that emanates from accessories. To accessorize is to make a useful sign out of a practical superfluity: the word *accessory* suggests not only a surplus or an excess (as in a bejeweled purse too small to hold anything, for instance) but also an oblique but significant instrumentality (as in an "accessory after the fact"). To accessorize a costume is thus to furnish it with the supplementary but nonetheless crucial items that serve to identify or locate the wearer. In matters of class and gender, Augustan fashion had already attained the status of science in this regard.[10] In matters of ethnic identity, it was still more tentative, but the expansion of colonization and trade (and the travel books associated with them) gradually had increased the repertoire of signs.[11] When the portraitist John Greenhill, for instance, depicted Betterton in the role of Solyman the Magnificent, he showed the actor dressed in a conventional English waistcoat along with a big, fluffy turban and a most formidable (and unsheathed) dagger in his hand.[12] The accessories, as specifying adjuncts, stand in for the costume as a whole, and, if clothes may be thought to make the man, they perforce stand in for the Turk in the geohistorical atlas of the mind.

The *Tatler* shows how such accessories can take on a life of their own even beyond the specific occasion of their use in performance. In a number devoted to satirizing the exceptionally venal theatrical manager Christopher Rich, who is shown auctioning off choice items from the property closet of Drury Lane Theatre, Joseph Addison lists, among other famous memorabilia for sale, "The Whiskers [fake beard] of a *Turkish Bassa,*" "The Complexion of a Murderer in a Ban-Box; consisting of a large Piece of burnt Cork [the favored method of blacking up], and a Cole-black Peruke," and "*Aurenzebe*'s Scymeter [scimitar]" (1:304–5). Properties such as these were reused for as long as the show was in the repertory, and they were also available for use in other productions when the need arose. Addison's inventory of Rich's sale also includes "A Plume of Feathers, never used but by *Oedipus* and the Earl of *Essex*" and "An Imperial Mantle, made for *Cyrus the Great,* and worn by *Julius Caesar, Bajazet,* King *Harry* the Eighth, and Signior *Valentini* [Valentino Urbani, the operatic castrato]" (1:304–5). From out of the stock inventory of such familiar objects, an Englishman of Steele and Addison's "polite Age" could select the exotic accessories (the authenticity of which was only occasional)[13] from which to fashion a global ethnoscape, dividing the world between alien and nonalien localities and interests.

Operating within the conventions of the mental atlas as well as the printed or the staged one, synecdoche and metonymy did yeoman service in mapping the global eighteenth century. Addison devotes another *Tatler* number to a report of a geopolitical dream, replete with localized settings and very suggestive accessory-properties. In this imaginative ethnoscape, the Switzerland-like bastion of the Alpine Goddess "Liberty" is besieged by the menacing alien figures of "Tyranny" and "Barbarity." They enter on cue at the head of two armies of supernumerary transnationals, costumed as if for the stage and well equipped to perform the obligatory fifth-act carnage. Addison's principals are all female, as they usually are in the famous mapmakers' cartouches of the four corners of the world, except that the *Tatler* transforms the benign voluptuousness of the seminudes into a specter of alien menace by clothing and accessorizing them with items issued from the deep property closet of xenophobia: "*Tyranny* was at the Head of one of these Armies, dressed in an Eastern Habit, and grasping in her Hand an Iron Scepter. Behind her was *Barbarity*, with the Garb and Complexion of an *Aethiopian; Ignorance* with a Turban upon her Head; and *Persecution* holding up a bloody Flag, embroidered with Flower-de-Luces. These were followed by *Oppression, Poverty, Famine, Torture*, and a dreadful Train of Appearances, that made me tremble to behold them. Among the Baggage of this Army, I could discover Racks, Wheels, Chains, and Gibbets, with all the Instruments Art could invent to make human Nature miserable" (2:401). Addison's head is a map. His synecdochic inclusion of La Belle France, "embroidered with Flower-de-Luces," among the Near Eastern, Far Eastern, and African Amazons raises the time-honored phobia whereby Englishmen situated French people and culture among the alien races on their mental map of the world.[14]

Based on the popular lucubrations of Addison and Steele, which rely on the complicit knowledge of their readers, I infer that the mental map carried about by other theatergoers in Betterton's London featured certain accessory-enhanced demispheres: here the violent Surinam of Aphra Behn's account, as dramatized by Thomas Southerne in *Oroonoko* (1695), or the eroticized Africa of Settle's *Empress of Morocco* (1673); there the sun-drenched, blood-drenched Mexico of Dryden and Howard's *The Indian Queen* (1664) and Dryden's sequel *The Indian Emperour* (1665), or the ritualized and intrigue-ridden India of Dryden's *Aurengzebe* (1675), from which the eponymous character's scimitar ended up as a notorious prop. Less frequently revived plays in this genre include Dryden's *Amboyna* (1673), Settle's *The Conquest of China* (1676), Behn's *Abdelazer* (1676) and *The Widow Ranter* (1689), Henry Purcell's operatic setting of *The Indian*

Queen (1695), Mary Pix's *Ibrahim* (1696), and Delarivier Manley's *The Royal Mischief* (1696).[15] By the thoroughness of their global distribution, I also infer from these examples that theater audiences shared an interest with atlas readers in wide-ranging geographical coverage, however fragmentary it may have been. The cluster of plays produced in the mid-1670s, which included the eye-popping *Empress of Morocco*, overlaps with the publication of Ogilby's extra-illustrated atlases. Chief among these were some that ended up in Thomas Betterton's book collection: *Africa* (1670), *America* (1671), *Asia* [India and the Near East] (1671), *China* (1673), and *Japan* (1673). Boasts of accuracy aside, the repertory of tragic drama set in exotic lands ran approximately abreast of Ogilby's stated agenda, which was "the Reducement of the whole World, viz. A New and Accurate Description of the Four Regions therof, the first of which being Africa."[16]

After his death in 1710, Betterton's books, prints, and paintings were auctioned for the benefit of his widow. The catalog, printed by the auctioneer Jacob Hooke, was titled *Pinacotheca Bettertonaeana. Pinacotheca* is a Latin word, derived from the Greek, meaning a small picture gallery or museum. For my purposes, that definition supplies a helpful characterization of the collection's import, especially when the geographical scope of the items is considered in connection with a conjectural reconstruction of a mental atlas that places Britain in the context of the larger world.[17] The largest single category, containing 145 of the approximately 600 items, is European history, especially English history, including major seventeenth-century works dealing with the search for the racial origins of the British people, notably Richard Verstegen's *Restitution of Decayed Intelligence in Antiquities Concerning the Most Noble and Renowned English Nation* (1605), which, citing fossil evidence, argues the geohistorical purity and superiority of the Anglo-Saxons.

As if to complement (or complicate) the anglocentrism of the history volumes, another large category in Betterton's collection—and obviously the most germane to my point—consists of travel books and geographies or "histories" of places and peoples from the four corners of the world. The commendatory verses for one such book, Richard Ligon's account of the island of Barbados, include a couplet that well describes the implicit invitation of many others in Betterton's library: "The Scite, Clime, Flood, the Customs, Laws, and Trade, / To each inquisitor is open laid."[18] In that spirit, Betterton owned George Sandys's *Travels [in the Ottoman lands and Egypt]*, "illustrated with 50 maps and figures," Tavernier's *Voyages into Persia and the East-Indies*, and Rycaut's translation of De la Vega's *Royal Commentaries of Peru*, with its meticulous accounts of comparative ritual practices.[19] There were also John Smith's *Travels*, Hackluyt's *Navigations*, Aaron Hills's *Present State of the Ottoman Empire*, Sir John Chardin's *Travels into Persia and the East-Indies*, Thomas Gage's *Survey of the West-Indies* ("with Maps"), a general *Geographical Dictionary*, and the very specialized Bible translated into the Algonquian tongue by Eliot. Jacob Hooke advertised Betterton's copy of John Ogilby's atlas set "with maps and other sculptures" as *The History of America, The History of Asia, The History of China and East-Tartary,* "with curious sculptures in 2 vols," *The History of Japan,* and *The History of Africa,* "illustrated with Notes and Adorned with Sculptures."[20]

There is no way of proving with certainty that Betterton's gleanings from this library of vicarious tourism influenced his stage productions. Among the drawings and paintings offered in the *Pinacotheca,* there is a tantalizing item, however: "Mr. Betterton in a Turkish Habit, by Greenhil [sic]," which might well have been the finished portrait of the actor as Solyman the Magnificent for which the preparatory sketch survives. There is also an item called "The Habits of the World, finely colour'd, 100 Prints."[21] However, the most suggestive concordance between the printed atlases and what can be known about the stage picture in the period of Betterton's spectacular productions resides in the ubiquity of one accessory in particular—the parasol. Ogilby's plates show the identical conical umbrella appearing not only in the cartouche on the large foldout map in the front matter of *America* (see fig. 6.1) but also in the plate marked "Habit of a Floridian King" (fig. 6.2).[22] It appears over the head of the Mogul Schah Iehann in *Asia* (fig.

Figure 6.2. John Ogilby after Arnold Montanus, "Habit of a Floridian King," *America* (1671).

Figure 6.3. John Ogilby, "Schah Iehann," *Asia, the First Part* (1673).

6.3)[23] and yet again shading the path of a Chinese noblewoman (fig. 6.4).[24] In the theater, the conical parasol appeared as the prop used by the aforementioned ballet of the Moors in *The Empress of Morocco,* but its chief glory in the history of stage came with the publication of the mezzotint by J. Smith and W. Vincent showing the actress Anne Bracegirdle in the role of "The Indian Queen" (fig. 6.5). Bracegirdle was adopted as a child and raised within earshot of the theater by Thomas Betterton and his wife. She grew up to play the heroines in some of the actor-manager's most successful productions. Most theater historians accept the "Indian Queen" mezzotint as a representation of Bracegirdle playing Semernia in *The Widow Ranter* (1689), Aphra Behn's tragicomedy set in Virginia during the time of Bacon's Rebellion.[25]

Not generally associated with Native American material culture, the royal or sacred umbrella figures prominently in the iconography of ancient art in the Mediterranean and the Middle East.[26] Christian saints carried by devouts in holy processions rode un-

Figure 6.4. John Ogilby, *Atlas Chinensis* (1671).

der the protection of such ambulant architecture. Yet here the parasol is not so much an American or European icon of authentic identity as it is a global one, a visual metonym for the concept of difference itself. In "The Indian Queen," as in the other images in which it appears, the parasol betokens the sovereignty of an alien noble, registered by the high degree of deference shown to her as one who deserves the labor-intensive perquisite of portable shade. But that is not the only work the umbrella does. A tableau of sacrificial excess with the parasol at its compositional apex, the staging depicted by "The Indian Queen" piles up accessory on accessory like the offerings at a potlach. Not all of them are inanimate objects. A Restoration tragedienne had to depend on a boy whose job it was to mind the lengthy and heavy train of her gown. He remained onstage as long as she did. Exits were particularly tricky because of the wide turning radius required by the train, and if the departure was abrupt, as when the character was in a rage or a pout, the boy had to be everywhere at once—except in the way. In his humorous complaints about overproduction in the staging of English tragedy, Joseph Addison sets up against the superfluity of its train bearers, as he does against its literally

Figure 6.5. W. Vincent, *Anne Bracegirdle as Semernia.* Engraving. By permission of the Harvard Theatre Collection.

feather-headed heroes: "As these superfluous Ornaments upon the Head make a great Man, a Princess generally receives her Grandeur from those additional Incumbrances that fall into her Tail: I mean the broad sweeping Train that follows her in all her Motions, and finds constant Employment for a Boy who stands behind her to open and spread it to Advantage. I do not know how others are affected by this Sight, but, I must confess, my Eyes are wholly taken up with the Page's Part; and, as for the Queen, I am not so attentive to anything she speaks, as to the right adjustment of her Train."[27] With the accessory object, though, superfluity is in the eye of the beholder. The less practical it is, the more it means. Even today, a tie is required of gentlemen because it has nothing useful to do, and no suit, however chic, is proof against a bad one. The Indian Queen merits two accessory boys, one for the train, the other for the parasol. Each of their tasks takes two hands, but the real work they do here is symbolic—like that of the train itself. It works its magic by transforming an excrescent detail into a crucial sign. The parasol does no less. Evocative of prestige, luxury, and pampered excess, it locates Semernia in the crowded stage picture of the global ethnoscape.

As it so often occurs in performances of difference, contact in "The Indian Queen" is mediated through an exemplary figure, typically a royal one—a summary instance of the one standing in for the many, a synecdochic embassy. The Queen has turned *contraposto* and opened out in fourth position to make an interesting line of the body. The silhouette of her gown is European, and she is tightly corseted, but her sandaled feet show skin beneath the hem of her dress, an erotic provocation in the Restoration playhouse. She holds her arms daintily in opposition: with her right hand she manages the salvage of her overskirt; with her left she raises a fan made of feathers, which in turn draws the attention of the beholder to her feathered headdress and to those of the boys.[28] In fact, all the accessories here—the feathers, the train, the parasol—lead the eye back to the exoticized children. Their race, and thus their *raison d'être* in seventeenth-century North America, is ambiguous. Like costume pieces, dispensable objects attached to the properties they manage, their role as metonymic substitutes is to efface the necessity of the real labor required to make and remake their world. Semernia's fan of plumes seems unlikely to make much of a breeze, the practical effect of the parasol against the heat of the day is countered by the weight of the gown, and the smiling boys were accurately minstrelized by the exclamation of a great theater historian of the early twentieth century: "How proud they are, and what fun they are having!"[29] Africans or Americans, their flesh stands in for an atlas of accessories under the expansive coverup of the global parasol.

Ogilby, the theatrical entrepreneur, explicitly connected his atlases to the Restoration stage on at least one significant occasion. In his introductory matter to *America,* he quotes the passage from Dryden's *The Indian Emperour* that describes the Spanish approach to the coast of Mexico. Strangely, Ogilby shifts the locale of the action to Peru, as if somehow his own misalliance of historical event and geographical space would counterbalance Dryden's attachment of Pizarro to the Mesoamerican expedition of Cortez. In his report speech to Montezuma, as Ogilby cites it, the wonder-struck Guyomar relates what he saw when he looked out at the horizon "To see that Shore, where no more World is found." Rather than the end of the world where dragons might rise at the margin of water and sky, however, what he saw was an anomaly approaching from the European corner of it, an ominous shape separating itself "like Bluish Mists" from the distant ranges of clouds—a warship, sails full set, broadsides thundering, which looked to him like a breaking wave of newborn gods. Montezuma wonders what forces these "Divine Monsters" represent, but Guyomar can only answer with a description of the particular parts (masts, sails, hulls, and guns) that signify and manifest the approach of the incomprehensible whole:

More strange than what your Wonder can invent.

The object I could first distinctly view,

Was tall straight Trees, which on the Waters flew;

Wings on their sides in stead of Leaves did grow,

Which gather'd all the Breath the Winds could blow:

And at their Roots grew floating Palaces,

Whose out-blown Bellies cut the yielding Seas.[30]

The wave-breasting galleon with full-blown sails and fire-belching cannons, sometimes pushed from behind by the breath of a big-cheeked Aeolus, is a favorite mapmakers' detail. In the mental map that Dryden's theatrical description evokes, it might be thought to stand in a general way as synecdoche for the European approach to the four corners of the world.

For Ogilby, Guyomar's visual encounter with the Spanish ship, which the Aztec-turned-Inca can only report in terms of its salient (but accessory) parts, reverses the implied direction of the colonial gaze without expanding its repertoire of tropes. The figure of the ship, which balances the parasol in the iconography of Ogilby's map of America, links the map to the text and to the stage through the quotation from *The Indian Emperour*. Recalling the Royal Cosmographer's relocation of the scene of the Spanish arrival, the ship appears on the Pacific side of South America and opens fire off the coast of Peru. Such accessories can long remain in mental maps of the world, illustrating global ethnoscapes with vivid parts, even if their relationship to the truth of the whole rests on no greater authority than the stage.

CHAPTER SEVEN

Oceans and Floods

Fables of Global Perspective

Laura Brown

Samuel Johnson's *The Vanity of Human Wishes* (1749), the eighteenth century's most canonical poetic inquiry into the scope and efficacy of metaphysical explanation, opens expansively with an imaginative circumnavigation of the world:

> Let observation with extensive view,
> Survey mankind, from China to Peru;
>
> . . . .
>
> Then say how hope and fear, desire and hate,
> O'erspread with snares the clouded maze of fate.

This global inquiry comes to a problematic close in the poem's last verse paragraph, which begins with a figure that evokes a much more precipitous voyage:

> Where then shall Hope and Fear their objects find?
> Must dull Suspence corrupt the stagnant mind?
> Must helpless man, in ignorance sedate,
> Roll darkling down the torrent of his fate?[1]

The paired passions of hope and fear give rise to a sudden "torrent" that rushes the poem's subject, and its reader, toward a seemingly irresistible fate. The following lines

of the poem negotiate that destiny without refuting its evocation of human helpless-
ness or confirming any alternate notion of human agency. Through unassuming
prayer, humankind can seek consolation in resignation, love, patience, and faith: "With
these, celestial Wisdom calms the mind, / And makes the happiness she does not find"
(ll. 365–68). The "torrent" is transformed by an act of faith into a beneficent "calm."
The *Vanity* provides an expansive survey of an unpredictable world, a world that im-
pels its citizens through a fluid irresistibility toward an end beyond their agency or
knowledge, and that is conditionally, perhaps even ironically, ordered by powers of
imagination.

Written twenty-one years earlier, Edward Young's *Ocean: An Ode* (1728) depicts a
similar scenario of conditional consolation and fluid turbulence, hope and fear:

> How mixt, how frail,
> How sure to fail,
> Is every pleasure of mankind!
> A damp destroys
> My blooming joys,
> While Britain's glory fires my mind.

> For who can gaze
> On restless seas,
> Unstruck with life's more restless state?
> Where all are tost,
> And most are lost,
> By tides of passion, blasts of fate?

> The world's the main,
> How vext! how vain
> Ambition swells, and anger foams;
> May good men find,
> Beneath the wind,
> A noiseless shore, unruffled homes![2]

Young's is an occasional political poem, Johnson's a speculative moral work. Yet these
texts share a set of linked images: the conjunction of a conception of "fate" with the
figure of a fluid waterway—a torrent, a tossing sea, a foaming main; the projection of
a world of global compass within which that nautical fate is performed; the evocation
of a contrastive structure of fear and hope, joy and frailty, glory and loss provoked by
that fluid, rushing, or restless fate; and the conditional assertion of a state of tranquility in the midst of that headlong waterway—the wishful vision of a maritime calm. Un-

likely cohorts though they certainly are, these poems share a story about an experience that neither directly names, a story that assumes that "the world's the main" and that torrents, oceans, and the global expanse they signify somehow define the terms of human fate.

The ocean was increasingly a fact of life and a foregrounded object of national and cultural contemplation in this period. Commerce, both overseas and domestic, was first and foremost an oceangoing enterprise; its local site was the urban port, notably the Port of London, where the most visible locus of maritime contact was the Thames and the open sea beyond. The prominence of the sea and of shipping in English life is a distinctive development of the early modern period. In the early seventeenth century, England was a rural and agricultural nation; in the course of that century, and especially after 1660, shipping emerged as one of the fastest growing national industries. Indeed the image of the Thames, so crowded with ships that their masts make up a "floating forest," becomes a trope for the expansionist destiny of the nation in the first half of the eighteenth century.

The sea was an immediate presence in English life in this period in many other ways. At the end of the seventeenth century, the shipping industry maintained 50,000 men in the service of the merchant marine, out of a national population of one and a half million. London was the nation's major entrepôt, and the massive businesses of transshipment, distribution, and repackaging, and the warehouses required by these businesses, were another prominent dimension of the port's presence. The Port of London was home to myriad related industries—including shipbuilding; rope, sail, and mast making; and warehousing, sugar refining, and importing—as well as the factors, brokers, trading companies, and marine insurance companies dependent upon the ports. At the beginning of the eighteenth century, as much as a fourth of the population of London was employed in trades related to the port and the business of shipping.[3]

In this context, it is not surprising that the ocean pervades the popular print culture of the eighteenth century. It is the ubiquitous fluid roadway of the travel narrative from John Churchill's, John Atkins's, and Thomas Astley's voyages to James Cook's, Joseph Banks's, and George Forster's epic journals of the exploration of the Pacific (1768–80). The sea is the defining instrument of emblematic isolation in the eighteenth century's single most influential vision of modern experience, *Robinson Crusoe* (1719), as well as in the subsequent castaway novels by Ambrose Evans, Penelope Aubin, and others. This is also the period of accounts of piracy and the "high" seas of violent, communal, alternative heroism. Naval adventure is featured in various forms of prose narrative in the course of the century, from Tobias Smollett's picaresque *Roderick Random* (1748) to Olaudah Equiano's autobiographical *Life* (1789). Jonathan Swift chooses the form of the oceangoing travel narrative as the frame of *Gulliver's Travels* (1726) and names Gulliver as a cousin of the well-known travel writer William Dampier and a traveler "instructed by the oldest mariners."[4] This general cultural engagement with the ocean finds a discursive focus in the many images of rivers, torrents, floods, oceans, and seas that become a staple, especially, of poetic discourse. In the decade of the 1660s, the sea becomes the national rhetorical element, taking the place of the isolationist image of the fortified island prevalent during Elizabeth's reign.

John Denham's *Cooper's Hill* (1642, 1655, 1668) makes the Thames the centerpiece of its claims to a global vision of prosperity, exchange, and political stability. Here, as elsewhere, the Thames is England's and the poem's access to the larger ocean, of which this river is a local manifestation and rhetorical synecdoche:

> My eye, descending from the hill, surveys
> Where Thames among the wanton valleys strays.
> Thames, the most loved of all the ocean's sons
> By his old sire, to his embraces runs;
> Hasting to pay his tribute to the sea,
> Like mortal life to meet eternity.[5]

Denham's poem, like Johnson's *Vanity,* connects the representation of this global waterway with an expansive "survey" that seems to extend to the whole world and that evokes in the process a notion of fate or destiny. The expansiveness of this image of the Thames projects the promise of a new style of mercantile imperialism: the world-benevolent mode of English commerce, in which exchange brings prosperity, wealth, and civilization wherever it goes:

> Nor are his blessings to his banks confined,
> But free and common, as the sea or wind;
> When he to boast, or to disperse his stores,
> Full of the tributes of his grateful shores,
> Visits the world, and in his flying towers
> Brings home to us, and makes both Indies ours;
> Finds wealth where 'tis, bestows it where it wants,
> Cities in deserts, woods in cities plants.
> So that to us no thing, no place is strange
> While his fair bosom is the world's exchange.   (ll. 179–88)

No torrents here. This is the calm and glorious course of English national destiny, linked in Denham's poem to the political balance installed by parliamentary monarchy, and to the historical dialectic that produced an increasingly prosperous mercantile imperialist state out of absolutist oppression and revolutionary excess. We might be surprised then, to see this promise of "no unexpected inundations" (175) suddenly withdrawn in the last lines of the poem, with a repudiation of precisely that evocation of balanced tranquility:

> When a calm river, raised with sudden rains
> Or snows dissolved, o'erflows th'adjoining plains,
> The husbandmen with high-raised banks secure
> Their greedy hopes, and this he can endure.
> But if with bays and dams they strive to force
> His channel to a new or narrow course,
> No longer then within his banks he dwells:
> First to a torrent, then a deluge swells;
> Stronger and fiercer by restraint he roars,
> And knows no bound, but makes his power his shores. (ll. 349–58)

This final figure makes conditional those earlier images of calm. This waterway has the power to impose a global apocalypse. The paradoxical conjunction of headlong fluidity and conditional calm in Denham's rivers expresses—in a cultural form more subtle and prescient than the poem's particular political allegories—an historical experience that we can find again, in different terms, in Dryden's early poetry on the Stuart monarchy.

In the prefatory essay to his major maritime work *Annus Mirabilis. The Year of Wonders, 1666* (1667), Dryden frankly acknowledges the sudden prominence—rhetorical and material—of the sea in his writing and in the world he represents: "For my own part, if I had little knowledge of the Sea, yet I have thought it no shame to learn."[6] Not surprisingly, then, the sea pervades Dryden's poetry of the 1660s; his celebratory works on the return of Charles II and the future of England prominently feature invocations of bodies of water, which link maritime events with historical and nationalist reflections, and in which we can locate the full cultural installation of this maritime fable. For Dryden, as for Denham, the sea is the medium of economic and political expansion, and this gives it a ubiquitous presence in imperialist apologia. Of all Dryden's early poems, *Annus Mirabilis* expatiates most fully upon that imperialist panegyric, locating not only naval conquest—the primary topic of the poem—but also global exploration, commerce, empirical science, the advances in chronometry that enabled the measurement of longitude, and even astronomy in its representation of the sea. This "British ocean" (st. 302), like Denham's, is an extension of the Thames, "her own domestic flood" (st. 298), and it produces the same global "emporium" (st. 302), the same benevolent system of commerce, and the same conditional calm:

Thus to the eastern wealth thro' storms we go,

    But now, the Cape once doubled, fear no more;

A constant trade-wind will securely blow,

    And gently lay us on the spicy shore.   (st. 304)

This image has an allegorical significance: the voyage around the Cape of Good Hope suggests the progress of England toward imperialist supremacy in Europe, and thus "Hope"
forms an unstated but, to contemporary readers, clearly present contrast to "fear." Indeed,
hope and fear are so persistently counterposed in the many accretions of this cultural fable that one inevitably implies the other. Yet despite the hope and peaceful seas evoked
here, "fear" is a powerful constituent of this voyage, even as it anticipates future commercial "triumphs" (st. 302); the calm of those gentle trade winds lies only in prospect. Hope
and fear converge here in a striking defiance of fate—"the utmost malice of [the] Stars"
(st. 291)—with the effect of proposing a new destiny that extends to "all the world" (st.
301). The fate evoked by the figure of the ocean in this poem entails a metaphysical propo-
sition; at the same time it projects the global fate of an imperial vision.[7]

The complexity of Dryden's construction of the figure of the "*British* Ocean" (st. 302)
is even more fully evident in his earlier poems written on the occasion of Charles's return. Most notably, in *Astrea Redux* (1660), the sea presides with paradoxical implications over the king's return across the channel from France. This is of course a providential voyage, with "willing winds," "joyful" ships, and "merry Seamen." Nevertheless,
the representation of an obedient sea and a calm voyage is systematically complicated.
The sea suggests dangers, reversals, and powers of rapidity and turbulence beyond human control. Even as it seems to provide him calm passage to the throne, the sea evokes
for Charles the tragic fate of his father in a striking image of drowning that haunts Dryden's picture of the sea: "Secure as when the *Halcyon* breeds, with these / He that was
born to drown might cross the Seas" (ll. 235–36).[8]

The nationalist histrionics of these poems quickly become the formulaic poetic
rhetoric of the first era of English imperial expansion; this early locus provides a striking glimpse of the complexity of the cultural fable of torrents and oceans even as that
fable, in its nascent iterations, shapes imperialist apologia. Taken together, these representations of rivers and seas begin to develop a story of an expansionist destiny, a cultural fable that has both a protagonist and a narrative movement toward a climactic and
surprising conclusion. It is a story that seeks to name and understand a powerful force
by seeing it as a fluid entity, inexorable, expansive, exhilarating, and dangerous. It represents that force in motion on a career characterized by radical irony or profound un-
decidability, conditionality, or contradiction. Finally, it projects the end point of this career as an unavoidable and apocalyptic fate in which triumph is matched with disaster,

fulfillment with destruction, optimism with despair. This climax emanates from the specific character of the fable's fluid and complex protagonist, but it comes to include the whole world that this protagonist seems to shape and to embody. If we trace this cultural fable over the next half century as England moves to a secure place as the pre-eminent imperial nation in the world, it can show us how an expansionist culture absorbs, explains, and uses the experience of global power.

In the two decades following the Peace of Utrecht (1713), the treaty that ratified British mercantile supremacy among the European powers, torrents and oceans are firmly installed as a ground of imaginative experience. As a figure for mercantile imperialism, the ocean comes to embody a complex system that perfectly unites the physical and the metaphysical in a way that gives its evolving narrative glory, momentum, and expanse, reaching beyond political discourse to scientific inference, metaphysical supposition, moral contemplation, and even social criticism. The Peace of Utrecht generated a set of celebratory works that develop the central claims of this fable. In Thomas Tickell's *On the Prospect of Peace* (1712), for instance, the sea becomes an active projection of British imperial destiny.

> Great queen! . . .
> From Albion's cliffs thy wide-extended hand
> Shall o'er the main to far Peru command;
> So vast a tract whose wide domain shall run,
> Its circling skies shall see no setting sun.   (105)

Here the ocean is the enabling figure for a global perspective that, by asserting a "watery kingdom," extends to "far Peru," laying claim to the whole globe. This elusive and symptomatic rhetorical movement—in which intermediary and destination, fluid and firm, sea and land, change places, substituting a "watery" empire for a solid one—is a persistent constituent of the fable of torrents and oceans in this later period, generating a powerfully evocative expansionist fantasy that represents an imperialism without geographical acquisition.

Pope's poem on the Peace of Utrecht, *Windsor-Forest* (1713), develops the same systematic global vision, through the celebratory speech of Father Thames:

> Thy Trees, fair *Windsor!* Now shall leave their Woods,
> And half thy Forests rush into my Floods,
> Bear *Britain*'s Thunder, and her Cross display
> To the bright Regions of the rising Day;
> .   .   .   .

The Time shall come, when free as Seas or Wind
Unbounded *Thames* shall flow for all Mankind,
Whole Nations enter with each swelling Tyde,
And Seas but join the Regions they divide;
Earth's distant Ends our Glory shall behold,
And the new World launch forth to seek the Old.

. . . .

Oh stretch thy Reign, fair *Peace!* From Shore to Shore,
Till conquest cease, and Slav'ry be no more:
Till the freed *Indians* in their native Groves
Reap their own Fruits, and woo their Sable Loves,
Peru once more a Race of Kings behold,
And other *Mexico's* be roof'd with Gold.   (ll. 285–412)

Pope's Thames is an active agent that carries the power of the British navy around the world, and his ocean is a force that "joins" the terrestrial nations together in a euphoric affirmation of peace and mutual benefit. The Thames thus purveys a benevolent world system, emanating from British mercantile prosperity, extending to "Earth's distant Ends," and bringing the Pax Britannica to "all Mankind." Peru and Mexico, the only "Nations" named in this global vision, exemplify the benevolent efficacy of the Pax Britannica. The Thames even has the power here to rewrite the colonial past of Aztec and Inca civilizations, replacing brutal Spanish colonial conquest with the mutual "admiration" of British imperialism.[9] In this poem, as in Tickell's and indeed throughout the literary culture of this period, "Peru" is the recurrent emblem of transforming power, condensing in one geographical referent the world historical claims of British mercantile capitalism: to see the globe from the single perspective of Britain and to remake history in its own image.[10]

Windsor represents this transforming power with a matching rhetoric, an evocation of motion, energy, and even violence like that in the torrent of *Cooper's Hill* that made "his power his shores." The power of Pope's Thames, which also stretches "from Shore to Shore" of the globe, though apostrophized as "*Peace*," is no less sudden and overwhelming than Denham's. In this final passage it comes as a tidal wave of expansionist strength, as the forests of Windsor, metamorphosed into the ships of the British navy, "rush" into the floods of the Thames and through the oceans of the globe, bearing "*Britain's* Thunder . . . and Cross." The "Reign" of "fair *Peace*" is not necessarily a tranquil one. This counterposition of tranquility and energy, peace and power in the figure of torrents and oceans is connected to the rhetorical and ideological superimposition of land and sea that becomes a fundamental undercurrent of this fable.

Even the understanding of the physical materiality of the ocean was a function of its role in this deeply significant story. Defoe in his *Review* entry for 3 February 1713, describes the behavior of the natural world in terms of British trade: "there is a kind of Divinity in the Original of Trade . . . How naturally does the Water, mov'd by the mighty winds, flow into every Hollow, and fill up every vacant Part in the Sea; the innumerable Particles diligently croud on the Heels of one another, to supply the Place of those forc'd away, and those that are forc'd from their Place by an unusual Gust, immediately return to fill up the first Emptyness they find? . . . Thus obedient Nature, true to its own Laws, preserves the Communication of one part of the World with another, and lays the Foundation of commerce, which would otherwise be altogether Impracticable and Impossible."[11] Here, in one breath, Defoe proposes a physical science, which explains the tendency of the crowded "particles" of the sea to "fill up" the empty space that would otherwise stand between one part of the world and another, and also a metaphysical system, which places the characteristics of the natural world in the context of a benevolent providential plan.

Edward Young's *Imperium Pelagi* (1729), or "the empire of the sea," represents the identification of commerce and Britain with the geographical vastness, the mercantile significance, and the material immediacy of the ocean. Like Defoe, Young sees a physical and providential ordering in that identification:

> Britain! behold the world's wide face;
> Not cover'd half with solid space
> Three parts are fluid, empire of the sea!
> And why? For commerce, Ocean streams
> For that, through all his various names:
> And if for commerce, Ocean flows for thee.   (353)

For Young, as for Defoe, ocean is the material substance whose fluidity makes possible both commerce and a global empire, the solid, land-based British *imperium* that in this poem appears only as an "empire of the sea." Ocean is the largest and most evident indication that "all Nature bends" (344) to advance the exploitation of commerce, and, by the next step of this expansionist logic, to promote British commercial supremacy:

> Luxuriant isle! what tide that flows,
> Or stream that glides, or wind that blows,
> Or genial sun that shines, or shower that pours,
> But flows, glides, breathes, shines, pours for thee!   (342)

Providence shapes the laws of nature to encourage trade, but, as in *Windsor,* providence also operates through commerce to benefit all humankind by circulating goods and materials among "different lands" to which "Heaven" has imparted "different growths" and needs (344). Here Young echoes the commonplace contemporary notion that trade benefits the world by distributing goods and uniting people in its shared cause. "The empire of the sea" is in this popular construction at once the agent of a providential system of distribution and a proxy for British global power. Indeed, as we have seen in *Windsor,* the claims for the benevolence of that system depend on that movement of superimposition of sea and land that generates the displacement of power from the "solid space" of the globe to the nonspace of the flowing, gliding, foaming ocean. The representation of the solid *imperium* cannot be so pacific. By displacing imperial violence in this way, the fable of torrents and seas performs an essential service to the ideology of the Pax Britannica, sanctioning its assertion of the peaceful imposition of empire on the world.

Imperium Pelagi develops an image of the ocean as a strangely populous space, "peopled" and "swarming" with life—a thronging *imperium* of its own. In this sense, the ocean stands in for the vast global empire that the poem proposes for Britain, a deflected embodiment of the energy of the "solid" mercantile empire currently in formation. As the alter ego of the solid *imperium,* the ocean contains all its energy and resistless activity. In the figure of the ocean, that image of the thronging, prosperous metropole is projected over the whole world:

> Hast thou look'd round the spacious earth?
> From Commerce, Grandeur's humble birth:
> To George from Noah, empires living, dead,
> Their pride, their shame, their rise, their fall,—
> Time's whole plain chronicle is all
> One bright encomium, undesign'd, on Trade.   (368)

The rhetoric of the global survey, here and elsewhere in its many manifestations in the poetry of this period, has two related implications. First, it contains, in a compact gesture, that movement of superimposition and consequent displacement of power that constitutes the formal and ideological complexity of this figure. Thus it stands rhetorically as the site for metaphysical speculation and moral contemplation. To "look round the earth" in this period is to project a providential system defined by the physical nature of the ocean and located in the commercial preeminence of Britain. Such a system undertakes to account not only for the British empire but also for reason, virtue, and human fate.

Thus in the last long section of *Imperium Pelagi,* the man of reason, who is the incarnation of benevolent commerce, when faced with the "hopes and fears" (345) of fortune, puts his faith in the "empire of the sea" and expects to be launched on "the flood of endless bliss" (345) at the passing of the present day. This metaphysical assurance is derived from the boundless efficacy of Young's ocean, in which the image of the "streams of Trade" (368) is identical to that of fate itself:

> Oh for eternity! a scene
>
> To fair adventurers serene!
>
> Oh! on that sea to deal in pure renown,—
>
> Traffic with gods! What transports roll!
>
> What boundless import to the soul!
>
> The poor man's empire, and the subject's crown!   (371)

Here, in a rhetorical transport that reproduces the "rolling" of the torrents and oceans that we have seen throughout this poetry, human fate is a serene sea that sublimates trade into a "traffic with the gods," and thus imagines a "pure" metaphysical realm where rich and poor are common subjects of a higher national destiny in which material acquisitions are replaced by spiritual ones.

Young's *Ocean* (1728) develops this metaphysical dimension of the story at greater length than does *Imperium Pelagi*. Here Young elaborates more fully not only the vitality but also the explicit dangers of this fluid medium of expansionism, describing scenes of sudden reversal in which serenity turns to destruction, peace to dread. *Ocean* is full of "storms" and "tempests," alternating with "peace" and "silence." The sea "tempts" sailors, then turns upon them with "black'ning billows." The turbulent ocean has the power of "Chaos" to "blend . . . seas and skies" (157) in a repudiation of all order and structure. However, like in *Imperium Pelagi,* Young here pursues the image of the ocean into the realm of moral speculation. An apparently abstract "Virtue" is said to save the "daring" enterprise of British imperialism from the terror and shipwreck attached to the image of the sea; actually, this virtue is itself a product of imperialist ideology, the name for the benevolent system of the Pax Britannica. The circularity of the interconnected physical and metaphysical structures generated by the figure of the ocean defines the virtuous system of British mercantile expansion, which generously distributes goods throughout the world and also guarantees the reward for that virtue—safety and serene seas. This maritime calm, and the virtue that earns it, guarantees that "the British flag shall sweep the seas" (163) as long as stars and suns and the solid globe survive.

The conjunction of virtue, commerce, and empire in the image of the peaceful sea directly inspires the metaphysical contemplation that opens the concluding passage of *Ocean:* "How mixt, how frail, / How sure to fail, / Is every pleasure of mankind!" (164). These are the stanzas that see "the world [as] the main." They propose an earthly state of hope and fear, a maritime scene in which "all are tost, / And most are lost," but where "good men" may be rewarded with a "noiseless shore" and "unruffled homes" (165). This is the serenity of mercantile virtue, in which, as we have seen, both a morality and a metaphysics are generated from the material and commercial image of "the empire of the sea." Yet in *Ocean* it is a forced, conditional serenity—a hope rather than an assurance. This ocean, like the "mighty cause" (164) of the British empire that it embodies, is too close to "Chaos" to be so readily tamed. Thus, upon raising the question of the fate of "good men," this poem in its final stanzas repudiates the "public scene" (165) and embarks on a pastoral contemplation of the "humble life" (166), which ends with a familiar evocation of eternity:

> Unhurt my urn!
> Till that great turn
> When mighty nature's self shall die!
> Time cease to glide,
> With human pride
> Sunk in the ocean of eternity.   (168)

Like Denham's Thames, which flows to the sea "like mortal life to meet eternity," Young's ocean is nothing less than fate itself. Furthermore, this metaphysical figure contains the whole of the ocean's complex character: its material vastness and physical ubiquity, its assertion of a national destiny, its projection of a moral system, its imposition of an expansionist global paradigm, and its ultimate power to overwhelm the speaker and the world. "Eternity" in this poem is the product of an imaginative confrontation with the material forces of history. It is the climax of the fable of torrents and oceans, in which the complex and ambiguous character of that story's unnamed protagonist is finally uncovered.

The story collectively told here takes on the transforming power of capitalist economic expansion, attempting to understand its nature and to project its effects. In the image of torrents and oceans, the fable locates an examination of this historical force, its irresistible energy, its momentum, its danger, its promise, and its threat to engulf everything. In the shape of its action, the fable shows how this force makes the world over in its image, generating from its own nature a system whose logic reflects, explains, and justifies that nature. In the course of its unfolding, the fable enacts the contradictions attendant upon this historical moment. Variously and paradoxically, it demonstrates the undecidable demeanor of its protagonist and the unpredictable effects of its action, alternating hope and fear, threat and subservience, unity and chaos, and mixing glory, peace, danger, and despair. Nevertheless, its final claim remains, throughout the vicissitudes of its plot, an attempt to come to terms with modern fate.

Johnson's poem is staged against this representation of fate. The passage from *The Vanity of Human Wishes* with which we began can be seen, from the hindsight of this reading of earlier torrents, as a metaphysical reflection upon the culture of global expansion. Though the poem does not take up the themes of empire, ocean, or Britain as explicitly as Denham's, Dryden's, Pope's, or Young's works do, the *Vanity* demonstrates the pervasiveness and power of expansionism in a way that those more explicitly political works cannot. Its opening couplet—"Let observation with extensive view, / Survey mankind, from China to Peru"—engages the same rhetoric of global survey that we have seen to be a central constituent of the fable of torrents and oceans. This "extensive view" is a projection of the theory of the physical propensity of water to fill the spaces of the globe and thus necessarily impel geographical expansion; it is the basis for the displacement of power from land to sea that produces the ideology of the Pax Britannica and the consequent distancing and denial of the political and the historical in this period of expansionism; and it serves as the systematic basis for metaphysical speculation, in which the assumptions of this global perspective are extended into the realm of moral inquiry. The specific naming of "Peru" here, echoing Tickell's and Pope's global surveys, signals the historical underpinnings of this metaphysics: we are observing a world mapped out by a historical force, a world whose fate is framed within the moral system generated by that force and whose reference points are the landmarks of that force's transforming power.

In this context, the subsequent couplet resonates with the ambiguous implications of the fable that we have seen repeated in the literary culture of this period from Dryden to Young: "Then say how hope and fear, desire and hate, / O'erspread with snares the clouded maze of fate." Hopes and fears—abstractions from those images of drowning, shipwreck, storm, and flood, on the one hand, and of survival, daring, glory, the advances of navigational science, and even the navigation of the Cape of Good Hope itself, on the other—signal the tensions and contradictions of this cultural fable's implications. The "fate" that this poem evokes at its outset projects the paradoxical outcome of the fable of torrents and oceans.

"Hope and fear" leads the poem to the central image of our fable, the "torrent" that signals the imaginative representation of British imperial fate:

> Where then shall hope and fear their objects find?
> Must dull Suspence corrupt the stagnant mind?
> Must helpless man, in ignorance sedate,
> Roll darkling down the torrent of his fate?

The figure of torrents and oceans comes full circle here: it belongs to the material world of shipping, commerce, and the seas, and we have seen how that material category generates a science, a metaphysics, a morality, and a story with a climax corresponding to the undecidable fate with which the *Vanity* concludes. Here that very "fate" is figured as a "torrent," in a metaphor that brings back the material experience of the fable as if it were an illustrative analogy. The story of torrents and oceans tells us as much as it told its contemporary audience. It tells us how the distinctively modern experience of global economic expansion was understood at a time of dramatic and explosive growth. It demonstrates the intimacy of that experience with the material conditions of contemporary life, and it shows us how a culture might grasp the complexities and explore the contradictions of a historical transformation imaginatively, even as it clings to a simple, celebratory, or apologetic rationalization.

Part II / Crossings

CHAPTER EIGHT

Proxies of Power

Woman in the Colonial Archive

Betty Joseph

If we want to imagine the "global eighteenth century" as a means of challenging the cultural dominant, there must be some attempt to connect this historical revisioning with the accelerated pace of globalization today. While the geographical reach of this volume reminds one with some irony of the Peking-to-Peru generalizations that characterized the globe-girdling ambitions of much Enlightenment historiography, its critical approach no doubt reaches toward an audience that already understands that history as having staged and excluded women, non-Christians, and non-Europeans while it put forward the white, Christian male of property as the universal man. However, this historical consciousness is also constantly neutralized by the repetitions-with-displacements we encounter in globalization today which make it more difficult to place the power of those Enlightenment discourses securely in the past. In other words, today, as a Peking-to-Peru is often replaced with a Beijing-to-Belarus, the Enlightenment is brought on stage again, this time clad in the garb of transnationality and economic development. In this round, however, instead of European Man we may have the European Woman as the new human norm.

Consider one such setting for the active construction of this human norm. A few years ago, while speaking at the Center for National Policy in Washington, D.C., a month before the Fourth World Conference on Women in Beijing, Madeleine Albright, then

Permanent Representative to the UN, listed for her breakfast audience the U.S. delega-
tion's proposed goals for the conference. She ended the wish list with a reminder that
"traditional and authoritarian societies" had a long way to go toward becoming societies that were inclusive of women. While preparing for the conference, she was re-
minded, she said, of an "old Chinese poem" in which a father addresses his young
daughter with these words:

> We keep a dog to watch the house
> A pig is useful too;
> We keep a cat to catch a mouse;
> But what can we do
> With a girl like you.[1]

The use of this cultural text as historical evidence suggests that there are two Chinas for
Albright and Washington. There is the China that exists as a deviation from a desired
norm (capitalist modernity) but that is still conjurable today through an anonymous "old
Chinese poem," and there is another China that one deals with as a business partner. Popular culture and journalism warn the American public about the China that is catching
up while official discourse exhorts another China to catch up. In this shifting field,
women's rights as human rights can become a rhetorical strategy in "Eurocentric strategies of narrativizing history" in which the industrialized West can congratulate itself for
showing the way without acknowledging any achievements in past social formations.[2]
This does not mean we should support older modes of production uncritically, but it
means we are in a position to analyze how certain universalist terms may disguise the
specificity of what is actually emerging in other places beginning to globalize. For instance, the explanatory power of concepts like "uneven development" may be limited
when delineating historical conjunctures in other countries. If a global theory is premised on a Eurocentric and teleological narrative of modernity, this may, as Liu Kang puts
it, "ultimately exclude possibilities of historical alternatives and/or alternative histories."[3]

This essay takes as its point of departure the belief that women's history has decon-
structive potential when reading the cultures of globalization and especially so at a time
when women deploy (for women) new forms of transnationalist thinking and action.
Further, we may learn much by revisiting textual sources from the time that first gave
such global projects their legitimacy and power. During the second half of the eighteenth
century, the great Enlightenment histories were organizing the world into three- and
four-step programs such as Montesquieu's despotism-monarchy-democracy program in *The Spirit of the Laws* (1748), or, later, John Millar's savage-pastoral-agriculture-
manufacturing program in *The Origin of the Distinction of Ranks* (1778). This great

swath of historiography effectively staged the woman as a measure of a civilization's advancement but excluded her from its modern political configurations. Thus, in my reading of the records of the East India Company and British parliamentary papers, I pick up the trail of a female subject as she was caught up in a massive Enlightenment experiment in the 1770s. At this time the company, having just defeated Bengal's local rulers and acquired the right to its revenues, was confronted with a choice: Should its territorial acquisition be remade in a normative metropolitan image (agrarian capitalism) or shuttled back into feudalism (a system already under attack back home by bourgeois radicalism)?

The resolution of this dilemma at this historical moment provides, as we shall see, a classic case of what Gayatri Spivak has called the "improper imposition of an Enlightenment episteme."[4] The case also demonstrates that the unevenness of European implementation on the ground produces "woman" in the colonial encounter as a complex site of many negotiations; she is never a unilinear movement toward a European norm but a result of many different configurations and linkages that weave together a subject from various strands of the economic, the political, the sexual, the linguistic, the religious, and so on. As a historical subject, she can be put together today only by a meticulous diagonal reading that moves across the body of discourses as well as up or down its temporal axes. Finally, in an attempt to undo Enlightenment historiography's foreclosure of the woman as native and other, I have deliberately picked as the historical agent in my discussion that history's most pathetic case—the so-called confined or secluded woman of despotic societies.

On 30 December 1774, a petition from the Rani of Burdwan arrived at Fort William in Calcutta where the Governor General of India, Warren Hastings, sat in council with four other members: Clavering, Francis, Monson, and Barwell. In the petition, the Rani informs the gentlemen that she, Bishnukumari, the widow of a recently deceased zamindar of Burdwan (Tilak Chand) and mother of his eight-year-old son and heir (Tejchand), has suffered "oppression," "treachery," and "injustice" at the hands of the company-appointed dewan (minister), Bridjoo Kishore, and John Graham, the chief revenue collector.[5] The Rani goes on to report her attempts to resist what she perceives to be illegal attempts by outsiders to gain control of her family's traditional privileges. The Rani, we deduce from the letter, apparently refused to hand over the zamindary seals—seals bearing her son's name—customarily used to authenticate all notices and orders originating from the house. By keeping them with her in the inner apartments, the zenana, out of reach of the dewan and the Resident, she was subjected to more punitive measures by the men:

Bridjoo Kishore [the Dewan] used every manner of persecution to get the Seal from me, I did not however yield it up. At last in the year 1797 [*sic*], Bridjoo Kishore having brought Mr. John Graham from Calcutta to Burdwan, took my son, who was from eight to ten years of age, and got him confined under a guard of sepoys; and having prevented me from eating for seven or eight days, till I was on the point of death, I found myself without remedy, and gave the seal into his possession . . . Bridjoo Kishore having thus got the Seal, granted away land . . . and took some lands likewise to himself. . . . All the measures adopted by him are intentionally to ruin me; besides this, he affixes the Seal to Papers, with the nature of which I am unacquainted, according to his pleasure. It never before this happened, that a servant, having got the management of his master's business, engrossed the lands which yield a Revenue. (*ER* 741)

With this petition to the company's council, the young widow began her twenty-five-year campaign to keep control of her family's zamindary. (Here, I avoid using the word "estate" because of a significant distinction. The "zamindar" translates as "landholder" and differs from feudal landlords in that this person did not own the land but was a revenue collector who paid taxes directly to the state. The zamindar's position could be made hereditary but could also be terminated if public responsibilities to the zamindary inhabitants were not upheld.)[6] In the 1770s, when the company had gained ascendancy in Bengal and the right to all its revenues, women managed three of the largest zamindaries. This was not unusual because patrimonial inheritance and religious and social rituals required surviving sons, and because territorial consolidations through matrimonial alliances encouraged polygamous marriages. The combination of the two often left young widows outliving their husbands for decades, ruling over the landholdings in their sons' names or even getting sunnuds (leases) from the state to run them on their own. The Mughal State's priorities were to ensure peaceful governance and the maintenance of its vast civil infrastructure rather than military conscription. Thus, without the requirements of primogeniture or male management, one could say that the state was relatively indifferent to gender.

It is tempting to read the Rani as someone who was simply trying to maintain the status quo when a foreign power appeared in her backyard. Yet the trail of effects rippling through the records as a result of her petition show that her presence in the initial company archive, and later in the Parliamentary Select Committee reports, is not a result of bureaucratic meticulousness. The Rani's entanglement with the company had important consequences. It became the subject of more than one parliamentary investigation and a major catalyst for the dispute between Warren Hastings and the council majority led by Philip Francis (who later became the key instigator of the impeachment hearings against the former).[7] It is not unwarranted to surmise that Rani Bishnukumari may have been among the many unnamed parties in one of the substantial charges against Warren Hastings in the parliamentary trial of 1788—the charge of accepting private presents and bribes. I explain in some detail how the Rani drew Hastings into this quandary, but first let us look at the zamindary seals that Bridjoo Kishore and Mr. Graham took by force from the Rani.

The seal was an important tool of proxy that did not require the authenticating presence of the body on display. It could be given and held in the name of a child, used by a woman, or even appropriated by a servant or foreigner. Yet its symbolic power was undeniable; the seals not only allowed the zamindars to issue instructions from within their houses to various parts of their provinces but also prevented the issuance of spurious documents in their names. They were also mediating tools in the transfer of power. In the transitional period, the revenue structures of the old Mughal imperial order that the British army had defeated was phantasmally kept in place without being fully replaced. Thus, capital accumulation could go on uninterrupted, as instructions still seemed to issue from a place that connoted the locus of power for the peasantry. The elite zamindary class to which the Rani belonged was not only a collaborating class in alliance with the alien power but also the class that mediated between English capital and native labor, temporarily bridging the radical rupture effected by the transfer of power. Thus, the Rani was still important for the company and could not be summarily dismissed, ignored, or mistreated. She was a valuable proxy for the English who had to rule over a population separated from them by language, culture, and religion, with a complex system of land tenures, revenues, allocations, and distributions that they did not fully understand but that they could not change in one swift move.

Let us look at the response to the Rani's petition. The council's minutes, which were later recorded in the revenue consultations in London, show a very detailed sequence of events.[8] When the petition is read out before the full council, Hastings and his supporter Richard Barwell clearly show signs of not wanting to pursue it any further. They protest vehemently against the majority's decision to grant the Rani's request to be released from the forced confinement within her home and removed to Calcutta, where, closer to the council, she could feel safe from possible harm. Barwell objects, arguing that reversing the orders of "past governments" would give natives the impression that British law could be repealed at any time and thus would endanger British authority in the countryside. Meanwhile, Hastings, referring to the Rani as "a violent woman," suspects her motives. He insists that her charges against the *dewan* and the British Resident, if investigated, would "only serve to disturb the peace and quiet of the settlement" and "excite factions among the Banyans and dependants of every person of power or supposed influence" (*ER* 734). Hastings's second objection is especially significant because it shows the company's active involvement in keeping the zamindary class as props and proxies: "I object to her bringing her son with her, because, by a solemn and repeated Act of Government, the charge of her son has been taken away from her and committed to proper guardians, both for the benefit of his education, and to destroy the influence which she possessed with his person. This Act cannot be regularly repealed, but by an express act of the administration passed for that purpose; and any resolution taken in breach of it must be publicly condemned as an indignity offered to the last government" (*ER* 734).

What Hastings is referring to here is the stopgap measure adopted by his administration when the incumbents of a zamindary were "minors, idiots or females." As considerations of revenue were paramount for the company in the first two decades of rule in Bengal, the board of revenue required certification that proprietors were "capable of management."[9] However, because the Bengal agricultural landscape was being made over in the image of English feudalism with its preservation of private property through male inheritance and primogeniture, the company was not averse to tinkering with the relative indifference to gender the Mughal State had shown in its award of zamindary leases. Under Hastings, the company began to intervene in zamindary child rearing. When widows were left with young sons, they came under company stewardship until the sons were ready to assume control. As mentioned earlier, at a time when the countryside was dotted with young widows, many with minor sons, the board of revenue moved in as substitute householder to appoint tutors and remove sons from their mothers' influence.[10] In this instance, the Rani got her way as the council's majority decided to ignore Hastings's and Barwell's warning and allowed her to proceed to Calcutta with her son.

Meanwhile, after receiving copies of the Rani's petition, the two accused, Bridjoo Kishore and Graham, were given the opportunity by the council to reply to the various charges, which included (besides manhandling the Rani) embezzling from the zamindary treasury and bribing company officials. Their replies arrived two days later. Kishore's is terse and alleges that the Rani is a woman "totally unacquainted with the nature of accounts, or even of common writing," and therefore capable of fabricating the charges (*ER* 742). Graham's response, on the other hand, indicates his years of experience as a company bureaucrat schooled in the art of correspondence.[11] Graham's letter is divided into two sections and resembles in format Pamela's response to Mr. B's prenuptial contract in the novel *Pamela*.[12] Indeed, Samuel Richardson's epistolary novel may be of some use to us here as a "discursive precursor" of sorts. In *Pamela*, we have a graphic representation of the ledger cum contract staged as the transformation of an economic relation into a gendered one, and by implication the social contract into a sexual contract. Mr. B's demands are placed side by side with Pamela's responses, thereby semiotically transforming the "minority" representation of sexual relations, in which a servant girl has had to steadfastly resist the advances of her employer, into an instrument of power that gives voice to the previously subjugated subject.[13]

Here, in the colonial archive, a kind of self-production reverses momentarily the relations of power that exist between the two letter writers. Graham had initially resisted the board's attempts to make him respond to the Rani's charges. In a memo that preceded this letter, he protests the ignominy of having to respond to a person of "such notorious character as the Ranny"[14] and declines to give an answer, saying that he would not do it without being on the "grounds of equality" (*ER* 735). By pointing out that the Rani and her *vackeel* (lawyer) were not British subjects and thus exempt from the jurisdiction and law of British Acts of Parliament, Graham in effect suggests that they should never meet on the same page.

They do, however, because Graham, as we see here, ultimately does reply to the petition. There is some indication in the records about why he underwent this change of heart. Graham was on his way back to London after fifteen years of service in India, expecting to reap, as most former civil servants did, the benefits of this long tenure with a permanent job at the company headquarters. Aware that the council's minutes were sent to London every week, Graham panicked. His departure was not for another two weeks, and the dispatches (with the Rani's petition as an enclosure) could conceivably arrive before him and have his reputation in shambles before his own ship docked. To minimize this lag between accusation and defense, Graham asked that the copies of his letters and his answer to the Rani's petition be forwarded in the next packet to the company headquarters.[15]

Though Graham does not recognize a member of the colonized native elite as a signatory to his own social contract, the graphic representation of his response to the Rani's petition does enact a momentary reversal of the usual relations between colonizer and colonized. Graham singles out the paragraphs in the Rani's petition that mention his name or allude to him in some way and copies them out in his letter to represent a sort of face-off with the Rani (whom he has never seen). Yet Graham is also forced to assume the place of the defendant as he counteracts the Rani's accusations with his own responses. Being on the right side of the page is clearly to be at a disadvantage; it puts him in the position of having to prove his innocence even before the Rani has furnished proof of her charges against him. There is an inescapable irony in Graham's words when he describes his letter as an exercise in following "the wanderings of falsehood" (*ER* 740). A bureaucrat who reproduced the power of the company through his official acts of inscription and signature is now no longer the self-possessed subject. His text, as it follows the Rani's charges, unravels the power of his previous subject position.

On the other hand, the Rani's appearance on the left side of the page as the initiator of the complaint is also the textual production of a new subject position. By appealing to the council as a previous beneficiary of its decisions (the confirmation of her son's succession to the zamindary, for instance), the Rani comes before British law without being a British subject. Her appeal depends for its force on the accusation that her two tormentors have also disobeyed the will of the company. As the space within which the confrontation takes place, the archive becomes both the guarantor of truth as well as the place of its production. The Rani's words accusing Graham (on the left-hand side) are replaced at the end of the letter by Graham's references to archived material, which he believes will provide testimonies of his conduct over the years. The archive is also cited by Graham to establish the other's dishonesty when he accuses the Rani of "premeditated" falsehood by lying about the date of her husband's death. "Rajah Tilook Chund," he declares to the council, "did not die in the Bengal Year 1174 but in the Bengal Year 1177" (*ER* 741).

This counteraccusation by Graham, however, illuminates a difference that can be obscured by the momentary equality enacted by the face-off on the page. What is declared to be a lie is actually a mistake in translation. Three weeks later, when the Rani responded to Graham's countercharges, the first point in her letter was that in translating the Bengali year into the Christian calendar, her translator had made a mistake. The real date can be verified, she says, by consulting the Persian copy that accompanied the English translation. The company's official translation of the Rani's petition by Alexander Elliot is included in the records and indeed states that the Bengal year of the Rajah's death is 1176 rather than the 1174 of the first translation (or 1177 as alleged by Graham) (*ER* 741). The Rani explains the discrepancy of a year as resulting from the zamindary custom of not declaring a year completed until the annual adjustment of revenues was completed (*ER* 743). The Rajah apparently died before this was done and so was regarded as having died in the previous financial year (1176).[16] In the margins of the text, we now notice the act of translation; it shows the precarious nature of the native's speech and writing and the risks of being misunderstood. The Rani, however, does not miss a chance to take a swipe at her former tormentor, even as she acknowledges the mistake: "Mr. Graham's pardon upon this occasion I need not ask," she writes. "[H]e has more than sufficiently made himself amends by the unjust and ungenerous conclusions he has drawn from it" (*ER* 743).

The verbal assault aside, the Rani's most important calculation is the timing of her application to the company's council in 1774. This act on the Rani's part thus has a time line that goes back a few years. After Warren Hastings's appointment as Governor General in 1773, unexpected transfers and deaths depleted the council and left Richard Barwell as sole surviving councilor. When Monson, Clavering, and Francis, two soldiers and an ex-war-office clerk, arrived in Calcutta in October 1774, the manner and tempo of decision making changed drastically. The newly appointed councilors, who were opposed in principle to Hastings's recently completed military campaigns and what they perceived to be his corrupt administration, blocked many of his initiatives in council meetings.[17] Bitter quarrels soon broke out between the newcomers and Hastings, who was now in the minority with Barwell. It was into this climate that the Rani's petition arrived barely two months after the council's reconstitution in December 1774. References in the records to earlier meetings indicate that she had failed on two previous occasions to persuade the council to act against the *dewan* and Graham, both of whom were, incidentally, Hastings's appointees. The resubmission of the petition for the third time in two years seems a deliberate attempt to test the waters again.

Even after all this, the persistent Rani's most important maneuver was yet to come, and it was one that would shift in a decisive way her standing with the company. On getting Bridjoo Kishore's and Graham's responses to her charges, the Rani, now probably aware that a divided council could be worked to her advantage, was no longer satisfied with a partial victory—whereby she had effected Bridjoo Kishore's dismissal and been reunited with her son. A whole month passed before the Rani finally furnished the proof demanded by the company. In March 1775, a letter arrived at the council with copies of accounts showing the "embezzlements" by John Graham and Bridjoo Kishore. Also enclosed in the letter was another item, one that had not been specifically requested. It is described in the revenue consultations as "Enclosure No 4" and is titled "Account of monies paid to Cantoo Baboo, the Banyan [accountant] of Governor Hastings" (*ER* 745). In the accompanying letter, the Rani's tone is considerably different from that in the first petition. There is little trace of the helpless widow without protection, the mother deprived of her only child, or the secluded woman of rank whose virtue and honor are threatened by strange men. Instead, we see signs of an emerging strategy to regain full control over the management of the zamindary without the direct supervision of appointed *dewans* or company officials.

In the letter accompanying the enclosures, the Rani appeals to the council as a potential manager whose competence can right the damage done to the company's revenues by the two corrupt officials. For a woman whose petitions show a rather excessive use of formal addresses, this letter makes its point without much ado: "[T]he Revenue of the Company has suffered much by these alienations; I therefore beg I may be empowered to resume these lands."[18] Her next letter, which arrived a day later, as though sensing the uproar created by Enclosure #4, attempts to minimize her action with these words: "In surrendering the papers which mention the name of the Governor General, I beg I may be understood to do it in compliance with my duty and a regard to my own safety, I must condemn or be condemned; no alternative is left me" (*ER* 751). The Rani clearly alternates between calculated acts of subterfuge and declarations of submission, even as she tries to temper the charge of corruption against the highest-ranking representative of British power in India. The letter ends with this assurance of loyalty: "Whatever favour and indulgence shall be shewn to me and my family will, I flatter myself, be fully repaid to the Company in their revenue; being well assured that the antiquity of my house will always operate to the Company's advantage, by the influence it will have in establishing that authority over the *ryots* [peasants] necessary in the collections and in securing that obedience which will be chearfully [*sic*] yielded to a family who has so many years presided over them."[19]

I leave the Rani, for now, in the subject slot she carved out for herself as a member of the collaborating elite. In exchange for keeping her traditional class and caste privileges, the Rani put her family's economic position and familiarity with the peasants to use in harnessing their labor for the company's revenues for years to come. I catch up with the Rani briefly at the end of this chapter. Her attempts to regain control over the zamindary—after the company subsequently made her son the primary manager—show that she could not be eased into retirement. Though the Rani escaped a fate that awaited others of her kind, her actions make her an example of potential gender trouble in Bengali zamindary management. In 1793, when the company converted the zamindars into "landlords" and installed private property in land with the enactment of "Permanent Settlement," women zamindars were removed from the official plans for nineteenth-century Bengal. Why did this happen? The last section of this chapter addresses this historical paradox. As a preamble to that discussion, I want first to look at the production of the theoretical fiction that facilitated this removal—Oriental despotism.

An awareness of the Orient has been at the heart of European political philosophy, political economy, and cultural self-representation since the eighteenth century. While the Oriental despot figures in Montesquieu's work as an emblem of political absolutism, representations of the harem and women's seclusion serve not only as political allegory (of absolutism) but as a trope of absolute female submission. These figurations of despot and harem were hitched together and energized through cross-cultural comparisons, debates about the social contract, and female enlightenment in eighteenth-century England.[20] As the age of colonialism got under way and Britain acquired political and economic sovereignty over Eastern lands and peoples, the earlier opposition between the Turkish despot and the enlightened ruler functioned not to shame European absolutism but to justify control over non-European peoples by replacing their "oppressive" governments with British colonial rule.[21] Once the British Empire became a political and economic reality, exercises in cultural hegemony began to supplement military consolidation, and the native woman emerged out of this older political allegory to become the privileged object of civilizing. She now became a cultural signifier of the difference between Europe and its others and the measure of the stage of development both had reached.

Let us begin with a hypothesis. When revenue maximization in a large and thriving district like Burdwan met the company's objectives, the company was relatively indifferent to gender as a criterion for selecting zamindars. However, as colonial rule failed to maximize revenue according to various physiocratic or free-trade principles, that is, as it met resistance in native structures, we see the deployment of culturalist arguments about the natives' essential difference. These arguments, in turn, justified new proposals for far-reaching changes in existing social relations. In the archive of colonial rule or the records of governance, this deployment of culturalist arguments is signaled by the explicit entry of secondary material into its deliberations. Here, I use a distinction that Ranajit Guha has made between various types of colonial writing based on their appearance in time and their filiation. For Guha, primary discourse is marked by its identification with an official point of view, its close proximity in space and time to the events it describes, and its purpose. It is usually written with a view to urge or direct action. Secondary discourse, on the other hand, draws on primary or official discourse, is a more processed product, and is often written by former officials well after the events described within them.[22]

Harry Verelst's monograph *A View of the Rise, Progress, and Present State of the English Government in Bengal,* written in 1772, is a good example from this secondary archive. Verelst, who was governor of Bengal from 1768 to 1771, before Warren Hastings's term, preempted his successor's policy of keeping the British Parliament at bay in Bengal. Like Hastings, he had sought severe limits on the application of British law in the territories administered by the company. Chapter 5 of Verelst's book is thus unambiguously titled "The Impossibility of Introducing English Laws into Bengal with some Observations on Native Customs."[23] Because Verelst had read and assimilated Montesquieu's ideas into his own thinking, law for him was a reflection of the "spirit" of the people. He believed that transplanting British law to the Indies would never work: "As well might we transplant the full-grown oak to the banks of the Ganges, as dream that any part of a code matured by the patient labours of successive judges and legislatures in this island can possibly coalesce with the customs of Bengal" (134). It is when Verelst investigates what he calls "the domestic relations of private life" to provide instances of the natives' acornlike existence, that the woman emerges as an important figure in the discussion of law. The biggest obstacles to British law, Verelst argues, are polygamy and the seclusion of women. He generously sprinkles his text with quotes from Montesquieu about the rapid maturing of girls in hot climates, the need to confine them, and the natural facilitation of polygamy. British law, on the other hand, is "formed in a temperate climate, where the charms of women are better preserved, . . . and their reason accompanies their beauty, and all have adopted the natural equality between the sexes" (137). Then, in order to clinch his argument about the total incompatibility of British law with Indian spirit, the secluded or "confined woman," as he calls her, is brought on the scene: "Shall our writs of liberty unlock these sacred recesses? Shall no reverence be thought due to the honour of a husband? Or shall we disregard the condition of a wife, incapable of governing herself? Shall our courts of justice become the authors of outrage, which the bloody ruffian would fear to commit? Thus, in despite of nature, shall we dissolve the ties of domestic life without substituting any government in their place and force the servant, the child and the wife, to renounce their dependence, unable to afford them protection" (141). Verelst defends the seclusion of women as a necessary precondition for maintaining not only the patriarchal honor of Indian men but also the very forms of civil society existing in India. Yet, with the typical self-contradiction that characterizes Orientalist discourse, Verelst then goes on to assert that under British law and standards all sexual intercourse in India is rape: "Women in the East are transformed with little ceremony and whether they be wives or concubines, their men seldom await their consent. Were our laws of rape and rules of evidence enforced, one half of the males would incur the penalty of death. I mean not to justify their practice, but beg leave to suggest that the sword of justice when too deeply stained with blood may prove but an indifferent corrector of the morals of a nation" (141). Whereas Verelst first brings the native woman to the fore to cast her as the impossible subject of British law (she can never "govern" herself), here it is the native male who is the impossible subject of the same. As rapist and raped, both are locked in an embrace that is impervious to the liberties of English law.

My point, however, is not to turn Verelst against himself. Rather, it is to demonstrate that even as the Rani's petition reached the company headquarters in 1774 and became part of the primary discourse, company officials in retirement were already creating an archive of secondary discourse. Here, the Rani could never have access to the subject positions that were available to her in Graham's letter or through the various epistolary engagements with the board of revenue and council. On the ground, where revenue maximization was the company's first priority, it was not Montesquieu but other issues and debates that produced the elite, secluded woman as a subject of history. Yet, within a few years, as British rule began its stranglehold on both the elite class and the peasantry, and revenue extraction reached supra-levels to pay for colonialist wars elsewhere on the subcontinent, zamindars themselves became obstacles to capital accumulation. Then, they were no longer treated as elites but were also regularly placed under guard and confined every time they failed to meet projected revenue amounts. (Later records show that the Rani's son, after coming of age, was put in jail three times by the company for failing to meet annual revenues.)[24] When this happened, it was Montesquieu who provided the discursive crossover so that the theoretical fiction of the secluded woman in despotic societies could replace a known historical subject—the Rani of Burdwan. I discuss the role of Montesquieu as a "discursive precursor" at some length elsewhere; here, I attempt a shorthand account of how company officials used him to effect the Rani's effacement.[25]

In late-century policy discussions by company officials, quotes from Montesquieu signaled that a discourse of cultural difference was already in play (as opposed to a discourse of comparative polity). Once this difference was acknowledged, culture became synonymous with what had to be avoided and surmounted at the same time. It was the site not only of native degradation but also of potential resistance. Thus, as company rule got increasingly despotic and company officials more relentless about collecting the exorbitant revenues, punitive measures increased against the former collaborators—the zamindars. As harsher measures were adopted against the native elite, however, the company also ran the risk of trampling on powerful cultural codes of social respect and propriety that had helped consolidate the company's position in the countryside. Many of the public functions of the zamindar, for instance, often involved religious rituals done for the rural community as a whole. Building temples and public works had given other zamindars like the Rani of Rajshahi an almost deity-like standing amongst the local peasantry.[26]

In this scenario of increased repression, the subject least available for control through confinement was the secluded woman. Her body remained within the female apartments, where, closed to strange men, she was ensured protection from undergoing public imprisonment by Englishmen under English law. Company records show that these women managed on numerous occasions to elude their harassers and other officials sent by the company. The secluded woman thus became a perfect example of what Jean-François Lyotard has termed a differend—a site of alterity or a subject position that cannot appear within the idioms that regulate the conflict.[27] While the company was willing, during the Rani's tussle with the board, to use native legal procedures under which secluded women could give their testimony through a curtain to a native judge, this was no longer a satisfactory scenario for the company. Now, under English law, the female zamindar's seclusion made her a nonwitness without the corroborating presence of her body. Her writing never carried the force of her signature as author. The voice behind the curtain could never be established as that of a free-willed or consenting subject, as her speech and writing came mediated through munshis and translators.

After Verelst, the argument gained force that the very notion of a secluded woman was incompatible with the idiom of British law and that her lifestyle was incompatible with the management of a zamindary. Official discourse (for instance, John Shore's famous Minute of 1789) exhibited long enclosures showing why women should not be given these positions. Despite the Rani's success in holding onto the Burdwan zamindary for twenty-five years, after 1793 the company's frustrations about its inability to punish her with physical confinement resulted in rules to restrict female management of zamindaries.

By replaying the case of the Rani of Burdwan and showing its imbrication in a complex discursive network that is only occasionally shot through with strands of what we often identify as Orientalist discourse, I have argued that we need to look more carefully at the texture of colonialism itself. When we distinguish between official or primary discourse and secondary or derivative discourse, and reveal the slow movement of seclusion as a category from one to the other, we learn another lesson: that gender is constitutive of the story of colonialism rather than a metaphorical vessel into which that story is put. We see that the discourse of confinement was not gendered when English law was used on the ground but was conflated with the Enlightenment discourse of seclusion only when the company's plans ran into resistant native customs. When the revenues of Bengal met with the demands of mercantilist and free-trade principles, the woman as a real agent and facilitator of economic practices (on the ground) was not an issue. Yet when revenues were kicked up into levels that were clearly beyond the reaches of the customary methods of exploitation, then theoretical fictions entered the scene to warrant the transformation of social relations that would make bigger profits possible. The secluded woman as an incapable agent of a despotic system was the theoretical fiction that ensured the unobstructed penetration of the company's punitive measures into all spaces. This lesson could forestall attempts, today, to rewrite the violence of such epistemic changes as "progress."

When we look at the ways in which the textual production of empire involves the simultaneous production and assignment of subject positions, the archive emerges as a differential relationship between texts and subjectivities rather than an absolute, institutional entity. In our reading of the Rani's case, we have seen how the very grammar of power that underwrites various kinds of colonial writing (letters, dispatches, testimonies, bills, receipts) can also be understood by tracking a gendered subject who appears only infrequently and intermittently in the archive. However, the scarcity of her appearance gives her an inversely proportional importance. How does this happen?

Because the colonial archive is expectedly one that teems with male subjects, when the woman appears she also exposes the conditions, rules, and constraints that have operated to keep her out of the action. By thus exposing the archive to be a "patriarchive," the figure of woman allows us to read one important aspect of this grammar of control—its ability to assign subject positions to those who enter its textual web. It then becomes possible for us to ask: What conditions have made it possible for a woman to appear in the colonial record? What constitutes her dispersal from one level to another?

How does she move from official discussions where she is a secluded subject into missionary tracts or novels where she is the object of religious conversion? From universalist Enlightenment histories where she is sexual slave to parliamentary discussions where she is promiscuous sexual predator and degenerate mother? All in all, the faintest presence of the figure of woman in official records is a sign that some significant discursive shifts have taken place. This figure thus can help us track the relationships between historical changes and discursive changes on the textual surface of the colonial archive.

There is one more important lesson to learn from the gendered historical subject in the archive. The story of the gendered subject is always a partial story and her history a partial one tied up with the grand narratives that accumulate their own "legitimate" stores of textual evidence. Yet, feminist historians and critics cannot wait till "all the facts are in" for women's histories to be written. Reconciling oneself to a partial history is ultimately a call for producing a new kind of narrative. Such a critical position suggests that though marginalized and instrumentalized, the woman does not need to appear as the subject of universal history. Rather, her appearance will expose the limits of such a totalizing desire. Her continuous use as instrument or as ruse can expose the role of fabrication in the production of subjectivity, and her fabricated history can expose the reality of (colonial) history as fabrication. A reading for woman is thus ultimately not only a quest for rethinking the relationship between literature and history but is always already a call for a new narrativization of history itself.

CHAPTER NINE

The Narrative of Elizabeth Marsh

Barbary, Sex, and Power

Linda Colley

It was late July 1756 when the *Ann* set out from the British colony of Gibraltar en route to London. A small ship, some 150 tons, it sailed in convoy because Britain was now at war with France, but there was nothing its crew could do about the weather. Once in the Straits of Gibraltar, fog closed around them like a shroud, confusing the navigator and severing them from the other ships. A week after leaving the Rock, they were still adrift off the coast of North Africa. The *Ann*'s only female passenger, Elizabeth Marsh, remained however determinedly unconcerned. Thinking of the new clothes her father had allowed her, and of what these portended when the ship reached England, she clutched at the delay and pretended it would last. The sailors snickered as she passed, holding her damp skirts close to her twenty-one-year-old body, but nothing kept her from seeking out one of her fellow passengers, a young merchant named James Crisp. The unaccustomed company, like the white mist pressing around the ship, kept at bay that other world that must surely soon possess her.

When the Moroccan cruiser thrust through the fog on 8 August, no defense was possible. The *Ann* was outgunned and outmanned some ten times over. Its crew and passengers, Marsh and Crisp included, were taken captive and brought to the corsairs' base at Salé, on the northern coast of Morocco, before being forced to ride 300 miles to its administrative and royal capital, Marrakech. London was not able to secure the captives' release until the end of 1756; and it was much later than this, in 1769, when the woman who had once been called Elizabeth Marsh published her two-volume account of what had befallen her: *The Female Captive: a Narrative of Facts which happened in Barbary, in the year 1756.*[1]

In almost all respects, this is an exceptional and unusual text. It is unusual because Elizabeth Marsh's existence and how she came to be captured can be authenticated by other sources. Marsh was born in Hampshire in 1735, the daughter of a ship's carpenter and dockyard official employed by the Royal Navy first at Minorca, then at Gibraltar, and finally at Chatham. Through her father, then, Marsh was connected both to the British state and to the business of empire. Partly because of this, her captivity attracted official attention, and at least some of the details in *The Female Captive* can be checked against correspondence in the state papers. Marsh's narrative is also extraordinary because some of the circumstances and progress of its composition are known. The copy in the British Library contains a manuscript note by a one-time neighbor of Marsh to the effect that she wrote it while living with her parents in Chatham in the mid-1760s. Her then husband had gone bankrupt and been forced to seek a position in India, and she was short of funds to maintain herself and their two children. Moreover, a manuscript exists in a copyist's hand of what is clearly an earlier version of this narrative of female capture and release.[2]

Yet what is most remarkable about this text is that it is a Barbary captivity narrative written and published by a woman who is known beyond doubt to have been herself a captive. As Joe Snader has recently described, Barbary captivity narratives had been published in England since the 1580s, anticipating by almost a century the first Indian captivity narratives published in America.[3] Such narratives were numerous because Barbary corsairs represented a protracted threat to English, Scottish, Welsh, and Irish shipping, just as they did to the Mediterranean and Atlantic trade of other European states. Between 1622 and the 1640s, privateers operating out of Algiers, Tripoli, Tunis, and Morocco captured at sea some 7,000 subjects of the English crown. Between 1670 and 1730, at least another 5,000 Britons fell foul of these privateers, and were confined and in some cases enslaved in North Africa.[4] Barbary corsairing's seriousness declined thereafter as far as Britain was concerned. Nonetheless, between 1756 and 1758, some 400 Britons were held captive at different times in Morocco, of whom Elizabeth Marsh was one. But although Barbary captivities were numerous and spanned four centuries, women formed only a minority of such captives, while authenticated narratives of the experience of Barbary captivity by women of any nationality may be counted on one hand with fingers to spare.[5]

Marsh's title makes the exceptionality clear. *The Female Captive* is reminiscent of Daniel Bellamy's *The Female Politician* (1741), Hannah Snell's *The Female Soldier* (1750), or Henry Fielding's *The Female Husband* (1746). The very wording underlines the point that Barbary captivity was an aberrant female experience. Just how aberrant, however, is less certain than it superficially appears. Lists of British captives redeemed from North Africa in the seventeenth and eighteenth centuries confirm that women were very much in the minority. Thus in 1637, a group of 293 captives redeemed by English envoys from Algiers included just 11 women.[6] Nineteen more women, eight of them Irish and two of them Scots, were redeemed in 1646; while the last substantial English redemption of captives from Algiers in the 1680s brought out only five women.[7] However, the number of British and other European captives redeemed from North Africa was always smaller than the total seized by Barbary corsairs in the first place, and there were particular reasons why this was the case as far as female captives were concerned.

Individuals seized by North African corsairs risked undergoing varieties of enslavement, especially before 1720. Male victims might be employed as galley slaves, or be sent to forced labor on public works, or sold to a private owner—fates from which the only likely escape was being ransomed by their home states. For the comparatively few women seized, however, Barbary captivity could mean something very different. Under Islamic law, a female slave became the sexual property of her owner, though she could not be put out to prostitution. This was what Elizabeth Marsh meant when she referred in her printed narrative to "the dangers my sex was exposed to in Barbary."[8] However applicable this was to her own situation (and this is a point we will return to), it seems certain that some British and other European women taken captive by North African powers disappeared into households there that never subsequently gave them up.[9] Hence the difficulties that the English envoy Edward Casson experienced reclaiming women from Algiers and Tunis in 1646. The authorities there insisted that captives could only leave if their respective owners were reimbursed for what they had paid for them in the local slave markets, and the women involved proved conspicuously expensive. Fewer than one in four of the 245 male captives Casson retrieved cost him 700 doubloons or more, but well over half of the nineteen women he won back cost more than this sum, and six of them were only redeemed for 1,000 doubloons apiece.[10]

This would seem to confirm evidence from other sources that female captives of Barbary were rare commodities and commanded—if young and healthy and brought to a slave market of some kind—a substantial price. Once purchased and made use of, their owners might refuse to give them up even for ransom, and the women themselves, particularly if they had children by their owners, might not wish to be let go. This said, much depended—as with male captives—on the class and economic status of the individuals involved. In the 1720s, firm evidence exists of three British and Irish women being seized by Moroccan corsairs. Two of these were Jewish, Blanca and Rachel Franco, captured along with their menfolk on a voyage from London to New York. Prosperous traders, they were redeemed and brought home by a Royal Navy ship in 1728. Margaret Shea, a working-class woman sailing on her own from Cork to Lisbon in 1720, had a very different experience. According to one version, having been captured by corsairs, she became the property of Moulay Ismaïl, then the Moroccan sultan, who forced her to convert and then into his bed before handing her over to a European renegade soldier. In terms of its details, this may be just one of the many European atrocity stories that circulated about this particular powerful Moroccan ruler, but Shea was undoubtedly captured, converted, and impregnated by someone in Morocco. Toward the end of the 1720s, a British envoy encountered her and the child there "almost naked and starved." "She had been a Moor upwards of 9 years," he reported, and "had almost forgot her English." She never got back home.[11]

So women, as well as men, could be shipwrecked by Barbary—their virtue, lives, and freedom put in danger—though I stress that this seems to have been a rare experience. The question arises, then, of how exactly we should approach and interpret Elizabeth Marsh's narratives of captivity. There can be no doubt that she was seized suddenly and by force at sea in August 1756 while traveling with an all-male crew and set of passengers, and was held against her will in Morocco for four months. We can assume that she was traumatized by the experience and that it was sometimes physically as well as psychologically arduous. This said, for the most part she appears to have been reasonably well treated by her captors. Official British reactions to her captivity at the time verge indeed on the phlegmatic. There is no mention by any British official writing of Marsh in 1756 of her being in physical danger because of what had befallen her, and no reference to lustful "Turks" or any sign of apprehension that she might end up in someone's harem. "Mr. Marsh has had [a letter] from his daughter [in Morocco]," an envoy wrote from Gibraltar that autumn, "and they all agree in their having been hitherto very well treated." "There is no matter of danger," agreed an English merchant writing from Morocco later in the year, although he did add a request: "Desire Mr. Marsh to send [his daughter] a small firkin of good butter, some cheese, tea and sugar." An attractive, single, twenty-one-year-old Englishwoman had fallen into the power of the Moroccan sultan, but the only thing her father was apparently to concern himself with was ensuring that she had continued access to dairy products and a cup of tea.[12]

When Marsh published her account of what had befallen her in 1769, however, she selected a very different emphasis. The book's darker and more dramatic passages may in part be attributed to her suppressed anger at what had happened to her, and to her genteel poverty at this stage, and consequent desire to boost sales. Nonetheless, the hostility she displays to almost all aspects of Moroccan society is striking. It appears still more so once one recognizes that Marsh almost certainly modeled some of the episodes in this published version of *The Female Captive* on Lady Mary Wortley Montagu's famous account of her expedition to Turkey, the *Embassy Letters*, originally written in 1717–18 but only published posthumously in 1763.[13] Yet whereas Montagu had been conspicuously admiring of some Islamic societies, often contrasting them favorably with the West, the former Elizabeth Marsh was almost invariably negative. Whereas Montagu made a point of wearing Turkish costume during and after her travels, and famously had herself painted thus attired, Marsh claimed repeatedly to have resisted during her captivity all suggestions that she should adopt Moroccan dress. Whereas Montagu sought out and savored the company of elite Ottoman women, Marsh's references to Moroccan females were almost invariably scathing, regardless of their social rank and relationship to the Moroccan sultan's court. Whereas Montagu had questioned Western presumptions about Ottoman despotism, Marsh's verdict on her captivity was that it had reduced her "to passive obedience and non-resistance," the worst fate possible for a Whig like herself. She referred, in her printed text, to ordinary Moroccans as being like "so many infernals" and alluded to her "dread of being exposed to those merciless Moors."[14]

She also made it titillatingly clear that the source of this dread was the sexual danger to which captivity had exposed her. She claimed that her fellow passenger on the *Ann*, James Crisp, was obliged to masquerade as her husband during their joint detention in Morocco so as to prevent her from being absorbed into the seraglio of the soon-to-be sultan and already de facto ruler, Sidi Muhammad, and she described two dramatic encounters between the latter and herself: "The Prince was tall, finely shaped, of a good complexion, and appeared to be about five and twenty . . . His figure, all together, was rather agreeable, and his address polite and easy."

This eligible creature ("I was amazed at the elegant figure he made") attempted— she claimed—to persuade her to join him in the splendors of his Marrakech palace. Solid bourgeois that she was, Marsh assured him that she preferred the equal relationship she enjoyed with her pretended "husband," James Crisp. She resisted the prince's subsequent anger as steadfastly as his appeals, refused to convert to Islam, and—so her narrative tells us—was at last released: "The Prince, being asked if he would not see the fair Christian before her departure, after a pause, replied, No, lest I should be obliged to detain her."[15]

At what levels are we to understand all this? The literary influence on *The Female Captive* not just of Wortley Montagu's writings but also of novels of single, respectable, unfortunate women undergoing ordeals and persecution such as *Pamela* and *Clarissa* is clear. Even more influential, apparently, is the set of conventions we now label as Orientalism. For Joe Snader, indeed, British Barbary captivity narratives were always Orientalist and therefore imperialist in intent: "As the captives describe their subjugation to foreign masters, their isolation from home within an alien environment, and their self-reliant efforts to regain native 'English liberties,' their voices of individualistic autonomy take shape against a detailed representation of the Orient as debased and despotic. Both the debased Oriental setting and the plot of subjugation and escape enforce an expansionist ideology by suggesting that autonomous and self-reliant Western captives possess a natural right and ability to resist and control the alien cultures that have enslaved them."[16] One may question how far resisting captivity and enslavement is necessarily tantamount to advocating expansionism. The wider problem of this kind of analysis for a historian, though, is not so much that it is inaccurate as that it is insufficiently specific. As Edward Said has acknowledged, one of the problems of charting expressions of racial and cultural prejudice is often their very antiquity. The idea that Eastern regimes inclined toward despotism, servility, and effeminacy was familiar to the Ancient Greeks. Moreover, as far as the British were concerned, this sort of condemnatory language was reinforced by Protestant insularity and by no means applied exclusively to Islamic states. In K. N. Chaudhuri's words: "After the Reformation . . . Protestants invested the Catholic Other with a range of 'debased' characteristics . . . which were very close to those attributed to Turks, to Arabs, to Asians, and to Africans (and indeed by the English to the Germans during and after the First World War)."[17]

Because the perception of alien societies as despotic, tyrannical, cruel, decadent, effeminate, superstitious, and so on had such an ancient pedigree, and often obtained in regard to Christian as well as to non-Christian societies, its precise contribution to any particular phase or direction of British imperialism becomes perforce problematic. There is a further difficulty. As Kenan Malik has remarked, focusing on Orientalist notions or on any other derogatory and clichéd epithets used by one society or people against another is inappropriate without also considering very carefully the respective levels of material and coercive power possessed by these societies over time.[18] The old children's rhyme "sticks and stones may break my bones, but names can never hurt me" applies as well to the dynamics of imperialism. Ancient languages of contempt and stereotyping, and collections of real and bogus knowledge, could only contribute toward effective imperialism when those deploying them had access as well to the requisite physical and economic power, and the will to make use of it in a particular direction. If we want to understand the history of empire over time, we need to be highly specific about when this situation of sufficient power and sufficient will was achieved. Consequently, always to analyze Barbary captivity narratives, or any other writings about British contacts with non-Europeans, primarily in terms of colonialist and imperial ideologies is overly casual and may even be perverse. By definition, the very fact that substantial numbers of Britons and other Europeans were taken captive at certain periods by non-Europeans (in this case by the North African powers) was a demonstration that—at these points in time—the power of the former had limits while the latter retained an ability to be predatory in fact.

There are obvious Orientalist motifs in *The Female Captive* that merit analysis. Yet to approach this text only or even primarily in terms of enduring tropes about Oriental despotism and sensuality would be to miss what it reveals more specifically about a particular historical moment, indeed a particular imperial moment, and the particular circumstances of Elizabeth Marsh herself. I want to devote the rest of this essay to identifying and exploring these various particularities.

It has become a commonplace that Western Europeans often, though not invariably, viewed Islamic cultures in terms of predatory sensuality and sexual excess. Yet what Britons and other Europeans were actually saying about power relations between themselves and Islamic societies when they eroticized the East in this fashion seems to have changed markedly over time. Literary treatments of male and female captivities in North Africa reinforce this point. As far as British female captives in Barbary are concerned, what is striking—at least before the mid–eighteenth century—is the paucity of literary references to them. To be sure, female captives in the North African powers were, as we have seen, very much a minority. Nonetheless, sufficient women were seized by Barbary corsairs over the years for dry, government documents regularly to make mention of them. Popular and polite literature, by contrast, contains few references to English or British female captives of Barbary. William Rufus Chetwood's *The Voyages and Adventures of Captain Robert Boyle* (1726) is one of very few novels to refer to them.[19] Elizabeth Marsh's 1769 volumes were the first female Barbary captivity narrative ever published in Britain. To my knowledge, there are no popular ballads in the English language about female Barbary captives, though there are many about male captives, and British men's captivity narratives rarely allude to female experiences in North Africa, even when the authors make it clear that women were captured alongside them.

Given preconceptions about Muslim sensuality, how is this apparent reticence before 1750 about British female captives and their possible sexual danger in North Africa to be understood? We must realize that, until the early eighteenth century, British Barbary captivity literature was more concerned with emphasizing the sexual threat to male captives supposedly represented by North African and Muslim men. For every reference to forced heterosexual sex I have seen in British discussions of Barbary before 1750, there are at least five to sodomy. This is true of polite as well as popular literature, public statements, and the most private of writings.

The notion found its way into petitions. "The said [Algerian] patrons [that is, slaveowners]," some captives' wives complained in the 1670s, "do frequently bugger the said captives, or most of them." It was the stuff of parliamentary speeches. Algerian captivity, an M.P. told the House of Commons in 1614, meant "children taken, kept for bug-gery and made Turks."[20] It informed diplomats' reactions to North African missions. The editor of the journal of Thomas Baker, English consul in Tripoli 1677–85, remarks that Baker was obsessed with male "homosexuality, which according to him, was quite acceptable in Tripoli, with homosexual rape . . . openly and violently practiced." Natu-rally, the claim surfaced in captivity narratives. "They are said to commit sodomie with all creatures," writes Francis Knight of his Algerian captors in 1640.[21] It can also be found in more substantial texts like Paul Rycaut's famous *Present State of the Ottoman Empire* (1668), where the Ottoman world's need to import Christian captives from without is ascribed to its own failure to reproduce because of "that abominable vice of sodomie." Moreover, these ideas circulated in all kinds of imaginative literature. In Chetwood's *Robert Boyle*, published in 1726 and reissued a dozen times over the cen-tury, a Moroccan informs the properly appalled British hero that sodomy "is so com-mon here that 'tis reckon'd only a piece of gallantry."[22]

For my purposes, it is immaterial whether these perceptions of North African and Ottoman sexuality were accurate. Even at the time, some sterner spirits were prepared to argue what is sometimes suggested now: namely, that accusations of sodomy on the part of Britons and Continental Europeans transposed to the Islamic world desires that the former secretly nurtured.[23] But most Britons who accused North African and Ot-toman males of sodomy in the 1600s and early eighteenth century were not, I believe, giving vent to suppressed desires, or seriously interested in delineating the sexuality of those they were denouncing, or merely using assertions of sodomy so as more thor-oughly to "other" Islamic peoples.[24] In this context, sodomy acted as a metaphor, a par-ticularly acute expression of the fear and insecurity that Britons and other Western Eu-ropeans continued to feel in the face of Islamic power and, as they saw it, aggression. The claim sometimes made that the West eroticized the Islamic world in order to fem-inize and dominate it, is therefore suspect, as far as Barbary and the Ottoman empires before 1750 are concerned. Indeed, this claim might almost be reversed. Those who threw out accusations of sodomy when discussing British captivities in Barbary were rarely primarily concerned with whether North African males allowed themselves to be sodomized. Rather, the burden of these expressed anxieties was that it was captive British males who were the potential victims. It was *they* who might be penetrated and invaded; *they* who might be forced into the passive role. Accusing the Barbary powers and the Ottoman empire (of which Algiers, Tripoli, and Tunis were technically military provinces) of sodomizing male Christian captives was one more way in which Britons and other Europeans gave vent to ancient fears that these societies and Islam generally might undermine and threaten them.[25]

Nor should these fears be dismissed simply as paranoia and prejudice. It is now broadly recognized that much of what was once believed about the rapid collapse of the great Islamic empires after 1600 was overstated and that these territories' capacity for internal reform and renewal remained in evidence well into the 1700s. There was decline, but it was slow and uneven, just as Western recognition of the Islamic empires' decline was slow and uneven. As far as the Ottomans were concerned, their territorial expansion into Europe only reached its furthest extent in the 1670s. Ottoman armies were finally turned back from Vienna in 1683, but the Ottomans remained strong enough to regain Belgrade in 1739 and did not experience major territorial losses until the 1770s.[26] As for the Ottoman satellites—Algiers, Tunis, and Tripoli—these together with Morocco have been sadly neglected by scholars writing in English, but it is clear that their capacity not just to resist European incursions but also to prey upon European trade was a markedly protracted one. The only British attempt to move into this region before 1800, the brief occupation of Tangier after 1662, proved a complete fiasco. Even in the 1720s, Morocco's well-armed land forces were more numerous than Britain's own peacetime army. As a Moroccan official told an envoy seeking to ransom British captives in 1718, "he knew very well [that] by sea the English would be too hard for them, but by land he did not at all fear 'em."[27] This persistent military capacity among the North African powers was one reason why corsairing persisted. The Royal Navy could and did sporadically bombard North African coastal ports, but the British lacked the power and the desire to launch a land invasion against these regions and suppress corsairing at source. This remained the case even in the early 1800s. Hence, to assume and concentrate on identifying a colonialist or imperial intent in seventeenth- and eighteenth-century British writings on Barbary is inappropriate and ahistoric.

By the time Marsh published *The Female Captive* in 1769, however, things were beginning to change. The Seven Years War, which began (as far as Britain was concerned) in the year of her capture, 1756, massively transformed and expanded British national self-regard and imperial power. For the first time ever, in conquering Bengal, Britain achieved decisive land victories and subsequent authority over Islamic powers. The onetime Miss Marsh would depart for India shortly after the publication of her narrative, dying in Calcutta in 1785. On the other hand, Turkey's disastrous wars with Russia, which began in 1768, encouraged Western Europeans increasingly (though still not invariably) to view the Ottoman empire as a rusting, antique titan. We should not be surprised, then, that from the 1750s there was a marked rise in Britain of "Oriental" literature, music, and art of a certain kind, of which *The Female Captive* is a minor example. Confections full of scantily clad harems, Christian damsels in distress, and masterful and strangely attractive sultans were by no means new, but these now flowed far more easily off the pen and sold more readily in Britain because the Islamic world, at least as represented by Barbary and the Ottomans, was losing much of its power to frighten.

References to sodomy—to the Islamic world's capacity to assault European males—shrank and became muted, along with British and European fears of penetration from without.[28]

At one level, then, *The Female Captive* must be situated on the cusp of what would prove to be a long, drawn-out, and always partial shift away from residual British apprehension of Islam to low regard for, and condescension toward, at least some of the states associated with it. But like every other text about cross-cultural contacts and imaginings, this one needs to be approached as well in the light of the personal imperatives of the writer and the mode of writing adopted. Elizabeth Marsh was briefly and astonishingly a captive of Barbary, but she was also constrained far more durably by other forces that influenced how and what she wrote. She was constrained, to begin with, by her lack of original literary talent. Marsh clearly enjoyed writing, but she lacked literary confidence and was markedly derivative in much of her style and emphasis. Marsh was constrained too by her gender and by her social class. Lady Mary Wortley Montagu, like another famous female visitor to and commentator on the Islamic world in the eighteenth century, Lady Craven, was the daughter of a peer of the realm. Marsh by contrast was lower middle class and possessed no independent income. This made her at once far more vulnerable than Montagu and Craven in the public sphere and, in some respects, freer in the private. Unlike these female patricians, Marsh did not enter an Islamic state by choice, and she had no servants or powerful relations to protect her on her travels. As she writes piteously, in her emergency, she had "no body near me that I knew."[29] Her hostility toward a Muslim power derived in part from a sense of personal insecurity within its boundaries that Montagu and Craven were too grand and too well guarded to experience. Yet, whereas Montagu and Craven were both victims in different ways of the aristocratic marriage market, Marsh expected to choose her own mate. By her own account, she left Gibraltar in July 1756 to journey to England and marry an officer to whom she was engaged. On returning from her Moroccan captivity at the end of that year, however, she broke this engagement and married her onetime fellow passenger on the *Ann,* James Crisp. She may indeed have become Crisp's lover while they were both held captive in Morocco. Claiming in her published narrative that she had clung to Crisp and that he had been compelled to masquerade as her husband in order to help her repel the lustful advances of a virile and imperious Moroccan prince and avoid being "detained in the seraglio" was at one level a means of getting herself off the hook. It helped to excuse to others and to herself her inconstancy to her original fiancé and her impetuous marriage to another man, who at the time of her writing was bankrupt and in disgrace.

Reading the published text of *The Female Captive* and the earlier manuscript version against each other suggests indeed that Marsh felt acutely torn between her desire to publish her own version of what had happened to her and make some money from it, and deep anxiety about how exactly she could best describe and seek to vindicate her experiences during and immediately after her captivity. Significantly but unsurprisingly, she published anonymously. She also left out from the final printed version much of the local Moroccan detail she incorporated in her earlier draft and much of the detail of her supposed encounters with Sidi Muhammad. (We have no way of establishing now whether these encounters ever took place.) Marsh also shifted the emphasis. In the earlier manuscript version of her captivity narrative, she refers regularly to the Christian God, to her reliance on his providence, and to her abiding fear that she will be forced by her Moroccan captors to convert to Islam. In the published version, however, there are only a few allusions to religion, or indeed to Marsh's wider Moroccan experiences and perceptions. The information she had initially included on Morocco's topography, costume, consumer goods, cuisine, linguistic patterns, and on the complex interplay in its port cities of Christian, Jewish, and Muslim merchants is almost entirely discarded. Her whole story becomes instead a rather formulaic account of how a young woman's virtue is exposed to trial and danger, and how she keeps herself separate and secure from her menacing surroundings.

The desire to present and publish her story in these terms may well explain Marsh's repeated insistence that she had refused to wear Moroccan costume. Whereas for Montagu, Ottoman dress had represented a kind of liberation, and whereas for the elite women who wore it at masquerades in the 1760s and 1770s, "Oriental" costume was a glamorous form of conspicuous consumption, Marsh's perspective was necessarily very different and far more tense. Unlike these privileged women, she had actually been in some danger in an Islamic society and had moreover compromised herself in the eyes of some in her own society. Consequently, her most urgent concern when committing herself to print was to stress her arduous aloofness from all things Moroccan. Given her evident taste for novels and literary borrowing, indeed, she may well have called to mind Daniel Defoe's *Roxana,* in which the (anti)heroine wears "the habit of a Turkish princess," including a turban, at scandalous parties.[30] Fearful that "the ill disposed part of the world would censure my conduct," Marsh may have felt obliged to repudiate "Oriental" costume in her own story lest it be viewed as an emblem of a lapse into disrepute on her part.

In commercial terms, this rewriting and distancing from things Moroccan proved to be a mistake. Contemporary reviewers seem to have recognized, despite *The Female Captive*'s anonymity, that it contained a core of authenticity, but they also judged that there was "nothing marvellous in the narration" and "very few interesting events."[31] Marsh had simply not been free enough, or powerful enough, or a sufficiently accomplished writer, to be able to publish comprehensively what had indeed been marvelous about her extraordinary experiences. Instead, she sought refuge in self-censorship and in standard literary forms, and, it seems, still failed adequately to redeem herself. Having left for India and the hapless James Crisp in the early 1770s, she never returned to England, and her deeply religious father left both her and her husband out of his will.[32]

So, like all texts, *The Female Captive* is culturally porous. It is influenced by the political circumstances of its writer and time of composition, and crafted in accordance with highly personal and specific imperatives. However, this text needs to be placed in yet another context. It is not enough to explore why the one-time Elizabeth Marsh, controversially and unluckily transformed into Elizabeth Crisp, wrote her narrative in the ways that she did. We need as well to locate what happened to her in the broader context of power relations and power perceptions between Morocco and Britain in the eighteenth century.

In her published text, Marsh actually refers to the reason why Morocco seized the crew of the *Ann* as well as some 400 other Britons between 1756 and 1758. Early in 1756, a British naval envoy called Captain Hyde Parker had behaved disrespectfully to the same Sidi Muhammad whom Elizabeth Marsh claimed to encounter, and rejected his demand for a British consul to be established permanently in Morocco.[33] The subsequent wave of captive-taking was on Morocco's part an act of retaliation against British arrogance and an attempt to exert political pressure. It succeeded. Between 1734 and 1756, the British state had paid over £60,000 to Morocco in ransoms for captive nationals. In 1760, Britain paid a further 200,000 Spanish dollars to retrieve this latest batch of Moroccan captives. It also apologized to the now sultan, Sidi Muhammad, for Hyde Parker's behavior and appointed a consul to Morocco.

This is not the sort of behavior one might expect in the middle of the Seven Years War when British imperial power was incontestably on the roll. Just why it occurred however is straightforward enough. The British had little choice. As we have seen, the potential for them to deploy physical force in order to curb Moroccan pretensions was limited at this point, and for their own strategic reasons, they had no desire to adopt such a course. They needed the assistance of the North African powers too much to wish to offend them, or to refuse them ransoms or consuls if they demanded them.

Scholars have badly neglected Britain's Mediterranean empire—perhaps because of an assumption that British empire was something that only happened outside Europe. Yet before 1750, more British troops were stationed in Gibraltar and Minorca than in the whole of North America, never mind in India. Without regular supplies from Morocco and the other North African powers (grain, cattle, fish, fresh fruit, etc.), these troops would have starved, and Royal Navy ships would not have been able to use these Mediterranean bases for essential reprovisioning. *The Female Captive* is a colonialist text, therefore, partly because of what it reveals about Britain's persistent need to placate Morocco in the eighteenth century so that it could continue to garrison and occupy territory seized from and inhabited by Catholic Europeans.[34]

This essay has been concerned with demonstrating the value of a close but deliberately diverse reading of a minor text, *The Female Captive,* and the insights this can provide into perceptions of sexuality and Islam, the vital and often neglected Mediterranean zone of encounter, naval and imperial power and their paradoxes, and the reading and writing styles of a lower-middle-class Englishwoman under pressure in the mid-eighteenth century. I take it for granted that historians need to learn how to mine literary and quasi-literary sources such as these, just as they need to learn how to read and deploy visual images. As a historian I have wanted in this essay, among other things, to problematize the relationship between Western representations of the Islamic "other" (which was by no means invariably perceived or presented as such) on the one hand, and Western coercive power and colonial intent on the other. It is certainly possible, as we have seen, to detect in the 1769 published version of *The Female Captive* a more dismissive and less tremulous tone emerging toward Barbary and Islam than had characterized many published English and British statements on this subject in the seventeenth and early eighteenth centuries. By the 1760s, Barbary and the Ottoman world had lost much of their power to arouse fear, and this made it easier at once to dismiss and to romanticize them. Yet this shift in cultural tone—which can be seen in music, art, drama, and costume after 1760 and not just in publications like Elizabeth Marsh's narrative—was not accompanied by an upsurge in British physical coercion and colonial power in the North African or Ottoman region. Even in the nineteenth century, Britain remained diffident about moving into or challenging either of these broad territorial areas.[35]

All of which is to say that literary and cultural representations of other societies are one thing and an important and a fascinating thing. But the capacity and will of states and peoples to impose and act upon their constructions and understandings of other societies, religions, and peoples are often quite a different matter.

CHAPTER TEN

The Lama and the Scotsman

George Bogle in Bhutan and Tibet, 1774–1775

Kate Teltscher

On the 8th of November 1774, after a seven-month journey from the plains of Bengal, across the Himalayan range and onto the plateaux of Tibet, a young Scotsman arrived at the court of the Panchen Lama of Tibet. George Bogle was the first British traveler to enter the region. Sent as the envoy of the governor-general of Bengal, Bogle aimed to negotiate a trade treaty and gather as much information as possible about Bhutan and Tibet. The opportunity to expand British influence in the Himalayan region arose in 1772 when the Bhutanese Desi, Zhidar, invaded Cooch Behar, a small state on Bengal's northern borders. The deposed Raja of Cooch Behar sought military assistance from the British. The terms of the agreement compelled the Raja to bear the cost of the campaign and cede sovereignty of the state to the East India Company. Defeated by a British regiment, Zhidar retreated to Bhutan, where he was met by a rebellion against his notoriously harsh regime. To escape the uprising, Zhidar claimed sanctuary with the Panchen Lama who initiated peace negotiations between the British and the Bhutanese. In response to these overtures, Bogle was appointed envoy to Tibet.

Bogle left Calcutta in May 1774, accompanied by two agents sent by the Lama, Purangir Gosain and Paima, a Scottish surgeon, Alexander Hamilton, and a large retinue of servants. They traveled northwards, through Bhutan, where they were received by the new Desi, Kunga Rinchen, at his capital fortress of Tashichö Dzong. Bogle remained at the Bhutanese court for several months, growing increasingly exasperated at the Desi's intransigence in their lengthy negotiations. Under pressure from the Tibetan regent in Lhasa, the Panchen Lama had written declining Bogle permission to enter Tibet. Bogle despatched Purangir Gosain to argue his case with the Lama. Finally receiving consent for the mission to proceed, the party headed for the Lama's summer palace, the monastery of Dechenrubje.

Lobsang Palden Yeshé, the third Panchen Lama, had risen to a position of religious and political preeminence in Tibet and the neighboring states during the minority of the eighth Dalai Lama. The Lama spoke Hindustani (Urdu), so he and Bogle were able to communicate without an interpreter. During Bogle's five months' residence with the Lama, he was granted numerous private audiences. From the many conversations recorded in Bogle's journal and letters, both seem to have been equally eager to gather political, commercial, and cultural information. As Tzvetan Todorov notes, it is only through talking to the Other (as opposed to issuing orders), that the Other is granted a subjectivity comparable to the Self.[1] Throughout Bogle's writing, the Lama is described in the most glowing terms: intelligent, attentive, charitable, affable, unaffected, and humane. In a private letter to Warren Hastings, the governor-general, Bogle observed, "I never knew a Man whose Manners pleased me so much or for whom, upon so short an Acquaintance, I had half the Heart's liking."[2] Unfortunately, the only Tibetan account of the encounter is a scant record of Bogle's first official audience. The Lama's "Autobiography" is a kind of court diary listing religious ceremonies and court business; it simply notes that Bogle offered presents, took tea, and made conversation at their first meeting.[3] The Lama's point of view can thus only be imagined through Bogle's writings. From these it appears that what began as an exercise in diplomacy turned into a friendship between the twenty-eight-year-old Glaswegian and the third incarnation of Amitabha, Buddha of Boundless Light.

In this chapter I interrogate the idea of cross-cultural encounter and intimacy. How important is Bogle's Scottish background to his representation of Tartars, Tibetans, and Bhutanese? The Tartars were classified as barbarians by the social taxonomies of the Scottish Enlightenment. I ask how far Bogle challenges these notions of barbarism and whether this in turn qualifies the idea of European civility. What part does the figure of the Lama play in this process of cultural questioning? As we shall see, Bogle tends to focus on his own relationship with the Lama, excluding the roles of the Lama's agents and Hamilton in the narrative of cultural exchange. Bogle represents the relationship with the Lama as one of reciprocal affection, rewriting the trading alliance in the language of sensibility.

Himalayan Highlands

George Bogle's Scottish origins may have initially recommended him to the governor-general. Warren Hastings was unusual in disregarding the prevailing anti-Scots feeling of the period to favor Scottish appointments in his administration; indeed he termed his inner circle of advisors and confidantes his "Scotch guardians."[4] As the youngest son of a prominent Glasgow trading family, Bogle was well equipped with the commercial and political connections that Hastings particularly valued. His father, also George, was one of the so-called Tobacco Lords, who made (and lost) a fortune importing tobacco from Virginia for reexport to Europe. The wealth of this merchant elite transformed eighteenth-century Glasgow into one of the most prosperous and elegant cities in the country, stimulating the cultural activity now known as the Glasgow Enlightenment.[5]

Unlike other mercantile groups in Britain, the Glasgow merchants were unusually well educated; many of them followed a course of study at university.[6] George Bogle senior played a prominent role in Glasgow's commercial, educational, and civic affairs, serving terms of office both as Dean of Guild and Lord Rector of Glasgow University during the 1740s and 1750s.[7] From 1751 to 1764, Adam Smith held the Chair of Logic at Glasgow University, teaching, among others, George's eldest brother, Robert, and one of his friends, William Richardson.[8] Bogle himself briefly attended Edinburgh University in 1760–61 before pursuing a more practical course of mercantile education at a private school in Enfield. Although his university career only lasted six months, Bogle's connections ensured that he was well versed in the ideas of the Scottish Enlightenment. His Calcutta library included works by Adam Smith, David Hume, William Robertson, and Adam Ferguson.[9] William Richardson, Bogle's friend and correspondent, was a poet, critic, and playwright, who became professor of Humanity (Latin) at Glasgow University.

The Scottish literati were preoccupied, perhaps to a greater extent than other Enlightenment thinkers, with the attempt to define and distinguish primitive and refined societies. Drawing extensively on travel literature, writers like Smith, Robertson, and Ferguson sought to chart human development by dividing society into various stages, usually corresponding to the savage, the barbaric, and the polished. It has often been remarked that this concern was related to the nature of Scottish society itself, split between the sophisticated Lowlands and "rude" Highlands.[10] To most eighteenth-century Lowland Scots, Highlanders would have appeared as the barbarous Other. Indeed, in the writing of the period, Highlanders were often identified with North American Indians as part of a widespread habit of cultural comparison.[11] Following the ruthless post-1745 destruction of the Highlands, the clans' military threat was defused. The figure of the Highlander could then be endowed with a nostalgic nobility, given particular currency by James Macpherson's poems of Ossian.

In appointing Bogle envoy to Bhutan and Tibet, Hastings was in part motivated by a desire for information, the kind of empirical evidence favored by the theorists of the Scottish Enlightenment. The mission was both an exercise in reconnaissance and an intellectual project. During his period as governor-general, Hastings was an active patron of scholarship, both British and Indian.[12] The studies that he commissioned from figures such as Nathaniel Halhed, Charles Hamilton, Charles Wilkins, and Radhakanta Sarma furthered the ends of the company administration by extending British knowledge of Hindu and Muslim law, history, and culture. In a letter addressed to Nathaniel Smith, chairman of the East India Company, prefacing Wilkins's translation of the *Bhagavad Gita,* Hastings asserted that "[e]very accumulation of knowledge, and especially such as is obtained by social communication with people over whom we exercise a dominion founded on the right of conquest, is useful to the state . . . it lessens the weight of the chain by which the natives are held in subjection." Yet for Hastings the immediate aims of government were complemented by the higher ends of moral and intellectual advancement. Arguing that the study of Indian culture "imprints on the hearts of our own countrymen the sense and obligation of benevolence," Hastings claimed that such works "will survive when the British dominion in India shall have long ceased to exist, and when the sources which it once yielded of wealth and power are lost to remembrance."[13]

The prestige and fame attached to intellectual projects always attracted the governor-general. The mission to Tibet offered Hastings the opportunity to act as a literary and scientific patron. In a list of private commissions, Hastings instructed Bogle to carry a pencil and pocketbook with him at all times, to make notes on everything he encountered, "the people, the country, the climate, or the road, their manners, customs, buildings, cookery &c."[14] For Hastings, the significance of the mission was as much textual as commercial or diplomatic. Writing to Bogle en route, he encouraged his literary pursuits: "I feel myself more interested in the success of your Commission than in Reason perhaps I ought to be, but there are thousands of men in England whose good will is worth seeking, and who will listen to the story of such enterprizes in search of knowledge with ten times more avidity than they would read Accounts that brought Krores [tens of millions] to the National Credit, or descriptions of Victories that slaughtered thousands of the National Enemies. Go on and prosper—Your Journal has travelled as much as you, and is confessed to contain more Matter than Hawkesworth's three Volumes."[15] The comparison with Hawkesworth's 1773 collection of voyages (which included a version of Cook's journal of the first Pacific voyage) flatters Bogle with a vision of national celebrity. The public appetite for scientific adventure, whetted by South

Seas exploration, Hastings suggests, will ensure an eager reception for Bogle's Himalayan expedition. Narrative plays its part in cultivating Hastings's—and Bogle's—political interest at home.

Bogle evidently appreciated the emphasis that Hastings placed on keeping a detailed journal (although he later confided to a friend that his notes had become faded, "so much effaced by the frequent opening and refolding the Paper, by rubbing in my Pocket, along with crumbs of Bread, Seeds of Trees &c. that I could only make out words here and there, and as these were unconnected & only catch words, I was often unable to find out what they aluded to, still more to recollect the general Idea which had occasioned them").[16] However partial and inadequate the original record, Bogle's mission was massively documented. In addition to the voluminous official correspondence and private letters preserved in the Oriental and India Office Collection in the British Library and Mitchell Library Glasgow, Bogle compiled various versions of the journal which formed part of his official report. Hastings sent a transcript of the journal to Samuel Johnson in the hope of securing influential literary patronage for his protégé.

Despite Hastings's encouragement, Bogle never managed to prepare a final manuscript for publication. A version of the journal, edited by the honorary secretary of the Royal Geographical Society, Sir Clements Markham, was finally published a century later when the British once again became interested in the area (in 1876 Bogle's narrative remained the fullest account of the region available). How, then, are we to explain Bogle's failure to publish? For more than a year after Bogle's return from Tibet, Hastings was in no position to provide him with the kind of appointment that would have allowed him to complete the work (as was Hastings's practice with other scholars he supported). Outvoted on the Bengal council, the governor-general was effectively rendered powerless, and it was only in 1777, with the death of one of his opponents on the council, that Hastings could once again exercise his patronage. This was an anxious period for Bogle, whose fate was closely linked to that of Hastings, as he explained to his brother Robert in a letter justifying the delay in completing the manuscript. There were further reasons for postponing the work:

> I dont despair of again visiting that part of the World, I am solicitous to avoid saying any thing where I am not well founded or where I might be contradicted by others who may at some time or other come after me. And besides I have doubts of the propriety of publishing to the whole world an Account of a Country hitherto little known. It is putting other Nations in possession of Knowledge which may be of use to them, and I am not certain of the world enough to be of that Mind. It is sacrificing real advantages perhaps to idle Curiosity or Vanity. However if I had more leisure on my hands I would very probably get the better of these Scruples.[17]

In attempting to account for his reluctance to publish, Bogle reveals both the text's ambivalent status and his own uncertain role. His apparently contradictory concern that the journal might be both inaccurate and a valuable source of intelligence suggests its hybrid nature: at once a literary account, a record of scientific observation, and a commercial and political report. This generic instability is mirrored by Bogle's own complex position: he is an ambitious intellectual and a loyal servant of the East India Company. The discussion's self-deprecating conclusion exemplifies this ambivalence by undercutting the preceding arguments.

Hastings, however, did not share Bogle's anxieties over the political sensitivity of the journal. In forwarding the narrative to Johnson, Hastings writes simply of his pleasure in the text and the attractive figure of the Lama. The accompanying letter opens with a reference to Johnson's own recently published work: "When I read the account of your visit to the Hebrides, I could not help wishing that a portion of that spirit which could draw so much entertainment and instruction from a region so little befriended by nature, or improved by the arts of society, could have animated Mr. Bogle, the author of this journal, but I flatter myself that you will find it not unworthy of perusal. I confess that I received great pleasure from it, and I assure myself, that whatever originality you may discover in the description of the countries and inhabitants of which it treats, you will at least be pleased with the amiable character of the Lama."[18] By alluding to the merits of Johnson's *Journey to the Western Islands of Scotland,* Hastings suggests a parallel between two equally harsh and unpolished regions: the Himalayan states and the Scottish Highlands and Islands. Indeed, Bogle draws freely on the trope of the Highlander in his account of the mission.

For Bogle, the northerly, mountainous state of Bhutan preserved the martial spirit of the old Highlands. Every man is a soldier, "dressed in short Trouze; like the highland Filabeg; woollen Hose, soled with Leather and gartered under the knee; a jacket or Tunick, and over all two or three Striped Blankets . . . They sleep in the open air, and keep themselves warm with their plaids and their whisky."[19] Sporting the symbols of Highland identity—the philabeg, plaids, and whisky—the Bhutanese exhibit manly virtues of resilience and courage. Bogle imagines that they express themselves with "all that Loftiness and Sublimity of Stile used by Ossian, or any other hilly writer"; the final phrase casually links topography and literature in a generalizing move typical of the Enlightenment habit of cultural comparison.[20]

Significantly, the Bhutanese do not conform to the paradigm of barbarism. In Bogle's account, the country is well policed, and although rebellions are frequent, armed uprisings guarantee the people's rights rather than threaten the polity. Writing to his father, Bogle notes:

So far from that Barbarism which with transalpine Arrogance is too often considered as the Lot of every Nation unknown to Europeans: I found a little State governed by a regular and strict Police, independent by the Situation of the Country, and subject to an elective Government, which though absolute was checked by the free Spirit of the People, unawed by Mercenary Troops, and apt to rebell when treated with Oppression. The Inhabitants, living in a Country where a Subsistence is with Difficulty obtained; with little Money, with less Ambition; bartering the different Necessaries of Life, uncorrupted by Trade, or an Intercourse with Strangers and under a strong Sense of Religion, are industrious, faithful, hospitable, honest, grateful, and brave.[21]

In Bhutan the attractions of primitivism—a mountain kingdom untouched by modern commercial greed—are united with the rule of law and an elective government. Significantly, Bogle completely elides his own role as trade emissary, apparently failing to see the disruptive implications of his presence for this Rousseauesque idyll.

For Bogle, as for Adam Ferguson, to condemn the unknown as barbaric was a manifestation of cultural arrogance.[22] Ferguson used the term *barbaric* to denote warlike societies and despotic regimes although, unlike many of his contemporaries, Ferguson found domestic virtues of hospitality and kindness among barbarians.[23] However, the power of the Lama among the Tartars is cited in Ferguson's "Essay on the History of Civil Society" as an example of the "despotism and absolute slavery" that barbarians are subjected to by superstition.[24] Throughout his writing, Bogle contests the notion of the Tartars as barbaric and celebrates the authority of the Lama as pacific and humane. In a letter to his friend William Scott, Bogle describes the chess games he enjoys with visiting Tartar opponents (who confer on every move) and speculates that the game might have a Tartar rather than Trojan origin: "Let no man say they are too rude and too stupid a People to find out so ingenious a Game. If I may judge by those I have seen and by what I have learnt they merit a very different Character. They are merry, acute, good humoured and possess that plainness and honesty of manners which I prize before all others. But they are to be reckoned Barbarians by us upstart sons of three Hundred Years because they know nothing of Greek and Latin, of Painting and Sculpture, and are ignorant of all those frivolous Arts which 'occupy and distinguish polished Nations.'"[25] Compared to the manly sincerity and antiquity of the Tartars, Europeans appear as affected parvenus. Contemporary European art is lightweight, and even the classics, those great cultural touchstones, are demoted to mere local significance. The attack on European refinement, semiserious though it is, challenges the value placed on the polite arts by writers like David Hume. For Hume, the spread of refinement was determined by the growth of commerce. Yet in this passage Bogle seems to resist this connection, once again effacing his own role as trade envoy.

The notion of European civility is most extensively questioned in a long letter to William Richardson in Glasgow. To write to his academic friend, Bogle adopts a wide-ranging historical view—one indebted as much to Voltaire in its criticism of European cruelty, as to Rousseau in its denunciation of luxury and idealization of the simple life. The discussion begins with the suggestion that it is the so-called Christians who are the true barbarians:

> I confess the more I see of what our European arrogance is pleased to stile the Barbar-
> ian Nations, the more I envy their Simplicity of Manners and that Contentment which ac-
> companies it. But these forsooth are involved in darkness and ignorance and not to be
> compared to us. "We are destined to rule and command; they to serve and obey"—I will
> allow that Europeans have carried their Arms into almost every Corner of the Earth, and
> that their restless Ambition or rather insatiable Avarice has disturbed the Peace of
> Mankind. That Nations professing a Religion which inculcates Humanity and Mercy, and
> distinguished by the Name of civilized, have committed Crimes and inflicted Calamities
> on their Fellow Creatures which Alexander, the Romans, or the barbarous Tamerlane
> would have shuddered at the Thought of . . . The Inhabitants of most of the West India Is-
> lands were extirpated before we became masters of them; but how many Thousands of
> People are doomed to Slavery and Death that we may drink Sugar with our Tea or take
> Snuff? The Dutch India Company for the sake of Cinnamon & Cloves have imposed the
> yoke of misery upon Numbers of States, and the English—but I will say nothing upon that
> Subject.[26]

Before he takes refuge in silence, Bogle alludes to the offenses of his own employer, the English East India Company. The refusal to speak is perhaps as much an anticipation of censorship—letters sent by company packet were subject to official scrutiny—as a rhetorical ploy. The silence is ambiguous; it seems to imply both Bogle's professional reticence and the indescribable extent of British crimes. Certainly Bogle is more forthcoming in condemning slavery; what he does not mention, however, is that much of his own family's wealth derived from slavery. The Bogle family was involved in the production of two of the luxury goods mentioned: tobacco (the main ingredient of snuff) and sugar. The Virginia tobacco that his father imported was partly cultivated by slave labor, and George's eldest brother, Robert, was the manager of a slave-worked sugar plantation in Grenada. But on the issue of slavery, as on so many others, Bogle remains elusive and contradictory; in another letter, he congratulates his brother on the flourishing state of the plantation.[27] It would be naïve to seek for consistency in a collection of letters where the correspondent's role shifts to suit each addressee, but Bogle is notably protean.[28]

The letter to Richardson continues with an extended condemnation of the pursuit of wealth:

> But if this Lust for Riches gives Birth to a thousand imaginary Evils which Providence never designed; if it tends to stiffle many of the most natural and laudable Passions of the Soul; if a large Proportion of the People are forced to lead a life of Celibacy because they are unable to support a Wife and Family in that Pomp and Ostentation which Vanity prescribes; if they are to be banished their Freinds, & home and have to pass many years in a joyless Industry and an inhospitable Climate; if all our Discoveries and Conquests, instead of contributing to the welfare of Mankind, serve only to render them miserable; if our Name which is known throughout the World is attended with the Curses of Nations, if our standing Armies, and our Improvements in War impose intollerable Burdens upon the Inhabitants; let the People of Europe return to their former rude State and learn from Barbarians to be happy. Let them live in Tents like the Calmucks [Tartars]. Let them feed on the Flesh and Milk of their Flocks, on the Deer which their Arrow has slain. Surrounded by their Families and their Friends, let them pass the Day in Hunting and the Night in dancing and merriment, and let Age steal on free from Care and free from Ambitions.[29]

Bogle transposes Rousseau's account of the evils of luxury in the *Discours sur l'origine de l'inégalité* to a colonial setting.[30] But with its insistently repeated "ifs," the condemnation of colonialism remains hypothetical. The passage builds to a great rhetorical climax where the only possible solution is a reversion to the nomadic life of the Tartars. Yet, just as Rousseau did not literally propose a return to nature, as Peter France has noted, so Bogle's vision of a pastoral Europe remains a grand rhetorical flourish.[31]

The many inconsistencies, silences, and elisions that we have traced through Bogle's writing point to the tensions inherent in his situation, to the collision between Bogle's mercantile and intellectual pursuits. He is a servant of the East India Company sent to establish trade links with Rousseau's idyll. These contradictions are at their most acute when Bogle is about to leave Tibet. In March 1775, he wrote to his sister Elizabeth of his life in Tibet, representing it as a "fairy dream" spent "without Business." Bogle concludes with a valedictory address to the Tibetans, possibly drawing on the Johnsonian trope of an enclosed Happy Valley: "Farewell ye honest and simple People. May ye long enjoy that Happiness which is denied to more polished Nations; and while they are engaged in the endless pursuits of avarice and ambition, defended by your barren mountains, may ye continue to live in Peace and Contentment, and know no wants but those of nature."[32] The speech of farewell is particularly important because, reprinted in Clements Markham's 1876 edition of Bogle's journal, it became one of the earliest sources for the notion of Tibet as an unspoiled mountain fastness, one of the origins of the myth of

Shangri-La.[33] However, Bogle had earlier reported to Calcutta on the demand for European goods, including firearms, in the area. The mountains that Bogle mentions as defending the region from the malign influence of "more polished nations" figure in Bogle's official "Observations on the proper mode of attacking Bhutan" as obstacles to supplying a British invading force.[34] There is perhaps a recognition that, even at its inception, this vision of Tibet is already obsolete in the use of the archaic "ye." Primitivism is of course inherently nostalgic, its end is always already spelled out, but in this case, the agent of its demise is the writer himself. Bogle's predicament reflects what Peter France has identified as a central paradox of the Enlightenment—that a modern commercial society should be beguiled by myths of ancient simplicity.[35]

The Lama

It is striking that the figure of the Panchen Lama does not readily fit the model of primitivism established for his compatriots. In a strategy familiar from many accounts of noble non-Europeans, the Lama is distinguished from the people by virtue of his rank. Bogle repeatedly insists that previous European missionaries and travel writers have misrepresented the lamas of Tibet. His main target was the Scottish doctor and traveler, John Bell, who, like Bogle, originated from just outside Glasgow. Bell accompanied a Russian embassy sent by Peter the Great to the Kangxi Emperor in 1719–22, traveling overland from St. Petersburg through Siberia and Mongolia to Peking. His *Travels from St. Petersburg* was published in 1763 by the Foulis Press, one of the central institutions of Glasgow's cultural life. Bell includes a description of the process of identifying a reincarnated lama and briefly mentions the Panchen Lama. According to Bell, lamas are "little better than shamans of superior dignity," and shamans are "a parcel of jugglers, who impose on the ignorant and the vulgar."[36] Bogle cautions his father against Bell: "The disrespectful manner . . . in which he [Bell], and most Writers, speak of the Lamas, appears to me highly unjust: and I may, like Lady Mary Wortley Montague, pretend to Advantages, which no traveller before me ever possessed."[37] In contesting Bell's account, Bogle engages in a specifically Scottish dispute, here claiming the authority of the eyewitness. By allying himself with Wortley Montagu, Bogle suggests the view of one who is admitted to prohibited spaces and cross-cultural intimacies. This feminized position allows for the possibility of conversation, admiration, and exchange.

Bogle continues the letter to his father with an account of the qualities of the Panchen Lama (here called the Teshoo Lama):

> In judging a Man's Knowledge and Abilities, it may be necessary to consider the Age
> and Country in which he lived. A Lycurgus or a Solon are justly called wise, although they

were ignorant of all those Arts, and all that Learning, with which Printing and Geography have deluged the world. In this light Teshoo Lama will appear to be endowed with very superior Parts, and an enlarged Mind. He is well acquainted with the state of China, of all the different Countries of Tartary, and also of Hindostan. He has the more Merit in this knowledge, on account of the Difficulty of acquiring it. As there are no Books from which he can derive this Information, he entertains Facquiers and Pilgrimes from all Quarters, and collects an Account of different Countries from them. He is said to be well acquainted with the learning of the Hindoos. He is entirely Master of his own Affairs, he writes and dictates Letters; he sees everybody himself; and gives a ready answer to all Representations that are made to him. In conversation he is extremely affable and entertaining. He is very charitable and generous. He is humane to his People, and employs all his Authority in settling the Quarrels which arise, not only in this Country, but in the Neighbouring States. On all these Accounts he is universally beloved, and is generally allowed to be the best, and most noble Lama, that Thibet has ever produced.[38]

By suggesting a parallel with Lycurgus and Solon, both types of the wise legislator, Bogle insists on the Lama's character as temporal ruler rather than religious hierarch. It is notable that the same classical sages feature in Adam Ferguson's discussion of civil liberty. Ferguson suggests that these two "heroes of political society" would never have achieved fame among a warlike people like the Tartars.[39] By contrast, Bogle's account demonstrates Tartar reverence for a pacific statesman. The classical analogy may transport the Lama to ancient times, but Bogle also stresses the Lama's contemporaneity. Far from being trapped in an archaic world, the Lama is very much au courant. Always hungry for intelligence, always ready to intervene, he is a prominent player in the region's political affairs.

The Lama was eager to establish contact not only with the British but with other neighboring powers. At the time of Bogle's mission, the Lama was also entertaining envoys from the court of Cheyt Singh, the Raja of Benares. The Lama's overtures to the East India Company were in part an assertion of Tibetan independence from China. The Manchu emperor, although acknowledging the spiritual authority of the Panchen Lama, stationed Chinese *ambans*, or residents, at Lhasa to monitor the direction of Tibetan policy. It is clear that these ambans and Bogle viewed each other with mutual distrust. The Lama may also have had religious motives for cultivating the British. For the Lama, India was the holy land of Buddhism, the source of Tibet's religion, literature, and culture. He sent monks to visit Indian sacred sites and negotiated with Bogle for the gift of a plot of land to establish a monastery in Calcutta, a permanent testimony to the alliance between the two powers.

Bogle, of course, shared the Lama's desire for intelligence. For both parties, the mission was an information-gathering exercise. While Bogle was accumulating materials on Tibet, the Lama requested that Bogle compile an account of Europe. To write the European history, Bogle suggests that he had to undertake a remarkable feat of cross-cultural identification. He observes: "I had to fancy myself a Tibetan, and then put down the things which I imagined would strike him."[40] The draft account is, however, considerably more partial than this implies. The French are given short shrift: the people are subjected to absolute rule, oppressive taxation, and a corrupt legal system; they are more polite than the British but showy and insincere. The much longer catalogue of British institutions, manners, arts, and sciences includes descriptions of the judicial system, the navy, Britain's conduct in war (honorable), the provision of stage coaches, popular entertainment, the theater (with a detailed summary of the plot of Otway's *Venice Preserved*), the practice of medicine, and the institution of poor houses. It also contains a paragraph on the "bad" customs of Britain: the prevalence of drunkenness and gambling, the large number of capital offences, and a practice which, Bogle writes, "although I am affraid to mention I must not conceal"—that of dueling. In this concern for a custom involving loss of life, Bogle may indeed be attempting to adopt a Tibetan-Buddhist perspective.[41]

Sometimes British patriot, sometimes Tibetan-influenced critic, Bogle occupies a number of shifting subject positions. There are moments when he turns from Tibetan institutions to interrogate British practice, as for instance in the account of Tibetan law: "If a Man kills his Slave it is a great Crime if another Man kills him it is a small one . . . The Reason for this arises from more generous Principles than what are to be found either in the Law of England or its West India Plantations."[42] At other times Bogle embraces a kind of cultural relativism, suggesting, for example, that to judge any system of government or jurisprudence, one must attend to the particular genius of the people.[43] Translated into practical terms, this cultural relativism is manifested as respect for local custom. In his journal, Bogle alludes to that maxim of appropriate conduct, "I always like to do at Rome as they do at Rome," and writes to his sister Martha of his delight in discarding tight, impractical European clothes for the comfort and warmth of Bhutanese and Tibetan robes.[44]

It was in Bhutanese dress that Bogle chose to pose for a painting by the Calcutta artist, Tilly Kettle, commemorating the alliance with the Panchen Lama (ca. 1775) (fig. 10.1). The scene depicts the Lama's reception of Bogle. At the focal point of the painting, the cross-legged Lama accepts a ceremonial white scarf (*khatag*), one hand receptively outstretched, the other holding a rosary, the sign of his religious character. The formality of the scene is undercut by the presence of the two figures sitting on the ground who, as Michael Aris has noted, are incongruously puffing on pipes.[45] No one would have actually smoked in the Lama's presence, but the informality of this pair sug-

Figure 10.1. [Tilly Kettle], *The Teschu Lama (d. 1780) Giving Audience* (ca. 1775). Courtesy of the Royal Collection © 2001, Her Majesty Queen Elizabeth II.

gests those qualities that Bogle associated with the Tibetans in general: unaffected good humor and jovial bonhomie. Bogle is represented on the left in front of a window opening out onto a view of romantic, rugged mountains (his position perhaps signaling his status as Himalayan traveler). Strikingly, he is wearing Bhutanese robes and is bare-legged. Although the green and cream of his robes differentiate Bogle from the other figures clad in various shades of orange and brown, his dress clearly suggests a cultural identification. The painting is now in the royal collection and is thought to have been presented by Hastings to George III, a sign of the political significance attributed to the alliance between Bogle and the Panchen Lama.

Cultural cross-dressing is a recurrent feature of Bogle's letters to female correspondents. Writing to his sister Martha, Bogle describes his dress in sensuous detail: "I wear a Sattin Night Gown lined with Siberian Fox Skins, a Cap lined with Sable, and a pair of Russian Red Leather Boots—What with this and a pair of Whiskers you would hardly know me."[46] Playfully turning himself into a spectacle of Otherness, Bogle both addresses and contains the anxiety of cultural alienation. With male correspondents, Bogle performs a similar feat, teasingly suggesting that the Lama has so impressed him that he is tempted to convert: "It requires all my strong Knoxical orthodoxy to prevent me from becoming one of his votaries."[47] Elsewhere, the identification with the Lama's devotees draws on the language of sensibility. Viewing a rapturous public reception of the Lama, for instance, Bogle observes in his journal, "One catches affection by Sympathy, and I could not help, in some measure, feeling the same Emotions with the Lama's votaries."[48] Bogle represents his own response as heartfelt, an almost involuntary access of emotion. As the time for Bogle's departure approaches, a final audience with the Lama is worked into a sentimental farewell scene: "I never could reconcile myself to taking a last leave of anybody; and what from the Lama's pleasant and amiable character, what from the many favours and civilities he had shown me, I could not help being particularly affected. He observed it, and in order to cheer me mentioned his hopes of seeing me again. He threw a handkerchief about my neck, put his hand upon my head, and I retired."[49] While the cultivation of harmonious relations is obviously part of the diplomat's role, Bogle turns the Lama into a sentimental friend.

The story of friendship may stand in place of the unrealized "mutual and equal communication of trade" that it was Bogle's mission to initiate between Bengal and Tibet.[50] The route through Bhutan, although open to Indian merchants, remained closed to East India Company servants. Bogle attributed this restriction to the Bhutanese suspicion of British motives and fear of Chinese disapproval. In the Panchen Lama, Bogle saw a possible future mediator between the company and the Emperor of China. Five years later, the Lama visited Peking and was to arrange a passport for Bogle to join him to conduct negotiations with the Chinese authorities, but these plans came to nothing. The Lama succumbed to smallpox at Peking and died there in 1780, and Bogle himself died in Calcutta the following year. The narrative of friendship between Bogle and the Lama was all that remained of the proposed trade agreement between the East India Company and Tibet. As Mary Louise Pratt has observed in her discussion of sentimental travel writing, "[r]eciprocity has always been capitalism's ideology of itself . . . While doing away with reciprocity as the basis for social interaction, capitalism retains it as one of the stories it tells about itself."[51]

CHAPTER ELEVEN

The English Garden Conversation Piece in India

Beth Fowkes Tobin

Johann Zoffany's painting of Warren Hastings and his wife belongs to a genre known as the conversation piece, specifically the outdoor or garden conversation piece (fig. 11.1). Enormously popular with the English gentry, especially in the mid–eighteenth century, the garden conversation piece was also a favorite with British colonial officials in India in the last decades of the century. Painted in Bengal in the mid-1780s, this conversation piece of Hastings and his wife standing on the parklike lawn of his Alipore house performs ideological work around the issues of land, labor, and colonialism, utilizing a particular visual and verbal discourse that had been developed domestically in Britain and then was transferred to India. I begin by reviewing some of the pictorial conventions of the traditional English garden conversation piece, and I then examine colonial garden conversation pieces in a global context, in particular those painted in India by Johan Zoffany and Arthur William Devis, son of Arthur Devis, himself a prolific painter of conversation pieces.

The Traditional Conversation Piece

Typical of the garden conversation piece is the depiction of the family on the grounds, usually the gardens or parkland, of their estate; sometimes glimpsed in the dis-

Figure 11.1. Johann Zoffany, *Mr and Mrs Warren Hastings* (1783–87). Courtesy of Victoria Memorial Hall, Calcutta.

tance is the family's palatial country house (fig. 11.2). In terms of subject matter, the garden conversation piece lies somewhere between two distinct genres: the conversation piece and the country house portrait. The conversation piece depicts family members and/or friends in domestic interiors or outdoors on terraces, lawns, and pleasure grounds of estate parkland. Ronald Paulson suggests that the indoor conversation was "more conducive to the portrayal of a middle-class family and exact socio-personal definition," while the outdoor conversation "displays an aristocratic family, garden imagery, and symbolism relating to art and nature."[1] A prolific midcentury producer of family portraiture, Arthur Devis painted both indoor and outdoor conversation pieces as well as country house portraits and garden views for his gentry clients.[2] Devis employed a somewhat archaic style that emphasized "clarity of detail" over expression of personality. The key to his success was his ability to define his patrons in terms of their possessions—houses, gardens, horses, dogs, children, and wives—for, as Paulson suggests, the "thrust" of the conversation was social and economic definition.[3]

The garden conversation may also be understood as a subgenre of the country house portrait. Indeed, art and architectural historian John Harris regards the garden conversation, which grew out of owners taking delight in being represented in their gar-

Figure 11.2. Arthur Devis, British, 1712–1787, *Thomas Lister and His Family* (1740–41), oil on canvas (115.1 × 103.8 cm). Gift of Emily Crane Chadbourne, 1951.203. Photograph © 2001, The Art Institute of Chicago. All Rights Reserved.

dens, as "never more than a minor vehicle for the display of the country house or garden."[4] Garden conversation pieces share with country house portraits and estate portraiture a concern with the politics of the visual representation of landownership. Portraits of landed families in the gardens and parklands of their country houses were painted to celebrate, commemorate, and legitimate a family's exclusive possession of a landed estate. In Arthur Devis's *Thomas Lister and His Family* (1740–41) (see fig. 11.2), the smooth lawns and parkland woods indicate Lister's mastery over the terrain that extends beyond the house and garden gate to the estate and agrarian community. Like country house portraiture, garden conversation pieces performed important ideological work in that they underscored the connection between land and lineage, a connection that was crucial to the eighteenth-century construction of social and economic elites based on dynastic landowning families.

    I argue here that the country house portrait and the garden view attempted to resolve on an aesthetic level the political, economic, and moral tensions aroused by the privatization of English property during the eighteenth century. These genres provided pleasing visual resolutions to class antagonisms produced by the enclosure of common land, the engrossment of farmland, the dispossession of the peasant-occupier, and the pauperization of the small farmer. Undergirding these changes in property relations was the redefinition of land as a commodity and the reconstitution of landholding as mere legal possession. Prior to this movement to intensify the privatization of property, landholding involved a complex set of moral, social, and economic relations between the lord of the manor and his dependents, who included relatives, servants, tenants, villagers, peasants, and wage laborers. Landholding could not be reduced to ownership—the possession of a commodity—for, as Nigel Everett argues, landholding was, at least ideally and in the minds of a disappearing tradition of "Tory" landlords, an affective relation to the land and people of the estate community, one that was based on tradition, local custom, and inherited responsibilities.[5]

This change in property relations from a moral to a political economy surfaces in country house portraiture and garden views in the form of alienation.[6] According to Ann Bermingham, the garden conversation piece celebrates the "self-identity of the proprietor and property" but also "betrays an alienation" between the proprietor and his property.[7] This alienation is inherent to private property, the foundation of which is the transformation of land into a commodity. When land is reduced to a commodity, it is shorn of all historical, social, cultural, and affective ties that encumber property and reduce its ability to circulate freely on the market. The new capitalist definition of property rights permitted landowners to do what they liked with their land—to enclose, to drain, to plant, and to build—without regarding traditional feudal obligations or rights.[8] Strict game laws were passed to protect the landowners' hunting and shooting privileges, and enclosure acts restricted access to land that had supported traditional activities such as gleaning, grazing, and gathering that were crucial to the well-being of small farmers and landless agricultural laborers. By the mid–eighteenth century, landowners exerted an unprecedented control over their property, using scientific agriculture and landscape design to force the land (and its inhabitants) to conform to their needs and desires.

Privatizing their land and transforming it into a discrete physical commodity were strategies the gentry used to dispossess the yeomanry and the laboring poor. But in erasing customary and traditional relations to land, the gentry also undermined their own affective and social relations to the land. In an eagerness to rid themselves of feudal-like encumbrances (the cottager's right to glean the fields and to forage for dead wood, for instance) and to limit access to their land with the enclosure acts and punitive game laws, landowners, in privatizing their property, also stripped it of historical and cultural meaning. The peasantry's customary ties to the land were erased as well as the gentry's customary relations to their land, which included the obligation to superintend the estate community, exert moral authority over cottage and village life, and perform disinterested acts of charity with an expectation of receiving gratitude and respect in return. Possessing private property stripped of its social and moral relations, landowners had to face the psychological and ideological consequences of possessing a commodity rather than a legacy or heritage. While it is entirely possible that many landholders, especially those of the Whig oligarchy, welcomed with enthusiasm the redefinition of property and the privatization and commodification of land, I believe that some landowners were anxious, even defensive about the implications of the privatization of property. They dealt with this anxiety, in part, on the visual level by commissioning various kinds of paintings—country house portraits, garden views, estate portraiture, sporting art—that would reassert an organic relation between landholders and their land and articulate a sense of historical and traditional connection with their property.

The traditional country house portrait and the garden conversation piece usually dealt with these class tensions by referring to the agrarian landscape with a view of a harvest scene, a field dotted with cattle, or a church spire of a distant village. These references to a world beyond the gates suggest that the country house and its gardens were a part of a larger organic community, participating in what Nigel Everett has called the "Tory view of landscape," an ethos that stressed the landed's responsibility to their communities, their paternal roles as custodians of the agrarian landscape and as superintendents of the rural community. Jan Siberechts's *Bifrons Park*, a country house portrait, and Paul Sandby's *Hackwood Park*, an estate portrait, portray landowners as superintendents of an organic community that includes the poorest and least privileged members while asserting the landlord's right to govern and to order the rural moral and political economy.[9] The country house portrait and the estate portrait, like the garden conversation piece, assert the power of the landed classes to rule the rural scene, but such pictures soften this expression of power by alluding to an organic community knit together by reciprocal ties of duty and deference. Retaining the visual vestiges of a quasi-feudal communal life, country house portraits, estate portraiture, and garden views present an idealized version of the country—bountiful harvests, happy and industrious peasants, and the comforts of village life—that suppresses the brutal economic reality of capitalized agriculture and the commodification of land.

Colonial Garden Conversations

Garden conversation pieces that portray the Anglo-Indian equivalent of country houses and their owners sitting in English-style parkland grew in popularity when artists such as Johann Zoffany and Arthur William Devis (the elder Devis's son) arrived in India in the 1780s and 1790s (fig. 11.3).[10] Zoffany and Devis produced outdoor conversation pieces for their Anglo-Indian patrons, who were prosperous British colonial

Figure 11.3. Arthur William Devis, *Mr and Mrs Fraser* (ca. 1785–90). Courtesy of the Yale Center for British Art, Paul Mellon Collection.

officials eager to establish their credentials as a ruling elite. Drawing on familiar forms of visual imagery associated with social status and political power, company employees chose to be portrayed as if they were landed gentry. In suggesting organic and hereditary ties to land, the garden imagery of the outdoor conversation piece lent a landed pedigree to these company employees. In addition to giving colonial officials a means by which to augment their social status, the garden conversation piece also provided them with a way to express and resolve on a visual level some of the tensions produced by living in a conquered land. Because Anglo-Indians used the garden conversation piece for reasons both similar and dissimilar to their English counterparts at home, my discussion of the colonial garden conversation piece will attend to ways it resembles and diverges from the traditional conversation piece, focusing on the treatment of house and grounds as well as the portrayal of family members and servants.

While traditional estate portraits depict an agrarian landscape, suggesting that the country house and its environs are part of a larger organic community, the garden view focuses on the gardens and grounds of the country house, making only slight reference to what lies beyond the garden gate. However, because of its association with other forms of estate portraiture, the garden conversation, though its scope was limited to the house's grounds, could imply an estate beyond the boundary. In this way, the garden conversation piece could confer on its patrons a social status beyond their material conditions. For East India Company officials, the garden conversation piece was the perfect pictorial medium in which to figure themselves as an elite equivalent to the landed gentry back home. It is not accidental that such country house and garden views became quite popular in India at the end of the century, long after the midcentury affection for such paintings had subsided in England. What was so attractive about garden views to this colonial elite was that the genre, in addition to gentrifying company employees, could express for them in familiar, almost comforting visual terms their very complicated and rather fraught relations with India, its people, and the land.

Johann Zoffany's *Mr and Mrs Warren Hastings* captures the social ambitions of the Anglo-Indian community as well as the contradictions surrounding landholding under colonial rule (see fig. 11.1). In its representation of what appears to be a Palladian mansion set in parkland, this painting partakes of the tradition of country house portraiture. Its pictorial conventions allude to Tory ideas about landholding as a form of social responsibility based on local, inherited, and reciprocal ties of duty and obligation. Standing in the foreground with a vast lawn stretching behind him, Hastings poses with his wife and her maid as if he were a member of the landed gentry and the mansion behind him were a manor house. In figuring himself as a country gentleman, Hastings lay claim to a heritage and tradition that was not exactly his. In fact, he became, for many of his contemporaries such as Edmund Burke, the antithesis of the English paternal ideal. To them he was the quintessential nabob—the corrupt, rapacious, wealthy figure often portrayed in plays, novels, poems, and prints either as a gauche, naïve, upstart outsider, or as a degenerate and despicable adventurer, whose presence could endanger the morals and manners of traditional English society.[11]

Like all garden conversation pieces, Zoffany's painting of Hastings defines the man in terms of his possessions: his property, his house, his wife, and his dependents. However, unlike the elder Devis's painting of Thomas Lister, who asserts his command over the people and things that define him, Zoffany's painting of Hastings is so full of contradictions that the formal codes and visual idioms of the conversation piece cannot quite contain them. The contradictions at work in this painting are those that Edmund Burke identified in his indictment of Warren Hastings for high crimes and misdemeanors against the Indian people. Though we must recognize that Burke was biased and had been influenced by Philip Francis, Hastings's enemy on the Supreme Council of Bengal, Burke rightly portrayed Hastings as the enemy to traditional Indian and English landholding practices.[12] According to Burke, Hastings had violated the English code of gentlemanly conduct when he employed harsh techniques and corrupt agents to collect revenues for the East India Company. Hastings's quest for revenues was productive of, in Burke's famously inflated rhetoric, "arbitrary, illegal, unjust, and tyrannical Acts," which were responsible for the "Destruction, Devastation, Oppression, and Ruin" of the provinces of Bengal, Bihar, and Benares.[13]

Of the many charges of corruption that Burke and the managers of this impeachment trial lodged against Hastings, most pertinent to our discussion are those surrounding Hastings's methods of revenue collection.[14] Burke accused Hastings of setting the revenues too high considering the condition of the land in Bengal and Bihar, which had been ravaged by warfare, famine, and depopulation in the years previous to Hastings's taking office as governor-general. He accused Hastings of instituting a system of land tenure that promoted rack renting, a practice with which Burke, as an Irishman, was well acquainted. Burke translated the remnants of the Mughal system of tribute collection into the more familiar language of British landholding practices with phrases such as "quit rents" and "ground rents" (6:189), turning zamindars into English country squires: "Zemindars have a perpetual Interest in the country; that their Inheritance could not be taken from them; that they are the Proprietors; that the Lands are their Estates, and their Inheritance; that from a long Continuance of the Lands in their Families, it was to be concluded . . . that solid advantages might be expected from continuing the Lands under the Management of those who have a natural and perpetual Interest in their Prosperity" (6:190). By figuring zamindars as country gentlemen whose relation to property is one of heritage and attachment, Burke had hoped to create sympathy for the zamindars in his audience, the House of Lords, and to stir up resentment against Hastings for his dispossession of the zamindars. Hastings's policies encouraged strangers and adventurers instead of hereditary landlords, and short-term leases instead of "perpetual interest"; both techniques were aimed at extracting the maximum revenues from the land in a short amount of time without providing assurances that any of those revenues would be reinvested in the economy from which it was extracted. (Again, the ghost of Anglo-Irish landholding practices haunts Burke's description of the events in Bengal.) According to Ranajit Guha, Hastings's policy of "revenue farming" did indeed undermine native landowning elites and hereditary property rights by auctioning "estates at the end of each term of settlement" and farming "them out to the highest bidders for leases not extending beyond five years."[15] Francis's critique of Hastings's system was, as Guha explains, "that a lack of permanence was inherent in the farming system itself. The farmers had no abiding interest in the lands settled with them; their leases were far too short to permit this; and all that was achieved in this process was the expropriation of zamindars of long standing. In short, the consequence of revenue farming was the subversion of property and there could be no form of instability more dangerous than this."[16]

For Hastings to commission a portrait of himself as if he were a gentleman visiting his country estate seems ironic given Francis's and Burke's charges against him as a destroyer of hereditary property. Hastings represented to country Tories and even some Whig landowners all that was wrong with the new "monied interest" and with returning "nabobs," whose wealth and ability to buy landed estates and seats in Parliament threatened the landed classes' control over government.[17] Zoffany's portrait was painted before the impeachment trial and Burke's attack on Hastings as the enemy of tradition, but well after Hastings's institution of land redistribution and rapacious revenue collecting policies. That Hastings allowed or even encouraged Zoffany to employ the visual trope of estate parkland to represent this governor-general of Bengal must have seemed outrageous, even scandalous, in its assertion of hereditary landed status, especially to someone like Philip Francis.

Zoffany's treatment of shrubbery in *Mr and Mrs Hastings* raises questions concerning affective and historical ties to land. Most traditional garden conversation pieces contain judiciously placed and ideologically resonant trees that convey ideas about a sitter's roots in an ancient, organic community.[18] Zoffany's use of trees in this picture is reminiscent of his handling of vegetation in another of his paintings, *The Drummond Family,* which, as Ronald Paulson has suggested, conveys a sense of the timeless, organic relation between land and family (fig. 11.4). In fact, Paulson's reading of the Drummond painting, in stressing the placement of the children around the "enormous old tree, signifying the continuity of the generations," relies on Edmund Burke's idea of society as "a carefully balanced whole which embodies the accumulated wisdom of the past."[19] However, the tree behind the Hastings group is not an oak or an elm, as in *The Drummond Family;* it is a jackfruit tree, which produces pendulous and aromatic fruits, larger than human heads, that sprout from its trunk. This tropical tree does not carry with it the English associations of patriotism, family heritage, and traditional ties to place that an oak tree would have. Though the jackfruit tree works on a visual level, framing the figures, mimicking their upright posture, and offering a dark background with which to contrast and highlight Mrs. Hastings's white skin and Hastings's white breeches and waistcoat, it thwarts the chain of associations that trees usually set into motion in conventional outdoor conversation pieces. It unsettles the formal correspondences that would link the figure to the landscape setting, and, in fact, highlights the "alien" quality of this landscape, thereby undercutting any allusion to affective, historical, or organic ties to this land.

An extensive vista in an outdoor conversation piece usually implies mastery over terrain and people subject to the landowners' authority. For instance, in Gainsborough's

Figure 11.4. Johann Zoffany, *The Drummond Family* (ca. 1769). Courtesy of the Yale Center for British Art, Paul Mellon Collection.

Mr and Mrs Andrews, Mr. Andrews, who has just returned from a day of shooting, towers over his demure wife and demonstrates his power over his land which has benefited from the latest agricultural innovations.[20] His dog stands obediently at his feet, ready for his commands. Unlike Andrews, Hastings does not appear to be in control of the scene portrayed. Rather, he seems to be showing his wife their home, as if it were a gift he was bestowing on her. His extended arm points in the direction of the house, and his hat in hand, a sign of deference, implies that all that stands behind him is hers. His eyes look to her face for approval, and his right hand clasps hers in an unusual gesture of intimacy. In most conversation pieces, the husband stands while his wife sits, or if he sits, he is the central figure; such placements stress his authority within the family and establish gender and generational hierarchies. This convention is subtly overturned with Hastings's upward glance into his wife's face and tender grasp of her hand. Her elongated body, her height—at least as tall or taller than her husband—and her placement between her maid and her husband make her the apex of a slight triangle, suggesting that her power derives from being the focus of her husband's attentions.

Instead of this painting establishing Hastings as lord of the manor, as is the case with most garden conversation pieces, *Mr and Mrs Warren Hastings* suggests that Marian Hastings has control over her husband's affections and can extract from him such tributes as the house behind him. Indeed, Hastings's affection for his wife was well known.

As Mildred Archer reports, "adored by Hastings who lavished love and money on her, Marian had a passion for opulent and eccentric dresses not wholly relished by Calcutta gossip."[21] One of her satin riding habits, trimmed with pearls and diamonds, was said by contemporaries to be worth between twenty-five and thirty thousand pounds sterling. Such gossip hints at Hastings's enormous expenditures, which aroused suspicions, especially in critics such as Burke, about his abusing the perquisites of his office; in particular Hastings purportedly was extracting huge sums of money in the form of gifts or unpaid loans from Muslim and Hindu rulers and landowners. Zoffany's treatment of Mr. and Mrs. Hastings provides just enough detail to encourage speculations, which still linger, connecting Hastings's adoration of his wife with accusations against him of corruption.[22]

Employing the conventional features of garden conversation pieces to portray this couple, Zoffany produced an image that is deeply conflicted. The essence of country house portraiture and the garden view is the celebration of inherited property and the assertion of an organic relation between the proprietor and the property. The historical facts concerning Hastings contradict this cultural tradition: Hastings did not inherit the property in this portrait; there was no organic or traditional relation between him and the land, nor any reciprocal relation between him and the surrounding community. Money, not inheritance or tradition, was the foundation of his relation to this land, and money, for many eighteenth-century political philosophers, was "precarious and uncertain," the very opposite of Burke's notion of a "natural and perpetual Interest" in the land.[23] For Burke, all the solidity of property—weighted with tradition, anchored in the past—was lost when land became a commodity. Even for Adam Smith, promoter of the new political economy, land was the foundation of social and economic relations, the basis of true wealth and civic virtue; money was unstable because it was mobile and ultimately based on imaginary credit. Smith argued, as did Burke, that landowners, unlike merchants, had a "fixed and permanent interest in their country of residence" and a "permanent interest . . . in seeing that society is prosperous and well-governed."[24] With his policies of "revenue farming" and his own extravagant expenditures, Hastings represented someone who acted, in the words of clergyman Thomas Gisborne, in a "sordid and ungenerous manner" by putting his "private advantage" over the needs of the country he was charged with governing.[25] Hastings himself remarked that the company's policies "conflict with the interests of the Indian peoples who are subject to its authority."[26] Hastings's charge was to produce revenues for the company, and to achieve this he instituted revenue farming, which undermined hereditary property relations. For Hastings to be portrayed as if he were lord of the manor was insulting not only to Tory notions that linked landownership with social responsibility but also to traditional Mughal landholding practices.

Labor in Anglo-Indian Conversation Pieces

Having traced out some of the contradictions that inhere in Zoffany's representation of land in *Mr and Mrs Warren Hastings,* I would like to turn to the representation of Indians in Zoffany's as well as the younger Devis's conversation pieces portraying company officials. If, as Hastings implies, the goals of the East India Company necessarily conflicted with the welfare of the Indian people, then how, if at all, is this conflict represented in these portraits, most of which are filled with the figures of Indian servants and some with minor Indian officials and company employees? To understand the relationship between master and servant as represented in colonial conversation pieces, we must return again to the codes and pictorial conventions that traditional conversation pieces employ to depict agricultural as well as domestic labor.

Rarely are English servants depicted in traditional indoor or outdoor conversation pieces.[27] Though a huntsman holding the reins of a hunter occasionally appears in a sporting scene, very rarely do domestic servants—maids, footmen, butlers, housekeepers, messenger boys, scullery maids, or cooks—appear in the conversation piece, with the significant exception, however, of "black" servants, that is, servants from Africa, India, and the Caribbean. As literary critics and art historians have argued, it was quite fashionable in the earlier part of the century for the upper classes to be portrayed with a black servant, frequently a boy dressed in Oriental garb with a gold or silver collar about his neck. The Oriental costumes of black servants featured in paintings such as Kneller's *Duchess of Ormond* and Richardson's *Lady Mary Wortley Montagu* were not necessarily referring to new world slavery, but that of the Ottoman empire. The Orientalized black servant set into motion discourses that linked women's beauty and sexuality to international trade and imperialism through the trope of women's appetite for exotic luxury goods such as silk, brocade, sugar, coffee, chocolate, and tea. In addition to these associations of exotic commodities and imperial trade, the black servant later in the century referred more specifically to wealth derived from the West Indies. A conversation piece of Sir William Young and his family includes the figure of a black servant, a slave judging from his silver collar, to mark the Youngs' pride in their legacy as owners of West Indian sugar plantations.[28]

The inclusion of Indians as household servants in Anglo-Indian conversation pieces grew out of these visual conventions depicting the black servant, an emblem of colonial labor and imperial trade, in domestic scenes. In Zoffany's *Mr and Mrs Warren Hastings,* a servant, a young Indian woman attired in modest European dress, stands next to Mrs. Hastings and holds her feathered hat. The browns in the servant's dress offset the lustrous sheen of the satiny yellow of Mrs. Hastings's expensive gown. Marian Hastings, as consummate consumer of exotic luxury goods, is rendered fetishistically as the beneficiary of an excess of colonial labor.

Though colonial conversation pieces, which contain one or two black bodies, can be explained as an extension of conventions already established in traditional conversation pieces, the proliferation of Indian servants in several other paintings suggests an additional dynamic at work, one having to do, as Richard Leppert suggests, with representing a "microcosm of imperial order."[29] Though Zoffany's *Impey Family* is crowded with eleven Indians—four of whom are servants and others who, as musicians, are entertaining the five members of the Impey family—Sir Elijah Impey, chief justice of the high court in Calcutta, dominates the scene with his height and his physical command of space (fig. 11.5). Clearly under command of their British masters, Indian servants are depicted as nonthreatening, deferential, and dutiful with placid, still faces and empty distant looks in their eyes as if they have accepted this new regime of conquering masters.

Though the black body, if Orientalized and made decorative, could be incorporated into the representation of ruling elites, no such pictorial conventions existed within

Figure 11.5. Johann Zoffany, *The Impey Family Listening to Strolling Musicians* (ca. 1783–84). Private Collection. © Christie's Images, New York.

portraiture to aestheticize white domestic labor. This absence of white domestic labor in traditional conversation pieces is puzzling, but perhaps portraying the upper classes' triumph over their "own" people, celebrating their right to the working classes' labor, might have seemed inappropriate, unseemly, or even imprudent and provocative. Such images might have stressed rather than harmonized class divisions in England, revealing exploitative relations too openly. Or perhaps, as Nigel Everett implies, class-based feelings of disgust for the "common" people operated in the upper-classes' desire to erase the bodies of white servants.[30] However, georgic pictorial conventions enabled the representation of white labor as long as that labor was clearly marked as agricultural. For instance, in Siberechts's country house portrait of Bifrons Park, agricultural workers—reapers, plowmen, shepherds, milkmaids, haymakers, and gleaners—dot the landscape. As John Barrell and Michael Rosenthal have noted, the georgic landscape, peopled with industrious laborers, is a landscape invested with virtue.[31] If white servants were represented not as dots of color in an agricultural scene but as fully rendered individuals complete with facial expressions, these servants would lose their invisibility, their status as objects, and rise into subjecthood. Perhaps feelings of unease dictated the absence of white servants in conversation pieces—an unease that grew out of a recognition that representation and subjectivity are intertwined. Class hierarchies based on difference are threatened when objects become subjects. However, in conversation pieces containing black servants, difference is maintained through racialist and nationalist categories as well as visual traditions that relegate them to the realm of the decorative; for these reasons, their presence does not threaten colonial hierarchies in the same way that the depiction of white domestic servants could have threatened class hierarchies at home.

The absence or presence of white laborers in traditional country house and garden conversation pieces seems to be determined by whether the labor is performed indoors (absence) or outdoors (presence). Another causal factor seems to be the proximity of white laboring bodies to the landed sitters; the farther away they work, the more likely they are to be represented. With colonial conversation pieces, these dynamics are reversed: Indian domestic servants are abundantly present, while Indian agricultural laborers rarely appear. One obvious explanation for this absence is that most Anglo-Indian outdoor conversation pieces do not portray the landscape beyond the house and its grounds. Even in the few that contain extensive views beyond the garden, the panoramas do not include the figures of Indian laborers. For instance, Devis's *The Honorable William Monson and His Wife, Ann Debonnaire* contains, along with the Monson couple, an Indian man, clearly a servant, who stands at attention with a blank stare on his face, patiently holding his master's hat (fig. 11.6). Other than these three people, the landscape is empty; the expansive view stretching behind them across a lawn with a

Figure 11.6. Arthur William Devis, *The Honorable William Monson and His Wife, Ann Debon-naire* (ca. 1786). 47.29.16. Courtesy of Los Angeles County Museum of Art, William Randolph Hearst Collection. Photograph © 2001 Museum Associates/LACMA.

columned villa contains only a wide river with a small boat and the river's distant shores. Even when the garden can be identified as part of an estate, as is the case with *The Auriol and Dashwood Families,* a conversation piece that Archer places on John Prinsep's indigo plantation, no Indian labor other than domestic and bureaucratic is represented. Agrarian and even commercial Indian labor as well as Indian communities seem to be unrepresentable, at least within the conversation genre. With one exception, Devis's *William Dent with his Brother, John, and an Indian Landlord, Anand Narain,* the colonial conversation piece focused exclusively on the families and friends of the Anglo-Indian elite. Only those Indians who were structurally incorporated into British systems of command, such as household staff and company employees, were represented. British painters occasionally depicted an India beyond British circles. Both Zoffany and Devis did, in fact, draw and paint Indian life; Devis even began a large project of painting pictures of Indian occupations with the idea of producing a book of engravings that recorded Indian life and work.[32]

An explanation as to why Indian agrarian and commercial labor is rendered invisible in the Anglo-Indian estate portraiture and outdoor conversation pieces lies in Hastings's own formulations about the conflict of interests between the Indian people and the British Empire. In short, what was good for the East India Company was not good for the Indian people. During Hastings's tenure, there was little attempt to hide that the goal of the company was to extract as much wealth from India as possible. The British in India dominated through exploitation enforced by a police state and the military. Not yet developed was Cornwallis's institution of a supposedly disinterested bureaucracy nor the nineteenth century's imperialist ideology of the white man's burden, which would help to obscure the contradictions of a commercial entity, the East India Company, acting in a judicial and administrative capacity in India.[33] As Marshall contends, "in the last resort social justice was of less concern to the Company than the security of its revenue."[34]

If the exigencies of the East India Company dictated a conflict of interests with the Indian people, as Hastings maintained, then why were garden views and outdoor conversation pieces so popular with company officials? Though Zoffany and Devis represented Anglo-Indians through traditional genres that had been developed out of a need to resolve tensions surrounding landownership and domination of rural economies within Britain, they tended to restrict themselves to garden views, which were better suited than estate portraiture to the political reality of India. The garden view, with its narrow focus on the grounds of the mansion, avoided depicting a landscape that could not convey through Indian laboring figures the georgic virtue so often evoked in traditional country house and estate portraiture. In short, the garden view simultaneously implied through association but avoided representing what was impossible in India: the ideal of an organic, hierarchical, but mutually constitutive community, one based on reciprocity and shared goals. The Anglo-Indian ruling elite could not pretend, as had their counterparts in Britain, that they existed in some harmonious relation with the populace, nor did they gesture toward some shared past or refer to a future built on common goals. Company officials in India did not possess traditional practices or residual rituals that referred to the moral economy of a quasi-feudal past, which the gentry could call upon to temper or mystify the relations of exploitation that undergirded the English rural economy.

Why was the garden conversation piece so popular in British India? Why employ a genre laden with imagery that evokes organic ties to land and moral ties to a rural community? One reason, perhaps, was that the garden conversation provided Britons a visual vocabulary that articulated in familiar terms their mastery over an alien terrain. The discourse on English country life enabled them simultaneously to convey their mastery and to mystify their violent and exploitative relations with India. Even more importantly, perhaps, for its patrons was the kind of ideological functions that the garden conversation could perform around identity issues. The garden imagery of the outdoor conversation piece helped to obscure the mercantile and bureaucratic occupations of these employees of the East India Company. Finally, and most importantly, the garden conversation piece signaled their status as a ruling elite on a par with the landed gentry back home in Britain. Anglo-Indians, like their West Indian counterparts, always intended to return home, bringing enough wealth to marry or buy into the landed ruling classes of Britain. To be portrayed as if they were English country gentlemen may have been premature and even presumptuous for these company employees, but such portraits allowed them to imagine simultaneously the world in which they lived and the world in which they hoped to live, giving them a double sense of place and identity. Yet we can see in this colonial mimicry of the domestic landed elite the potential for unintentional parody of not only the conventions of the traditional conversation piece but also these company employees' own desires, for in their repetition of English formulas, they reveal their desperation to legitimate their power over this alien land.

CHAPTER TWELVE

Black, Yellow, and White on St. Vincent

Moreau de Jonnès's Carib Ethnography

Peter Hulme

> "Todos los seres humanos sin excepción somos
> mestizos de incontables cruzamientos."
> FERNANDO ORTIZ

In Leslie Marmon Silko's wonderful novel *Almanac of the Dead,* the black Cherokee character called Clinton traces his spiritual ancestry back to the children born to escaped African slaves and indigenous Carib Indians during the colonial period.[1] His reference is to the so-called Black Caribs who supposedly dominated the island of St. Vincent in the second half of the eighteenth century until they were defeated militarily by the British during the revolutionary wars of the 1790s and deported en masse to the Atlantic coast of Central America, where their descendants still live. The story of the Black Caribs has often provided a standard example of ethnogenesis, the creation of hybrid groups or "new peoples" generated out of the maelstrom of colonial history.[2] From the day they were dumped off the coast of Honduras, the Black Caribs could certainly be considered as a "new people," so radically different from anything they knew were the circumstances in which they found themselves. What interests me here, however, are the stories that were told during the second half of the eighteenth century about the origins and development of the Black Caribs on St. Vincent, and—to the extent to which we can access them—the cultural and political realities that lay behind those stories. My particular focus is on a soldier from the French Revolutionary army that fought alongside the Caribs against the British, whose firsthand evidence about the disposition of indigenous people on St. Vincent casts doubt on the traditional picture and helps pose new questions about cultural and ethnic "crossings."

In recent years postcolonial studies has readily become identified with an emphasis on crossings and mixtures—as Salman Rushdie writes, "hybridity, impurity, intermingling, the transformation that comes of new and unexpected combinations, . . . mongrelization, mélange, hotchpotch, a bit of this and a bit of that" is, in short, "how newness enters the world."[3] Beyond that reflection of ethnogenetic "newness," Rushdie's celebratory phrase has its general anthropological equivalent in the greater attention given in the last two decades, especially by writers such as James Clifford, to cultures that are impure, adulterated, transculturated—not, in Clifford's case, particularly to celebrate the impure but rather to try to shake anthropological discourse free of its fascination with the ideal of the pure, the untouched, and the authentic.[4] The Caribbean as a cultural region occupies something of a pivotal role in these debates: once seen as of little interest because it was culturally so mixed, now the Caribbean is seen as offering an exemplary case study precisely because of its history of vertiginous cultural crossings. Though debates about *métissage* have held center stage, a different introductory example here suggests that not all crossings are between white and black, however defined.

In 1998 the Museo del Barrio in New York organized an exhibition called "Taino," dedicated to pre-Columbian art in the Caribbean. The lead item in the exhibition, displayed in a case at the entrance and pictured on the cover of the catalogue, was a piece called the Pigorini zemi.[5] This remarkable object was constructed by native craftsmen on Hispaniola in the early years of the sixteenth century from Caribbean cotton, Venetian glass, and African rhinoceros horn: in other words it is the very embodiment of the tricultural mix out of which colonial Caribbean culture developed. Of special interest is that *this* piece was chosen by the exhibition curators to represent Taino culture, not one of the unequivocally precontact pieces. This would not have happened twenty years ago, when the Pigorini zemi would have been seen as "inauthentic" because of its use of non-Caribbean materials. What I would like to draw from the example is that transculturation, to use Fernando Ortiz's phrase for cultural crossings, can have at least three component parts, a necessary reminder of the powerful indigenous presence in the Caribbean up to the end of the eighteenth century and of the need to think beyond the limitations of the genealogical metaphor when considering cultural process.[6]

Sir John Fortescue, author of the multivolume *History of the British Army,* calls what happened in the West Indies in the 1790s the "darkest and most forbidding tract" in the whole of that history.[7] Britain ultimately won what it called the Brigands' War, defeated the French and their native allies, took back possession of islands that it had almost lost, and extirpated its Black Carib enemies. Yet the experience was apparently so horrific, even for the victors, that, according to Fortescue, the few survivors had no desire to talk about what they had been through.[8] Perhaps as a direct result of this sense of the war as a journey to the heart of darkness, there has been little historiography about it; most writers have been content to see the Brigands' War as an unfortunate offshoot of the French Revolution, a series of disturbances instigated by *agents provocateurs* in an attempt to destabilize British islands that a benevolent plantocracy had previously shared amicably with contented slaves and happy natives. As the *Cambridge History of the British Empire* puts it, with laconic inaccuracy: "A serious crisis had arisen in St. Vincent in March 1795, when the Caribs (now mainly Negroid) broke loose from their reservation. Previously contented, they were roused by the levelling propaganda of Victor Hugues from Guadeloupe, and for a time threatened to master the whole island."[9]

In 1748 Britain and France had agreed to regard St. Vincent as neutral, outside the limits of each other's penetration in the Caribbean, and therefore effectively in possession of the Caribs. After 1763, however, at the end of the Seven Years' War, the island became—as far as the British were concerned—British, and commissioners were sent out to organize the surveying and sale of land for the plantation of tropical crops, especially sugar. One of the commissioners, William Young, thought that the island had the potential to become the most valuable British sugar colony after Jamaica.[10] The activities of these commissioners occasioned several major incidents in the 1770s in which the Caribs, with an acute sense of what was at stake, destroyed surveying equipment and maps in order to prevent a road being built into the fertile windward valley that the British planters especially coveted. With Carib help, the French took back control of the island between 1779 and 1783.

For many years before 1795 the planters and commissioners had clearly wanted the Caribs removed altogether from St. Vincent, but the British government was, in the eyes of the planters, too sensitive to the opinion of sentimental do-gooders, including missionaries, who knew little about the realities of Caribbean life and who tended to have a low opinion of West Indian slave-owners. The native uprising in March 1795 convinced the government of the need to remove the Caribs from St. Vincent once they had been militarily defeated, and Carib collusion with the French enemy silenced humanitarian voices. Once that removal had taken place, the only voices who wanted to tell the story, *their* story of suffering and eventual triumph, were the British planters and their allies. Through their pens, the planters' version of the ethnography of the Vincentian Caribs entered the historical record, where it has never been seriously challenged. William Young produced what he called an "authentic account" of the Black Caribs, providing evidence which, he writes, "a British court of justice would admit as competent, and decide upon as true."[11] In effect, Young's version has become historical truth because he appeared to be the only witness prepared to give testimony.

At the center of the planter description of the free non-European population of St. Vincent is a division between what it calls the Yellow Caribs and the Black Caribs. From the 1770s onward, the planters described a situation in which the westward side of the island was occupied by a small number of *Yellow* Caribs largely under the protection of French settlers, while the eastward half—desired by the planters—was controlled by a much larger number of *Black* Caribs. William Young stressed that the Yellow and Black Caribs were "two nations of people of very different origin and pretensions,"[12] although actual descriptions have remarkable difficulty in locating these differences.

Stories about the origin of this supposed division are frequently repeated, although not always consistent. They usually involve the shipwreck of a slaving ship, sometimes dated to 1675, with the Caribs enslaving the shipwrecked Africans, the Africans revolting, setting up their own community, stealing Carib women, joining forces with existing Maroons, becoming stronger than their erstwhile captors, and taking over the most fertile parts of the island. So completely, according to this account, did the Black Caribs come to dominate their former native masters that British population estimates for the middle of the eighteenth century are of around 3,000 Black Caribs and somewhere between 100 and 500 Yellow Caribs.

The planter evidence for two distinct nations or races, for how that division came about, and for how completely the Black Caribs dominated by 1795 is not without certain self-contradictions, not least that—even by the planters' own account—the Black Caribs spoke the same language as their Yellow counterparts and had adopted the entire repertoire of their cultural practices, such as flattening infant heads and upright burials. The planter story of Africans made slaves by Caribs before rebelling and capturing Carib females is also suspiciously similar to stories of supposed *Carib* settlement in the islands vis-à-vis the indigenous Arawaks.[13] There is little evidence of what the Caribs thought of all this, but one colonial office document quotes the Black Caribs as refusing to give up any of their lands, "which lands were transmitted to them from their ancestors and in defence of which they would die"—suggesting that they saw themselves very much as Caribs first, at least on this issue.[14] Yet if, linguistically and culturally, Black and Yellow Caribs were identical, the British planters were still determined that the Black Caribs should be *seen* as distinctly African. They were sometimes simply described as a "colony of African Negroes"[15] on the assumption that the "Africanness" of the maroon men had overwhelmed the "Caribness" of the women they had kidnapped for sexual partners, although occasionally—remembering that the Caribs themselves had also had a reputation for fierceness—the Black Caribs might be called that "doubly savage race."[16] Agostino Brunias's painting of the meeting between the Carib chief Chatoyer and the British General Dalrymple in St. Vincent in 1773 depicted the Caribs as so dark-skinned that lithographs of the painting could be used in subsequent years to illustrate British negotiations with Jamaican and Dominican Maroons.[17] William Young neatly summed up the four important divisions on the island as the planters saw them: "aboriginal Indians, Negro colonials, French intruders, and British settlers."[18]

So the British planter account Africanized the group it called the Black Caribs. This had a number of advantages for the planters. It emphasized the Black Carib role as usurpers. It helped avoid a repetition of the groundswell of British liberal opinion in defense of the *indigenous* Caribs during the war of the 1770s—which had forced the British to sue for peace. It reduced the number of indigenous families to a handful, and it drew upon the traditional association of blackness with savagery and evil, heightened by the success of slave revolts in the Caribbean in recent years, especially in St. Domingue after 1791.

Douglas Taylor described the problems with this picture very well some fifty years ago in asking "why this fortuitous assemblage of fugitive African slaves . . . should have prospered," and why, having been deported by the British, they should have clung with such tenacity "to the language and traditions they adopted from a breed so little of whose blood they inherit, and whom they themselves helped to defeat."[19] Taylor's language actually hints at how he tried to avoid these questions: for him the Black Caribs were "really" Africans who adopted indigenous cultural practices but remained phenotypically and psychologically separate from their "host" community. The complexities of the historical record of transculturation were only "solved" by positing an African truth behind an indigenous mask.

In the first half of the nineteenth century, slavery began to become the subject of scholarly analysis. The earliest statistical study in France was published in 1842 by Alexandre Moreau de Jonnès, already a distinguished historian of the French Caribbean islands and author of a study of yellow fever, the disease that had devastated the islands at the end of the eighteenth century. Moreau was appointed head of the new French Bureau of Statistics in 1833 and went on to crown his academic career with a book on the general principles of statistical analysis. He became a member of the French Academy and died as the grand old man of French social science in 1870, aged ninety-two. However, in 1858, at the age of eighty, he published a memoir of his first career as a soldier, *Aventures de guerre au temps de la république et du consulat.*

Moreau had an extraordinary early life. He left school in Rennes to go to Paris to serve the revolution: he was present in the Tuileries at the meeting between Louis XVI and Lafayette; he fought against the Breton resistance; he was in Toulon when it was burned by the English in 1793. He took part in both French invasions of Ireland, meeting Fitzgerald in Munster in 1796, and Wolfe Tone on another occasion in France; he was a spy at the Nore during the great British naval mutiny, actually witnessing Samuel Parker's execution. In the Caribbean he served as a gunner and military commander; but he was also forced by circumstance to act as an engineer, a surveyor, a lawyer, and a doctor. He worked under cover on Martinique during the British occupation and took part in the French attack on Dominica in 1805. He crossed the Atlantic ten times during the Anglo-French wars, the last being in 1809 on his way to a prison ship in Portsmouth where he drafted a first version of his memoirs. He returned to France aged thirty-five, after spending a remarkable twenty-two years as a soldier. During that time he had taught himself geography, botany, and mineralogy: he was the first person to prove that the Caribbean islands were volcanic in structure.

Moreau's adventures included several extended tours of duty in the Caribbean, the first of which lasted from August 1795, when he crossed the Atlantic in a privateer, until June 1796, when he was taken prisoner by British troops in St. Vincent and deported to France. His most extended visit to St. Vincent lasted for three months after he was appointed by Victor Hugues to strengthen Carib forces in preparation for an attack on Kingstown, the capital of St. Vincent.

During this period—from September to December 1795—Moreau stayed in a Carib village near the east coast, offering weapons training to Carib warriors. Over those months fighting almost ground to a halt as both British and French armies, with soldiers dying by the thousands from yellow fever, waited for reinforcements. Moreau—just eighteen years old, but a child of Linnaeus and Rousseau—reveled in his tropical idyll, fascinated in equal degree by the social life of the savages, the tropical vegetation around him, and the beauty of the chief's daughter, Eliama, also eighteen. In his memoir, he calls the village a paradise and says that it has always stayed in his memory as the place where he spent the happiest moments of his life: "During the three months I spent in the mountain carbet with my Carib friends, my days were a tissue of silk and gold. This was truly Eden, as Milton describes it, with its perpetual spring, its shady forests, its magnificent views, its flowering groves, its singing birds, adorned with the most varied and brilliant colours. Nothing was missing, since a second Eve lived in this pleasant retreat."[20]

In writing about the Vincentian Caribs, Moreau recalls Rousseau's "eloquent pages" and offers his own "humble tribute," consisting of what he calls "eyewitness observation and evidence."[21] "Fighting with these natives and for them," he writes, "and living in the same carbet, sharing opinions, interest, and affection, I got to know them, and I could determine, through the exploratory procedures of the modern sciences, the curious elements of their social condition and the highly controversial problem of the goodness of their hearts."[22] His statement should not, of course, be taken to imply that this French source is authoritative: Moreau wrote his memoir more than half a century after the events it describes; he wrote as a friend to the Caribs just as the planters wrote as bitter opponents; he looked to Enlightenment science for his rhetoric of authority just as the planters looked to English jurisprudence. Neither stance, neither rhetoric, delivers truth on its own account. In particular, the apocalyptic events of the 1790s mean that all evidence about the disposition of Black and Yellow Caribs or their relationships with the French or British needs to be read as extremely context-specific. That certainly goes for Moreau, who joined a community on a war footing. However, Moreau's friendship with the Caribs did undoubtedly lead to greater intimacy and arguably, therefore, to greater knowledge. During these four months, Moreau certainly lived in much closer daily contact with the Vincentian Caribs than any other outsider at this time, possibly during the whole course of the eighteenth century. Moreover, Moreau's time in St. Vincent coincided with that historical moment when the conjunction of the abolition of slavery with the development of those "exploratory procedures of the modern sciences" was leading to the development of ethnographic methodologies. In 1799 the Société des Observateurs de l'Homme was established in Paris, and Joseph-Marie Degérando wrote his treatise on the observation of savage peoples, directed at Baudin's forthcoming expedition to Tasmania and sometimes seen as the first primer for anthropological fieldwork.[23] So there is other evidence for seeing the late 1790s as an ethnographic moment of some importance.

The national difference is also significant. The French had massacred many Caribs, especially while ruthlessly annexing Martinique and Grenada during the seventeenth century, but they had also developed the commercial tradition of the *coureurs des îles,* which had brought them into closer contact with the Caribs: the *coureurs* would often dress as Carib, have Carib wives, speak Carib, and presumably, at least on occasion, simply *become* Carib. Also, French settlers on St. Vincent had small plantations on which they grew coffee, tobacco, indigo, and cocoa, none of which had a deleterious effect on the environment, from a Carib point of view. The British drive in the four islands they gained in 1763 was to develop sugar plantations, involving the large-scale destruction of the islands' forest, which was productive land for the Caribs but which the planters tended to see as likely to harbor savages who might attack them.[24] As a result, British contact with Caribs was infrequent, limited, and often antagonistic.

There are a number of ways in which Moreau's evidence changes our picture of the Vincentian Caribs. Living with them so intimately and having a lively interest in botany, Moreau gives a full picture of the crops the Caribs grew, which the British were largely unable to understand, partly because of their ignorance of the terrain in which the Caribs lived—thus Carib gardens were invisible to British eyes even when they were looking at them—and partly because of British conviction that the island had been simply *occupied* by the Caribs without ever being made productive.

We also get some sense from Moreau of the extent of Carib integration into the larger Caribbean world of the 1790s. After a storm in September 1795 destroyed Carib crops, Moreau accompanied a group of Caribs on an overnight canoe trip to Trinidad. With a supply of Spanish gold coins, gathered after a shipwreck, the Caribs bought food and chartered three schooners to carry the supplies back to St. Vincent.[25] They operated perfectly happily within the money economy of the Caribbean. In addition, Moreau says, Carib pirogues were constantly on the move between the mouth of the Orinoco and the islands of the Bahamas, which meant they were well informed about everything that was happening in the Caribbean. They were, he says, Victor Hugues's eyes and ears, the intelligence force for revolutionary insurgence.[26] He also has much to say about the prominent role that women played in the Carib councils and in the actual fighting; of which there is no hint in the British sources.

Yet the most striking—and puzzling—aspect of Moreau's evidence is that he lived and fought with a group he regarded as Yellow Caribs. He meets Black Caribs and even describes a kind of national council at which all indigenous leaders are present, but the picture that emerges from his account is of Yellow Carib dominance, both ideologically and numerically. The British estimated around 5,000 Black Caribs and a very small number of Yellow Caribs; Moreau's numbers are 1,500 Black Caribs and in excess of 6,000 Yellow Caribs.[27] This is an enormous discrepancy, even taking into account the difficulty of estimating population numbers at this time and in this terrain.

Moreau was, however, just as convinced as British observers of the presence of two ethnic groups on St. Vincent. He says about the Yellow Caribs: "It was the first time I had seen indigenous people from the New World . . . The first thing I noticed was their serious demeanour, dignified and proud . . . It was easy to recognise a people never disgraced by slavery, who clearly regarded themselves as anyone's equal. Their looks were assured, and in them could be read the indomitable courage which had stood the proof of three centuries . . . Their skin was copper colour, very like the hue that the leaves of certain trees take in autumn before they dry out."[28] This is Moreau on the Black Caribs:

> I had not previously seen the [Black Caribs] and from misleading accounts I had formed quite a false idea of them. I believed, from the missionaries' tales, that they owed their origin to negro slaves escaped from neighbouring colonies. I was much surprised to find them of quite another race. In place of woolly hair, flat nose, and gaping mouth set with thick out-turned lips, they possessed Abyssinian features: smooth hair, long and black, more like

a mane; straight nose, standing out from the face but slightly curved at the end, and such as you would never see from Cape Bon to the Gulf of Guinea; and finally, a mouth furnished with thin lips in no way like that of a negro, except for the beauty of the teeth.[29]

Just as the British wanted to associate the Caribs with Africa and Negroes so, it seemed, Moreau was equally keen to *distance* them, Yellow and Black alike, from any such association. His anxious negatives are close in content and tone to Aphra Behn's description of her fictional hero, Oroonoko, the classic instance of an African who does not look like an African, or even, more appropriately, close to Robinson Crusoe's description of his Carib slave Friday. For Moreau the Black Caribs in some way have to be given an African origin, otherwise they could not be distinguished at all from the Yellow Caribs, so he gives them African features that are black but not Negro, without any explanation of how Abyssinian features could be found in the Caribbean islands. By Abyssinian Moreau probably referred to the Amhara, reputedly mixed descendants of the Semitic conquerors who had crossed the Red Sea from southern Arabia into Ethiopia and the native Cushitic population (the folk-etymology of "Abyssinian" being precisely "mixed," supposedly from the Arabic word "habash").[30]

It would be difficult to overestimate the precariousness of the political situation in the late-eighteenth-century Caribbean, as manifested by large-scale population movements that probably made the Vincentian Caribs the most firmly rooted of all Caribbean groups at this time. If the eastern Caribbean had begun the eighteenth century with relatively well-defined groups—English and French planters, European merchants and soldiers, African slaves, indigenous Caribs—then by its end the movement of people, breeding patterns, and political revolution had thrown all these classifications into turmoil. By 1795 the British planters established on St. Vincent shared the island with a few French-speaking planters, a group of *petit blanc*, French-speaking traders and farmers, small free colored and free black populations (mostly French speaking), a large slave population (divided between English and French speakers), an indigenous Carib population of various hues (many speaking French), and small groups of black Maroons. When the rebellion broke out in 1795, most of these groups divided. Some part of each fought against the British (and no doubt a larger part of each had anti-British sympathies); some of each group, apart from the Caribs and Maroons, fought on the British side; some individuals changed sides. Into this already confused situation came a variety of French-speaking free coloreds, blacks, and white French soldiers, like Moreau, to fight with the rebels. As part of British reinforcements came not only white British soldiers and black British soldiers in new slave regiments but also French-speaking ex-slave black and colored militia recruited in Martinique and commanded by white French officers with royalist sympathies who wanted to oppose the revolution.[31] The quantity of crossings over the years already meant it was difficult to tell who people were by looking at them. Increased population movement now also meant it was difficult to account genealogically for particular individuals. An acculturated Carib, living as a farmer, wearing European dress and speaking French, might be indistinguishable, in English eyes, from a free colored; yet, at the drop of a hat and with an application of body paint, he could be transformed into a Carib warrior. Just when it became absolutely crucial for the British to be able to recognize friends and enemies, the complexity of the social and racial mix on the island was becoming disconcerting. Rarely can some form of classification have seemed more desirable or necessary.

In a very real sense this was the age of classification, a crucial component in what Mary Louise Pratt has described as the age of "planetary consciousness."[32] Linnaeus's *Systema naturae* had classified the natural world by making observable differences codified by language. Classification was the domain of the visible, and skin color had become crucial for the description of human differences. Writers such as Moreau de Saint-Méry—cousin to Moreau de Jonnès—had evolved monstrous tabular classifications giving names to the minute distinctions of color that result from the almost infinite number of possible racial crossings that can be produced by simple multipliers of two. This charting in theory provided a way to identify those who, though descended in part from Africans and slaves, might have the audacity to possess seemingly white skins.[33] ("Moreau" in French, as neither impeccably white Frenchman of that name mentions, actually means "as brown as a Moor.")[34]

Racial typology was developed at the same time as tabular classification and would prove an even more powerful tool for representing non-Europeans. Just as the Caribs went to war in 1795, the influential third edition of Johann Friedrich Blumenbach's *De generis humani varietate nativa*—the foundation text of physical anthropology—was published. For Blumenbach there were five principal varieties of the single human species: the middle, or Caucasian, variety; two extremes, Mongolian and Ethiopic; and two intermediate varieties, the Malay and the American. Five skulls, one for each variety, took pride of place in the engravings illustrating this treatise; the American was represented by the skull of a Carib chief from St. Vincent. This skull was a gift to Blumenbach from Sir Joseph Banks, who had received it from the director of the botanical garden in St. Vincent, who had dug it up at dead of night from a sacred burial site. Unlikely as it might seem, there were very real connections between the earliest European centers of ethnological classification and the political realities of the small island of St. Vincent.[35]

Moreau's ethnographic evidence exacerbates the contradictions already apparent within the British story.[36] The first and most important conclusions to be drawn from his memoir are negative. The contradictory evidence produced by British and French sources suggests that we know much less about ethnic and cultural crossing in St. Vincent in the late eighteenth century than we thought we did, and that the notion of ethnogenesis has tended to obscure rather than illuminate the processes involved in such contact. As always, we underestimate at our peril the work needed to unravel accepted stories and the deep and misleading assumptions they help maintain.

Positive conclusions must be tentative. Even if one assumes some homogeneous Carib appearance in 1492 (which would mean leaving aside a whole history of mixing with other Native Americans before that date), by 1795 the Caribs on St. Vincent had been mixing with Africans and Europeans—both heterogeneous categories themselves—for nearly 300 years. Carib response to Africans, however they arrived on the island, undoubtedly varied over time and according to circumstance. Semiautonomous black communities may have been allowed to form; shipwrecked slave ships would after all have contained women as well as men. As Carib numbers declined, Africans were doubtless inducted into Carib communities, probably through an initial period of submission, which European observers misidentified as "slavery." However, there would not have been a *single* Carib response: the European invasion of the islands was socially and economically—as well as demographically—devastating for the Caribs, and different villages probably responded pragmatically to changing circumstances. There is some evidence that the British were well aware that when they were dealing with, say, the Grand Sable Caribs, they should not assume a similar response from other villages. Villages were autonomous and no doubt came to different kinds of accommodation with the Europeans, one form of which involved recapturing escaped slaves or even stealing slaves from the French to sell to the British.

Proximity to European settlements would have been an important factor, but there is also evidence that individual Caribs sometimes opted for a new relationship with Europeans—taking employment, for example, in ferrying goods from ship to shore on the windward coast. (Young actually calls these "domesticated Caribs.")[37] There is also evidence of Caribs, possibly the children of French traders and Carib women, setting themselves up as cultural intermediaries, living in European-style houses, wearing European clothes, but identifying as Carib. One French source, the royalist exile Jean-Jacques Dauxion-Lavaysse, visited a Carib called Larose in 1793 and described the properties of the Caribs as "divided by hedges and orange trees," with "houses built of squared timber, and covered with shingles"—not exactly an indigenous style. He was served lunch "on fine white table linen, in dishes and plates of Wedgwood, with silver cutlery and cut glass."[38] Even Eliama, the Carib chief's daughter that Moreau fell for, had been educated in a convent on Martinique. This aspect of Carib transculturation—with European culture—is something about which the British sources are resolutely silent, so keen are they to stress the process of Africanization.

By the 1790s there were about twelve main Carib groups, mostly but not exclusively resident on the eastern side of the island. The individuals belonging to these groups would, in terms of appearance, have covered a wide spectrum from the relatively pale to the relatively dark, in accordance with the random relationship between genetic make-up and skin color. In discussing mestizos in Latin America, Schwartz and Salomon note that, "Up to a point, mestizo was as mestizo did. Dress, association, custom, and appearance could make the difference."[39] Carib individuals, families, and even larger groups may have responded to the dramatic changes on St. Vincent by using dress and appearance to move into and out of social relationships and perceived ethnic identities in a way that was much too rapid and subtle to adhere to the rigid classification deployed by Europeans.

After the fiasco of the failed attack on Kingstown in December 1795, Moreau was recalled to Guadeloupe by Victor Hugues. While on St. Vincent, Moreau—an inveterate walker—had sketched a map of the island, showing all its tracks and paths, and indicating the best military positions.[40] Hugues was impressed enough to send Moreau on a perilous mission to British-occupied Martinique to map the British defenses around St. Pierre in preparation for a French attack, which never happened. Moreau entered Martinique disguised as a traveling doctor with a taste for botany and drew forty-five sheets of maps, which he kept in a leather case disguised as an herbal.[41] After the maps had been sent back to Guadeloupe, Moreau was taken prisoner by the British and exchanged for a captured English officer. On board the French ship taking him to Guadeloupe, Moreau learned of the arrival of the British reinforcements under General Abercromby, which had turned the tide of the insurrections on Grenada and St. Vincent. Moreau's sense of honor insisted that he return to St. Vincent so he had himself dropped off on the windward coast, close to the village where he spent those four idyllic months the previous year. The first thing he found was a massacred village—men, women, children, old people—all hacked to death and their houses burned. Then he came across Zami, maid to Eliama, and learned that both the chief and his daughter had been killed in the recent fighting.[42] Some Caribs had surrendered at this point, but most regrouped and joined the French in time to suffer a final defeat in June 1796.

On St. Vincent, the classificatory schema introduced by the British and French created a situation in which visible indigenous skin tones were reduced to two—yellow and black—with these skin tones corresponding to two supposedly distinct ethnic and

racial groups on the island: two types, two attitudes, two politics. The inherent unlike-
liness of this scenario has been obscured only by the insistent repetition of its key terms
in subsequent historiographical and anthropological literature.

Black and *yellow* applied to Caribs are colonizers' terms, ideological fictions built
around the unmarked centrality of imperial whiteness. When able, the indigenous
groups thus designated have rejected those terms, which do not, the contradictory evidence suggests, correspond to any clear racial or ethnic division. Caribs on St. Vincent
did mix with a small number of Europeans and a larger number of Africans, but these
new individuals and small groups were culturally assimilated. For the British, it seems,
a one-drop rule was already in place; any inkling of African ancestry was enough to turn
a Yellow Carib into a Black Carib—even if that one drop was in the British imagination rather than the Carib bloodstream.

The British persisted in their determination to recognize their enemies by sight,
sending 102 Yellow Caribs back to St. Vincent from the small island where they were
awaiting transportation purely on account of their lighter skin color, despite the fact
that they had fought against the British.[43] In Central America, the Vincentian Caribs
have always regarded themselves as Indian but were classified as Negroes by the constitution of the Republic of Central America in 1823.[44] They still call themselves Carib or
Garifuna or Garihagu, are identified by others as Indians, speak an indigenous language, and have cultural practices that are uniquely the result of their indigenous origins. Anthropologists and historians persist in calling them Black Caribs, but the final
suspicion has to be that their story, as currently told, is yet another chapter in that long
denial of the continuity and survival of indigenous American traditions through the
travails and crossings of the colonial period.

CHAPTER THIRTEEN

Marketing Mulatresses in the Paintings and Prints of Agostino Brunias

Kay Dian Kriz

In 1770 Sir William Young, newly appointed governor of the islands of Dominica, St. Vincent, and Tobago, set off for the West Indies accompanied by the Italian artist Agostino Brunias.[1] Brunias's presence in Young's entourage requires some explanation, for prior to this time there was little demand for professional artists in the British West Indies. Indeed there was little in the way of "art" that actually represented the West Indian landscape or its inhabitants; maps, natural history illustrations, and a few schematic topographical prints and drawings constituted the bulk of visual imagery relating to the British islands until the 1770s. In this chapter I argue that the paintings and prints of slaves and free people of color that Brunias produced over twenty years can best be understood by considering the particular nature of the colonial project there. Given the fierce, ongoing competition between the British and the French in the Caribbean, the primary goal of Young and other colonial officials was to encourage British immigration to these islands, newly ceded to Britain by France at the end of the Seven Years War.[2] Maintaining a British presence was essential because of the strategic location of the islands vis-à-vis the French colonies (especially Martinique and Guadeloupe); therefore it was crucial for Britons to settle there rather than to serve as absentee landlords. In order to foster settlement the islands' appeal as a potentially civilized as well as profitable space had to be emphasized. Through his depiction of the social life

of slaves and free people of color—shown promenading, conversing, and trading in local markets and along market pathways—Brunias attempted to promote these newly
won colonies as a place where people, as well as raw materials, could be cultivated and
refined.[3] These scenes of West Indian life were well suited to luring potential colonists
from Britain and the older West Indian colonies at the moment when the first organized effort to abolish the slave trade emerged, roughly coinciding with the important
Somerset case of 1772.[4] Within the context of a nascent abolitionist movement, successfully promoting these islands through art had to involve demonstrating the happiness and well-being of the slaves who lived there.

At first glance, Brunias's images would seem to be an unproblematic contribution
to Young's project of making a "jovial part[y] of colonization" by showing happy slaves
enjoying island life.[5] Closer examination of these images reveals their repeated focus
around one particularly vexing figure within contemporary colonial discourse: the mulatto woman. An example is *Market Day, Roseau, Dominica* (ca. 1780) (fig. 13.1), in which
buyers and sellers at a market run by people of color in Dominica's major port are
shown variously clothed and variously pigmented.[6] Skin tones range from the dark
brown of the two figures seated on the ground to the right, to the light beige complex-

Figure 13.1. Agostino Brunias, *Market Day, Roseau, Dominica* (ca. 1780). Oil on canvas (14 ×
18 1/4 in). Courtesy of the Yale Center for British Art, Paul Mellon Collection.

Figure 13.2. Agostino Brunias, *A West Indian Creole Woman with her Black Servant* (ca. 1780). Oil on canvas (12 × 9 7/8 in). Courtesy of the Yale Center for British Art, Paul Mellon Collection.

ion of the mulatto woman in the center that they are so intently watching. Unlike the other figures in the scene, who are involved in commercial transactions, conversation, or watching, she engages no one directly with her eyes, yet solicits the gaze of everyone, including the viewer of the picture.

The mulatress's dominance is effected by her central placement in the composition, the brilliance of her white dress, and her size. She is the tallest figure in the scene by virtue of her elaborate turban; her dress and gestures further enhance her visual importance. As if her placement, size, gestures, and elaborate costume were not enough to draw viewer attention, Brunias places a slightly darker-skinned male figure directly behind her, his body bracketing hers, knees bent, eyes raised, and hat off, in a pose of deference and desire. This same female figure, or a variation thereof, is repeated in work after work, as, for example, in *A West Indian Creole Woman with Her Black Servant* (fig. 13.2), where she is shown on a path with a smaller, darker-skinned female attendant.

Although Brunias painted West Indian scenes that do not feature this figure, the frequency with which the mulatto woman not only appears but also dominates is quite striking and requires some explanation, considering what a problematic figure she was within contemporary written accounts of the West Indies. Janet Schaw, a Scotswoman writing about her sojourn in Antigua in the mid-1770s, displays a typical reaction toward people of color when she complains about "the crouds of Mullatoes, which you meet in the streets, houses and indeed every where."[7] For Schaw, mulattoes were the visible signs of "licentious and unnatural" liaisons between white masters and black slave women. Furthermore, Schaw, and a host of other British, French, and white West Indian writers, perceived mulatto women to be lascivious and intent on seducing white men. While these were qualities associated with all women of color, these writers claimed that mulatto women were distinguished by their vanity, passion for fancy clothing and jewelry, and pride in possessing a light complexion that bespeaks a white forebear.[8] According to William Young the Second, who inherited his father's West Indian estates and many paintings by Brunias, a manifestation of that pride was an unwillingness to perform manual labor, even minor tasks such as snuffing a candle or opening a window.[9] Brunias's pictures reinforce these written representations of the mulatress's pride, love of finery, and seductive power, but their mode of address is not one of social or moral critique. That is, they do not solicit viewer disapproval of these vain but elegant creatures. Why, then, the recurrence and dominance of such a troubling figure in the first substantial body of visual images celebrating the social life of people of color in the British West Indies? I argue that Brunias mobilizes the mulatress's ambiguous social and racial status—her in-betweenness—in order to represent civilized society "under development" in a place more commonly associated with base pleasures and profit taking.

A comment on the choice and the connotations of the racialized terms used in what follows is essential. While *mulatto* was strictly defined by the Spanish *sistema de castas* as the offspring of a pure white and pure black person, in the British West Indies it was the only term used generally to designate light-skinned individuals with a part-European and a part-African background.[10] I use the contemporary term *mulatress* in this essay to signal that the adult women of mixed race pictured by Brunias were most likely taken to be of French-African heritage due to the predominance of French over British colonists on the islands in question in the mid–eighteenth century. In the passage by Young (cited above) decrying the refusal of certain West Indians to perform simple tasks, the baronet's specific reference is to whites and the "Mulatto free Person." While not all mulattoes were free people of color, nor all of the latter mulattoes, there was a slippage in colonial discourse between the idea of the mulatto and the idea of the free person of color, who disdains labor and has the financial resources for luxuries such as fine clothing. I argue that it is precisely this tendency to assess the legal and social status of persons according to racialized categories based on an aesthetic and ideology of Whiteness that Brunias capitalizes on in his representation of the well-dressed, light-skinned mulatto woman.

In using a female figure to promote a refined and prosperous society based on commerce, Brunias was drawing on a discourse linking the condition of women to social evolution; this discourse was widely disseminated through travel literature and social philosophy, as well as natural and civil histories of the Old and New World, including the West Indies.[11] Scottish physician William Alexander put the case most succinctly in his *History of Women*, first published in 1779: "the rank . . . and condition, in which we find women in any country, mark out to us with the greatest precision, the exact point in the scale of civil society, to which the people of such country have arrived; and were their history entirely silent on every other subject, and only mentioned the manner in which they treated their women, we would . . . be enabled to form a tolerable judgment of the barbarity, or culture of their manners."[12] This gendered assessment of societies was an extension of four-stages theory, which posited that all human societies began with a primitive hunting and gathering stage; some of these progressed to the pastoral state, later evolved to the agrarian stage, and finally reached the most advanced and civilized form, the commercial stage. In primitive societies women were virtual slaves to their men, who forced them to perform arduous physical labor and to satisfy their base sexual urges. By the time the commercial stage was reached, women's function and relationship to men was removed from the realm of fulfilling material or purely sexual and reproductive needs. Here this theory of civilization intersected with the associated discourse on civility or "politeness." Women were at the center of this discursive network, or rather a particular type of woman—one who could provide those forms of sociability that would soften the brutish manners of men. Due to this social theory designed to privilege commercially developed societies, European women were encouraged to think of themselves as superior to women from the non-European world.[13] In the case of the newest additions to the British West Indies, the issue was even more complicated. Who was to stand for "Woman" in a place where widely divergent cultures from Britain, Europe, Africa, and America clashed and intermingled? It seems that there were a number of possible candidates among these populations, as well as a number of possible visual modes that were conventionally used to depict them.

Since the European "discovery" of the New World, the West Indies, along with the rest of the American continent, was figured allegorically as an Indian woman, a representative of the least evolved stage of societal organization. Shown nearly nude, with a feathered headdress, she took her place on maps and seals, in paintings and prints, and on decorative objects. As one of the four continents, she was often shown in company with a primitivized Africa, an exoticized Asia, and a Greco-Roman figuration of Europe, such as in the frontispiece of the 1774 edition of Malachy Postlethwayt's *Universal Dic-*

Figure 13.3. "Africa, Asia, and Europe Offering their Riches to Britannia" in Malachy Postle-thwayt, *Universal Dictionary of Trade and Commerce* (1774). Engraving. Courtesy of the John Carter Brown Library, Brown University.

tionary of Trade and Commerce, where allegorical figures are offering up their riches to Britannia (fig. 13.3). Such images of "America" obviously served well the interests of European colonizers who could thus avail themselves of the natural resources that these female figures so willingly relinquish.

Indians specifically associated with the West Indies were depicted via what we would now call an ethnographic format in travel literature and New World histories, and Brunias produced a number of such paintings and prints of the Caribs of St. Vincent. They are posed in polygamous family groups on forest paths and in front of native huts; their peaceful demeanor belies the conflicts the Caribs had with the English after the Treaty of Paris was concluded. These conflicts so threatened British colonial interests that

William Young made a concerted attempt to remove the Caribs from the island altogether.[14] Brunias represented both the "Yellow Caribs" (fig. 13.4), the supposedly original Indians of St. Vincent, and the "Black Caribs," composed of the descendants of escaped African slaves who intermixed with the indigenous population and took up their way of life.[15] Like the allegorical images of Indians, these ethnographic scenes suggest that left to their own devices, Indians and Indians intermixed with Africans are only capable of forming societies at the most primitive stage of social evolution. Accordingly, Brunias's Carib women often appear to be barely distinguishable from the men, who use them as beasts of burden and force them into polygamy.[16] Joseph Senhouse, the official in charge of customs in Dominica, made a direct connection between the treatment of Carib women and the primitiveness of their society when he wrote in his diary in 1776 that the more uncivilized these "savage communities" were the more inhumanly their women were treated: "and here we find the Indians, who are still in a deplorable state of ignorance and barbarity, oblige their Wives to carry all burdens whatever."[17]

Figure 13.4. Agostino Brunias, *A Leeward Islands Carib Family outside a Hut* (ca. 1780). Oil on canvas (12 1/8 × 9 3/4 in). Courtesy of the Yale Center for British Art, Paul Mellon Collection.

If the female Indian body could not represent societal evolution in the British West Indies—and actually was used to make quite the opposite point—neither could the African woman's body. Pressed into service as an allegorical sign of a continent invariably represented at the lowest stage of social evolution, despite that the very existence of the slave trade depended upon active and ongoing African commerce, the female African body was severely compromised as a sign of the civilizing process by its enslavement, as well as the lowly status of African slave women as producers and reproducers of arduous physical labor. When islands like Dominica, St. Vincent, and Tobago moved away from diversified and small-scale farming to large sugar plantations, women slaves lost ground. After the British assumed control, female slaves occupied proportionally fewer domestic and skilled positions, the majority working alongside men in the cane fields.[18] As Senhouse observed, such female labor is precisely what marks a less "civilized" society. It is not surprising, therefore, that when Brunias does include African slave women in images designed to show both the abundance and the potential refinement of the new colonies, he represents them as "free" agents in a market economy, selling fresh produce grown in their provision grounds after their day's work for the master was done (see the lower right of fig. 13.1).

While significant numbers of women in Britain and the West Indies were directly involved in this form of marketing activity, they did not serve as the primary visual sign of an advanced commercial society. In Britain women of elevated social status who had a facility for sociability—especially the art of conversation—assumed that status. James Forrester, writing in 1734, explains: "It is the Conversation of *Women* that gives a proper *Bias* to our inclinations, and, by abating the *Ferocity* of our Passions, engages us to the *Gentleness* of Deportment, which we style *Humanity*."[19] British artists visualized such women in a variety of genres, but the family conversation piece was especially suited to this purpose. The companionate marriage is frequently figured in these scenes as the source of those affectionate sensibilities that bind together the entire family gathering, and by extension, the whole of society.[20]

Similarly, one might expect to find a proliferation of portraits of white West Indian families, featuring their women as the sign of a new, potentially prosperous, and refined colonial society. In fact, white women in the new British colonies proved to be even more resistant to visual representation than their black slaves or domestic servants. Part of the problem was the widespread knowledge of West Indian demographics: the ratio of white women to white men in the Caribbean colonies was minute compared to that in England. Colonial administrators such as Thomas Atwood, who wrote the first history of Dominica, complained that enterprising Britons who traveled to the lesser Antilles in the latter part of the eighteenth century did not expect to stay there but hoped to make a financial killing and return to Britain as quickly as possible.[21] Consequently, the married men left their wives at home in Britain, and single men tended to remain unmarried during their stay in the West Indies. In either case, once in the islands, many of these men took black and colored mistresses and produced racially mixed offspring. One outcome of this state of affairs was that the domestic sphere in the West Indies proved to be a highly fraught space, offering little opportunity for the celebration and visualization of British virtue, refinement, or even wealth. For not only did adventuring colonists form illicit unions with women of color, but also they tended to save any profits they made for their return to England, or more likely reinvested them, rather than build large, richly furnished plantation houses. Indeed, even though the elder William Young's commitment to the new British Caribbean islands prompted him to appropriate—or as the crown later charged, misappropriate—government funds to promote land development, he did not settle in the West Indies nor did he commission Brunias or anyone else to paint him on his West Indian estates. (Young did engage Johann Zoffany to paint a portrait of the baronet and his family on his English estate prior to his leaving for the West Indies; the painting is now in the Walker Art Gallery in Liverpool.)

The problem of imaging the domestic sphere in the British West Indies was not simply that women of color were displacing or supplementing white women in their sanctioned roles of wife and mother. Even more troubling for a wide range of contemporary writers was the sense that the white creole woman's own identity was being altered by her prolonged contact with women of color who served in her household.[22] In his *History of Jamaica* (1774), Edward Long launches perhaps the most vehement tirade against this negative influence: "We may see, in some of these places, a very fine young woman aukwardly dangling her arms with the air of a Negroe-servant, lolling almost the whole day upon beds or settees, her head muffled up with two or three handkerchiefs, her dress loose, and without stays . . . her ideas are narrowed to the ordinary subjects that pass before her, the business of the plantation, the tittle-tattle of the parish; the tricks, superstitions, diversions, and profligate discourses, of black servants, equally illiterate and unpolished."[23] Here the civilizing process seems to be operating in reverse—all the most negative aspects of "illiterate and unpolished" black people were imprinting themselves on the body, mind, and character of white creole women.

For his part Brunias privileged women of mixed race in his paintings and refrained from representing women who could securely be identified as white creole or European. A useful comparison can be made between any of the women who populate Brunias's paintings and an eighteenth-century portrait of an unknown lady, which may have been set in Jamaica and is attributed to Philip Wickstead, a British artist who worked in there in the latter eighteenth century (fig. 13.5).[24] The whiteness of this figure is emphatically declared by her extremely pale complexion, her upswept powdered hair (or wig) styled

Figure 13.5. Attributed to Philip Wickstead, portrait of an unknown lady. © Christie's Images, New York.

in the English fashion, her shoes and richly embroidered dress, the shaping of her body with stays and petticoats, and especially by her hat, which bears no resemblance to the turbans adopted by African and African creole women in the Americas. Even though Brunias's pictures feature women of color, these images, like Wickstead's, are also about whiteness. Unlike Wickstead's portrait, they are about the fantasy of possessing a body that both is and is not white, bearing the marks of refined whiteness and the promise of savage sexual pleasure so closely associated with blackness. My use of the ambiguous phrase "possessing a body" is intended to suggest that such an image permits possible viewing options that involve fantasies not only of subjection via a master/slave encounter but also of identification. It is all too easy to assume that Brunias's images were designed to appeal to white heterosexual men, but they equally, if perhaps more surreptitiously, invite the gaze of white women, who might fantasize about "possessing" (in either sense) a body understood to offer "dark" sexual pleasures.[25]

The challenges and problems in picturing this white/not-white body are especially apparent in *Linen Market, Dominica* (fig. 13.6). With his customary attention to sartorial detail, the artist displays an undulating frieze of various individuals buying and selling at the portside Sunday market in Roseau, where domestically produced fruits and vegetables are sold alongside linens imported from Europe. Scanning the colorfully dressed crowd, the viewer's eye is drawn to the centrally placed woman dressed in white and shaded by a bright pink parasol. She is both like and unlike Brunias's typical mulatta figure, as exemplified by the brightly dressed woman on the left wearing a straw hat set rakishly atop her checkered turban. The skin of the woman in white is pointedly lighter than that of her dark-skinned servant, but not markedly different in hue from that of the mulatto woman on the left or the female figure standing at the right, holding a vegetable. The central figure's loose-fitting gown boasts more ruffles and lace than the skirt and blouse of the mulatta on the left; similarly she wears a highly elaborate white headdress, still recognizable as a turban but having little in common with the striped and checked kerchiefs the women around her are wearing. Her hair lacks the tight curl marking Brunias's other women of color, yet it is neither lighter in color nor more elaborately coifed. The pink parasol also visually emphasizes the woman in white, but a bright blue version of this useful accessory also shades the market woman opposite her, providing welcome relief from the sun and a mark of social distinction within a hierarchically ordered community of people of color.

Figure 13.6. Agostino Brunias, *Linen Market, Dominica* (ca. 1780). Oil on canvas (19 5/8 × 27 in). Courtesy of the Yale Center for British Art, Paul Mellon Collection.

Based on these observations one might "read" the woman in white *as* white, and therefore as an exceptional figure within the artist's oeuvre and within the physical spaces of a market that white women would have been unlikely to frequent. Is she or isn't she? The uncertainty of this woman's "race" is surely one of the pleasures this figure offers its viewers. What makes this ambiguous figure exceptional is not only her appearance but also the way she is constructed through the gazes within the picture. Those gazes register anxiety as well as desire. Note that she is actively looking at the goods offered by the market woman, unlike the mulatress on the left, who, more typically, turns away from the business at hand to chat with a foppishly dressed mulatto man. Absorbed in a commercial transaction, the woman in white is under close surveillance. Tucked into the background and the shadows is the figure of a bewigged white man tensely gripping his cane. From his position and the manner in which he intently watches the woman in white, he appears to be the woman's companion (the term *sugar daddy* seems even more apt in this context) rather than a casual admirer. His piercing gaze contrasts pointedly with the glance of his companion's dark-skinned servant, who confirms her mistress's status as a free woman and person of means. She seems distracted by the sights and sounds of the market, however, and positions the parasol so that it shades both her mistress and herself—an action that possesses some measure of insubordination.

Is that what so unsettles him, or has his wariness to do with the intensity of his companion's gaze on the commodity displayed before her? By the 1770s colonial officials and entrepreneurs recognized the importance of women as consumers for the perpetuation of a healthy and wealthy commercial society. One of the arguments a colonial official made in 1763 for turning Roseau into a free port was that the British would be able to undersell the French and Dutch in printed linen and cotton, which were worn by "the fair Creolls [and] their servants, who imitate their mistresses."[26] Conversely, the most common criticism of a society based on commerce was that unchecked consumption could spawn a descent into luxury, into a feminine and feminizing love of sensuous things that would doom the individual and fatally weaken society. It is not clear whether the piercing gaze of the gentleman represents this social anxiety about the perils of female acquisitiveness, or whether it registers a pressing concern about his ability to maintain her as his possession in the context of a competitive market where both things and bodies are for sale. The woman in white, it appears, has nowhere to look and no way to look without engendering a form of colonial anxiety that derives from her highly precarious position of power based on her gender, "race," and social status. Is that what this picture is also about—not only the aesthetic and erotic pleasures offered by such an ambiguously marked body but also the precariousness of whiteness as an absolute value in an island culture where the possibility of "passing" depends on local knowledge of genealogies and social performance, rather than the lightness of one's skin? Or, even more worryingly, does it threaten to expose whiteness as the fantasy that it really is—a fiction designed to secure the power and, as Kalpana Seshadri-Crooks has recently argued, the psychic wholeness of the Anglo-European subject?[27] In any event, Brunias did not depict a woman manifesting this degree of racial ambiguity in any of the other market scenes that I have encountered thus far in my research in Jamaica, England, and North America.

In this analysis I have resorted to a "process of elimination" as a method for understanding what sort of woman might best be able to represent the prosperity and promise of the newest British colonies in the West Indies. I am not claiming that this is how Brunias arrived at a solution; it is much more likely that he developed his compositions intuitively rather than by some abstract deductive process, although that intuition was also socially formed and ideologically conditioned. Instead, my purpose in taking this approach is to show what problems were associated with the alternatives and why visualizing such a problematic figure as the mulatto woman might have seemed a viable solution—more viable, in fact, than the white woman who fulfilled the role of representing Britain as a highly civilized society but could not serve the same function for its West Indian colonies. We have examined some of the difficulties of representing white creole women "in public." The domestic sphere was unavailable, and there was not a wide array of polite social spaces in the new British islands that could be mobilized as an alternative. If the markets and paths that Brunias depicts were not polite spaces, they were perhaps the next best thing—important sites of social and commercial exchange among slaves and especially among the women of color who largely ran the weekly markets held on Sundays and were their dominant attractions.[28] Rendered in a cursory and generalized manner, these settings mark out a space that is neither familiar and civilized (not urban or quite rural) nor savage and threatening. There are just enough signs—a palm tree here, a thatched hut there—to locate the scene within the imaginative geography of the torrid zone. Like the people of color who populate it, this is a creolized landscape that is underdeveloped and under development.

If, as I am arguing, one of the important ideological functions of these multivalent images was to promote these islands as potentially civilized settlements for enterprising Britons, it is important to attend to the particular way that refinement is produced within an economy based on slave rather than wage labor. In a slave economy, social refinement depends upon disavowing the violence and coercion involved in the laborious extraction and transformation of raw materials into finished products. Brunias's proud, lavishly dressed mulatress seems designed to banish all thoughts of forced labor, rape, and brutal punishment. Appearing outside of the plantation house and the cane

Figure 13.7. After Agostino Brunias, *A Negro Festival, Drawn from Nature, in the Island of St. Vincent* in Bryan Edwards's *History of the West Indies.* Courtesy of the John Carter Brown Library, Brown University.

field, her figure commands the space of the market while being actively disengaged from commercial transactions. Like the figures in English conversation pieces, she is involved in conversation or polite recreations, such as dancing (see, for example, fig. 13.7, *A Negro Festival in the Island of St. Vincent* after Brunias from Bryan Edwards's *History of the West Indies*). Even when she is not dancing (as in figures 13.1 and 13.2), her pose is often more suited to that activity than to buying goods at market. In referring to forms of dance that were discernibly Europeanized, this figure serves as a substitute for slave performers who could not so easily be imaged—either within the physical spaces of polite sociability in which these paintings were viewed or within the representational space of an image attempting to forge some form of West Indian refinement. According to one account from the late 1780s, foreign slave ships would anchor just off shore from Roseau (like the ships in the background of figure 13.6), and the shipmasters would bring the slaves on deck at certain times of day and oblige them to sing in chorus a "yo-yo" that could be heard for more than a mile.[29] Such forced music would form a weird accompaniment to the fashionable mulatress who, while operating as a surrogate for these slave performers, seems to be dancing to an altogether different tune. I am using here

Joseph Roach's notion of surrogation, which addresses the attempts by a society to authenticate itself in the process of filling vacancies that occur when crucial members of a society die or leave.[30] In this case the members in question (slaves) were neither dead nor gone but disavowed as subjects actively involved in the production of a refined civilization. Roach argues that the attempt to provide substitutes is rarely successful because they usually either fail to fulfill expectations or exceed them. As a surrogate for slaves forced to perform music (and labor and sex) the "dancing mulatress's" sheer excessiveness—her inflated body, dramatic gestures, and ornate costume—are signs of colonial anxieties that continue to surface despite attempts to banish them via replacement, disavowal, and repetition.

Just as the figures of the mulatress can be seen as a refined substitute for those slave performers who could be heard but not seen, Brunias's Sunday markets, populated with happy, well-dressed people of color, serve as surrogates for those unrepresentable slave markets that deal in human flesh. It is the setting and performance of the figures in these scenes rather than their legal status that enables this substitution to take place, as most of the slaves and free people of color involved in the Sunday markets as buyers and sellers had been, were, or could all too easily become goods sold at market.[31] Within these flesh markets, economic value is determined not by voluntary display of fine clothing but by forced exhibition of the naked body; there buyers and sellers assess the capacity for productivity, reproductivity, pleasure, and pain via a complex semiotics of physical attributes, including skin color. Brunias also attended to gradations in skin color in order to register social distinctions as well as racialized difference. Light-skinned women of color are usually more lavishly dressed than their darker-skinned counterparts and are often accompanied by darker-skinned attendants (as in figure 13.2). They also are less likely to be shown selling fruits and vegetables or seated close to the ground, and are more often represented as purveyors of dry goods or as consumers. Such differences represent not merely a division of labor but a system of power relations in which personal freedom, as well as socioeconomic status was at issue, for as Barry Higman has shown, as slaves approached whiteness, their (very slim) chance of manumission increased.[32] Brunias's images suggest that such a social hierarchy based on an aesthetics and ideology of whiteness functions even in situations where the white body is visually absent.

As a site for staging such hierarchical relations through a complex set of social performances and economic exchanges, the market is apposite because it is a place where meanings are particularly labile. A commodity can mean whatever its buyer wishes it to mean—it is value that counts.[33] Brunias's lavishly dressed mulatress serves as the perfect polysemous commodity: her sheer size and repetitiveness, as she travels from painting to painting virtually unaltered, are testimonies to her connotative oversaturation. Refusing manual labor and soliciting colonial desire, she operates as a sign of a developing civilization at the rudest margins of empire. She is, of course, a racially hybrid figure—with both her Africanness and her Frenchness enhancing her exoticism and sexual desirability. Yet she is also a subject who occupies that ambiguous and highly precarious position between the political freedom of the white European or creole, and the abject state of the slave. Such ambiguity permits the mulatto woman to be read quite differently by, say, a British viewer with little knowledge of the West Indies, who might mistake her for a happy, well-treated slave, and a West Indian creole, who could appreciate both the very real constraints and opportunities afforded such an individual within the context of a society based upon African slavery. As a polysemic sign set within a landscape under development, the mulatress operates as a surrogate for the other female bodies—African, Indian, and European—that were too abject or unruly to represent these new British colonies that themselves would be riven by conflict throughout the remainder of the global eighteenth century.

CHAPTER FOURTEEN

Archipelagic Encounters

War, Race, and Labor in American-Caribbean Waters

Nicholas Rogers

On a Saturday night in October 1744, in the English harbor of Antigua, the crew of the *Mercury* were living it up. The occasion was the capture of a Dutch sloop, or at least of a sloop flying Dutch colors that had been marauding colonial shipping, and the seamen were no doubt looking forward to receiving the windfalls of the prize. Between ten and eleven o'clock, the sentinel spied a smaller craft approaching and hailed it to little avail. Amid the noise of drums, trumpet, and general merrymaking, the watch could neither identify the approaching vessel nor comprehend the muffled response of its seamen, some of it in French. The *Mercury*'s captain was alerted. "Warm" with drink and armed with a pistol, he demanded that the boat heave to. The commander of the small vessel, the master of a local tender, pleaded with the captain not to fire "for there were only Negroes that were with him in the boat."[1] Nonetheless, Captain Montague, concerned that the intruders might be French, "snapped his piece" indiscriminately into the boat and on his second attempt severely wounded one of the seamen in the thigh. The injured man was brought on board, but the ship's surgeon was too drunk to dress his wounds properly and so the surgeon from HMS *Lynn* was called for. By the time he arrived, the injured man had lost a lot of blood. The second surgeon patched him up as best he could, but the man died the following morning. His wound crudely sutured with needle and thread, with only a small "roller" over the dressing, he bled to death on the deck.

Captain William Montague of the HMS *Mercury* was hardly perturbed by this incident. The dead man was a slave, one of the "King's negroes" belonging to the yard at Antigua whose job it was to careen the vessels of the Royal Navy. As far as Montague was concerned, his action merited at most a fine and some monetary compensation to the government for the loss of one of its slaves. This was all the laws of Antigua demanded, he informed the Admiralty. He had not committed a willful killing, "much less was it done illegally or wantonly," he continued. It happened because of the "wilful default of those in the Boat, in not answering when haled to." In his opinion, the "whole island" and other crews in the harbor "looked on it in this light."[2]

Montague was astounded when Commodore Charles Knowles, the illegitimate son of the fourth earl of Banbury, sent him home to face a court martial. Not only did Montague lose his share of potential prizes and his place in the officer hierarchy, he complained, he also suffered "greatly in his Honour and Reputation."[3] The lords of the Admiralty, for their part, sympathized with Montague's predicament, and they were no doubt influenced by Knowles's dispute with the crown over the distribution of two Spanish prizes.[4] While they did not question Knowles's decision to send Montague home, they did not initiate a court martial either. Indeed, the only court martial to eventuate from the affair concerned the surgeon of the *Mercury,* who was charged with professional negligence.[5] Rather, the Admiralty quickly restored Captain Montague to the command of another vessel at the Deptford yard and had him carry volunteers and pressed men down to the Nore. Within a month or two, Montague found himself reconnoitering off the French and Spanish coasts, where he picked up a French ship bound for Bordeaux loaded with cacao and cayenne: a catch, he informed their lordships, "which I believe will turn out to be a very good prize."[6]

The incident at English harbor is a tragic story of racial contempt and of the incredible insouciance of a naval officer who, by the racist standards of the day, thought himself above reproach. It is also about the predatory world of the mid-eighteenth-century Caribbean, where the spoils of war were fierce and competitive. Furthermore, it throws an oblique light upon the different labor regimes that made up that world and shaped the manner in which great power struggles could be fought in it.

More than one servile labor force faced one another at English harbor in October 1744. Apart from the poor slaves who were subjected to Captain Montague's intemperate actions, his own ship contained seamen who had been brought to the Caribbean against their will and were consigned to serve in his majesty's navy for the duration of the war. Precisely how many impressed men were aboard the *Mercury* in 1744 is uncertain, for the muster books provide no reliable indication of the numbers who were coerced into service rather than taken as volunteers. However, it seems likely that approximately a third of the *Mercury*'s crew were impressed.[7] They were part of a larger resistance to naval service that at its most violent generated widespread anti-impressment riots, the most dramatic occurring at Gravesend where a "great Mob of People" rescued pressed men from the local gaol.[8] In fact, there were at least fifty-five anti-impressment affrays reported by the recruiting officers from the inception of the war to the incident at English harbor. Despite the excitement that surrounded the war at home and the jubilations that greeted Admiral Vernon's early victories, despite hard winters and soaring bread prices, the reality was that the Admiralty had to scour the jails and streets to find a sufficient quota of men. As Sir Charles Wager remarked to Vernon at the very outset of the war, "We must do as well as we can, but we find great Difficulty in getting Seamen enough for our ships, which has been our Case in all our considerable Sea Armaments."[9]

Serving on his majesty's ships was a poor substitute for the high wages that a seaman might enjoy on a merchantman, or for the windfalls of war that might be won on a privateer. But the reluctance to serve in the 1740s was amplified by the fact that the main theater of war was in the Caribbean. This torrid zone was well known to be a deathtrap. The risks of war were underscored by the popular comparison between Vernon's victory at Porto Bello and the fate of Admiral Hosier's expedition some twelve years earlier, when 4,000 seamen died of yellow fever. In the 1740s the death toll never reached these dizzy heights, at least for seamen; although it has been computed that at least two-thirds of the soldiers who embarked on Caribbean expeditions in the 1740s died of tropical diseases.[10] Yet in proportion to the number of seamen borne, the death rate was formidable enough. In the cramped quarters of the lower deck, an early exposure to malaria could quite literally decimate crews. Of the two squadrons stationed at Jamaica in 1741, some 2,514 men, more than 17 percent of the total, were discharged dead, while another 5 percent were off-duty sick.[11] On some ships the proportion of men who went down due to either scurvy or malaria topped 30 percent. Without adequate hospitals in which to house them, the lower decks were seething cellars of disease, as Tobias Smollett, a former surgeon's mate, so graphically represented in *Roderick Random*.[12]

In an effort to offset the inevitable mortality of crews in Caribbean waters, the Admiralty adopted a number of strategies. To begin with, crews were supplemented with supernumaries on setting sail from Britain, but this was only accomplished with difficulty when hostility to impressment ran high.[13] Another alternative was to impress men in the colonies, either from the colonial ports or from homeward-bound vessels. The crews of Guineamen were especially vulnerable on this score, for slavers routinely augmented their complement in anticipation of slave revolts on the middle passage. Indeed, the Royal Navy customarily attempted to impress up to one in three Guineamen on their return voyages and up to one in five from other merchant ships. Sometimes

there were complaints that commanders were taking more.[14] Admiral Davers, for instance, was criticized for pressing too many men from outward-bound vessels in 1745,
although he claimed he only did so where they were regarded as "mutinous and dangerous fellows."[15]

The difficulty with this policy was that the flow of men frequently ran in the opposite direction. Once hospitals were built in the major ports of the Caribbean, men-of-
war frequently anchored to discharge their sick men, and because all ships were regularly infested with the toredo worm in tropical waters—at least until the introduction
of copper sheathing in the 1770s—they frequently had to be careened in dry dock.[16]
The consequence was that naval seamen had real opportunities to desert—and desert
they did. About 4 percent of the Jamaica squadron deserted in 1741, over 6 percent in
1747. These figures approximated those who disappeared while on general leave at
home, but on some ships the proportion was in excess of 20 percent.[17] One storeship,
the *Astrea,* lost virtually its whole crew between March and December 1741. Lured by
the high wages offered by merchants for homeward-bound runs, or by the prospects of
privateering, seamen were ready to jump ship.

Naval officers did all they could to prevent this drain of labor. In April 1744, five men
belonging to HMS *Plymouth* were given three dozen lashes each for desertion, a punishment that must have drenched the gratings in blood. Very occasionally a deserter was
hanged from the yardarm; "to deter others" remarked Commodore Knowles in 1744,
"for no corporal Punishments have been able to do it."[18] In the following year Admiral
Davers executed two men because "the continual Desertions from his Majesties ships
& the hospital obliged me to make examples of them, as Offenders of the worst kind."[19]
Yet punishments of this magnitude could only be used sparingly, for the navy wanted
men, not bloody backs and broken necks. Consequently, the Admiralty also attempted
to deter seamen from desertion by recommending that they should lose not only their
wages but their prize money, the latter being regarded as a form of private property that
seamen could claim through the prize courts. This prohibition was achieved by parliamentary act in 1744.

None of these actions diminished the level of desertion as long as local merchants
offered high wages for the homeward-bound trade and privateers inveigled men from
the service with the promise of ever larger spoils. Every commander on the Jamaica station recognized this to be the crux of the problem, yet none proved able to resolve it.
Admiral Vernon attempted to bully the merchants into compliance, only to witness the
desertion of more than 500 men from the hospital at Port Royal, lured, so he claimed,
"through the temptation of high wages and thirty gallons of rum."[20] When he scoured
the taverns of Port Royal and cracked down on the North American traffic in his quest

for men, he so alienated the Jamaica merchants that his second-in-command, Sir Chaloner Ogle, nearly came to blows with the governor over the issue and suffered the indignity of a prosecution for assault.[21] Commodore Knowles, for his part, strove to persuade the merchants that the privateers were seducing their crews and that it was in their mutual interest to restrain their commissions. However, he failed to convince them this was so and had to tolerate the harassment of his gangs at the hands of privateers and conniving magistrates. His captains, he complained, were "insulted by 50 Arm'd men at a time" when they came on shore looking for men, and were "obliged to take shelter in some Friends houses." He was bitterly critical of the magistrates who, rather than quelling the riots, "encouraged the Privateers Men to knock the Men of Warr Dogs (as they call them) on the head."[22]

Part of the manning problem in the Caribbean was that the local imperatives of commerce did not easily square with the imperatives of war. Island planters and merchants wanted safe convoys for their sugar, rum, and molasses; open channels of trade with the North American colonies upon whom they were dependent for provisions and lumber; and a sufficient privateering force to ward off enemy predators and to capture enemy cargoes. In other words, they wanted the best of all worlds. They were quite willing to take naval officers to court over matters of impressment. The captain of the *Deal Castle,* for instance, found himself facing damages of £2,000 for an alleged "trespass" upon merchant property following an aggressive impressment exercise in St. Kitts.[23] Moreover, in its efforts to keep the navy at arm's length, the colonial elite threatened to revive an old 1708 statute that prohibited the impressment of seamen in the colonies save those who were technically deserters.[24] Although the act was declared null and void in 1740 on the grounds that it had expired at the conclusion of the War of Spanish Succession in 1713, there was still considerable disagreement over its legal status. In the northern colonies the act had been used to stiffen popular resistance to impressment, leading to a full-scale riot against the press gang in Boston in which the council chamber was besieged and the regulating officers run out of town.[25] In the islands, there was less insistence upon the act's legality but considerable resistance to impressment none the less. In St. Kitts and Antigua, naval officers were prosecuted for riotous recruitment while in Barbados the governor only prevented a pitched battle between the press gang and the mob by calling out the militia.[26] Under the circumstances, the powerful West India interest pressed for the reenactment of the 1708 act. It did not entirely succeed. The new act of 1746 allowed the navy to impress deserters, as before, but it also permitted impressment where an invasion was imminent or where there was "any other unforeseen and emergent necessity."[27] Loosely interpreted, this clause might well have nullified the whole act, yet it also specified that impressment could only be undertaken with the assent of the governor or colonial assembly. In the incessant wrangling over impressment in Caribbean waters during the 1740s, the colonial authorities had secured the upper hand.

The Caribbean elite's hostility to impressment was fueled by fear that the islands would be starved of crucial supplies from the North American colonies as the naval presence in Caribbean waters intensified.[28] Within the planter elite there was the further anxiety that the islands would be stripped of white men, disrupting the ratio of whites to blacks that was thought necessary to sustain social stability.[29] The urgency of the problem was accentuated by the growth of the great plantations on the major sugar-producing islands, and by the lower ratio of whites to blacks that resulted from British competition with the French, whose sugar economy had overtaken the British in the 1720s and 1730s.[30]

The most critical issue was the fear of internal revolt. The onset of the war with Spain coincided with South Carolina's Stono rebellion, whose reverberations were felt down the Florida coast to St. Augustine, where the Spanish continued to entice runaway slaves with promises of freedom.[31] In Antigua, where there had been an island-wide revolt led by a group of Coromantees in 1735, it was reported five years later that white planters and their overseers "had a most narrow escape from having their Throats cut by their slaves."[32] Although the ferment in Jamaica had subsided with the conclusion of a decade-long war with the Maroons, the situation remained volatile. In the early years of the war it was still unclear whether the Windward and Leeward Maroons would uphold their bargain to return runaway slaves and aid the planters to defend the island from enemy invasion. Eventually, the Leeward Maroons under Cudjoe did help quell a Coromantee slave rebellion in 1742.[33] Two years later, however, Governor Trelawny discovered another slave conspiracy, encouraged, so he thought, by the recruitment of an independent militia to aid the war with France.[34] Clearly, Trelawny viewed the prospect of arming blacks with increasing concern, even though the Cuban expedition of 1741 had necessitated it because the British companies in the Caribbean had succumbed to yellow fever in such large numbers.[35] The outbreak of another slave revolt in St. David's parish in 1745 likely strengthened his reservations, and it was predictable that in the discussions for settling the Mosquito coast, Trelawny strenuously argued against large-scale slave plantations for fear of further slave revolts and Maroon havens.[36]

The prospect of slave revolt made the planter class unwilling to commit a large number of its white settlers to man his majesty's fleets. They were needed, Trelawny explicitly remarked, "to quell any rebellions that may suddenly arise among their Slaves,"[37] particularly in wartime when regular army garrisons were overstretched. Why, then, did the planters not concede its black slaves, just as they had conceded several black companies to the military expeditions to Cuba in 1741 and Porto Bello in 1742?

It was not a matter of skill. Black slaves were sometimes seasoned seamen, and some were hired out by their masters to provision plantations or ships in local harbors. Slave codes attempted to regulate their movements and to ensure that they sailed with white masters or overseers, or in the case of Jamaica, with certificates of leave.[38] Yet maritime slavery was certainly growing, constituting perhaps 3 percent of the total slave population in Nevis in 1765, and roughly the same proportion in Jamaica a decade later.[39] In the trade of the northern colonies to the Caribbean, the presence of black seamen was noticeable, enhanced perhaps by the reluctance of white seamen to sail to the Caribbean in wartime. A spot check of the vessels lying in Kingston harbor in mid-December 1743, from Boston, New York, Rhode Island, and Bermuda, revealed that 30 percent of the crewmen were black, and some of these slaves rather than freemen. In the Bermuda vessels, in particular, blacks routinely outnumbered whites aboard ship—a pattern that deeply disturbed Governor Trelawny.[40]

Blacks also achieved enviable reputations as pilots in Caribbean waters, where swift currents, shifting winds, and shoaled passages could be extremely dangerous to commercial traffic. In the windward passage between Jamaica and Hispaniola, for example, the currents were known to be "very irregular" and "seldom set in the same direction for two days altogether." At Plumb Point off Port Royal, it was imperative to get the aid of pilots, remarked Charles Roberts later in the century; they were "so useful [a] body of men that every encouragement ought to be given them both here and elsewhere."[41] Not surprisingly, black pilots were often venerated for their skills and knowledge of local waters, and were poached by Britain's enemies. At the end of the war, Spanish brigantines were reported off the Mosquito coast looking among the blacks for able pilots before they set off on a raiding expedition to the Cayman Islands.[42]

Placing slaves on board men-of-war was not unprecedented. French ships had recruited slaves from Saint Domingue during the war of the 1690s,[43] but the planters in the British colonies were very averse to following suit. They had only agreed to the recruitment of black auxiliaries for the 1740–42 military expeditions with the utmost reluctance, as exceptional concessions to the British war effort. Indeed, the vast majority of these slaves acted in an unarmed capacity, as "pioneers" or general drudges rather than as "shot negroes," as they were popularly known.[44] Given the general uncertainty about internal rebellion, and the fear that some slaves would avail themselves of the wartime situation to desert their masters, it was hardly surprising that the planters were averse to volunteering their slaves as naval seamen. Like their counterparts in Virginia and the Carolinas, they thought maritime slavery would corrode bonded labor because of the mobility and worldliness it encouraged.[45] If they did agree to set their slaves afloat, it was in privateering vessels rather than men-of-war, and only because of dramatic shortages of white seamen. In 1745, for example, John Curtin, a planter and owner of the privateer *Dowdall,* was forced to put fourteen of his own slaves on board his vessel because too many of his sailors had been impressed aboard HMS *Adventure.*[46]

In subsequent wars the planters deplored the way in which the navy inveigled slaves aboard men-of-war and kept masters at bay through the "licentious and uncontrouled Behaviour of the Seamen."[47] In the 1740s this practice was unnecessary because the navy had not proactively recruited runaways. The navy wished to placate a planter class bent upon reviving the 1708 act against impressment, and naval captains upheld the proprietorial nature of slavery. There may also have been a general reluctance to mix two servile labor regimes. Slaves were, after all, among the spoils of war. Although the war of the 1740s seldom degenerated into the general manhunt that characterized the War of Spanish Succession, when enemy plantations were raided with impunity, slaves were part of the prizes captured by British men-of-war. In 1744, for example, Commodore Knowles's fleet captured two slave ships from the Guinea coast and Angola, the first with 400 blacks on board, the second with 650.[48] These prizes would have been worth about £30,000 and shared, albeit very unevenly, among the crews involved. Such rewards were one of the few tonics that kept seamen aboard ship in these torrid climes, inducing, noted Admiral Vernon, "a good will for the Public Service."[49] Bringing large numbers of slaves on board to serve in the navy would likely have unsettled already fractious crews and complicated relations on the lower deck. Slaves capturing slaves was, of course, one of the historical paradoxes of Caribbean warfare, but it was best left to privateers rather than the large crews of the Royal Navy to negotiate the contradictions it might have involved.[50]

This did not mean that the Royal Navy did not bring slaves on board ship—only that it did not actively recruit them in large numbers. Naval officers were sometimes accompanied by black servants whom they had purchased, as was Captain Pascal by Olaudah Equiano during the Seven Years War.[51] So, too, was the odd ship's carpenter. In the muster book of HMS *Plymouth,* for example, James Caesar, a carpenter's servant, was entered on 25 July 1745 along with his master, who collected Caesar's wages until his discharge two years later.[52] Quite possibly a few runaways were recruited at Caribbean ports, especially when desertion rates ran high and complements were perilously low. On HMS *Lenox,* for example, which lost nearly a third of its crew through death or desertion on the Jamaica station, we find that William Quasshy was entered as an able seaman at Port Royal, and John Quamino as a boatswain's servant six months later. On HMS *Canterbury,* where the ship's complement was down by 25 percent, we discover entries at Barbados for Hilkia Moor and Black Emmanuel.[53] Whether these men were runaways or free blacks it is impossible to say. Free blacks certainly found their way onto men-of-war, either as impressed men or as volunteers who feared reenslavement on the islands if they were without work.[54] John Henzer was among those aboard HMS *Litch-*

field until his desertion in 1740. He was described as having "a swarthy mulatto complexion and black lank hair, aged about 28 years," five feet seven inches high with "a large scar on the inside of his shoulder."[55] Yet men like Henzer were not as visible in the Royal Navy as they would be later in the century, when the free black population in the British colonies was considerably larger.

Slaves and ex-slaves, then, did find their way on board British men-of-war but not in numbers that would have made them a very visible minority. The only exception to the rule was the Jamaican Maroons who volunteered for service aboard HMS *Princess Louisa*,[56] and after the 1739 treaty they were clearly a special case. By and large the British navy followed the army strategy of using slaves as auxiliaries. The captain of the *Deal Castle* reported in early 1744 that he sent his carpenter, a gang of men, and "8 Negroes ashore to Cutt Timber." Later a further "6 Negroes" were brought in from Spanish Town to assist in the work.[57] In Jamaica and Antigua, the British government even purchased its own slaves to careen, caulk, and repair the ships. With their own women and children, they formed small companies, thirty or so in size, known as "His Majesty's Negroes." From time to time the British navy hired other slaves to supplement this small but skilled work force. In Antigua, Governor Matthew arranged for a hundred blacks to help the navy rebuild its wharf and careen its ships. In Jamaica in 1748, Commodore Knowles asked Governor Trelawny for 250 blacks to assist "in heaving the ships" in order to careen them.[58] He was reluctant to commit his own seamen, he said, because too many of them had been enticed away by the high wages offered by merchants for the "run home." Besides, he added, echoing the prejudices of his day, blacks were acclimatized to heavy labor in the sun in a way most of his seamen were not. As one contemporary writer asserted, "Drudgery in the Sun cannot be borne by the *Europeans*."[59]

In segregating its servile workforce by race, the British navy inevitably found itself continually short of men on board ship. Ostensibly, the colonial authorities cooperated with the navy in its search for deserters. Laws were passed imposing heavy fines on anyone who harbored them.[60] Yet frequently these laws were honored in the breach. Too many colonial officials had links to merchants and privateers to take the regulations seriously, and when navy press gangs scoured ports to track down deserters, they were sometimes opposed by colonial forces. In 1746 the search party of the *Falmouth* was arrested by the militia in Spanish Town on the grounds that its unruly behavior threatened the town on what was a "negro holiday." When Admiral Davers complained, Governor Trelawny retorted that the actions of the militia officer were "prudent."[61] Davers thought otherwise. It was indicative, he informed the Admiralty, of the way in which the service was being compromised by officials whose first allegiance was to the merchant and planter elite.[62]

The tug of war over manning the navy inevitably led commanders to adopt other expedients. Prisoners of war were sometimes given the option of serving in his majesty's fleet rather than languishing in close quarters. Some accepted, for the muster books are littered with Spanish names in particular. Indeed, free black or mulatto seamen from Spanish vessels had a special inducement to enlist, for there was a very real prospect that they might be enslaved if they reached British ports, especially if they could be construed as part of British prizes.[63] Together with the pressing that took place off shore— from privateers, from merchant ships on the homeward run, even from vessels flying flags of truce—the navy strove hard to hold on to a minimal complement of men.[64] In 1744 Commodore Knowles complained that he could only man his squadron in the Leeward Islands by exchanging prisoners with the French, a frustrating experience because island governors deemed such exchanges to be within their jurisdiction and frequently turned the prisoners over to privateers.[65]

In these circumstances, the severe strain upon crews was registered by squabbles over prizes and near-mutinies when commanders lost sight of ships with valuable spoils, or were thought to be dealing with local merchants over contraband goods that would otherwise have been condemned.[66] One seaman, who had been pressed into service thirty-two months previously and had little respite from service beyond a brief sick leave in Gibraltar, was sentenced to thirty-six lashes of the cat for describing HMS *Eltham* as a "prison" (despite his having worked his way up to being a quartermaster).[67] In the following month, on another man-of-war that had done long service in the Leeward Islands, two men were hanged from the yardarm for deserting their ship and drowning the midshipman in the process. The bosun's mate who had abetted their escape was sentenced to 300 lashes of the cat o' nine tails, a punishment that if rigorously executed would have surely killed him.[68]

Deserting a ship in foreign waters was risky. It was especially so in the hurricane season between July and mid-October when merchant shipping virtually stopped, leaving seamen little choice but to linger in port. Without contacts, seamen could easily fall into the hands of local crimps, who would consign them to the highest bidder. A deserter's chances of getting home were best when the large merchant convoys were about to sail in the spring and early summer, although the chances of detection on the voyage were high. The other alternatives were finding some space for survival on the Caribbean frontier or joining a privateer; there were over 400 British privateers in Caribbean waters in the peak years of 1745–47, as well as those rigged out by the Spanish and French.

Historians have sometimes suggested that the profits of privateering were little better than the prize money that a seaman might obtain aboard a man-of-war. In the Caribbean, at least, the prospects were better because the distribution of prizes was more equitably shared among the crew, with only a third of the share going to the owner rather than the half demanded in European waters.[69] Much, of course, depended upon chance, upon the capture of a lucrative prize, for privateering crews were not always paid wages. Yet the rewards from captured cargoes of sugar, molasses, tobacco, coffee, and indigo were often more than double the average wage paid to merchant seamen and six times the Royal Navy's monthly wage.[70] Besides, there were opportunities for running contraband trade to enemy islands and even for trafficking in slaves. The Bahamian privateers, in particular, seem to have been notorious on this score. They routinely captured slaves from open boats and canoes off the coast of Hispaniola and supplied that island with much needed provisions.[71]

Naval officers sometimes expressed disbelief that seamen with two or three years' back pay would desert for a privateer, but the lure of spoils was great. In any case, the discipline aboard a privateer was not as harsh as on a man-of-war, where naval officers had armed marines to back up their decisions. The promise of shorter cruises, usually seven months in all, was also attractive. Among other things, it gave British seamen the opportunity of getting back to British North America and then home, for the principal ports from which privateers hailed were New York, Newport, Boston, and Philadelphia.[72]

As a last resort, a seaman might seek a haven in which to hide for the duration of the war. In the Caribbean of the 1740s, the number of places where one might eke out such an existence were limited. Most islands and isthmuses were rapidly becoming part of the plantation zone, in which there was a significant growth of large estates at the expense of poor white settlers. The one obvious frontier for British colonists in the mid–eighteenth century was in Central America among the logwood settlements of the Bay of Honduras or further south on the Mosquito coast, where handfuls of white settlers lived alongside the Miskito Indians and mustees descended from coastal Indians and shipwrecked black slaves. The Mosquito coast was of no economic importance. Rather, its significance was strategic, for the British had cultivated good relations with the Miskito Indians, paying for their good will in an effort to counter Spanish ambitions in the area and to cultivate a reserve force for putting down slave rebellions in Jamaica. On the other hand, the logwood enterprises and the valuable dyes they produced were important to the British woollen industry. They were largely seasonal settlements run with slave labor, despite the fiction of patriotic discourse in Britain which portrayed them as industrious territories of free-born Englishmen vulnerable to the lawless depredations of the Spanish. In fact, the Baymen were quite prepared to engage in illicit trading with the Spanish, who claimed the territory, and also with the Dutch and northern colonists who received the lion's share of the lumber. There was no semblance of government. "The modern settlers, as well as their predecessors," remarked Edward Long two decades later, "have lived hitherto in a kind of republican state, having no governor appointed over them."[73] Governor Trelawny of Jamaica thought that the whole coastline was "a retreat for Pyrates and disorderly people averse to all Government" and that it had been so for forty years.[74] Captain Nathaniel Uring, who had spent some time among the logwood cutters earlier in the century, was of the same opinion. He thought them a "rude drunken crew," a motley group of ex-pirates and seamen whose "chief delight" was "drinking."[75]

Naval deserters certainly ventured to the area during wartime. When the Jamaican government decided to build a port and garrison on the island of Ruatan as a center of operations against the Spanish, some of the seamen jumped ship.[76] A few may even have joined the various expeditions against the Spaniards that the adventurer Ralph Hodgson organized on behalf of the government; these expeditions were compromised by the Miskito preference for marauding and enslaving local Indians. Others may have joined the privateers who cruised the coast, or participated in the raids on Spanish settlements in Truxillo and Omoa in the aftermath of the war.[77] Some deserters would have been confronted by their own kind, for in the retaliations of the Spanish along the Mosquito coast by two brigantines, half of the crews were said to be English or Scottish. "A little hanging for these renegadoes, if they can be catched," remarked Hodgson, "would be extremely wholesome."[78]

The continuation of hostilities up and down the Mosquito coast in the early 1750s points to the difficulties that many seamen had in coming to terms with the armistice of the great powers. Seamen who became habituated to privateering or to trafficking in contraband goods under flags of truce sometimes found it difficult to return to normal commerce once war was terminated. Captain Henry Osborn remarked on the shift from privateering to piracy at Montserrat and recalled an attempt to do this off Barbados aboard the *Chesterfield* privateer.[79] The same happened at New York. When several French prizes were not condemned before the declaration of peace, a few crews mutinied and became "very arrogant & desperate," according to Governor Clinton, "& threaten publicly that they will cut out some Vessels, and hoist the Black flag."[80] Among those who did so was Owen Lloyd, a seaman who persuaded the masters of two Rhode Island sloops to steal the cargo of a Spanish galleon moored in Ocracoke inlet in Pamlico Sound and venture south to Caribbean waters. One of the sloops ran aground, but peg-legged Lloyd successfully charted the other to Spanish Town, Jamaica, and then onward to the Virgin Islands, where he reached his own treasure island—Norman's south of Tortola. There, on an uninhabited island that was a regular rendezvous for privateers with contraband goods, he unloaded 50 chests of Spanish dollars and church plate, 120 bales of cochineal, and 70 bags of indigo and tobacco.[81] It was a spectacular heist, worth perhaps £100,000. Lloyd's own share of the catch appears to have been a tenth, about £10,000, a princely sum for a seaman and one that likely set him up for life.

If he managed to get away with it, Owen Lloyd's haul paled in comparison to the windfalls of war that accrued to admirals—several of whom received £100,000 or more in prizes—and the risks were incomparably greater. The golden age of piracy was over. Under the vigilance of the Royal Navy, the pirate community had been broken in the 1720s, dwindling in numbers to little more than 200 men. The great powers of Europe were not about to tolerate its revival thirty years later once the war had been concluded. Although some captains feared that wartime privateering would "breed up a Nursery of Pyrates,"[82] policing operations and trials were the order of the day, aided and abetted by the privateer owners themselves, who in the last year of war transferred their investments to less predatory activities.

British seamen of the 1740s were more likely to go "upon the account" on Hounslow Heath than they were on the not-so-Spanish Main. As one English commentator remarked, the end of the war would "loose upon the Nation Twenty Thousand *Sixpence-a-Day Heroes,* with perhaps a Crown in their Pockets, and very little Inclination to starve for want of recruiting out of other People's Property."[83] In this struggle for survival there were few cross-cultural alliances that extended beyond the lower deck. Indeed, the camaraderie that seamen fostered during the war tended to be concrete and specific to their own crews. According to John Brown, a vicar from the thriving port of Newcastle-upon-Tyne, it was this sort of comradeship that made the British navy such a formidable fighting force.[84]

Although there have been recent attempts to situate Atlantic mariners at the center of a rebellious, multiethnic proletariat in the eighteenth century,[85] there is actually little evidence that seafaring solidarities extended to other subaltern groups in the Caribbean or indeed in North America. In the incident at English harbor with which I began this chapter, there is fleeting evidence that some of the crew disapproved of Captain Montague's intemperate actions. Several refused to fire into the longboat, and the mate attempted to intervene before Montague fired his second shot.[86] There were also a few occasions when blacks alerted white seamen to the threat of impressment, joining them (among many others, propertied and unpropertied) in their protests during the Boston riot of 1747.[87] Yet such support was fleeting and fragmentary. There is no evidence that seamen sympathized with slave revolts in the Caribbean during this decade. Although there was some collusion between Irish soldiers garrisoned at Fort George and the slaves who worked along the New York waterfront in the conspiracy of 1741, the New York seamen were conspicuously absent. The only seamen clearly implicated in the plot to burn the houses of the royal governor and other well-heeled citizens were Spanish-speaking free men of color who had been sold into slavery when their sloop, *La Soledad,* had been condemned as a prize of war. These men had a particular grievance against Captain John Lush, the man who had separated them from their white crew members and sold them in New York. They protested that "if the captain would not send them to their own country, they would ruin all the city." Amid threats of burning the town and "killing all the people," and boasts that they could kill twenty times as many people as an equivalent group of "York negroes," they looked forward to the possibility of the French or Spanish invading New York and facilitating their emancipation.[88] Their sentiments were hardly revolutionary or conducive to forging more permanent solidarities among the diverse subalterns of the Atlantic world. Rather, they were very much part of the particular conjuncture of eighteenth-century war, its adventure capitalism, and racial inequities. Nor did the other known sailor who was involved in the conspiracy show much solidarity with the New York waterfront. He was Christopher Wilson, an eighteen-year-old from the hospital ship, the *Flamborough*. He had been part of the fencing network at Hughson's tavern where the conspiracy was hatched, but he turned in one of the chief conspirators, a slave called Caesar who was owned by a New York baker.[89]

What is particularly damaging to the notion of a multiethnic Atlantic working class that features sailors and slaves prominently among its motley crew is that sailors were deeply implicated in the institution of slavery, both as pirates and privateers. Despite the existence of pirate "commonwealths" and more egalitarian relations aboard ship, pirates were not ideologically opposed to slavery. On the contrary, pirates in Madagascar and Sierra Leone owned and traded slaves. Similarly, seamen crewing for privateers had little compunction about selling slave cargoes in time of war.[90] This was also an era when Maroons tracked down runaways and when Miskito Indians, ethnic soldiers in the service of the British, enslaved their rivals and sold them to logwood cutters on the Bay of Honduras, or to Dutch and Jamaican planters. Briton Hammon, one of the few blacks to have left a record of his sea adventures during this decade, recalled being captured on the Florida coast by a band of Indians who "beat me most terribly with a cutlass." They taunted me in "broken English," he remembered, saying that "they intended to roast me alive."[91] Later they sold him to the governor of Havana.

This is not a picture that evokes interracial harmony or some international fraternity of the dispossessed.[92] It was a violent world of marchlands, to use Bernard Bailyn's phrase, in which relatively little space opened up for amicable relations between people of different cultures, let alone the cultivation of wider solidarities.[93] As Philip Morgan has argued, seafaring may have "blurred the binary terms in which British peoples generally encountered indigenous peoples on land," where scalping and ritual sacrifice accentuated cultural difference, but it never "overcame the fissures of race."[94] In fact the Atlantic world of the mid–eighteenth century threatened to degenerate into a dog-eat-dog society whose predatory actions flowed from the predatory nature of war, the state conflicts that licensed that predation within specific international divisions of labor, and the sheer struggle for survival among the marginal and exploited.

It is a picture, however, that should be contrasted with the prevailing discourse in mid-eighteenth-century Britain, which saw the 1740 struggle with Spain and subsequently France as a preeminently patriotic venture, a veritable derring-do. The fervor that greeted Admiral Vernon's victory at Porto Bello expressed a libertarian, bellicose mercantilism in which trade and the accumulation of wealth were revered as the highest national and individual good—a felicitous welding of national and imperial interest, of participatory politics and Protestant destiny. Within this context the Caribbean became the site of freedom of trade, freedom from Catholic absolutist rule, and, through the growing popularity of sugar and tobacco, of consumer desire. Slavery was deeply but elliptically implicated with production and colonial grandeur within this discourse. The slave was periodically recognized as the raw but necessary muscle of the sugar economy, surfacing abruptly in the Stono rebellion as a simpleton seduced by Catholicism and hopes of freedom at the hands of the perfidious Spanish.[95] The seaman, by contrast, was foregrounded as the victimized tar of the Spanish *guardacosta* or as the sturdy arm of a masculinist nationalism. In the same issue of the *London Daily Post* in which the Stono rebellion was reported, there was an account of Vernon's assault upon Chagre (the headquarters of the *guardacostas*), in which seamen stormed the fort and struck the colors. Such valorous tales were commemorated later in the year with a print representing Jack Tar as the British Hercules—the stuff of imagined communities but not a true representation of the experience of the lower decks in the torrid plantation zone.

CHAPTER FIFTEEN

Questioning the Identity of Olaudah Equiano, or Gustavus Vassa, the African

Vincent Carretta

Was Olaudah Equiano born in Africa, as he claims in *The Interesting Narrative of the Life of Olaudah Equiano, or Gustavus Vassa, The African. Written by Himself?*[1] First published in London in March 1789, his autobiography was quickly and widely reviewed, and immediately became a bestseller; a second edition appeared in 1789, and a ninth, the last published in the binomial author's lifetime, in 1794. Selling his book primarily by subscription, which required buyers to pay half the price of the book in advance, the author controlled the means of production and distribution of his book, and thus his public identity, even more than most autobiographers. In 1792 the newspapers the *Oracle* and the *Star* first raised what I call the Equiano question: was Olaudah Equiano an identity *revealed*, as the title of the autobiography implies, or an identity *assumed* by Gustavus Vassa around 1789 for rhetorical (and financial) ends? Consequently, any new information about the author's life may cast significant light on the author's self-creation through the inclusion, exclusion, misremembering, and perhaps even invention of evidence. For example, baptismal, naval, and other records discovered since 1994 enable us to correct the chronology of the author's early years in slavery and raise the possibility that he altered events in his early life for rhetorical purposes. More importantly, however, new evidence suggests that the author of *The Interesting Narrative* may have gone well beyond simply suppressing or manipulating some facts: he may have fashioned rather than recounted his African beginnings, in the process hiding his birth in South Carolina.[2]

In the first known published review of *The Interesting Narrative*, Mary Wollstone-craft noted the significance of the author's nationality. Her comments in the May 1789 issue of the *Analytical Review* opened with the observation that "The life of an African, written by himself, is certainly a curiosity, as it has been a favourite philosophic whim to degrade the numerous nations, on whom the sun-beams more directly dart, below the common level of humanity, and hastily to conclude that nature, by making them inferior to the rest of the human race, designed to stamp them with a mark of slavery."

In the June 1789 issue of the *Monthly Review,* the anonymous reviewer of *The Interesting Narrative* called the book "very seasonable, at a time when negro-slavery is the subject of public investigation; and it seems calculated to increase the odium that has been excited against the West-India planters." For this reviewer, too, the author's nativity was of primary significance: "We entertain no doubt of the general authenticity of this very intelligent African's story." Although the author of *The Interesting Narrative* originally published his book without authenticating documentation, he added re-views, including this one, and testimonials to preface each of his subsequent editions.

Pro-slavery writers also recognized that *The Interesting Narrative* was "calculated to increase the odium . . . against the West-India planters" at a time when Parliament was actively considering bills to abolish the slave trade. Yet for three years the apologists for slavery left the authority of the work and the binomial identity of its author unchal-lenged, watching the book become a bestseller. The fourth edition alone, published in Dublin in 1791, sold 1,900 copies. On 25 and 27 April 1792, however, while the author was in Edinburgh revising and promoting what would be the fifth edition of the *Narrative* (Edinburgh, 1792), the question of the author's true identity was raised in two London newspapers: the *Oracle* and the *Star.* The *Oracle* reported that "It is a fact that the Pub-lic may depend on, that *Gustavus Vassa,* who has publicly asserted that he was kid-napped in Africa, never was upon that Continent, but was born and bred up in the Dan-ish Island of Santa Cruz, in the West Indies [now St. Croix in the U.S. Virgin Islands]. *Ex hoc uno disce omnes* [that one fact tells all]. What, we will ask any man of plain un-derstanding, must that cause be, which can lean for support on falsehoods as auda-ciously propagated as they are easily detected?" Suddenly, both sides of the author's bi-nomial Afro-British identity had been challenged. But what was at stake?

In 1789, the author's rhetorical ethos—his authority to speak as a victim and eye-witness of slavery in Africa, the West Indies, North America, Europe, and the Middle East—was dependent upon the African nativity he claimed. His autobiography was offered and received as the first extended account of slavery and the slave trade from a former slave's point of view. With the exception of his friend and sometime collaborator Quobna Ottobah Cugoano, who had published his *Thoughts and Sentiments on the Evil of Slavery* in London in 1787, the author of *The Interesting Narrative* was the first writer of African descent to present his work as self-authorized, proudly announcing on the title page that the book was "Written by Himself." Cugoano and his friend published their works without any of the authenticating documentation or mediation by white authorities that prefaces the works of Phillis Wheatley or Ignatius Sancho and other black writers to reassure readers that the claim of authorship is valid and to imply that their words have been supervised before publication. Cugoano's *Thoughts and Sentiments* went unreviewed and unanswered, and hence his identity and authority went unchallenged. However, the claim of authenticity by the author of *The Interesting Narrative* was quickly recognized by his readers to be fundamental to the effectiveness of the autobiography as a petition against the Atlantic slave trade. If an African could write and publish with neither the help nor the authorization of European intermediaries, and if he could attest from personal experience to the cruelty and inhumanity of the Middle Passage and slavery, he was prima facie evidence against the major arguments made by contemporaneous apologists for slavery. Furthermore, the binomial identity found on the title page enabled the author to maintain his British identity, signified by the name Gustavus Vassa given him in slavery, as well as his newly announced African identity. Following the author's usual practice, henceforth in this chapter I refer to him as Gustavus Vassa, except when he himself writes of his Olaudah Equiano identity.

Ironically, Vassa reverses the traditional rhetorical relationship between authorizing white and authorized black writers. In his capacity as the victimized African Equiano, his descriptions of his experience of having been enslaved, especially of his life in Africa and the horrors of the Middle Passage, serve to verify and thereby validate much of the evidence conventionally cited in abolitionist discourse. Vassa's memory of Africa as a pastoral and idyllic land corrupted by European contact reinforces a convention frequently promoted by white abolitionists and disputed by apologists for slavery, who contended that slavery rescued Africans from a brutal existence and introduced them to Christianity and civilization.

Immediately recognizing the issues at stake in the challenge to his identity made by the *Oracle* and the *Star*, Vassa prefaced the fifth and subsequent editions of his *Narrative* with a letter addressed "To the Reader." He counterattacked the "invidious falsehood [that] appeared in the Oracle . . . with a view to hurt my character, and to discredit and prevent the sale of my Narrative" (5). Typically, he was as concerned for his pocketbook as he was for his integrity. Sales depended upon his authority, which derived from his Afro-British identity. To defend his "character," Vassa also added a short list of the names of "those numerous and respectable persons of character who knew me when I first arrived in England, and could speak no language but that of Africa" (5). The first of these six names is that of "My friend Mrs. Baynes, formerly Miss Guerin" (238), the former Mary Guerin, the younger sister of Maynard and Elizabeth Martha Guerin. Michael Henry Pascal's will (PROB 11/1142) shows that the Guerins were his cousins.

From the first edition on, Vassa tells us that he was born Olaudah Equiano in 1745 in what is now Nigeria, kidnapped and enslaved by fellow Africans after he "turned the age of eleven" (46), and was sold by them into slavery to Europeans "at the end of six or seven months" (54). After an unspecified amount of time waiting off the coast of Africa on an "African snow" (63), his new enslavers transported him to Barbados in the West Indies (a trip that usually took about two months). After staying "in this island for a few days; I believe not above a fortnight," he tells us that he was brought "in a sloop" to Virginia, "up a river a good way from the sea" (62). The voyage from Barbados to Virginia normally took three to four weeks. Approximately ten months had passed between his first capture in Africa and his arrival in Virginia, according to his account. In Virginia, the young slave was bought by Mr. Campbell, a local planter. After three months, Campbell sold him to Pascal, a lieutenant in the British Royal Navy who had been given leave to command the *Industrious Bee,* a commercial vessel. At this point, Pascal's new slave, soon renamed Gustavus Vassa, "could smatter a little imperfect English," enough "to understand [Pascal] a little" (64). Pascal intended to give Vassa "for a present to some of his friends in England" (64). After an unusually long "passage of thirteen weeks" (a transatlantic voyage from Virginia to England generally took about eight weeks), Vassa arrived at Falmouth, where, he tells us, he first saw snow. Vassa says that "[i]t was about the beginning of the spring 1757 when I arrived in England" (67). According to Vassa's account, about sixteen months had elapsed between his initial kidnapping in Africa and his arrival in England. He says that he spent "some months" (69) more in Guernsey before coming to London and meeting the Guerins in Westminster, where he was baptized in February 1759. Elizabeth Martha Guerin was Vassa's godmother.

Vassa recognized that his memory of when he first reached England was not precise. In the first four editions of his *Narrative,* he opens the fourth chapter by observing that, at the beginning of 1759, "[i]t was now between two and three years since I first came to England"; from the fifth edition (1792) on, he revised this opening to read "between three and four years" (77), perhaps in response to the challenge to his credibility by the *Oracle* and the *Star.* As an editor of Vassa's works, I have tried to verify at least some of the many details and dates found in his *Narrative.* Because my research has shown him to be remarkably accurate whenever his information can be tested by external evidence, his mistakes and omissions become all the more fascinating and possibly therefore more significant.

Admiralty records (ADM) in the Public Record Office (PRO), Kew, and surviving issues of the *Virginia Gazette* lend support to Equiano's credibility and prove that he had an extraordinary memory. Having already been on leave from the Royal Navy for six months, on 4 February 1752, Lieut. Michael Henry Pascal successfully petitioned to have his leave extended another ten months because he "had Now the Command of a Merch[an]t Ship, In the Virginia Trade" (ADM 1/2290; ADM 3/62). On 5 June 1752 Pascal advertised a reward in the *Virginia Gazette* for the return of four men, who had jumped ship from the *Industrious Bee*, out of a total of ten crew members who had sailed from London with him in February 1752 (ADM 7/87). Pascal's leave was further extended by the Admiralty board, so that he might stay in "Virginia in the Merchant's Service," for additional twelve-month periods, on 1 February 1753, 9 February 1754, and 30 January 1755 (ADM 3/63). However, as we shall see, by the last date Pascal was already back in England.

Vassa's comments that while in Virginia on Mr. Campbell's plantation he "was a few weeks weeding grass" before he was "sent for to [Campbell's] dwelling house to fan him" (62) suggest that Vassa probably reached Virginia during the summer season, and it must have been the summer of 1754. Pascal must have purchased Equiano from Campbell and renamed him Gustavus Vassa in early September 1754 because on 14 December 1754, about "thirteen weeks" later, the London newspaper the *Public Advertiser* reported the arrival of the "Industrious Bee, [commanded by] Pascall, from [Newfoundland], at Falmouth." A stop at Newfoundland on the way from Virginia to avoid crossing the Atlantic more directly during the hurricane season would account for the unusually long voyage. Furthermore, surviving meteorological data prove that Equiano would have experienced snow in Falmouth during the winter of 1754–55. Snow is infrequent enough to be noteworthy in Cornwall, where imported palm trees thrive in the mild climate. Analysis of the meteorological records kept by William Borlase, rector of Ludgvan, a small village approximately twenty-five miles west of Falmouth, reveals that "[t]aking the winter periods into consideration 1754/55, 1769/70 were the snowiest" years in southern Cornwall during the period 1753 to 1772.[3]

Colonial Office records in the PRO enable us to identify with a high degree of probability the vessel that would have brought Equiano from Africa to Barbados and the one that would have brought him from there to Virginia in mid-1754, if my calculations are accurate and Vassa's account of his life before meeting Pascal is true. The *Ogden*, a snow owned by Thomas Stevenson and Co., cleared Liverpool, England, on 5 June 1753, to go to Bonny on the Bight of Biafra (the main source of Igbo slaves) in Africa, seeking 400 slaves. Under James Walker's command, the *Ogden* arrived at Barbados on 9 May 1754, bearing a cargo of 243 enslaved Africans. On 21 May the sloop *Nancy*, owned by Alexander Watson of Virginia and commanded by Richard Wallis, left Barbados with thirty-one slaves and brought them up the York river in Virginia on 13 June.[4] Campbell very probably would have bought Equiano soon thereafter.

The first hard evidence we have of Vassa's existence is the appearance of his name on 6 August 1755 on the muster list of the *Roebuck* (ADM 36/6472). Not surprisingly, prior to that date no documentary evidence of Vassa's existence has been found. The names of Pascal and Vassa's young friend, Richard Baker, appear on the muster book of the *Roebuck* on 18 and 28 June 1755, respectively. The muster and pay books of the Royal Navy are reliable records of who was on which ships and at what time, whether members of the crew or not, because the ships' captains and pursers had to account for all expenses incurred onboard. Interestingly, although Baker is listed as Pascal's servant, Vassa is not. He is identified as a servant of the captain, Matthew Whitwell.

September 1754 is two years earlier than the date Vassa offers in the *Narrative* for his entry into Pascal's service, and December 1754 is much earlier than when he places himself in England in the first four editions. Other internal and external evidence also proves that he was in England before "spring 1757": he tells us that he saw Admiral John Byng during Byng's trial, which took place aboard the *St. George* in Plymouth between 27 December 1756 and 27 January 1757, and he served on the *Savage*, listed as "Gusta Worcester," from 12 to 21 January 1757 (ADM 36/6573). Recorders of muster lists often attempted to spell foreign-sounding names phonetically, with widely varying degrees of success. Vassa was discharged from the *Savage* on 21 January at Deal, where he "remained some short time" before Pascal ordered him to come to London.

Vassa probably first met the Guerins in February or March 1757, about three and a half years after he says he had initially been kidnapped in Africa. When they met he "could not stand for several months, and . . . was obliged to be sent to St. George's Hospital," Westminster, where "the doctors wanted to cut [his] left leg off . . . apprehending a mortification" (71) from the chilblains he had probably suffered while serving on the *Savage*. An inflammation of the ear, hand, or foot caused by exposure to moist cold, a chilblain in severe cases could lead to ulceration of the affected extremity. Immediately following his recovery from chilblains, Vassa contracted smallpox, requiring him to stay additional weeks in the hospital.[5] Although we cannot establish exactly when in 1757 Vassa first met the Guerins, Vassa had already been in English-speaking environments for approximately three years when he reached Westminster. On 10 November 1757, Vassa ("Vavasa"), fully recovered, joined Pascal aboard the *Jason* (ADM 36/6365). During the next two years, he served under Pascal mainly at sea aboard the *Jason*, the *Royal George* (ADM 36/5743), and the *Namur* (ADM 36/6253) before returning to London at the beginning of 1759.

At this point, questions about the place and date of Vassa's nativity first arise. The parish register of St. Margaret's church, Westminster, records the baptism on 9 February 1759 of "Gustavus Vassa a Black born in Carolina 12 years old," indicating a birth date of 1746 or 1747. During the eighteenth century, "Carolina" frequently encompassed both North and South Carolina. Vassa himself, of course, may not have been responsible for the information or misinformation regarding the place and date of his birth recorded at his baptism, but the correct information was presumably available to the future Mrs. Baynes, who Vassa later said first knew him as African. The question of his place and date of birth comes up again in the historical record. Vassa's accounts of his voyages and military engagements while serving Pascal during the Seven Years War (1756–62) are almost all verifiable and impressively accurate, so much so that he either must have kept a journal or had a uniquely retentive memory. At a later point in his recounted life, he tells us that he was keeping a journal during his voyage to the Arctic. He does not mention in the *Narrative,* however, that just before Pascal reneged on his promise to free Vassa and instead sold him to a slave trader bound for the West Indies at the end of 1762, "Gustavus Vassan" had been promoted by Pascal to the rank of able seaman, the highest-paid, most skilled, and prestigious position below an officer in the navy. As Vassa's owner, Pascal was, of course, financially interested in his promotion. The salaries of both Pascal and Vassa were sent to the same agent and, presumably, ultimately into Pascal's pocket (ADM 32/5). Consequently, we cannot ignore the possibility that Vassa's promotion may have reflected Pascal's self-interest rather than Vassa's abilities as a seaman.

However, that Vassa returned to service in the navy after an eleven-year hiatus and re-entered with the same rank he had when he left indicates that Pascal's promotion of him was probably prompted by a combination of self-interest and merit. Vassa tells us that seven years after he bought his freedom in the West Indies, he joined the expedition led by Capt. Constantine Phipps, later Lord Mulgrave, seeking a northeast passage through the Arctic Ocean in 1773. Yet in his account of the expedition he omits some information that greatly complicates the Equiano question. Although Vassa tells us in the *Narrative* that he "attended [Doctor Irving] on board the Race Horse," Alexander Mair is identified on the muster list as the "Surgeon's Mate." The muster book of the *Racehorse* records the entry on board, as of 17 May, of "Gustavus Weston," identified as being an able seaman, aged twenty-eight, and born in South Carolina (ADM 36/7490). The 23 April–19 May 1773 muster list of the *Racehorse* lists him as "Gustavus Feston," indicating the recorder's uncertainty about the spelling and pronunciation of his name.

Gustavus Weston/Feston was certainly Gustavus Vassa: Weston and Feston are both plausible approximate phonetic spellings of Vassa; the rank, age, and birthplace are consistent with those of Vassa found in earlier muster lists, in the *Narrative* itself, and in the parish register of St. Margaret's, Westminster; and Mulgrave was one of the original subscribers to *The Interesting Narrative.* The recorder of the *Racehorse* muster was unlikely to have had either access to or interest in Vassa's baptismal record. Since the personal data probably came from Vassa himself, now a free man, we must ask why, if he had indeed been born Olaudah Equiano in Africa, he chose to suppress these facts. He was not obligated to do so. He could have claimed any birthplace he wished. Among the *Racehorse*'s total complement of ninety men, most were able seamen. Virtually every place Vassa had lived or said he had lived was represented among the places of birth included for his peers. For example, besides the many English, Irish, and Scottish birthplaces recorded, one man lists London, one Virginia, and three Philadelphia. Yet Vassa's choices were not limited to the British isles or Britain's colonies. Twelve of the other able seamen were born in various parts of continental Europe. Nor was there any clear reason for Vassa to hide an African birth. As we can deduce from the names and places of birth on the muster list, Vassa was one of at least three black men among the able seamen on the expedition. Twenty-two-year-old Richard York (sometimes spelled Yorke on the lists) was born in "Guinea," and thirty-year-old Jonathan Syfax was born in "Madagascar."[6]

Vassa probably encountered his African-born former shipmate York again a few years later. York was serving under Capt. Stair Douglass on the *Squirrel* when Vassa sought Douglass's protection in 1776 to enable him to return to England (ADM 36/9078). In fact, York may well have vouched for Vassa to Douglass (the former owner of Julius Soubise, friend and correspondent of Ignatius Sancho). Given Vassa's apparent freedom to have chosen any place of birth, his improbable choice of declaring himself an Igbo of South Carolina paradoxically increases the probability that it is true. Why else choose the colony that actively tried to avoid importing Africans from the Bight of Biafra, in part because of their reputation for trying to avoid slavery through suicide or flight, rather than, say, Virginia, which preferred them? An Igbo-descended slave in South Carolina might well have been sent to Virginia for sale.[7]

Assuming that the birth date of 1745 he gives in the *Narrative* is accurate, Vassa must have been younger than he claims when he left Africa, younger still if he was born in 1746 or 1747, as the ages recorded at his baptism and on his Arctic voyage suggest. A date of 1745, 1746, or 1747, however, could only have been approximate for an undocumented birth in either Africa or South Carolina. The documentary evidence indicates that he was most probably between seven and nine years of age when Pascal first met him in Virginia, and thus he would have been between six and eight years old when he says he was initially kidnapped in Africa. Phillis Wheatley was approximately the same age when she was brought from Africa to Boston on 11 July 1761, but she later pointed out that she remembered nothing of her native language and little of Africa. The discrepancy between the ages and dates Vassa records in his *Narrative* and the external documentary evidence may simply be due to a confused memory of childhood events recounted some forty years later, though this explanation seems unlikely given the extraordinary accuracy of his memory for details when it can be checked against the historical record.

The discrepancy may have been rhetorically motivated: Vassa may have recognized that the younger he was thought to have been when he left Africa, the less credible his memories of his homeland would be. Even if Vassa was "a Black born in Carolina" rather than in Africa, he might still have spoken "no language but that of Africa" when Pascal first met him. During the first half of the eighteenth century, due to the low rate of acculturation of slaves born in low-country South Carolina, an African or creole language, not English, was likely to be such a slave's first language.[8] If he was a native of Carolina, his account of Africa may have been based on oral history and reading rather than on personal experience. The evidence regarding his place and date of birth is clearly contradictory and will probably remain tantalizingly so. Wherever and whenever he had been born, however, by the time he met the Guerins, Vassa should have been quite proficient in English and thus not restricted to speaking only the language "of Africa." There can be no doubt that Vassa manipulated some of the facts in his autobiography.

Besides the prefatory list of character references that the author added to the fifth and subsequent editions, what evidence external to the *Narrative* do we have that the identity of Olaudah Equiano existed before the name appeared in the first and subsequent editions of Vassa's book? As far as I have been able to discover, Vassa only twice used the name Equiano elsewhere in the published or manuscript writings he produced before, during, and after the imprints of the *Narrative:* in his solicitation for subscribers dated November 1788,[9] and in a cosigned letter published on 25 April 1789 in the newspaper the *Diary; Or Woodfall's Register,* writing as one of the "Sons of Africa," he identifies himself as "OLAUDAH EQUIANO, or GUSTAVUS VASSA" (344). Several cosigners, including his friend "OTTOBAH CUGOANO, or JOHN STUART," also reclaim African identities that had been erased by slavery and baptism. In all other cases, however, from the first entries of his name in the muster lists of ships on which he served during the 1750s, 1760s, and 1770s, to his will drawn up in 1796, he is identified or identifies himself only as Gustavus Vassa. Very rarely was he, to my knowledge, ever referred to or addressed as Equiano by others in print or manuscript during his lifetime.[10]

Although after 1786 Vassa became increasingly well known to both blacks and whites opposed to the African slave trade, none of them betrays any familiarity with his identity as Equiano. In his published and unpublished correspondence after 1787, Vassa uses the epithets "the African," "the Ethiopian," and a "Son of Africa" to identify himself, but he uses none of these in any known works before 1787, including writings reproduced in his autobiography. One of the leading abolitionists, Granville Sharp, who knew Vassa personally at least as early as April 1779, when he gave him one of his books, refers in his journal on 19 March 1783 to "Gustavus Vassa, a negro." Sharp subscribed for two copies of the *Narrative*. Another leading abolitionist and friend, James Ramsay, had probably known Vassa since the period when they had both lived in the West Indies. In a manuscript in the Rhodes House Library, Oxford, probably written in 1788, Ramsay includes some of the African biographical details that would appear the following year in Vassa's *Narrative*. Yet Ramsay, who also was an original subscriber to the *Narrative*, never refers to Vassa as Equiano, and he could not have met Vassa in the West Indies before 1763. Hence, Ramsay's knowledge of Vassa's early life could only have come from the adult Vassa himself. From the evidence I have seen, the presence of the name Olaudah Equiano on the subscription proposal and title page of the *Narrative* in 1789 must have come as a revelation to friend and foe alike of Gustavus Vassa. They may have known that he claimed an African birth, but we have no proof yet that they knew of Olaudah Equiano before 1788. As the evidence demonstrates, Vassa had no obvious reason before 1788 to suppress an African identity. Unless we argue that his memory of it was repressed until then, the new evidence obligates us to at least consider the possibility that *The Interesting Narrative* is an even more creative piece of work than formerly thought.

Part III / Islands

CHAPTER SIXTEEN

The Point Venus "Scene,"
Tahiti, 14 May 1769

Neil Rennie

Captain James Cook's first voyage to the Pacific and round the world in the *Endeavour* was certainly eventful, but one particular event in Tahiti received a great deal of attention in Britain.[1] One of the main aims of the voyage was to observe the transit of the planet Venus across the sun, and it was from Tahiti that the planet Venus was to be observed, but it was not the planet that excited the British public.

On Sunday, 14 May 1769, Cook proposed a divine service ashore in the fort he had constructed to protect the observatory on Point Venus, "so called," he explained, "from the Observation being made there."[2] Joseph Banks, the botanist, was keen that some of "our Indian friends," as he wrote in his journal, "should be present that they might see our behaviour and we might if possible explain to them (in some degree at least) the reasons of it."[3] His guests, however, politely "imitated my motions" but would not "attend at all to any explanation."[4] The symbolic significance for Tahitian society, if any, of the "Scene" that followed later the same day has never been satisfactorily explained, but in Britain it would become symbolic of Tahiti and of the whole South Seas. The Point Venus "Scene" is described by Cook but not by Banks (who presumably did not witness it). The whole entry for 14 May in Cook's holograph journal reads as follows:

> This day we perform'd divine Service in one of the Tents in the Fort where several of the
> Natives attended and behaved with great decency the whole time: this day closed with an

odd Scene at the Gate of the Fort where a young fellow above 6 feet high lay with a little Girl about 10 or 12 years of age publickly before several of our people and a number of the Natives. What makes me mention this, is because, it appear'd to be done more from Custom than Lewdness, for there were several women present particularly Obarea [Purea, a lady some of the British took for a Tahitian queen] and several others of the better sort and these were so far from shewing the least disaprobation that they instructed the girl how she should act her part, who young as she was, did not seem to want it [i.e., to need such instruction].[5]

That is Cook's own description of the "Scene," as he calls it, and we must now follow what became of it on the *Endeavour*'s return to England in 1771. The Admiralty had possession of Cook's journal as well as the journals of men aboard the ships *Dolphin* and *Swallow,* which had preceded the *Endeavour* into the Pacific, and the Admiralty was anxious to publish an official account of these voyages in order to establish British claims in that ocean. So, when Lord Sandwich happened to meet the musicologist Dr. Burney in September 1771, Dr. Burney "had a happy opportunity of extremely obliging Dr. Hawkesworth," as Fanny Burney recorded in her diary: "His Lordship was speaking of the late voyage round the world and mentioned his having the papers of it in his possession; for he is First Lord of the Admiralty; and said that they were not arranged, but mere rough draughts, and that he should be much obliged to any one who could recommend a proper person to write the Voyage. My father directly named Dr. Hawkesworth, and his Lordship did him the honour to accept his recommendation."[6]

Hawkesworth's *Voyages* was eagerly awaited. Boswell and Johnson, who provided a running commentary on Tahitian affairs in London, anticipated its publication in their different ways. Boswell spoke with enthusiasm of "the people of Otaheite who have the bread tree" (the breadfruit tree).[7] Johnson would have none of this nonsense about "ignorant savages": "No, Sir, (holding up a slice of a good loaf), this is better than the bread tree."[8] His opinion of his old friend Dr. Hawkesworth's forthcoming book was equally characteristic: "'Sir, if you talk of it as a subject of commerce, it will be gainful; if as a book that is to increase human knowledge, I believe there will not be much of that. Hawkesworth can tell only what the voyagers have told him; and they have found very little, only one new animal, I think.' Boswell: 'But many insects, Sir.'"[9]

What kind of *Voyages* was Dr. Hawkesworth—poet, critic, essayist, translator, author, jack of all literary trades—going to write? Sandwich, according to Fanny Burney, regarded the original journals as "mere rough draughts." He wanted "a proper person," a man of letters, not a seaman, to "write the Voyage." Cook admitted that he himself had "neither natural or acquired abilities for writing," but his claim to represent what he reported "with undisguised truth and without gloss" is justified by the plain if sometimes awkward prose of his journal.[10] Nevertheless, Hawkesworth had been employed to "write the Voyage" and to adapt the journals of Cook and other seamen to form a continuous and homogeneous narrative. He also obtained for this purpose the journal of Joseph Banks, promising Lord Sandwich, who had supplied it, to "satisfy the utmost Delicacy of a Gentleman to whom I shall be so much obliged."[11]

In the General Introduction to his *Voyages,* Hawkesworth gives us a glimpse of himself discussing narrative technique with the Admiralty. It was "readily acknowledged on all hands," he says, that the work should be written "in the first person," as this would "more strongly excite an interest, and consequently afford more entertainment."[12] Lest this impersonation of "the several Commanders" should restrict Hawkesworth to what he calls a merely "naked narrative," however, it was also agreed that he should be at liberty to "intersperse such sentiments and observations as my subject should suggest."[13] As his manuscript would be submitted to the persons in whose names Hawkesworth would express his sentiments and observations, and their approval secured, "it would signify little," according to Hawkesworth, "who conceived the sentiments that should be expressed."[14] This promise was properly kept, Hawkesworth assures the reader, but it is difficult to reconcile with the statements of Cook and others to the contrary. Cook recorded that "I never had the perusal of the Manuscript nor did I ever hear the whole of it read in the mode it was written, notwithstanding what Dr Hawkesworth has said . . . in the Interduction."[15]

The resulting *Voyages,* inevitably, was not a "naked narrative," so how did Hawkesworth present the "Scene" at Point Venus? His chapter heading shows the close connection as well as juxtaposition of events, and gives an idea of the kind of Tahitian entertainment his readers received for their three guineas: "The Indians attend Divine Service, and in the Evening exhibit a most extraordinary Spectacle."[16] Hawkesworth moves from the fuller account of the divine service in Banks's journal to the following "extraordinary Spectacle"—the "odd Scene" mentioned only by Cook—with editorial agility but without resisting the temptation to link the two events (which are merely separated by a colon in Cook's journal) by way of an amusing but irreverent metaphor. His description of the "Spectacle" is taken from Cook without much significant revision other than a slight reduction to the man's height, a slight increase in the girl's age, and a substitution of the phrase "performed the rites of Venus with" for Cook's naked "lay with," and it is followed by one of Hawkesworth's own "observations." The passage is best judged in its entirety, including Hawkesworth's introductory witticism (which is underlined in Banks's copy of the *Voyages*):

> Such were our Matins; the Indians thought fit to perform Vespers of a very different kind.
>
> A young man, near six feet high, performed the rites of Venus with a little girl about eleven

or twelve years of age, before several of our people, and a great number of the natives, without the least sense of its being indecent or improper, but, as appeared, in perfect conformity to the custom of the place. Among the spectators were several women of superior rank, particularly Oberea, who may properly be said to have assisted at the ceremony; for they gave instructions to the girl how to perform her part, which, young as she was, she did not seem much to stand in need of.

This incident is not mentioned as an object of idle curiosity, but as it deserves consideration in determining a question which has been long debated in philosophy; Whether the shame attending certain actions, which are allowed on all sides to be in themselves innocent, is implanted in Nature, or superinduced by custom? If it has its origin in custom, it will, perhaps, be found difficult to trace that custom, however general, to its source; if in instinct, it will be equally difficult to discover from what cause it is subdued or at least overruled among these people, in whose manners not the least trace of it is to be found.[17]

The public spectacle in Hawkesworth's text is ultimately no more explicable than the one in Tahiti, but we can at least make our own observations and consider whether the man of letters in his study has distorted the "odd Scene" the seaman described in Tahiti. Clearly, Hawkesworth's euphemistic "rites of Venus," in combination with his jest about Tahitian "Vespers," gives an impression—which Cook had not intended—of a Tahitian religion of sexual love, but this was probably the result of an attempt to make Cook's description more genteel and refined for the reader.[18] While the "odd Scene" is in its essentials unchanged, Hawkesworth's substitution for Cook's "lay with" and his slight changes to Cook's estimates of the man's height (Cook's "above 6 feet" becomes "near six feet") and the girl's age (Cook's "about 10 or 12" becomes "about eleven or twelve") do suggest some concern to moderate, if not expurgate, the "Spectacle" for the British public.

We can also observe, which Hawkesworth's public could not, that he has a justification for displaying the "Spectacle" and for his phrase "without the least sense of its being indecent or improper," and also for raising the philosophical issue, in Cook's own words: "What makes me mention this, is because, it appear'd to be done more from Custom than Lewdness." Cook writes as if he is an anthropologist in the field, and his vocabulary suggests he considered the "Scene" a kind of rite: just as the British "perform'd" their service, so did the Tahitian girl "act her part." Hawkesworth's vocabulary follows Cook's, giving "performed the rites of Venus" for "perform her part." The philosophical question itself, which Hawkesworth leaves open without pressing the conclusion that shame is unnatural, but also without preventing the reader from inferring it, is in keeping with Hawkesworth's sense of his editorial duty to supply philosophical reflections. However, his commentary has the rather more important functions of cloth-

ing the "Spectacle," otherwise a "naked narrative," and of distancing it as well as justifying it—no mere "object of idle curiosity"—by placing it in what Hawkesworth presumably believed was a safely balanced and neutral philosophical context. It was perhaps to excuse the public description rather than the public performance of "certain
actions," perhaps to cover himself rather than the Tahitians, that Hawkesworth added
his "observation" to Cook's observation at Point Venus. He had respected his source
more than his reader, even so, and had not sufficiently considered that what was public in Tahiti "without the least sense of its being indecent or improper" was now, by himself, to be made public in Britain.

The eagerly awaited publication of Hawkesworth's *Account of the Voyages undertaken
by the order of his present Majesty for making Discoveries in the Southern Hemisphere* took
place on 9 June 1773, and Mrs. Charlotte Hayes invited her clients to observe for themselves in London what Cook had observed in Tahiti: "Mrs. Hayes presents her most re-
spectful compliments to Lord—, and takes the liberty to acquaint him, that to-morrow
evening, precisely at seven, a dozen beautiful Nymphs, unsullied and untainted, and
who breathe health and nature, will perform the celebrated rites of Venus, as practised
at Otaheite, under the instruction and tuition of Queen Oberea; in which character
Mrs. Hayes will appear upon this occasion."[19]

While Mrs. Hayes supervised the "celebrated rites," and the *Covent-Garden Magazine; or, Amorous Repository* choicely excerpted from the *Voyages,* featuring what "we
[the editors] think will be worthy the perusal of our readers"—particularly the Tahitian "rites of Venus" and Dr. Hawkesworth's "own truly philosophical observations"—
other responses to Hawkesworth's book included disbelief and outrage.[20] A man calling himself "A Christian" harangued and castigated Hawkesworth in the press for ten
weeks, writing in the *Public Advertiser,* for example: "Our Women may find in Dr.
Hawkesworth's Book stronger Excitements to vicious Indulgences than the most intriguing French Novel could present to their Imaginations [and] our Libertines may
throw aside the Woman of Pleasure [Cleland's pornographic novel, better known as
Fanny Hill], and gratify their impure Minds with the Perusal of infinitely more lascivious Recitals than are to be found in that scandalous Performance!"[21] John Wesley, a
better Christian, took refuge in disbelief. Any text which contradicted the biblical account of postlapsarian shame must necessarily be fictional: "Men and women coupling
together in the face of the sun, and in the sight of scores of people!" he wrote in his diary.[22] "Hume or Voltaire might believe this, but I cannot . . . I cannot but rank this narrative with that of Robinson Crusoe."[23]

For all "A Christian's" fears on their behalf, some women were not excited by the *Voyages.* Mrs. Elizabeth Montagu, for example, doyenne of the Bluestockings, wrote wittily
to her sister: "I cannot enter into the prudery of the Ladies, who are afraid to own they

have read the Voyages, and less still into the moral delicacy of those who suppose the effronterie of the Demoiselles of Ottaheité will corrupt our Misses; if the girls had invented a surer way to keep intrigues secret, it might have been dangerous, but their publick amours will not be imitated."[24] One of Mrs. Montagu's friends, however, did not feel that the proud disclaimer she made of any firsthand knowledge of the *Voyages* should prevent her from expressing a widely held opinion: "It gives one great pleasure to find that this nation has still virtue enough to be shocked and disgusted by . . . an outrage against decency, such as Dr. Hawkesworth's last performance, which I find is most universally disliked."[25]

Dr. Hawkesworth, author of Tahitian indecency, for which he was held as guilty as if he had invented it or even perpetrated it, survived the publication of his "last performance" by less than six months. It was generally agreed that his *Voyages* had brought him not only £6,000 but also ill fame, ill health, and death. After a dinner Hawkesworth attended at the Burneys' in Queen Square in October 1773, Fanny remarked in her diary that the abuse of his *Voyages* "has really affected his health."[26] She, whose father had been so helpful, was certain of the cause of his death the next month, which she explained afterwards in a letter: "The death of poor Dr. Hawkesworth is most sincerely lamented by us all, the more so as we do really attribute it to the abuse he has met with . . . His book was dearly purchased at the price of his character, and peace . . . He dined with us about a month before he died, and we all agreed we never saw a man more altered, thin, livid harassed!"[27]

In the wake of Hawkesworth's *Voyages* came a series of anonymous poetical pamphlets. The first of these was *An Epistle from Oberea, Queen of Otaheite, to Joseph Banks, Esq.*, in which Oberea supposedly recalls to Banks how "oft with me you deign'd the night to pass / Beneath yon bread-tree on the bending grass."[28] This account of Oberea's fictitious idyll with Banks serves as the author's pretext for developing, with the firm support of footnotes from Hawkesworth's text, all the titillating Tahitian parts of the *Voyages,* including, of course, the notorious "Spectacle" at Point Venus, with the answer to Hawkesworth's philosophical question made plain:

> Scarce twelve short years the wanton maid had seen,
> The youth was six foot high, or more I ween.
> Experienc'd matrons the young pair survey'd;
> And urg'd to feats of love the self-taught maid;
> With skill superior she perform'd her part,
> And potent nature scorn'd the tricks of art.[29]

A continuing interest in the matter of Tahiti was demonstrated in the new year, 1774, by the appearance of *An Epistle (Moral and Philosophical) from an Officer at Otaheite to Lady Gr*s**n*r*, addressed to a notorious divorcée whose scandalous trial in 1772 was not the author's real concern. This time the initiation at Point Venus, Hawkesworth's "Spectacle," emerges more clearly as the most interesting and significant of the stock Tahitian topics and is given a lingering introduction, too long to quote in full:

> Lo here, whence frozen Chastity retires,
> Love finds an altar for his fiercest fires.
> The throbbing virgin loses ev'ry fear,
>
> .   .   .   .
>
> Unerring instinct prompts her golden dreams;
>
> .   .   .   .
>
> Her bed, like Eve's, with choicest flowers blooms.[30]

A scholarly footnote quotes Milton's lines describing the dubious delights of postlapsarian copulation in *Paradise Lost*. The Tahitian Eve, after lengthy and patently unnecessary instructions from Oberea, proceeds to enact the "Scene" originally witnessed in Tahiti and now described in full detail in London.

The author then calls for the expansion of Oberea's "empire, Love, from shore to shore" and, continuing in this apparently libertine vein, approaches the issues raised by Hawkesworth's philosophical commentary (which he quotes in a footnote):

> . . . here no shame imprest,
> Heaves with alarming throbs the female breast;
> Naked and smiling every nymph we see,
> Like Eve unapron'd 'ere she *robb'd the tree.*
> Immodest words are spoke without offence,
> And want of decency shews innocence.
> A problem hence Philosophers advance,
> Whether shame springs from Nature or from chance.
> The contest lasts; kept up by human pride;
> Where sages differ, how can I decide?[31]

The author does decide, however, and his sarcasm becomes more blatant, his irony more evident, and his answer to Hawkesworth's question explicit. "Is it great Nature's voice," he asks,

> Or is it custom? dubious is the choice?
> No; modest instinct proves *its* source divine
>
> .   .   .   .
>
> Tho' lewdness and unbridled lust combine,
> To counteract the Deity's design;
>
> .   .   .   .
>
> Custom indeed corrupts the human heart.[32]

The references to Eve and *Paradise Lost* should have prepared us to expect a changed note in this author's treatment of the Point Venus "Scene," featuring a Tahitian Eve now, not a Tahitian Venus, a biblical instead of a classical allusion. His "moral and philosophical" theme is clear: the corruption of Nature by Tahitian custom. The young girl's lack of shame is unnatural not natural. Tahiti is no paradise before the fall brought shame, but a perverse as well as fallen world. This is already, in 1774, the Tahiti to which the missionaries would be sent at the end of the century.

Meanwhile in France, Voltaire had been reading the French translation of Hawkesworth's *Voyages*, and he wrote to a friend: "I am still in the island of Tahiti. I admire there the diversity of nature. I am edified to see there the Queen of the country attending a communion of the Anglican church, and inviting the English to the divine service of her country; this divine service consists in making a completely naked young man and girl lie together in the presence of her majesty and five hundred male and female courtiers. One can be sure that the Tahitians have preserved in all its purity the most ancient religion of the world."[33] Voltaire had immediately recognized the main Tahitian topic. So what would he make of it?

The answer came the next year, 1775, Voltaire's eightieth, with the publication of one of his contes, *Les Oreilles du comte de Chesterfield et le chapelain Goudman* (The Count of Chesterfield's Ears and the Chaplain Goudman), in which the hero, Goudman, meets at dinner a Dr. Grou, who has supposedly been round the world in the *Endeavour*, and tells the guests of the Tahitian religious ceremony he and the whole of the ship's crew have witnessed. Dr. Grou relates Voltaire's version of Hawkesworth's version of Cook's version of the "Scene" at Point Venus:

> A very pretty young girl, simply dressed in an elegant gown, was lying on a platform that served as an altar. The Queen Obéira [Will Obey] ordered a handsome boy of about twenty to perform the sacrifice. He pronounced a kind of prayer and mounted on the altar. The two sacrificers were half-naked. The Queen with an air of majesty instructed the young girl in the most suitable manner of conducting the sacrifice. All the Tahitians were so attentive and respectful that none of our sailors dared to disturb the ceremony with a ribald laugh. That is what I have seen, I'm telling you, that is all that our crew has seen. It is for you to draw the conclusions.[34]

It is for us to draw the conclusions. Voltaire's point is precisely the point.

But Dr. Grou is a fictional traveler to Tahiti and his dinner-table talk is fictional talk. What were the actual facts? At a real dinner Boswell asked the very man we would like to ask. When Cook returned from his second voyage to the Pacific in 1775, Boswell was pleased to meet the "celebrated circumnavigator" at a dinner given by Sir John Pringle, the president of the Royal Society, on 2 April 1776.[35] Boswell "talked a good deal" with Cook and found that he "was a plain, sensible man with an uncommon attention to veracity," who "did not try to make theories out of what he had seen to confound virtue and vice."[36] Naturally, the subject of Hawkesworth's *Voyages* was raised, and naturally the Point Venus "Scene," and Cook, according to Boswell, "said Hawkesworth's story of an initiation he had no reason to believe."[37] Now this is odd, as of course we know that Cook had witnessed and described the famous "initiation," as Boswell calls it, Hawkesworth's "Spectacle," Cook's very own "Scene" at Point Venus. But Boswell's response to Cook reflects informed contemporary opinion: "'Why, Sir,' said I, 'Hawkesworth has used your narrative as a London tavern keeper does wine. He has *brewed* it.'"[38]

The following morning Boswell called on Johnson and found him "putting his books in order," enveloped in "clouds of dust": "I gave him an account of a conversation which had passed between me and Captain Cook, the day before, at dinner at Sir John Pringle's; and he was much pleased with the conscientious accuracy of that celebrated circumnavigator."[39] Boswell's skepticism about the "exaggerated accounts given by Dr. Hawkesworth of [Cook's] Voyages" was congenial to Johnson, but Boswell combined his skepticism about Hawkesworth's *Voyages* with enthusiasm about Cook's voyages: "I told him that while I was with the Captain, I catched the enthusiasm of curiosity and adventure, and felt a strong inclination to go with him on his next voyage."[40] "Why, Sir," replied Johnson, "a man does feel so, till he considers how very little he can learn from such voyages."[41]

Boswell conceded that the South Sea voyagers' own reports were also highly unreliable:

> I said I was certain that a great part of what we are told by the travellers to the South Sea must be conjecture, because they had not enough of the language of those countries to understand so much as they have related. Objects falling under the observation of the senses might be clearly known; but every thing intellectual, every thing abstract—politicks, morals, and religion, must be darkly guessed. Dr. Johnson was of the same opinion. He upon another occasion, when a friend mentioned to him several extraordinary facts, as communicated to him by the circumnavigators, slily observed, "Sir, I never before knew how much I was respected by these gentlemen; they told *me* none of these things."[42]

A fortnight later, on 18 April, Boswell dined with Cook again, making a terrible joke about "a good *Cook*."[43] He "placed [himself] next to Captain Cook" and pressed him on the difficulty of anthropological knowledge of South Sea cultures.[44] According to Boswell, Cook "candidly confessed to me that he and his companions who visited the South Sea Islands could not be certain of any information they got, or supposed they got, except as to objects falling under the observation of the senses; their knowledge of the language was so imperfect they required the aid of their senses, and anything which they learnt about religion, government, or traditions might be quite erroneous."[45]

Again Boswell's skepticism about "extraordinary facts" gave way to enthusiasm to observe them personally, and he "felt a stirring in [his] mind" while conversing with Cook: "We talked of having some men of inquiry left for three years at each of the islands of Otaheite, New Zealand, and Nova Caledonia, so as to learn the language and . . . bring home a full account of all that can be known of people in a state so different from ours. I felt a stirring in my mind to go upon such an undertaking, if encouraged by Government by having a handsome pension for life."[46]

Of Boswell's last meeting with Cook, a few days later, on 22 April, we have only a few notes. Boswell went early in the morning to Cook's house at Mile End and had tea in the garden. A blackbird sang, they talked, shook hands, and parted.[47] Boswell's notes give no details of the conversation, but when Cook sailed on his last voyage, later that summer, he sailed without Boswell.

The sexuality of Tahiti symbolized by the Point Venus "Scene" remained powerfully associated with the island in the public imagination. When Bligh reached London after the mutiny on the *Bounty*, reports were soon in the papers. On 16 March 1790 the *General Evening Post* printed an account of the "Mutiny on board the Bounty," giving, as the "most probable" explanation, that the young mutineers "were so greatly fascinated by the Circean blandishments of the Otaheitean women, they took this desperate method of returning to scenes of voluptuousness unknown, perhaps, in any other country."[48] Bligh's Tahitian explanation of the mutiny (the alternative explanation was Bligh himself) was popular and inspired in 1790 the first of three editions of *An Account of the Mutinous Seizure of the Bounty: with the succeeding Hardships of the Crew: to which are added Secret Anecdotes of the Otaheitean Females.* As the shameless sexuality of the Tahitian females was the cause of the mutiny, the anonymous authors considered "it necessary (in order to prove that there is no absurdity in the supposition) to offer our readers some authentic anecdotes respecting them."[49] The ensuing "Secret Anecdotes of the Otaheitean Females" consisted of select but hardly secret excerpts from Hawkesworth's *Voyages*, culminating, of course, in the Point Venus "Spectacle," complete with Hawkesworth's philosophical question.

Hawkesworth's "Spectacle" and philosophical commentary with its implication that sexual shame is artificial, not natural, that the shame that supposedly came to paradise with the fall did not come to Tahiti, are reflected not only in the *Bounty* story but also in the imagery of tourism, which invites us (to quote a typical sample) to "discover" Tahiti with a "special possessive pleasure."[50] A photograph of an attractive Tahitian girl illustrates the "special possessive pleasure" that awaits those who will follow in the wake of the eighteenth-century voyagers and "discover" Tahiti. Indeed, travel, after all the centuries of exploration, has come to this: an invitation to return to paradise, where we can lose our civilized inhibitions and our clothes, an invitation that is often explicitly female and sexual.

    This, we know, is a false paradise, an illusion, but perhaps the Point Venus "Scene" is evidence that something like it was true once, in Tahiti, before the Europeans came, as Diderot said, with their civilization and their shame.[51] Perhaps modern anthropology can enlighten us and explain the real Tahitian meaning of the "Scene"? There is a gulf of time now, instead of space, but the darkness Boswell remarked, of linguistic and cultural ignorance, has surely lifted by now. Well, unfortunately, so far as I can tell, the anthropologists have not paid much attention to Cook's Point Venus "Scene," which has sometimes been confused with accounts of other public copulations between Europeans and Tahitian women. Whether the "Scene" was part of the practices of the Tahitian Arioi cult is a question that cannot be satisfactorily or even usefully answered. James Morrison of the *Bounty,* who spent eighteen months as a participant observer of Tahitian society, thought that Purea's (Oberea's) membership of the Arioi may have contributed to the promiscuity of the Tahitian women's relations with the British sailors, as her followers were "such as preferd the Rites of Venus to those of Mars," but he was skeptical of the reports of "former Voyagers" and had never seen the Tahitians "holding Carnal Conversation in Publick."[52] If Arioi practices did indeed include public sexual acts, as some accounts have indicated, these were in the context of elaborate Arioi festivities, involving feasting, wrestling, acting, singing, and dancing.[53] Cook had heard of the Arioi, but did not connect them with his "Scene," writing that the "Arreoy's . . . have meetings among themselves where the men amuse themselves with wristling &ca and the women in dancing the indecent dance before mentioned [the "Timorodee"], in the Course of which they give full liberty to their desires but I believe keep up to the appearence of decency. I never saw one of these meetings."[54] One popular anthropologist asserts nevertheless that "what Cook, Banks and Solander had witnessed was undoubtedly one of the 'arioi' revival meetings" (although Banks does not mention the "Scene" in his journal and his colleague Solander did not keep a journal).[55] Another anthropologist, who has carefully collected and analyzed the early reports of Tahitian society, confuses Cook's and Hawkesworth's accounts of the "Scene" and quotes with approval the first anthropologist's "judgement," lacking any anthropological sense, or relevance, that acts of public copulation between "native women and European sailors . . . were doubtless due to the Polynesians' curiosity and, like all instances of sexual intercourse in public, must be regarded as a special form of entertainment."[56]

    It seems that anthropology has nothing to tell us about the Point Venus "Scene," but is there any other evidence that might enlighten us before we must, as Voltaire said, draw our own conclusions? There is another small scrap of evidence we should perhaps consider. William Wales, who was not on the *Endeavour* but sailed as astronomer on Cook's second voyage, published in 1778 some *Remarks* about that second voyage which contain an incidental note about the Point Venus "Scene": "I have been informed from the authority of a gentleman who was in the *Endeavour,* and saw the transaction here alluded to, that it is very imperfectly, and in some measure erroneously, related by Dr. Hawkesworth. Oberea *obliged* the two persons to *attempt* what is there said to have been done, but they were exceedingly terrified, and by no means able to perform it."[57] Wales's report is secondhand and in the tendentious context of defending the virtue of Tahitian women from the alleged misrepresentations of other published accounts—part of an argument, therefore, rather than a disinterested attempt to ascertain the truth—but it is perhaps suggestive enough to return us to the only firsthand account, Cook's own words, on which the whole issue turns: Purea (Oberea) and the others "instructed the girl how she should act her part, who young as she was, did not seem to want it."

Cook's syntax is confused. Is "it" the "part" or the instruction? Hawkesworth's syntax is not: "they gave instructions to the girl how to perform her part, which, young as she was, she did not seem much to stand in need of." In Hawkesworth's reading, Cook's "want" becomes "need" and Cook's meaning is that "it seemed that, although she was young, she did not need instruction in the sexual act." That is what I said Cook meant when I quoted the passage earlier, and it is what everyone has always taken Cook to have meant. But "want" in the eighteenth century can have its modern meaning of "desire" as well as its older meaning of "need," and in Cook's own usage, which matters more than the fine writing quoted in the *Oxford English Dictionary,* "want" has both meanings. So Cook may have meant the exact opposite: that "it seemed that, because she was young, she did not desire the part in the sexual act." She "did not want it" may mean what a modern reader would take it to mean, therefore. Or it may not.

Well, we must, after all, draw our conclusions. The only evidence we have is what Cook wrote, which is perfectly ambiguous, it seems to me, and could mean one thing or its exact opposite. And to add to the textual mystery and the anthropological mystery, there is yet another mystery even more profound: a psychological mystery. What was in that young girl's mind, so far away and long ago? What did she really want at Point Venus on 14 May 1769? How can we ever know?

CHAPTER SEVENTEEN

Island Transactions

Encounter and Disease in the South Pacific

Rod Edmond

The fear of contracting and communicating disease played a significant role in the encounters between European voyagers and the island peoples of the Pacific in the late 1760s and 1770s. There were a number of reasons for this. The eighteenth century had produced new forms of discursive entanglement between the body, travel, and health. As long-distance travel became more frequent, its effect on health was increasingly a matter for scrutiny and concern. Thus travel became pathologized as the body was being medicalized, and both became part of the construction of the bourgeois subject as a "mobile sovereign individual."[1] Closely related to this concern with the health of the European traveler was the revival of ancient theories that explained disease as primarily a geographic phenomenon. In the expanding global world of eighteenth-century colonialism this revival of environmental disease etiology resulted in new biogeographical understandings of the world. As Alan Bewell puts it, geography was being rewritten in terms of the language of health, disease, and medical technology.[2] These intersections produced complex effects. As Europeans ventured into parts of the world they had never previously visited, communicating as well as contracting disease became a concern. The historically belated arrival of Europeans in the southern Pacific meant that according to the constructions of the time an untouched geography rapidly became a pathogenic one. In this chapter I try to demonstrate how the voyages of Captains Samuel Wallis, Louis-Antoine de Bougainville, and James Cook to the Pacific in the 1760s and 1770s contributed to emerging biomedical definitions of the world through the complex disease exchanges they inaugurated.

First, some general remarks about islands and encounter. There is a very long tradition of imagining islands as places of health and beauty, cut off from mainland contamination and therefore "virus-free." The reports of Wallis, Bougainville, and Cook from Tahiti and other islands of the southern and eastern Pacific were influenced by this tradition and became assimilated to it as they were received in Europe. Subsequent eighteenth-century visitors' uneasiness when they learned of the extreme susceptibility of these islands to introduced diseases clearly contrasts with European attitudes to the Caribbean. In the Caribbean islands, where indigenous populations had been wiped out and slave-based European settlement was long-established, Europeans feared contracting disease rather than communicating it. There was little concern with the health of the slave population, and yellow fever, the main cause of European death in the Caribbean, was thought not to attack Africans.[3] In the "untouched" world of Oceania however, with indigenous populations whose physical beauty rapidly became a byword in Europe, attitudes were very different. These apparently salubrious cultures of ease and hospitality renewed older ways of thinking about islands. For example, J. R. Forster, the naturalist on Cook's second voyage, regarded islands as "more apt to . . . accelerate civilization than large continents" because they were circumscribed and hence more likely to promote sociality and prevent nomadism.[4] The geography of the Pacific, with its numerous island clusters scattered across a vast ocean, also invited comparison between the increasing number of island groups that Cook and other European voyagers encountered. As more and more such groups were collected, a taxonomy of islands began to emerge based upon their relative degree of civilization. Typically, Tahiti was at the top of this ladder of development, with New Zealand several rungs below, and the islands of the western Pacific toward the bottom.

In colonial and postcolonial studies the process of encounter is often conflated with that moment of first meeting when Europe confronts its other across some troubled or contested contact zone. This is particularly so in the Pacific where the beach provides such an obvious border between two worlds. I am more interested in reencounter, in what happened when later eighteenth-century voyagers returned to the islands of the Pacific and witnessed the effects of their previous visit. The experience of encounter always outlived first contact, persisting in the minds of voyagers and of indigenous populations between, as well as during, actual meeting. In memory, at least from a European point of view, this could take idealized forms. William Hodge's oil painting *Tahiti Revisited* (1776) is one notable expression of this idealization, which focuses on the eroticized Tahitian female body.[5] Actual return visits, however, seldom allowed such idealization. Encounter, therefore, was a complex and protracted process involving contact, memory, reflection, and the renewal of contact upon return. If we take Tahiti as an example, Cook's four separate visits during his three voyages were preceded by one each from Wallis and Bougainville, and punctuated by two from the Spanish voyager Boenechea. These eight visits between 1767 and 1777 can be thought of as one extended process of encounter, with European voyagers reading each other's accounts, comparing their own visits with previous ones, and refining that comparative habit of mind that the configuration of the Pacific encouraged. This is to say nothing of the Tahitian experience of this rash of visits. By 1777 they must have felt well and truly "discovered."

Disease and trade were central to this process of encounter, and they often substituted for each other. Trade could be regulated, up to a point. It was in the interests of both sides to protect what they most valued, to trade with the things they least valued, and to try and understand the system of valuation of the other culture.[6] Rules of exchange were established and policed, with some difficulty, on both sides of the beach. Disease, however, proved impossible to control; it was the invisible form of exchange. As voyagers returned to previously visited islands, disease confronted them with the damaging evidence of their earlier landfalls. Yet trade and disease were also mutually displaceable. Venereal disease was a consequence of sexual trade, for example, and the damaging effects of trade itself were repeatedly imaged in the language of infection and disease.

It was on native bodies, on the skin of indigenous populations that the evidence of contact was most visible. All the journals of early voyagers to the south Pacific noted the susceptibility of Polynesians to what Banks called "cutaneous distempers,"[7] and skin served as a kind of litmus for the transmission of disease and other effects of contact. Skin was to the body what the beach was to the island, a contact zone memorializing the signs of previous encounter. The voyagers' attention to the body surface was also heightened by their valorization of the Polynesian body. In the careful, increasingly elaborate comparisons they made between different island groups, beauty was as important a consideration as any. The most attractive and fascinating feature of these peoples—their physical appearance—was precisely the thing most threatened by the European presence. Accordingly, figuring, disfiguring, and refiguring became an obsession with the visitors.

On the earliest voyages, the health of those on the ships was the main concern. For Wallis and Bougainville, Tahiti was a health farm for scurvy-ridden seamen. Both captains put their ill ashore on arrival, Bougainville claiming that those with scurvy regained their strength after one night.[8] The healthy physical condition of the islanders was particularly noted. By Cook's first voyage however, with scurvy better under control and venereal disease on shore becoming the main concern, the sick were detained on board in order to protect both Tahitians and crew from the cycle of infection. Francis Wilkinson was one of only two journal writers on Cook's *Endeavour* who had sailed with Wallis, and as a returnee his journal is interesting because it uses his previous visit as a constant point of reference. As soon as he goes ashore, he notices the disappearance of "the Principle People" from the bay, something he puts down to the "Inveterate Ich or Yaws" which has become prevalent since his former visit. Soon he is recording that a number of the crew "begin to be very Bad with the Venereal Disorder," blaming this on the Spanish, with whom Bougainville had been confused.[9] So began a heated history of blame and counter-blame between the British, French, and Spanish for introducing venereal disease into the Pacific.

After the first three European visits to Tahiti, therefore, there was more risk to the health of sailors from going ashore than from sailing the oceans. They were more likely to contract diseases that Europeans had brought to the island in the first place than they were to come down with scurvy. Indeed, as early as Cook's first voyage this had become a reason for not jumping ship, as James Matra, midshipman and putative ringleader of a plan to escape ashore, understood: with "the Pox . . . being there . . . getting it certain & dying rotten [was] most probable."[10]

It was on Cook's second voyage, 1772–75, that the reflections prompted by reencounter were freshest and most concentrated. Those habits of observation and comparison resulting from Cook's first voyage were also taken further by the father-and-son team of J. R. and George Forster. Their concerted attempt at a comparative ethnology involved close attention to health and disease, and its relation to trade and civilization, and offers material for more sustained analysis. Of course, it was the Forsters' first voyage, but they had worked together on translating Bougainville's *Voyage* and had Cook and other returnees on hand through whom to experience first contact as if it were also reencounter. This created some elaborate patterns of encounter and comparison, exemplified by the visits to Dusky Bay and Queen Charlotte Sound in the South Island of New Zealand between late March and early June 1773. The visit to Dusky Bay, in the far south of the island, was a first for everyone. The immediately subsequent anchorage at Ship Cove in Queen Charlotte Sound, a few hundred miles north, was a return for Cook and a first visit for the Forsters, though, of course, their second New Zealand landfall. Taken together, these paired scenes have the structure of a controlled experiment, and this was how J. R. Forster, in particular, came to see the experience.

It was several days after anchoring in Dusky Bay before any inhabitants were seen. The first encounter with a man and three women took place on a small island in the bay. Nicholas Thomas has analyzed the visitors' confusion over the "family" relations between the man and the women.[11] I want to consider another aspect of the scene—something recorded in all the journal accounts—namely, the large wen on the upper lip of the eldest woman who was assumed to be wife and mother of the group. Cook noted that it made her look "disagreeable" and resulted in her being "intirely neglected by the man."[12] J. R. Forster, present with Cook at this first meeting, noted "a monstrous wen or excresence" on her upper lip.[13] When the group visited the *Resolution* several days later, this wen had grown and moved: William Wales described her as "rendered barely not frightful by a large Wen which grew on her left Cheek & hung down below her Mouth."[14] Forster and Cook were having skin problems of their own caused by sandfly bites that swelled and itched, resulting, as Cook wrote, in "ulcers like the small Pox."[15] Forster's hands became so swollen that he could hardly hold his pen or take off his jacket.[16] The wen, although disgusting to the visitors, neither troubles them nor prompts wider reflection, apart from providing a reason for the man's indifference to her. They were likely, I suppose, to have assumed it was caused by the vicious sandflies. The agency of her disfigurement is local, not imported, and therefore it can be observed and described without qualm.

Forster records there were "only three families in all this bay,"[17] and these small numbers made it easier to establish careful contact, and to observe and regulate its flow. Exchange of whatever kind was restrained, visible, and carefully described. Queen Charlotte Sound, by contrast, was teeming, and Forster, unused to the frantic trading that a visit from a ship to a crowded harbor normally prompted, was overwhelmed by the number of people and by the unregulated market, which dealt in everything imaginable. His uneasiness is reflected in the comparison he made between the two places. In his journal, he described the inhabitants of Queen Charlotte Sound as demanding and prone to theft, whereas "those in Dusky Bay had nobler Sentiments & made us presents of their own accord." In fact the virgin Dusky Bay was altogether superior to the shop-soiled Queen Charlotte Sound: "The Girl we saw at Dusky Bay had . . . principles of honour & virtue; she never suffered any indecency or familiarity . . . Those females in Queen Charlotte's Sound . . . would all willingly comply with any indecency."[18]

It is a surprise, therefore, to find this valuation reversed in Forster's *Observations*, written after his return to England. Here, the sparse population of Dusky Bay is described as rude and filthy in dress and habitation, contrasted with the better-housed and socialized inhabitants of Queen Charlotte Sound. In the *Observations*, Forster is developing an argument that toward the poles the human species becomes sluggish and "insensible to the dictates of virtue . . . incapable of any attachment."[19] The Dusky Bay and Queen Charlotte Sound comparison needs to be fitted into this geographic template of human development, and thus the contrast must be adjusted accordingly. Whereas the journal valorizes solitude and dignified restraint in its construction of a version of the noble savage—the prose equivalent of Hodge's famous canvas *Cascade Cove, Dusky Bay, New Zealand* (1775)—the *Observations* takes sociality and the eagerness to trade as evidence of a more advanced condition.[20] The previously ennobling re-luctance of the man and women in Dusky Bay to engage fulsomely in commerce has now become a sign of their backwardness, and their small number, formerly a safeguard against unregulated contact, has become in itself disabling. Similarly, the promiscuity of trade in Queen Charlotte Sound that so disturbed Forster has now become the hall-mark of a protocivilization.

However, this passage was written several years later, when Forster revisited the scenes in absentia. At sea, a fortnight after leaving Queen Charlotte Sound for Tahiti, venereal disease was discovered on board. Concluding that it must have been intro-duced by Cook's *Endeavour* three years earlier, Forster angrily denounces this wicked-ness: "every feeling heart must . . . detest the memory of the Man who first disseminated this venom among this brave & spirited Nation. They have acquired nothing . . . by the commerce and intercourse of our Ships crews . . . nothing is capable to compensate in the slightest manner the great injury done to their Society."[21] Cook similarly deplored the effects of trade on the inhabitants of the Sound and the manner in which "we de-bauch their Morals already prone to vice and . . . interduce among them wants and per-haps diseases which they never before knew and which serves only to disturb that happy tranquility they and their for Fathers had injoy'd."[22]

Both men therefore arrived in Tahiti—Forster for the first time—with the troubling experience of Queen Charlotte Sound foremost in their minds. Disease, its origin and transmission, was to shadow the rest of the voyage. At Matavai Bay, Tahiti, they discov-ered what was thought to be syphilis among the population. Forster denounced the French; Cook, more cautious and defensive, thought that the venereal was declining, and noted: "These people are, and were when the Europeans first visited them very sub-ject to eruptions of every kind, so that one may easily mistake one disease for a nother."[23] From here it was a short step to the argument, increasingly favored on Cook's ships, that venereal disease was indigenous.

The confusion over how to read skin symptoms spread. George Forster thought the disease at Matavai Bay might be "a kind of leprosy . . . it is certain, that there are several sorts of leprous complaints existing among the inhabitants, such as the elephantiasis, which resembles the yaws."[24] Such confusion was inevitable. Even today, diseases in-volving the skin and its underlying tissue are impossible to diagnose accurately with the eye. Late-eighteenth-century medicine had few means of distinguishing between syphilis, yaws, lesions caused by fungi, scabies, and so on. Syphilis and gonorrhea had not yet been established as distinct diseases. The treponemes responsible for yaws and syphilis were morphologically identical, making these closely related diseases impossi-ble to distinguish.[25] Although yaws was indigenous, and venereal disease introduced, there was no way of telling them apart, and this complicated the perceived patterns of disease exchange. Leprosy, whose Latin name *Elephantiasis Graecorum* added further confusion, was commonly used as a generic term for a wide range of skin disorders.

The next landfall after Tahiti and the Society Islands was Eua in the Tongan group. By now, Forster's scrutiny of native bodies had become intense: "one Woman had all the face eaten & ulcerated; the Nose was quite rotten away & only a hole left, the Eyes were sore & red, the whole face tumid & sore & running as Cancers do."[26] Leprosy stayed on Forster's mind as the ships sailed back from Tonga to New Zealand. Caught in a violent and prolonged storm off New Zealand, Forster turned to his books and to "the remarks of Prof. Michaelis on the Leprosy, & its various branches."[27] In a very long journal entry he tries to distinguish between the different kinds and degrees of leprosy he thought he had seen, in a manner that recalls the even more obsessive effort to describe and classify the disease in chapters thirteen and fourteen of the Book of Leviticus. Forster's journal passage rehearses a more developed discussion of the subject in *Observations*, where the implied relation between leprosy, elephantiasis, and venereal disease becomes more definite. Here Forster assumes that the disease he had observed on Tahiti must have been introduced by the Spanish:

> as this Spanish ship came from Lima and Callao, where a great number of negro slaves are kept, who are frequently and chiefly subject to the various kinds of leprosis and elephantiasis, it might perhaps have happened that one or more of the crew might be infected with that kind of elephantiasis, which they communicated to the natives of these isles: for it is well known, that some species of leprosy may be communicated by cohabitation, that many lepers are very immoderate in venery, even a few moments before they expire, and that especially the elephantiasis described by Aretaeus and Paulus Aegineta, had some symptoms that are perfectly corresponding with those pointed out by the natives.[28]

This mélange of scholarship and folklore, observation and supposition, illustrates how the attempt to discriminate between diseases in a context of ignorance about their etiology and transmission breaks down into further confusion. Here, as elsewhere, the anxiety prompted by medical uncertainty is heightened by unease about the infectious European presence. It was this, as much as patriotism, that prompted the British, French, and Spanish to blame one another for the introduction of diseases, some of which, like yaws—almost certainly the cause of the Euan woman's disfigurement— were indigenous.

In the western Pacific, Cook's ships sailed past Bougainville's Isle of Lepers, now Omba in Vanuatu. Bougainville had named it such soon after discovering that many of his crew had contracted venereal disease in Tahiti; Ahutoru, the Tahitian they were taking back to France, "was quite ruined by it."[29] Going ashore at Omba, Bougainville had described the islanders as "short, ugly, ill-proportioned, and most of them infected with leprosy."[30] Generally though, eighteenth-century voyagers were less preoccupied with skin disease in the western Pacific. Social negotiation was more difficult and became a main topic of the journals. Sexual commerce between ship and shore virtually ceased, and as the risk of infection receded, scrutiny of the native body became less intense. Another reason for this diminished interest was that the inhabitants of the western Pacific, still yet to be classified as Melanesians, were regarded as physically unattractive. Forster and Cook both echoed Bougainville's description, and Cook added simian comparisons as well.[31] With contact more distant and infrequent, the anxiety around disease abated along with curiosity about its various forms. Indigenous bodies in the western Pacific were not subject to the same intense regard.

I have already touched on some of the differences between Forster's journal and the *Observations*. Whereas the journal often expresses acute unease at the wake of illness and contagion that follows the voyagers, in the *Observations* this has either been smoothed out into a generalized contrast between a diseased Europe and a healthy Pacific, or else infections such as leprosy, venereal disease, and their cognates are ascribed to the indigenous population. "It is . . . no wonder," Forster remarks, "that in a hot climate, in a libidinous nation, inclined to the leprosy . . . a disease should pullulate, which may become contagious only by cohabitation." He describes a youth seen on Huahine (but not mentioned in the journal), "covered with ulcers . . . His eyes . . . almost extinct . . . the sad victim of brutal appetite and libidinous desire." Forster's insistence that this youth is the agent of his own condition enables him to conclude: "We need not wonder therefore that the disease should have made its appearance at Taheitee and its neighbourhood, long before the arrival of Europeans at their isle."[32] Forster's angry despair at having introduced venereal disease to Queen Charlotte Sound has by now been redirected.

There is little to be gained from assigning blame. Contact between island cultures, with their narrow range of human pathogens and lack of protective antibodies, and Cook's ships, with their full complement of virulent microorganisms, was bound to be devastating for the indigenous populations. Nevertheless, a brief summary of the medical evidence is necessary. On Tahiti and Tonga it seems likely that yaws was often mistaken for syphilis. Yaws, an indigenous disease, would have given considerable though not total immunity to syphilis. The venereal disease contracted by Bougainville and Cook's men would almost certainly have been gonorrhea introduced by Wallis's crew. In New Zealand, however, and in Hawaii on Cook's third voyage, both gonorrhea and syphilis were introduced. Neither group of islands had yaws, and therefore there was no indigenous immunity to syphilis. Leprosy was not an indigenous disease and was not introduced until the mid–nineteenth century.[33]

Whatever the facts of the case, journal writers on eighteenth-century voyages to the

Pacific came to believe they were spreading illness and disease. The sudden frequency of these voyages and the return visits paid by Cook's ships made the consequences of this exploration, whether real or apparent, unavoidable. Disease became the overdetermined focus of the doubts and uncertainties that accumulated with each return. It literalized the contaminating effects of contact and became a figure for these effects in general. These ungovernable effects of contact were intensified by the paradox that the more hospitable and receptive the indigenous culture, the more vulnerable it was to contamination through trade and disease. The degree of interest and curiosity in the culture of the ships was regarded as a mark of how far a native people had progressed toward civilization. Forster's comment that the Del Fuegians "looked at the ship and all its parts with a stupidity and indolence . . . and expressed hardly any desires or wishes to possess any thing which we offered" relegated them to the bottom of the human league table.[34] This lack of interest was a characteristic of savage cultures. New Zealanders, barbarian rather than savage, were interested in European artifacts but had no desire to visit Europe. The semicivilized Tahitians and Tongans, however, were keen to do so.

This paradoxical relation between the development of a culture and its vulnerability to disease was noted and theorized by George Forster in his remarks on New Caledonia. Remarking that the only disease he had noted at this island group was "elephantiasis, a sort of leprosy," and that it was less virulent here than on many other islands, he concluded: "Upon the whole, a great multitude of diseases are the consequences of unbounded luxury, and cannot take place among persons so little refined as those of New Caledonia."[35] The corollary of this was that the voyagers themselves were more vulnerable to disease from contact with their most sympathetic and advanced hosts. In describing the apparently leprous man and woman on Eua who had been noted by his father, George found the relationship between trade and disease becoming altogether too close for comfort:

> one man . . . had his whole back and shoulders covered with a large cancerous ulcer, which was perfectly livid within, and of a bright yellow all round the edges. A woman was likewise unfortunate enough to have all her face destroyed by it in the most shocking manner; there was only a hole left in the place of her nose; her cheeks were swelled up and continually oozing out a purulent matter; and her eyes seemed ready to fall out of her head, being bloody and sore. These were some of the most miserable objects I recollect ever to have seen; and yet they seemed to be quite unconcerned about their misfortunes, traded as briskly as any of the rest, and what was most nauseous, had provisions to sell.[36]

Although it was serendipitous that markers of civilization such as curiosity, hospitality, and willingness to trade should coincide with superior physical beauty, this correlation also underlined the damage caused by European landfalls. The more valued the culture, the more susceptible it was to deformation; the more diseased it became, the keener it was likely to be to trade. In this lies the beginning of fatal impact theory.

Disease, therefore, challenged, undermined, and rebuked the project of exploration. Everything the voyagers touched was likely to be spoiled, and as more islands were collected and described, and the differences between them were constructed, these careful comparisons and fine discriminations were threatened with erasure. In the subtle dialectic of similarity and difference that marked these early European observations of Pacific islands, disease and analogous forms of contamination seemed likely to reduce every island to the same kind of place. The evolving taxonomy of islands was itself in danger of collapse. This point is worth emphasizing. It is clear that disease narratives in the modern colonial period have repeatedly been used to produce and reinforce difference between Europeans and the indigenous peoples they colonized. It is also clear that the communicability of disease always threatened to undermine the very difference that such narratives were intended to establish. Yet in the case of the Forsters, and more generally with the later eighteenth-century attempt to describe and understand the new world of Oceania, the differences that were being constructed were as much between different island groups as between Europeans and some generalized Pacific people. In Oceania, at least, the concern with similarity and difference was more complex than Saidean-derived notions of othering can accommodate. The ubiquity of disease made it an especial focus of the attempt to understand the consequences of encounter and exchange.

This effort to understand expressed itself in preoccupation with skin, the most intimate of all contact zones and the surface on which previous contact was written. The journal writers of these later eighteenth-century voyages to the Pacific seem to have been far more concerned with skin lesions than with skin color. There was relatively little use of color to establish and explain difference, and when it was used, it was mainly to distinguish between the inhabitants of the eastern and western Pacific rather than between Europeans and Pacific islanders. Nineteenth-century colonial discourse was to establish color as an absolute marker of difference. Unlike color, however, the quality of the surface of the skin often provided no kind of marker at all. The attentions of the voyagers shifted uneasily between native skins and their own, and the result was confusion and anxiety. Both Forsters were assiduous medical observers, and J. R. Forster's reports on native bodies were often accompanied by accounts of his own. Syphilis was mimicked by yaws. Scurvy, the dominant everyday health concern on the ships, mimicked many of the skin conditions of the islanders. During the long sweep south "as far as I think it possible for man to go," as Cook wrote,[37] George Forster, like many of the ship's complement, was afflicted with scurvy. His description of its symptoms—"Excruciating pains, livid blotches, rotten gums, and swelled legs"[38]—recalls the accounts of indigenous ailments so frequently catalogued by father and son. Going ashore was the cure, and this was done with the confidence that scurvy was noncommunicable. Yet belief in the health-giving qualities of dry land also became insecure. Although New Zealand's Queen Charlotte Sound, with its abundance of antiscorbutic plants, could always be relied upon to "rekindle[d] a glow of health on our cheeks,"[39] George Forster also doubted the depth of the recovery it seemed to bring: "It may, however, justly be questioned, whether the continual hardships and labours which we had undergone, had not in reality made the shew of health deceitful, and impaired the body so much that it was not able to resist so long as it had formerly done."[40] In other words, although scurvy could not be brought onshore, its invisible consequences might expose the visitor to other shore-based disease.

This chapter opened with the suggestion that the pathologies of travel in the eighteenth century were part of the process whereby the bourgeois subject was constructed as a "mobile sovereign individual." What I have shown is that this process was less seamless and more conflicted than any such formulation can capture. Cook's second voyage was the most extensive and ambitious ever undertaken. Often presented as a supreme achievement of British exploration, the journals of those who traveled on it reveal what an edgy and disorienting experience it was. Jonathan Lamb has shown how scurvy, the bane of all such long-distance oceanic voyaging, produced violent mood swings and intense feelings of homesickness, "present[ing] in its most literal and material form the corruption of the seagoing self."[41] Drawing on Thomas Trotter's *Observations of the Scurvy* (1792), which argued that scurvy resulted from the reciprocal action of the mind and the body in which despair and physical degradation were interchangeable, Lamb uses the disease as a way of imaging the bewildering strangeness of the Oceanic world that late-eighteenth-century voyagers entered. He concludes: "They had things on their hands and a sickness in their bones they could not possibly trace or categorise."[42] This statement also applies to the communicable diseases they brought ashore and those they thought they might catch. At the other end of the world, European subjectivity, bourgeois or not, was as likely to dissolve as to consolidate, and the exchange of disease was always one of its potential solvents.

Alan Bewell has criticized Emmanuel Le Roy Ladurie for placing the unification of the globe by disease between the fourteenth and seventeenth centuries, pointing out that the peoples of Oceania had still to encounter Europeans at this time. Le Roy Ladurie's summary of this process as "a common market of bacilli" also betrays a sense that the world beyond Europe and its fringes barely exists.[43] It was not until the second half of the eighteenth century that evidence of globalization was written on the skin of the inhabitants of Oceania. By then disease had become a focus of anxiety, reminding those who journeyed of the damage they wrought and the risks they incurred. Disease, whether real or imagined, was as much on their minds as more visible forms of exchange; it was the invisibility of its transmission that proved so disturbing. Disease transgressed the boundaries between bodies and was impossible to police. It undermined the ordering of relationships that Cook was concerned to establish at every landfall, as well as the philosophical ordering of the relation between Europe and its others that J. R. Forster attempted. In this way it mocked the voyagers' good intentions and made palpable their more questionable ones. To return to J. R. Forster's observation with which the chapter opened, it seemed that the civilizable terrains of the islands of the Pacific were being infected even before they had been cultivated.

CHAPTER EIGHTEEN

George Berkeley the Islander

Some Reflections on Utopia, Race, and Tar-Water

Carole Fabricant

William Butler Yeats's portrayal of George Berkeley as a "God-appointed" figure who "proved all things a dream" derives its full significance from his insistence on viewing Berkeley within a specifically Irish framework, as a thinker whose refutation of John Locke's empiricism ("We Irish do not hold with this") initiated what Yeats hailed as the "birth of the [Irish] national intellect."[1] This chapter reconsiders Berkeley's role as Yeats's Irish dreamer, examining his significance as a thinker whose lifelong relationship to islands, of the world and of the mind, brought out utopian impulses that colored all aspects of his life and thought, and that help illuminate the contradictions at the heart of his class position as an eighteenth-century Anglo-Irish churchman, striving to create a utopia in the New World while complicit in the brutal *dis*topia of Old World social and religious conflicts.

Born in county Kilkenny, Ireland, Berkeley was (like Swift a generation earlier) educated at Kilkenny School and at Trinity College, Dublin. He took orders in the Anglican Church and spent much of his life as a Church of Ireland clergyman, first as Dean of Derry, later as Bishop of Cloyne, in county Cork.[2] Berkeley's life included mental and physical interactions with other islands as well—England, Ischia, Bermuda, Aquidneck—all of which reveal the idealizing tendencies of Berkeley's imagination and play a role in his quest to recreate Eden out of the shards of a fallen world. An avid traveler from his twenties on, Berkeley embarked on his second continental tour as tutor to the son of Swift's old mentor, St. George Ashe, in the year 1716. The bulk of his lengthy trip was spent traveling in Italy, during which time he stayed for several months on Ischia, the tiny island located about twenty miles southwest of Naples, in the Tyrrhenian Sea. Although he kept a journal of his Italian travels, it is primarily from two lengthy letters—one to his close friend John Perceval, the other to Alexander Pope—that we can discern the complex interrelationship of fantasy and reality in the constitution of Berkeley's earthly paradises. In his description of Ischia to Percival, he does not stint on physical details but assimilates them to a picture suggesting an ideal realm of harmony and plenty: "The fruit lying everywhere exposed without enclosures makes the country look like one great fruit garden . . . Nothing can be conceived more romantic than the forces of nature, mountains, hills, vales, and little plains, being thrown together in a wild and beautiful variety."[3] Viewing his surroundings through layers of biblical and literary convention, Berkeley paints a tapestry in which seeming oppositions—art and nature, wildness and order—are reconciled, revolving around the island as a small, self-contained place that yet proudly eschews suffocating enclosure, remaining open to the delighted spectation and senses of its visitors.

Perhaps not surprisingly, these descriptive tendencies become heightened in the letter to Pope, where Berkeley seems very conscious of writing to the author of a series of "Pastorals" as well as a poem—*Windsor-Forest,* published four years before—that celebrates the return of the "Groves of *Eden*" (7).[4] Prefacing his account with the observation that Italy is "an exhausted subject" about which he has nothing to add, Berkeley shifts his gaze to the island of Ischia, which he depicts as "an epitome of the whole earth, containing within the compass of eighteen miles, a wonderful variety of hills, vales, ragged rocks, fruitful plains, and barren mountains, all thrown together in a most romantic confusion" (*Works* 8:107). Berkeley presents a lengthy catalogue of the abundant fruits that "lie every where open to the passenger" and describes how, from a mountaintop in the middle of the island, one can obtain "the finest prospect in the world," including parts of Italy that "hath been sung by Homer and Virgil." All elements combine to create a "noble landscape" that Berkeley assures Pope "would demand an imagination as warm and numbers as flowing as your own, to describe" (108).

The picture of a veritable paradise on earth would seem to be complete but for one almost comically grotesque qualification that Berkeley casually drops into his account, as though noticing the serpent's tail behind the tree but not quite ready to acknowledge its significance. He portrays "the inhabitants of this delicious isle" as near-perfect beings who might well "answer the poetical notions of the golden age" were it not for "an ill habit of murdering one another on slight offences," which in one instance results in the shooting death of a young man on Berkeley's very doorstep (*Works* 8:108). His

"Fourth Travel Journal" elaborates on this subject, describing a brutal revenge attack on the island by 150 men of the Sbirri clan and concluding with the observation that the island's inhabitants are, for all their exemplary qualities, "blood thirsty & revengeful" (*Works* 7:313). Pope, dealing solely with a mythopoetic tapestry in *Windsor-Forest*, has no problem in temporally and spatially separating the age of barbarism from the restored groves of Eden, the savage hunter of men from the civilized hunter of beasts. Berkeley, however, dealing not only with the myth but also the empirical realities of island existence, is forced to reveal the inextricable links between barbarism and civilization, between the dream of paradise and the actualities of a fallen world where the brutishness of the savage cannot be separated from the innocence of the Arcadian dweller.

In the fall of 1720 Berkeley concluded his continental tour and returned to the "fair scepter'd isle" that had so enthusiastically welcomed him into its bosom only a few years before, offering him entrée to those writers who were celebrating the return of the Golden Age on the heels of the Peace of Utrecht. This time, however, he was confronted with dramatically changed circumstances, for his arrival in London coincided with the collapse of the South Sea Company, an event whose shocking revelations and disastrous consequences could not but put an abrupt end to Arcadian fantasies, especially in the case of a strict moralist of Tory leanings such as Berkeley. The result was "An Essay towards preventing the Ruin of Great Britain," which we might think of as the flip side of the coin to the letters from Ischia—the dark underbelly of the idealist's yearning for a return to Eden. For Berkeley, the so-called South Sea Bubble was far more than just a financial fiasco—it signified nothing less than an all-encompassing breakdown of Britain's religious and moral foundations. The tone of his essay is therefore not just somber but ominously prophetic, and it gradually takes on the shape of a full-blown jeremiad in which his audience is warned that "the finger of God will unravel all our vain projects . . . if we do not reform that scandalous libertinism which . . . is our worst symptom, and the surest prognostic of our ruin" (*Works* 6:71). After extended reflection on "the corrupt degenerate age we live in," Berkeley apocalyptically declares that "it is to be feared the final period of our State approaches" (*Works* 6:84–85). The essay suggestively anticipates the final stage of its author's life as messianic physician-alchemist by portraying England as a diseased body in desperate need of potent medicine to restore it to health because "Where the vitals are touched, and the whole mass of humours vitiated, it is not enough to ease the part pained; we must look further, and apply general correctives" (*Works* 6:83–84). Yet, even in the midst of delivering his prophecy of doom, Berkeley cannot resist nostalgically rehearsing the circumstances of a glowingly idealized past when England was "inhabited by a religious, brave, sincere people, of plain uncorrupt manners, . . . improvers of learning and useful arts, enemies to luxury, tender of other men's lives and prodigal of their own; inferior in nothing to the old Greeks and Romans, and superior to each of those people in the perfections of the other" (*Works* 6:85).

Reading this tract, one is struck by the remarkable tenacity of Berkeley's Golden Age dream while at the same time left wondering how it could ever be truly salvaged from such moral wreckage. The answer was not long in coming. The tract was published in 1721; by the end of the following year Berkeley had already conceived what was to become known as the Bermuda Project—his plan to found off the coast of America an ideal community, with a college for training Christian missionaries at its center. An early description of this plan appears in Berkeley's letter to Percival of 4 March 1723, which names as its two most important goals "the reformation of manners among the English in our western plantations, and the propagation of the Gospel among the American savages" (*Works* 8:127). In order to achieve these aims, Berkeley proposed the erection of a seminary where both English and Indian youth could be educated in the liberal arts and sciences, instructed in the Christian religion, and then sent out to spread the gospel in their respective communities.

One might have thought that an Anglo-Irish churchman would have had his hands full trying to convert the large body of Roman Catholics within Ireland itself, but in actuality Church of Ireland clergy, official rhetoric notwithstanding, were given little incentive to try to convert the Irish natives because without the continued existence of a Catholic underclass, there would no longer have been any justification for a Protestant Ascendancy. Men in Berkeley's position were in effect forced to look to other islands across the sea as territory ripe for their evangelical exertions. As the most fitting site for his seminary, Berkeley singled out the Bermuda Islands, which, in a way reminiscent of his portrayal of Ischia, he described as a place where "the summers refreshed with constant cool breezes, the winters as mild as our May, the sky as light and blue as a sapphire, the ever green pastures, the earth eternally crowned with fruits and flowers. The woods of cedars, palmettos, myrtles, oranges &c., always fresh and blooming" (*Works* 8:128). One need hardly point out that Berkeley had himself never been to Bermuda—a circumstance that protected it from those pesky facts on the ground (so to speak) that had earlier belied his picture of an Ischian Arcadia. Having duly located the "perfect" site for his college, Berkeley held it out as a tantalizing promise of a paradise on earth—or rather, on the ocean—a place where men can "enjoy health of body and peace of mind" and find "whatsoever the most poetical imagination can figure to itself in the golden age, or the Elysian fields" (*Works* 8:129).

It would be hard to exaggerate the appeal Berkeley's Bermuda vision exerted on his contemporaries. The project won the promise of a parliamentary grant of £20,000, and a number of well-placed people in England and Ireland agreed to leave their old lives behind in order to accompany Berkeley to his island paradise. The list of those raising funds for the project, as appended to "A Proposal for the Better Supplying of Churches in our Foreign Plantations" (1725), included such prominent figures in society as Dr. John Arbuthnot, Edward Harley, the banker Henry Hoare, the alderman of the City of London, and a number of notable churchmen such as the Dean of Ely and the Vicar of St. Martin's in the Field, with the Archbishop of Canterbury, the Duke of Newcastle, and the Bishop of London serving as trustees (*Works* 7:361). Berkeley's project not only enlisted the support of influential figures, it also captured the imagination of much of English society, becoming for a time synonymous with a romantic retreat from the ills of the world. Thus Lord Bolingbroke could write to Swift in July of 1725, asking him to leave his "Hibernian flock" and join Bolingbroke in Bermuda, where "we will form a so-ciety, more reasonable, & more useful than that of Dr Berkley's Colledge."[5]

It is perhaps not surprising that Berkeley, eager to exchange Old World decadence for the purity of a world reborn, should cast his eyes across the ocean to the Americas. But why Bermuda in particular? The answer no doubt lies in the island's history and textual representations during the previous century. Bermuda's settlement by the En-glish resulted from a shipwreck and miraculous rescue—a circumstance that must have held a special appeal for the Church of Ireland clergyman, eager to discern earthly signs of God's providence in a world he had only recently proclaimed on the verge of damna-tion. In late July 1609, the *Sea-Venture*, one of nine ships en route from Plymouth to Virginia, under the command of Sir George Somers, became separated from the rest of the fleet during a hurricane and was thrown onto the reefs off Bermuda, until then a group of uninhabited islands widely known as the Islands of the Devil. As Sylvanus Jourdan explains in his 1610 narrative of the shipwreck, the Bermudas were deemed "a most prodigious and inchanted place, affoording nothing but gusts, stormes, and foule weather, which made every navigator to avoid them . . . as they would shun the Divell himselfe."[6] Somers and his crew wound up staying on the Bermudas for almost a year, and while the outside world took them for dead, they not only survived but in many ways thrived, thanks to what Jourdan described as "ayr so temperat, and [a] countrey so abundantly fruitful of all fit necessaries for the sustentation and preservation of man's life" (*Memorials* 1:16). During these months they built two ships, pointedly named *Patience* and *Deliverance*, which finally carried them to their original destina-tion, Jamestown, in May 1610. From that point onward the Bermudas became known by the felicitously apt name of the Summer Islands.

The various first-person accounts written of this event—collectively known as *The Bermuda Pamphlets*—tend to underscore the widespread belief that Admiral Somers's shipwreck and deliverance were the working out of a divine script. One of these, pub-lished under the direction of the Council of Virginia, insists that the mariners' discovery of a safe harbor in the midst of the storm "was no Ariadnes thread, but the direct line of Gods providence," and it equates their rescue with the instance "when God sent abundance of Quayles to feed his *Israel* in the barren wildernesse" (*Memorials* 1:13). Similarly, "A True Reportory of the Wracke" written by William Strachey, a member of the *Sea-Venture*'s crew, declares that "it pleased our mercifull God, to make even this hideous and hated place, both the place of our safetie, and meanes of our deliverance" (*Memorials* 1:28). The fact that, at around the very time that Berkeley was conceiving of his Bermuda venture, he himself was caught in a storm at sea, "outrageous beyond description," and managed to survive only by what he construed as God's deliverance (*Works* 8:126–27), suggests that personal experience may have combined with religious ideology to influence Berkeley's selection of the Summer Islands as the site of his utopian design.

Reinforcing the providentialist view evident in *The Bermuda Pamphlets* were a number of celebrated literary works written in the decades following the shipwreck, such as Andrew Marvell's poem, "Bermudas," in which the island is characterized by "eternal Spring" (l. 13), and Edmund Waller's mock-epic poem, *The Battle of the Summer-Islands*, which portrays the island as a type of paradise: "Bermuda, wall'd with rocks, who does not know? / That happy island where huge lemons grow, / And orange trees, which golden fruit do bear, / The Hesperian garden boasts of none so fair" (I.5–8).[7] Berkeley specifically quotes Waller's poem to help authorize his choice of Bermuda (*Works* 7:352). Of course, the work that most famously uses the story of Somers's shipwreck is Shakespeare's *The Tempest*, which was performed at court less than a year and a half after the crew of the *Sea-Venture*'s seemingly miraculous return from a watery grave. Though Bermuda is mentioned only once in the play—in Ariel's reference to "the still-vex'd Bermoothes" (I.ii.229)—aspects of its physical description and the circumstances of its discovery likely informed the characterization of Prospero's island, as several critics have noted.[8] It is tempting to imagine Berkeley, as he was drawing up the plans for his island utopia, thinking of himself as a latter-day Prospero, setting forth across the ocean on a holy mission to bring salvation to the Calibans of a New World that was at once innocent and savage, a source of regeneration for European decadence even as it cried out for the Europeanizing influence of a Christian redemption.

Berkeley's utopian project in Bermuda generated as noble a vision as Old Gonzalo's ideal community, with which it had many features in common, such as the absence of both riches and poverty and a nature "bring[ing] forth, / Of it own kind, all foison, all abundance, / To feed [its] innocent people" (*Tempest*, II.i.163–65). Yet the dark side of this glorious vision, the dirty little secret that like a worm ate away at its ethical core, was its dependence on a system of belief that not only tolerated but actively defended the most *ig*noble and *in*glorious practices and institutions of the day—specifically, slavery and empire. In his "Proposal," Berkeley emphasizes as one major benefit of his plan the conversion to Christianity of the black slaves in the American colonies. Lamenting "the small Care that hath been taken to convert the Negroes of our Plantations," Berkeley assures slave owners that "Gospel Liberty consists with temporal Servitude," and he urges them to consider "That it would be of Advantage to their Affairs, to have Slaves who should *obey in all Things their Masters according to the Flesh, not with Eye-service as Man-pleasers, but in Singleness of Heart as fearing God* . . . and that their Slaves would only become better Slaves by being Christians" (*Works* 7:346). Berkeley returned to this point in the "Anniversary Sermon" he preached before the Society for the Propagation of the Gospel on 18 February 1732, less than four months after his return to England from America. In it he applauds a document, signed by the king's attorney and solicitor-general, which affirmed the compatibility of baptism with slavery and thus encouraged English settlers to attend to the presumed spiritual needs of those they owned (122). What Berkeley does not mention in the sermon is his own dubious exemplarity in this matter, based on his own stint as a slaveholder during his extended stay in Newport, Rhode Island, which was at the time the most important slaving zone in the North American colonies, using more slaves in small businesses, farms, and homes than any other Northern colony.[9] On 4 October 1730, Berkeley paid £80 to one Simon Pease in order to purchase a Negro named Philip, aged about fourteen, and three days later he paid William Coddington £86 for Edward, also known as Anthony, a Negro of about twenty years of age. Around this same time he apparently also bought a female slave called Agnes, although the exact details of this transaction have been lost. Consistent with his expressed views in this matter, he baptized all three in Newport's Trinity Church on 11 June 1731.[10]

It is against this backdrop that we must try to understand Berkeley's view that the Bermudas were the home of an "innocent Sort of People" who embodied more than a few hints of Golden Age virtues (*Works* 7:352). Writing to Percival, he explained that the Bermudans "have the greatest simplicity of manners, more innocence, honesty, and good nature, than any of our other planters, who are many of them descended from whores, vagabonds, and transported criminals, none of which ever settled in Bermudas" (*Works* 8:128). This statement refers to the 1615 charter for the islands (see *Memorials* 1:83–98), which proclaimed that all were eligible to be colonists there except for jailbirds and—what would have been of special interest (and no doubt satisfaction) to an Anglo-Irish churchman—Catholics. Although both groups did eventually come to the islands as indentured servants or as prisoners on the notorious "convict hulks" docked off the islands' northeasternmost tip, their formal exclusion from the original charter of Bermuda allowed Berkeley to wipe the slate clean, as it were, and present a picture of an uncorrupted (which is to say, a socially and racially unpolluted) society that in effect managed to prevent the serpent from entering the garden—a picture bolstered by Berkeley's portrayal of the islands as "the securest spot in the universe, being environed round with rocks[, with] all but one narrow entrance, [and] guarded by seven forts" (*Works* 8:128).

All of this suggests that Berkeley's Bermuda Project was as dependent on its omissions and exclusions as on its expressed, often lovingly detailed articulations. For already by the middle of the seventeenth century—and despite the charter's explicit provision that the island's inhabitants would "enjoy all libertyes franchesies and immunities of free denizens and naturall subjectes" (*Memorials* 1:94)—Bermuda's economy had become dependent on slave labor. First, it relied on the indentured servitude of Indian captives and later on the forced labor of black Africans, who by the Restoration period made up one-third of Bermuda's population and were being subjected to increasingly repressive legislation passed by the Bermuda Assembly throughout the 1660s (see, e.g., *Memorials* 2:216–19), designed to strengthen the "Act to restrayne the insolencies of the Negroes" first put forward in 1623 (*Memorials* 1:308–9). Indeed, in June 1730, at the very time Berkeley was writing from Newport to various correspondents, reaffirming his opinion that Bermuda was indeed "the proper place" to establish his utopia (*Works* 8:210), a mulatto slave on that island was being burned at the stake for allegedly plotting to poison the members of the affluent white family for whom she worked. The notorious Sarah Bassett trial and execution—with its overtones of Obeah, Satanism, and the threat of black resistance to white oppression—gave immediate rise to legislation directed at tightening control over "*Negroes, Indians, Mulattoes,* and other Slaves," and ensuring that Bermudan slave-owners would be protected from punishment for killing a slave, who was described as "no otherwise valued or esteemed amongst us than as our Goods and Chattels or other personal Estates."[11]

In the absence of viable plantations, Bermuda had long since become a maritime economy, its trading ships plying the coast of the Americas with crews that included black slaves and indentured seamen. This fact is at once alluded to and purged from Berkeley's "Proposal" concerning Bermuda. Listing the advantages of that group of islands over other places in the Caribbean, Berkeley remarks, "The *Bermudans* are excellent Shipwrights and Sailors, and have a great Number of very good Sloops, which are always passing and repassing from all Parts of *America*. They drive a constant Trade to the Islands of *Jamaica, Barbadoes, Antego,* &c." (*Works* 7:350–51). Here Berkeley presents a pleasing visual tapestry that features at its center the image of incessantly moving ships that seem to tell a story of freedom, not captivity—and certainly not the real story of the freedom of a few paid for by the captivity of many.

In short, black slaves are everywhere and nowhere in Berkeley's descriptions of Bermuda, haunting them with their absence in much the same way that the Catholics were often everywhere and nowhere in the writings of the Irish Protestants, even in their elided state threatening at any moment to break through the Ascendancy's magisterial style and disrupt its picture of a God-graced land basking in British-sponsored privilege and prosperity. The analogy I am suggesting here is not a casual one. The discourse of race was as potent a factor in Irish history as it was in the history of African (and later American) blacks. The common pictorial representation of Irishmen with pronounced simian features throughout the Victorian period reflected a set of attitudes that can be traced at least as far back as the late twelfth century, when Henry II's invasion of Ireland was justified by the historian Giraldus Cambrensis, who portrayed the so-called wild Irish as "a most filthy race, a race sunk in vice, a race more ignorant than all other nations of the first principles of the faith."[12] Among the many barbaric practices ascribed to the Irish was cannibalism—one of a number of characterizations that connected the wild Irish with the American Calibans in the minds of those who styled themselves exemplars of civilization. Thus in 1689 Sir Richard Cox could assert that there was "good reason to call *Ireland, The Barbarous Island.*"[13]

It is, then, hardly coincidental that ironic comparisons between the Irish and the Hottentots, Africans, and American Indians run throughout Swift's writings, which also exemplify how a rhetoric of slavery versus freedom was appropriated by eighteenth-century Irish nationalists—one thinks of the outraged query of Swift's Drapier: "Am I a *Free-man* in *England,* and do I become a *Slave* in six Hours, by crossing the Channel?"[14] Though this rhetoric was in many cases disassociated from the actual system of slavery in the New World, it could also insist on the grim parallels between enslaved Africans and Irish Catholics. Berkeley himself was well aware of these unsettling similarities: In "A Word to the Wise; or An Exhortation to the Roman Catholic Clergy of Ireland" (1749), he criticizes the absurd pride of his Irish "kitchen-wench" for refusing to carry out the cinders "because she was descended from an old Irish stock" and goes on to observe, "At the same time these proud people are more destitute than savages, and more abject than negroes. The negroes in our plantations have a saying, 'If negro was not negro, Irishman would be negro.' And it may be affirmed with truth that the very savages in America are better clad and better lodged than the Irish cottagers throughout the fine fertile counties of Limerick and Tipperary" (*Works* 6:237).

This epistle is noteworthy for the way in which it combines what was for the time a remarkably tolerant religious perspective—"I consider you as my countrymen, as fellow-subjects, as professing belief in the same Christ," Berkeley tells the Catholic clergy (*Works* 6:248)—with a deeply biased and stereotyped portrayal of the native Irish poor as "a lazy, destitute, and degenerate race" (238) whose tainted Scythian blood has produced "the native colour, if we may so speak, and complexion of the people" (243–44). Such remarks indicate that race at this time was not so much a matter of skin pigmentation as a constructed category used to regulate power within a social hierarchy and create clearly defined places for different groups within that hierarchy—a circumstance elaborated upon at length in Theodore W. Allen's monumental study, *The Invention of the White Race.*[15]

Berkeley's mechanism for asserting his whiteness and thus distinguishing himself from the Irish "negroes" included an inherently contradictory set of attitudes that called simultaneously for charitable treatment of the savage and support of the institutions—slavery in the Americas, the penal laws in Ireland—that ensured that the savage would remain a savage (even if a baptized one), thereby buttressing racial categories that perpetuated the existence of a ruling class. When, in attempting to garner sponsors for his missionary venture in the New World, Berkeley declared, "no Part of the Gentile World are so inhuman and barbarous as the savage *Americans*" (*Works* 7:359), the irony of his invoking the very same terms that the English had historically applied to the Irish was lost on him. It would not have been lost on Swift, who well understood that not only Irish Catholics but also the Anglo-Irish themselves were, from the perspective of God's Englishman, tarnished with the brush of "savagery"—that by the early eighteenth century, the marker of inferiority for the English was not so much Catholicism as Irishness. Berkeley's serene ability to police the boundaries between savage and civilian, white man and Negro, despite his own class's stigmatization as a kind of hybrid or mongrel race, underscores the ironies inherent in the Protestant Ascendancy's claims of racial superiority in the eighteenth century.

Berkeley's complicity in empire went hand-in-hand with his involvement with slavery and was a direct outgrowth of his peculiar brand of evangelical Christianity, which necessarily entailed a form of spiritual imperialism, founded as it was on a proselytizing zeal to spread the Word of the white Anglo-Saxon Protestant man's God throughout the furthest reaches of the New World. So fervently committed was he to achieving this goal, he sanctioned the act of "taking captive the Children of our Enemies" if such an expedient proved necessary for procuring young Indian students for his college (*Works* 7:347). Even when focusing on the spiritual benefits of his mission, Berkeley expressed his awareness of their political and economic implications, as when he warned that if the Protestant religion failed to be planted more firmly in America, missionaries from Spain and France would instead spread the Catholic religion, "which would probably end in the utter Extirpation of our Colonies, on the Safety whereof depends so much of the Nation's Wealth, and so considerable a Branch of his Majesty's Revenue" (354). He went on to proclaim that "the Honour of the Crown, Nation, and Church of *England*" was vitally concerned in his scheme because the latter would "cast no small

Lustre on his Majesty's Reign, and derive a Blessing from Heaven on his Administration and those who live under the influence thereof" (355).

Berkeley's attitude toward empire is further highlighted by a poem, "Verses on the prospect of Planting Arts and Learning in America" (*Works* 7:373), which he apparently wrote several years before actually departing for the new continent, though it was not published until much later. In it, he contrasts a decadent Old World, "Barren of every glorious Theme" (2), with the vision of "another golden Age" marked by "The rise of Empire and of Arts" (13–14), concluding on an emphatically prophetic note: "Westward the Course of Empire takes its Way; / The four first Acts already past, / A fifth shall close the Drama with the Day; / Time's noblest Offspring is the last" (21–24). (In the original version, the final line has more apocalyptic overtones: "The world's great Effort is the last.") While the poem's religious, and especially millennial, implications are clearly central to the work, we should not ignore the concrete worldly dimension of its prophecy—the political as well as biblical framework within which the word "empire" functions. In words reported by his daughter-in-law, Berkeley declared that unless episcopacy was introduced in America "that noblest, grandest part of the British Empire of the WHOLE world will be lost; [the Colonies] will shake off the Mother Country in a few years. Nothing but introducing Bishops amongst them *can* keep them together, can keep them loyal. Church and state, in every country, must stand and fall together."[16] Since for an eighteenth-century Anglo-Irishman the total interdependence of church and state was the indispensable cornerstone of society, the sine qua non for the survival of the ruling class, it is hardly surprising that Berkeley would have seen little point in differentiating a spiritual empire from a political one.

The optimistically expansionist and millennial coloration of Berkeley's "Verses on . . . America" clearly struck a deep chord in the continent they celebrate. By the middle of the following century, they had been cited so often, not least as support for the doctrine of Manifest Destiny, that Charles Sumner noted they had "become a commonplace of literature and politics."[17] The prophecy of empire's westward course was borne out in the spread of Berkeley's fame and that of his "Verses" to the westernmost reaches of the American continent. A decade after the College of California was chartered in 1855, its leading trustee Frederick Billings suggested that its site be called Berkeley, arguing for the appropriateness of naming it after one who "prophesied so truly of the Course of Empire." Taking his cue from Billings, college president Daniel Coit Gilman, in his 1872 Inaugural Address, applauded the institution's new name and told his audience, "It is not yet a century and a half since that romantic voyage which brought [Berkeley] to Newport, in Rhode Island . . . His fame has crossed the continent which then seemed hardly more than a seaboard of the Atlantic; and now, at the very ends of the earth, near the Golden Gate, the name of Berkeley is to be a household word . . . Let us labor and pray that his well-known vision may be true"; whereupon Gilman proceeded to quote the final stanza of Berkeley's "Verses" ("Westward the Course of Empire takes its Way").[18]

On 6 September 1728, having succeeded in obtaining a charter from the king for St. Paul's College, Berkeley set sail for the New World, after making plans to take up temporary residence in the town of Newport, Rhode Island, located on the island formerly known as Aquidneck, acquired from the Narragansett Indians a century earlier. Here he waited for the £20,000 promised him for his Bermuda venture. In letters written soon after his arrival in Newport, Berkeley depicted the island in the same romanticized way he had earlier portrayed Ischia and Bermuda, once again conveying the image of a kind of garden paradise marked by a profusion of fruit and what was reputed to be the "most delicious autumn in the world" (Works 8:194). Inevitably, however, Newport no more than Ischia could provide a real-life framework to support Berkeley's Arcadian dream. In this case, the snake in the garden took the form not of bloodthirsty Italian clansmen but of a wide variety of religious Dissenters, who were quite willing to welcome an Anglican dean (not to mention a famous European philosopher) into their midst but who had not the least desire or intention to allow episcopacy to take hold in their territory. Newport did, however, offer ready access to the mainland across the Narragansett Bay, where Berkeley, accompanied by the Rev. James McSparran, another Irish clergyman who served as rector of the Narragansett parish, pursued the chief aim of his mission, namely, to proselytize among the native Americans.[19] Despite a number of contacts with them, Berkeley does not seem to have made much more headway in bringing the Narragansett Indians over to Christianity than he did in persuading Newport's Nonconformists to embrace the Church of England. Nevertheless, it may well have been from these contacts with the Indians that he first learned of the use of tarwater to prevent and combat disease: an event that was to have profound repercussions for the final remarkable phase of his life.[20]

Berkeley remained in Newport for two years and eight months, waiting in vain for the government grant promised him. A combination of factors, including a changed political situation in England and the emergence of other New World schemes more directly useful to the colonial enterprise, diverted the Bermuda Project funds elsewhere. Writing to Perceval in March 1731, a disheartened Berkeley informed his friend he had given up all hope of ever seeing the money and hence of carrying out his design, adding that he felt "absolutely abandoned" by everyone involved in the project (Works 8:212). Within six months Berkeley was back in London, having left behind the New World for good.

It would seem that this disappointment could not but herald the final and irrevocable defeat of Berkeley's utopian vision. I would like to suggest, however, that the failure of his Bermuda Project provoked Berkeley not to abandon his vision but rather to reconceive it in other terms. No longer able to find a real-world geographic place to project his ideal society onto, he turned away from the land altogether and looked toward water as the site and agent of redemption. In this regard, I believe he was not only falling back on the obvious Christian symbolism associated with baptism but also responding as a lifelong islander whose existential experiences had always been shaped by his nearness to the sea, and who (in contrast to Swift) consistently displayed the sanguine side of an islander sensibility in relation to the natural elements. Thus his writings are filled with water imagery connoting purification and regeneration. As a typical example, Jeremiah's "fountain of living waters" appeared both as a pictorial and a textual reference on the title page of the first volume of *Alciphron, or The Minute Philosopher,* a work against free-thinkers that Berkeley wrote while in America. Several of the work's Dialogues take place in settings that strikingly evoke the island atmosphere of Newport and its vistas of Narragansett Bay, as if to suggest that Berkeley were directly absorbing the power and inspiration to refute godlessness from his watery surroundings. Given this sensibility, it is perhaps no wonder that in the final years of his life he exchanged his obsession with Bermuda for an obsession with what he saw as the all-encompassing medicinal virtues of tar-water.

In January 1734, Berkeley obtained the bishopric of Cloyne, took up residence there the following summer and—against all odds and expectations, given his earlier peripatetic existence—settled down in Cork for almost twenty years thereafter, remaining until shortly before his death. Cloyne, a small town about twenty miles east of the city of Cork, located near the long inlet of the sea that creates Cobh Harbor and two or three miles from the bay, placed Berkeley once again on land defined by its propinquity to the sea and its estuaries. Here he created for himself and his family a center of culture filled with imported art and music, and enjoyed the many perks available to one of his high social position. However, much of the area in which he resided was impoverished, inhabited mainly by Catholics and subject to the devastating famines that were already a recurring feature of Irish history, as well as to a series of epidemics that claimed many victims in the neighborhood. In February 1741 he recorded the arrival in town of an "epidemical bloody flux" (*Works* 8:248), and three months later he wrote Prior, "The distresses of the sick and poor are endless . . . The nation will probably not recover this loss in a century. The other day I heard one from the county of Limerick say that whole villages were entirely dispeopled" (251–52). Faced with the threat of illness all around him, including within his own domestic circle, and with no physician residing in the immediate area, Berkeley assumed the role of doctor, dispensing medical advice to his parishioners on a wide range of maladies, and carrying on medical observations that culminated in the 1744 publication of *Siris,* his remarkable treatise on the virtues of tar-water.

Subtitled "A Chain of Philosophical Reflections and Inquiries," the treatise contains a compendium of Platonic and Neoplatonic effusions culminating in an ecstatic vision of the celestial sphere and "the perfect intuition of divine things" (*Works* 5:164). It begins, however, on a very concrete and practical note by offering specific instructions on how to make tar-water, a liquid produced by mixing "a gallon of water [with] a quart of tar" obtained from tree bark and then allowing the result to stand forty-eight hours so that "the tar may have time to subside" (32). Simultaneously acknowledging his debt to what he learned in the New World and asserting his independent thinking on the subject, Berkeley explains how tar-water is made "in certain parts of America" but then quickly goes on to recommend his own, putatively superior method of composition (32). What follows is an extended description of the potion's wondrous powers, with examples of its near-miraculous cures recounted in detail, some supposedly based on Berkeley's own personal and family experiences. The list of ailments for which the tar-water is said to bring relief seems almost endless, assuming its most impressively fulsome form in his *First Letter to Thomas Prior on the Virtues of Tar-Water,* published in the same year as *Siris:* "But I am most sincerely persuaded, from what I have already seen and tried, that tar-water may be drank with great safety and success for the cure or relief of most if not all diseases—of ulcers, itch, scald-heads, leprosy, King's evil, cancers, the foul disease, and all foul cases, scurvies of all kinds, disorders of the lungs, stomach, and bowels, in rheumatic, gouty and nephritic ailments, megrims, inveterate headaches, epilepsies, pleurisies, peripneumonies, erysipelas, small-pox, and all kinds of fevers, colics, hysteric and all nervous cases, obstructions, dropsies, decays, and other maladies" (179). It is in this *Letter* too that Berkeley explicitly acknowledges what his earlier claims for tar-water inescapably imply: "I freely own that I suspect tar-water is a panacea" (175).

Given the sweeping curative powers ascribed to tar-water in his strangely seductive treatise, it is perhaps not surprising that in his own time *Siris* was Berkeley's most popular work and that it generated an enormous amount of excitement in the public at large—in certain ways reminiscent of the intense interest generated by his Bermuda project twenty years earlier. Once again Berkeley showed himself to be a consummate promoter of utopian hopes, managing to persuade numerous others to embrace his vision of a world cured of imperfections. The appeal of tar-water proved even more powerful than that of the Caribbean, extending to segments of society that had remained largely immune to the Bermuda craze on the strength of Berkeley's assurances that "this safe and cheap medicine suits all circumstances and all constitutions" (*Works* 5:65). As a contemporary observer noted in June 1744, "[Tar-water] is the common topic of discourse both among the rich and poor, high and low . . . Do you sell tar-water? a man asked an apothecary; tar-water, was the reply, why, I sell nothing else."[21]

The title *Siris*, a variation on the Greek word for "chain," most obviously refers to the interlinking series of reflections that make up the treatise, but, as Berkeley observed in a note to his *Second Letter to Thomas Prior on the Virtues of Tar-Water* (1746), it was also the name the ancient Egyptians gave to the Nile. His argument uses this fact to particular metaphorical effect: "The virtue of tar-water, flowing like the Nile from a secret and occult source, brancheth into innumerable channels, conveying health and relief wherever it is applied" (*Works* 5:185). The tracing of his panacea to "a secret and occult source" serves to obfuscate its specifically American origins—indeed, removes it from the geophysical world altogether and places it in a supernatural realm, on a par less with other medicinal substances than with the Eleusinian Mysteries. In this way tar-water is purged both of its gross nature and its ties to the savage continent—in a necessary if probably unconscious move, given Berkeley's Old World ambivalence about the New World as a simultaneous source of renewal and site of barbaric contamination.

The point to be emphasized here is the extent to which the idea of tar-water as a panacea performed a function similar to Berkeley's Bermuda Project, offering a cure for bodily corruption just as the latter had held out a remedy for moral corruption. If, as Berkeley wrote to a correspondent, "Political societies have their diseases as well as natural bodies" (*Works* 8:207), his new role as physician meant he could restore the health not only of ailing patients but also of a sick society and could thus carry on the utopian project in a reconfigured form. It may seem oddly disproportionate that tar-water should be made to bear the full weight of this redemptive act, but this circumstance can, I think, be explained by David Berman's observation that for Berkeley "tar-water is, in effect, drinkable God."[22] That Catholics as well as Protestants, the poor as well as the rich, had equal access to this divine potion, which offered a means of circumventing the increasingly remote and elitist medical profession—whose members, indeed, felt sufficiently threatened by this readily available layman's cure to rail against the "epidemical madness of drinking tar-water"[23]—suggests the more radical implications of Berkeley's treatise. At the same time, the promotion of tar-water as a cure-all offered no direct threat to the political status quo. One could even argue that taking tar-water, especially in its role as prophylactic, functioned as a safe alternative to the taking up of arms, which was, after all, a distinct threat in the months leading up to the final abortive Jacobite Rebellion of 1745: an event Berkeley forcefully opposed in two open letters published in the *Dublin Journal* in October of that year, one specifically addressed to the Catholics of Cloyne (*Works* 6:227–30).

The figure of Berkeley in the last decade of his life seems almost *too* resonant with ironies and contradictions that register on both the personal and the historical levels. A man intent on transforming his manse-house in the Irish hinterlands into an Italianate palace of art, Berkeley was at the same time animated by a more generous and less elitist vision of community, reflected in his medical ministrations to all members of his parish as well as in his sponsorship of local training programs for the poor and in his advocacy of a civic virtue that demanded active promotion of "the public prosperity" over pursuit of private interest (*Works* 6:254).[24] The ironies in this regard can, I think, be understood at least partly in terms of Berkeley's steadfast commitment to a utopian ideal, which by its very nature stands as a challenge to the status quo, pushing against the narrow bounds of any one class's self-interests by articulating the vision of a society transformed through its embrace of the collective good.[25] The many pictorial representations of Berkeley made during or shortly after his lifetime highlight this duality of outlook. While a number of them portray the Anglo-Irish cleric in full regalia, exuding an air of well-fed content and surrounded by the official trappings of authority that indelibly mark him as one of the ruling class, others present a figure seemingly far removed from the nexus of money and power that defined the governing mechanisms of eighteenth-century Ireland. In John Smibert's famous painting *The Bermuda Group* (ca. 1739), for example, Berkeley is shown looking up and out into empty space as he stands to the right of the other figures in an attitude of rapt contemplation, with the outlines of his utopian island visible in the background.[26] Although juxtaposed alongside family and friends in what conforms in most respects to a conversation piece, he seems a curiously solitary and detached figure, rooted not in earthly reality but in an otherworldly dimension, his visionary gaze moving beyond the picture frame just as his utopian imagination burst through the narrow confines of Irish Protestant ideology to reveal the outlines of a more spacious and inclusive vision.

The many ironies and contradictions of Berkeley's career can perhaps best be summed up by the following circumstance: In living out his final years in a "remote corner" of Ireland (*Works* 8:268), urging all in his neighborhood to imbibe the divine in a gesture suggesting nothing so much as a medically rationalized form of transubstantiation, Berkeley, though in many ways the quintessential embodiment of Irish Protestant values and privilege, became identified with an act combining the spiritual, nature-based practices of pagan and native American lore and the religious rituals of the Roman Catholic Mass. In so doing, he unwittingly underscored the extent to which the much-vaunted civilization that the Ascendancy laid claim to was inextricably bound up with putatively "savage" elements that belied the seamlessly coherent "white" identity it strove to foster, and that contained the seeds of its eventual demise.

CHAPTER NINETEEN

Inhuming Empire

Islands as Colonial Nurseries and Graves

Jill Casid

"The acquisition of a new plant is a sweet and humane conquest."
BERNARDIN DE SAINT-PIERRE, *Voyage à l'Isle de France*

The acquisition of plants, transfer of vegetable commodities, and seeding of the ground were the founding, paternalistic gestures in the European formation of colonies. Inseminating appropriated land with transplanted seed was a material act, a staking of geopolitical claims that, as a privileged scene, attempted to perform the imaginative labor of converting conquest into something "sweet and humane." Take, for example, the account of Admiral Anson's landing on the island of Juan Fernández in *A Voyage Round the World,* the narrative of Anson's naval escapades published in 1748. The commander and his crew do not merely survey, catalogue, and topographically render the island for European consumption as "the only commodious place in those seas" where British seamen sick with scurvy could recover after the passage around Cape Horn, but Anson himself is supposed to have planted seeds of European vegetables and fruit trees into the soil of the island: "Mr. Anson having with him garden seeds of all kinds, and stones of different sorts of fruits, he, for the better accommodation of his countrymen who should hereafter touch here, sowed both lettices, carrots, and other garden plants, and sett in the woods a great variety of plum, apricock, and peach stones: And these last he has been informed have since thriven to a very remarkable degree."[1] This scene of sowing seed is the founding paternal gesture of possession. With its attendant metaphor of heterosexual reproduction, the insemination of the ground ostensibly displaces the subjugating appropriation of the land with an act of potential momentary incorporation for future improvement or propagation. In Jean-Jacques Rousseau's *Émile ou de l'éducation* (1762) the exemplary youth Émile is taught a lesson about the importance of agriculture that becomes an emblematic performance of the contemporary assertion that lands belong to those who make productive agricultural use of them: "He took possession of it [the ground] in planting a bean; and surely this possession is more sacred and more respectable than that staked by Nuñez de Balboa to South America in planting his standard on the coastline of the South Sea in the name of the King of Spain."[2] Seeding the ground as the sign of cultivation replaces what was supposed to have been its opposite: the planting of a nation's banner into the earth. Just as the tale of Anson's carrot seed is narrated to establish British right to Juan Fernández, Émile's little bean usurps the place of the Spanish conquistador's standard on the moral high ground.

With this materializing metaphor of the practices of agriculture and landscaping as heterosexual reproduction, to plant was also to produce imperial subjects to populate or support these practices. However, given the material conditions of the sugar plantation with its forced slave labor, to plant or impress imperial subjects with a new ideology of empire as cultivation rather than conquest, the colony required reimagining. This new conceptualization was the island at a remove, the island as garden shifted from the plantation sites of slave labor on the colonized islands of the Caribbean to create what I call the *antiempire* of the island garden. The tendency in current scholarship to write of pre-Napoleonic France as the age of enlightened philosophy, voyages of discovery, and political revolution and emancipation, forgetting France's eighteenth-century colonial empire derives, in part, from the historical precedent for this elision, the eighteenth-century reimagining of empire as its seeming opposite, an insulated, self-sufficient island garden or *antiempire*.[3]

I argue that the most influential imperial landscapes of the eighteenth century were the island gardens of narrative fiction, particularly Daniel Defoe's *Robinson Crusoe*, Jean-Jacques Rousseau's *Julie ou La nouvelle Héloïse*, and Jacques-Henri Bernardin de Saint-Pierre's *Paul et Virginie*.[4] The island gardens of these novels have been most obviously linked by the extent to which they cite and revise one another. In his famous work on education, Rousseau declares that there is only one book of "natural education" required in the formation of the young Émile. "What is this marvelous book? Is it Aristotle? Is it Pliny? Is it Buffon?" Rousseau asks. The marvelous book is *Robinson Crusoe* and more precisely his island sojourn.[5] In *Julie ou La nouvelle Héloïse*, when Saint Preux steps into Julie's garden and invokes the island of Juan Fernández, the novel refers not only to Admiral George Anson's stopover on this island off the western coast of South America but also to other representations of the island, notably the celebrated accounts of Alexander Selkirk's sojourn from 1704 to 1709 as a castaway there.[6] Defoe's story of Crusoe marooned for years on an unnamed island in the Caribbean, that is, off the opposite coastline of South America, came to be associated with the early eighteenth-century account of Selkirk on the island of Juan Fernández.[7] While scholars make much of Bernardin de Saint-Pierre's refashioning of Julie's island garden in Clarens by shifting the garden as an island within the metropole to the tropics and specifically to the French colony of the Île de France, we should not forget that Bernardin de Saint-Pierre also wrote that *Robinson Crusoe* was the book that consoled him in his childhood.[8]

However, the garden spaces of these novels are not merely linked to one another by their reworking of the topos of island isolation and apparent insularity but by their strategies of dislocation and by what they are set against: the colonial sugar plantation islands of the Caribbean and their relation to empire. Despite the distancing, these island gardens are, nonetheless, linked both to one another and to the displaced sites of empire by their very techniques of transplantation (removing people and plants from one site and replanting them in another). By their seeming distance from the spaces of the imperial real, these narratives of imaginative displacement from the geographical space of the metropoles of England and France shaped the space of empire into an antiempire, into a seemingly innocent dreamspace of the Edenic island as garden or garden as island. Against the island perimeter's buffer of oasis-like enclosure and its naturalized boundary, I suggest that we endeavor to exercise a practice of anamnesis or countermemory retracing the connections between the floating islands and the metropoles in the resignification of eighteenth-century empire.[9]

I focus in this chapter on Bernardin de Saint-Pierre's fictional history of an alternative society in the midst of the French colony of the Île de France (now Île Maurice or the Republic of Mauritius); the novel was first issued as a separate illustrated edition in 1789. As the father-figure narrator of *Paul et Virginie* declares, the state may be "semblable à un jardin" (similar to a garden) but not just any garden.[10] The tale uses the setting of the East Indian island as a means to establish the ideal society or state as a particular kind of garden—a garden on the model of the isolated, insular, and autarchic island.[11] The ideal state in miniature, the little society of the "happy family" of Madame de la Tour, Marguerite, their children Virginie and Paul, and their slaves Marie and Domingue is explicitly founded in contradistinction to the plantation model.

Madame de la Tour, left behind on the island by her husband, resolves to cultivate a small piece of ground to provide the "necessities of life" with the labor of her slave, Marie, a woman from Madagascar whom she has brought with her to the island. Whereas her husband planned to build a plantation with black slave labor in order to support them, Mme de la Tour chooses land neither "in the most fertile districts" nor "those best adapted to commerce" (105). The society is a self-sufficient one, a subsistence landscape rather than one founded on the production of surplus for commercial exchange. Against the international trafficking of triangular trade, the little society is instead defined against empire by its seclusion. The valley may be secluded but the "asile caché" (refuge) of Mme de la Tour and Marguerite depends on enclosure to keep others from settling there. By enclosing, clearing, and planting, the little society takes possession of the terrain of the island valley, making the land their private "propriété" (109). The founding of the little society, though premised on retirement, is secured through a process that nonetheless repeats the means by which plantation colonies were established and justified. Set in the midst of a plantation colony in the process of development as a seat of government, shipping, and agriculture, the apparent necessity of exclusion and barriers in order to create the ostensible seclusion attests to the ambivalent status of the little society as separate and distinct from the plantation colony.[12]

Paul et Virginie opens with the authorial pronouncement, "I have tried to paint a soil and vegetation different from those of Europe" (77), and the tale is still vaunted for having introduced an alien, foreign, and exotic kingdom of vegetation into French letters.[13] However, the little society's garden, the site endlessly discussed as a refuge of all that is natural and indigenous, is represented, rather, as a cultivated terrain of transplantation filled with the plants that Bernardin de Saint-Pierre's own *Voyage à l'Isle de France* lists as fruits, vegetables, trees, and shrubs introduced to the island by the Dutch and the French. Unlike the forest habitation of the narrator, the settlements of this little society are cultivated by Marguerite's slave Domingue, described as a "Noir yolof" (110). Each of the kitchen vegetables with which Domingue sows the ground—cucumber, gourd, pumpkin, and potato—are foreign transplants from Europe and the Americas. Likewise, the banana trees arranged along the river and around the two huts were brought to the Île de France. The other planted crops—cotton, sugar cane, coffee, and tobacco—were, besides indigo, the principal commercial plants of eighteenth-century plantation agriculture and colonial trade and those that the government encouraged planters to cultivate on the Île de France.[14] The various grains—millet, maize, wheat, rice—that Domingue cultivates are all discussed in Bernardin de Saint-Pierre's *Voyage à l'Isle de France* (Letter 13) as transplants.

While most of these plants, he writes, were brought under government auspices, the letter also singles out the contributions of certain inhabitants: planter and savant Joseph François Charpentier de Cossigny, Intendant of the Île de France and Île Bourbon Pierre Poivre, the engineer Jean Auguste Thomas Gilles Hermans, and colonial administrator and botanist François Etienne le Juge.[15] In *Paul et Virginie* the little society takes the place of these official names and their large plantations and botanical gardens. Domingue's plantations are, indeed, "exotic" but in the reverse sense. That is, the little society's landscaped habitation represents not a tropical paradise of plants alien to French readers but a botanical garden's worth of plant transfers alien to the Île de France. The *Voy-*

age laments that such plant commodities brought to the Île de France for the purpose of testing the island's possibilities were not yet sufficiently under cultivation.[16] Read in this context, it is difficult not to see *Paul et Virginie*, the georgic of the tropics, as a primer for colonial transplantation in narrative form. However, by making transplantation the everyday practice of humble people, the slave Domingue and later the indigent Paul and Virginie, the tale transvalues this colonial technology as basic subsistence.

That such transplantation is not immediately obvious is an essential part of the tale's cultural work of turning imperial transformation into subsistence and preservation of the indigenous features of the place. One famous scene of self-sufficiency and harmony with nature is supposed to demonstrate the children's native ability to survive in the wild forest. They feed themselves on what (it would seem) simply happens to grow there to refashion consumption of the native and introduction of the foreign into a myth of regeneration that sustains the wildness of the native landscape. In this same episode Paul and Virginie attempt to find their way back home after having returned a Maroon to her master. Though Paul despairs of finding them food in the forest, Virginie will not return to the plantation, declaring that "The bread of the wicked fills the mouth with gravel."[17] Paul insists that the forest trees produce nothing but bad fruit and that there is not even a tamarind or a lemon tree to refresh them. As soon as Virginie invokes the idea that God will provide, the children hear the running of a spring and find water to drink and watercress ("cresson") growing on the banks to eat.[18]

This botanical manifestation of their "goodness" or favor is a sign not of the native and indigenous but a remnant of empire in the midst of the wild forest. Like the English book "discovered" on the empire's imagined periphery or the sign of imperial authority to be taken for a natural wonder, the European watercress, introduced by settlers and naturalized to grow "wild" on the island, is found in the midst of the ostensibly "virgin" mountain forest.[19] As evidence that the forest produces more than "bad fruit," Virginie discovers a young "palmiste" or cabbage palm, the fruit or "chou" of which Paul retrieves by setting fire to the base of the tree "à la manière des noirs." The fire not only fells the tree but also releases the "chou" and serves to cook the fruit. The lemon and tamarind, the fruits of trees transplanted to the island, would seem to give way to learning how to make use of the native palmiste.[20] However, the means of exploiting the "native" vegetation for subsistence comes from their apparent capacity to become Maroon. Their survival depends on the appropriative mimicry of the lifesaving techniques of those Africans who, after being taken by European colonists to the Île de France, ran away to seek their freedom in the mountain forests of the island. By making the forest a Maroon preserve and a site of imperial transplantation, the episode transvalues colonial incursions as a seeming preservation of liberty. The naturalized "cresson" (the European plant that abides even in the "wilderness") and Paul and Virginie's capacity to endure the experience of being marooned in the forest function as visible signs of the little society's capacity to integrate sustainably the alien and the indigenous, to become part of the "nature" of the place without altering its character.

The little society's island-garden habitation reimagines the plantation colony as an antiempire by representing transplantation as harmonious interbedding. The tale devotes pages to laying out the visual details of the transplantations and transformations involved in the slave Domingue's planting of the fields and garden of the family's habitation, and then describes Paul's landscaping embellishments. Yet the little society's claim to moral goodness rests, however paradoxically, on the ready apprehension of the habitation's fusion with the native terrain. Thus, the recognition of the "virtues" of the model society, as opposed to the taste for "malignant anecdotes" that characterize European colonies—specifically the colonial settlement of Pamplemousses on the Île de France—is made analogous to finding violets that one senses but cannot immediately see because thorny bushes conceal them.[21] The transplanted European flower becomes a token of virtue when interspersed with the indigenous flora to the point of concealment and to the extent that the sense of vulnerability is reversed. Here it is not the native vegetation that requires protection from encroachment by colonization but the European transplant that needs the sheltering defense of the indigenous bush turned into an enclosing bulwark of thorns.

The little society's habitation is created as a new and special site disjunct from metropolitan France and the colonial plantation in its purported harmonic blending of various species. This ostensibly anti-imperial tropical nursery for the production of subjects that would live in peaceful and generative unity brings together not merely a diverse mixture of people and plants but the very combination that characterized the colonial plantation system: European colonists, black slaves, coffee, indigo, and sugar cane. Paul's "embellishments" ("avait embelli") over and around what the black slave Domingue has "merely cultivated" ("ne faisait que cultiver") "compose a view" of elaborate yet "harmonious" diversity that works to diminish these obviously imperial elements established as part of the landscape at the habitation's founding (140–41). That is, around the coffee, cotton, tobacco, and sugar cane planted by Domingue, Paul transplants a varied bounty of vegetation that includes an array of fruit-bearing plants (i.e., citrus, orange, tamarind, custard apple, myrobalan, mango, avocado, guava, jackfruit, and jambo) along with grass, flowers, vegetables, and, in the distance beyond them, meadows and fields of rice and corn arranged according to height in a kind of "amphitheater of greenery" (141) that frames diversity within a figurative embrace.

However, this "happy harmony" (142) or general principle of "unity in variety" goes only so far. While the domestic may be united with the wild and the indigenous with the alien, each plant is placed in its "proper site" and "each site received from its planting its natural ornament" (142).[22] This guideline may sound like a simple variant of the then-common gardening principle of the "genius of the place" according to which any changes or introductions were to retain the specific character of the location. However, there is another principle at work: naturalized segregation within a picture of concord in diversity. "Proper site" also has a racialized cast. Mme de la Tour and Marguerite transplant wheat, strawberries, and peas to small portions of the territory that they demarcate as "Bretagne" and "Normandie" (146). Two other spots within the enclosure that Domingue and Marie use for the cultivation of grass for weaving into baskets and in which they plant a calabash tree, they name "Angola" and "Foullepointe" after their birthplaces in Africa. This subdivision of the habitation into miniature reproduced environments is sentimentalized as a means to help these expatriated families maintain the "sweet illusions of their countries" in a "foreign land" (146).

The separation on the basis of what is appropriate to their "climates" introduces eighteenth-century ideas of essential racial difference and concerns about the degenerating influence of the climate of the "torrid zones" on moral character under the seemingly innocent guise of sweet signs of home.[23] This racialized geography is literalized in the tale's description of the heavily settled area of the island, the quartier de Williams. After Virginie's death, the father-narrator takes Paul to see this landscape of white colonists and transplanted European vegetables that form a picture of industry and variety, due in part to the elevation and fresh air's appropriateness to "la santé des Blancs" (266). Despite the rhetoric of inclusion within the "family," which casts slave bondage as intimate voluntary labor, the establishment of the garden embeds racial division with the plural "families." Whereas the garden, as a whole, may embrace Europe, Africa, and the East Indies, the placing of each "family" under its own tree works to reinforce fictions of purity and distinctness. Ultimately, while the re-landscaping of the habitation into an elaborate garden nursery attempts to distance the little society from the metropole and the colonial plantation, it conceives the racial and class hierarchies and borders of empire as the order of nature.

As in the picturesque landscape gardens in France, the garden of the little society is subdivided to create different places within one larger scheme, each with its segregated inhabitants, its discrete plantings, and its own monuments.[24] In place of the stone monuments of the metropolitan landscape garden, on the suggestion of the father-narrator, inscriptions from Virgil's *Georgics* are incised over the door of Mme de la Tour's cottage and carved into the bark of a tacahamac tree. These Latin inscriptions are justified as a reminder of the soul's immortality and empire's passing: "If this inscription is of some ancient nation that subsists no longer, it draws our soul into the fields of the infinite, and gives us the sentiment of its immortality, in showing us that a thought has survived the very ruin of an empire."[25] But even these reminders of the ruin of empire fall to ruin. The *antiempire* empire of the little society fails. A hurricane devastates the little society's garden except for the two transplanted coconut palms named for Paul and Virginie. The little society itself is broken when Virginie is sent to France and comes back only as a corpse in the sand, part of the debris washed up on the shore of the island after the hurricane's destruction of the returning ship, the Saint-Géran. Not long after Virginie's drowning, Paul, Mme de la Tour, Marguerite, Marie, and Domingue all follow her to the grave. Though the last lines of the text represent the tears of the father-narrator as he bemoans the desolation of their habitation, which no one has dared to cultivate, the entire tale is governed by the logic of the remnant—specifically, the seed or body that can be buried to generate new growth.

Such remnants engender the old colonial order purified. After the hurricane's devastation of the little society's garden and Virginie's departure, Paul accidentally comes upon the site, not far from the old man's cabin, where Mme de la Tour, Margaret, Paul, Virginie, and the "father" used to dine. He is "filled with joy" at the sight of the large female, fruit-bearing "papayer" that had grown from no higher than Virginie's knee at her departure to twenty feet.[26] The "papayer" or pawpaw tree stands in metonymically for Virginie, who planted the seed, but it is also a material sign of a colonial order that conserves the environment by replenishing what it consumes. Virginie, we are told, used to make a practice of never eating a fruit in the country without burying ("mît en terre") the kernels or pips in the ground so that one day the trees would bear fruit for some traveler or bird. This fruit-bearing remnant is also a sign of the successful transplantation of the foreign or alien. Although by the eighteenth century papaya trees had been grown on the Île de France for two centuries, the papaya was not indigenous. The word *papayer* was derived sometime in the seventeenth century from the Carib designation, for this fruit native to the West Indies or French Antilles. The "papayer" joins the East and West Indian parts of French empire in a scene of renewal that replays consumption as regeneration of the landscape.[27]

Compared to the monuments of empire, the "papayer," sign of the good deeds of a poor young girl, is considered more worthy of veneration than the triumphal arches of the Romans. In taking the place of the imperial monuments of antiquity, these colonial transplants would seem to make of empire its opposite and yet work, on the contrary, to reinfuse a dead system with new life. As he embraces the "papayer," Paul cries: "O tree by which posterity lives on in your wood, I have viewed you myself with more interest and veneration than the triumphal arches of the Romans! May nature that destroys each day the monuments to the ambition of kings, multiply in our forest those of the good deeds of a poor, young girl."[28] The biblical injunction to be fruitful and multiply is transferred in the metonymy of girl and tree. When seeds are placed in the earth, the trees multiply and, through them, the empire has not only immortality but also posterity, in the sense of issue and even increase.

The substitution of living botanical specimens for the grand-scale, but dead, memorials of empire recurs throughout the work of Bernardin de Saint-Pierre. In the *Voyage à l'Isle de France,* the vine takes the place of the column, and simple food plants enrich the nation more than the silver shield of Scipio.[29] Valuing plant trophies above those of territorial conquest rests on more than replacing the arts of war with those of agriculture atop a sculptured memorial to empire. The idea of the botanical monument rewrites the discourse of discovery, as in the declaration in the *Études de nature,* "Certainly, if I had any wish to perpetuate my name I would prefer to see it born by a fruit in France than by an island in America."[30] Finding plants replaces the ostensible "discovery" of the islands in the Caribbean, and the exogamous traffic of empire would seem to be rejected in favor of the isolation of national boundaries. However, this seemingly anti-imperial reorientation of discovery from America to France forms part of a passage which asserts that the real heroes are those who introduce and reclimatize plants. While vaunted as a means to fill the baskets of French peasants, the transfer and embedding of the alien transplants depended on commerce with those rejected islands.[31] These vegetable monuments produced out of colonial commerce were to outlast engravings in marble and grant both the heroic botanist and the imperial nation an afterlife.

Transplants are endowed with the moral qualities of ideal persons (e.g., the heroic botanist, the poor young girl who plants the seeds of the fruit she consumes), whereas people attain the virtues granted to nature when they, like the transplants, seed the earth. These vegetable monuments function as grave markers in that they serve to remember the bodies in whose place they rest and, yet, as organic matter that is also inhumed or "mît en terre," these transplants perform the sacralizing and generating role of the buried body and vice versa. In the metonymic chain of *Paul et Virginie,* the inhumation of alien plants and bodies introduced into foreign soil take the place of architectural monuments in the symbolic and material sustenance of the colony of Île de France as representative of the imperial body politic. While the papayer substitutes for Virginie, this girl, whose virtue is restored through her death, stands in not just for the little society but for the entire colony of Île de France that mourns her death. She is both the botanist and, ultimately, the seed itself. From France she sends back stones, pips, and seeds of various European fruits and flowers, among which two are singled out for special mention: the violet, the flower of hidden virtue to which the little society is compared earlier in the tale, and the scabious, also called the "widow's flower" because it appears to be in mourning. Virginie specially instructs Paul to plant these two

European flowers in their garden (208). Yet this attempted intermingling of transplants is in vain as only a small number grow at all and even these are stunted.

When the violets finally do return, they appear with the shipwreck of the Saint-Géran as "the pale violets of death" joined with "the roses of modesty" on the cheeks of Virginie's corpse half buried in the sand.[32] In this tableau of traffic between the colony and the metropole washed up as a dead woman's body on the colonial shore, Virginie the violet is buried, but not, as one might imagine, as a dematerialized tragic allegory of condemnation. The flowers she sends fail, but she herself (that is, her body) becomes the transplanted flower interred to rejuvenate the colony. While inscriptions and ruins point to empires past and empires lost, the father-narrator explains to Paul that although everything on earth changes, nothing is lost (130). Virginie, he declares, "has suffered the fate reserved for birth, beauty, and empires themselves," namely, death.[33] Empires, like Virginie, are condemned to die as soon as they are born. However, in this discourse, death leads not to a separate, ethereal condition but rather, as part of nature's cycle, into the earth where it may resurface again. Death becomes not an end but a means to a materialized immortality. Within this scheme, the little society's garden must fall to a hurricane and its members die for this *antiempire* empire to survive. The family in a sense become fertilizer so that empire may achieve not just an afterlife in memory but a kind of physical eternity embodied in the colonial landscape of the tropical island into which these alien transplants, as at once corpses and seeds, are inhumed.

In this condensation of death and life into one enduring material stratum, past and future coalesce into a colonial landscape made eternal. The device of recounting the tale in the past tense but framing it as a present encounter between the father-narrator and a traveler from France visiting the island reinforces not just the idea of the remnant or souvenir—the seed, the tree, the book itself—but the transplanted colonial landscape as an enduring base. The tale opens with a lengthy description that lays out a preferred prospect of the French colony on the Île de France. Seen from the vantage point of arrival in the island's main port, Port-Louis, the scenic view positions its subject as a metropolitan traveler newly arrived by boat. The traveler's privileged view enjoys, at once, the solitude of enclosure and a "boundless view" or an imperial prospect of limitlessness and that which occludes it. Within the circumference of this single view, the landscape that opens to the metropolitan traveler's gaze joins colonial commerce, signified by the main port town of the colony "at the base" of the composition, with the ostensibly self-sufficient and insular society opposed to it, remembered in the center of the tableau by the ruins of "two small cabins" on "a piece of ground once under cultivation." The signs of the commercial life of the colony, the main point of contact with the metropolis—Port-Louis, the mountain Discovery Hill from which the signal is given when a ship is sighted, and an avenue of linearly ordered bamboos leading to the church and the settlement known as the Pamplemousses district—are offset and yet held in a kind of compositional balance by the geographic landmarks signifying death and loss, Tomb Bay and the Cape of Misfortune. Spatialized onto an exotic, tropical island terrain that the eye can take in all at once, empire appears no longer subject to the vicissitudes of time but instead occupies an eternal present. With the opening landscape device of the encompassing scene in which death appears as a necessary, ever-present, fertilizing feature of a thriving scene of plantation commerce, the tale comes full circle. By always already incorporating both the signs of colonial empire and their destruction, the prospect endeavors to neutralize the threat that all empires must decline and fall.

Yet, with the cottages as the central focal point of the landscape, this eternal imperial present is a domestic and familial one. Though Virginie dies without reproducing and the fatherless family unit of the little society is likewise destroyed, the tale nonetheless works to reproduce imperial subjects and the larger colonial order. By recycling birth and death and substituting plants for bodies, the tale separates reproduction from childbearing. Analogized to breastfeeding, the colonial technologies of transplantation and grafting are represented as an improvement on what heterosexual reproduction alone may produce. In the absence of branches connecting bodies on a family tree, grafting, like exchanging the care of babies, may generate familial ties of emotion that exceed those of endogamous relations: "Like two buds that rest on two trees of the same species from which the tempest has broken all the branches come to produce sweeter fruit, if each of them, detached from the maternal trunk, are grafted onto the neighboring trunk, thus these two infants, deprived of their parents, are filled with more tender sentiments than those of son and daughter, brother and sister, when they come to be exchanged at the breasts of these two friends who brought them into the world."[34] In propagating relations of "friendship" (such as that between these two "amies") that, unlike the institutions of heterosexual reproduction and marriage, do not depend on parentage or birthplace, the colonial technologies of grafting and transplantation are imagined to create familylike ties capable of binding across distance and difference. However, to hold in check the possibilities of exogamous alliances—miscegenation and queer relations—the tale reinstalls the father.

In the separate series of color prints published in 1795 after designs by Jean-Frédéric Schall and with engraving by Charles-Melchior Descourtis, the father-narrator makes a central appearance in the last two plates of the series.[35] The same scene is virtually rendered twice, underscoring the thematic importance of inhumation in the story. In plate five the father-narrator bends over Virginie's dead body in the sand (fig. 19.1), while in plate six the grave site takes the place of her outstretched body and the narrator kneels on the freshly filled dirt in almost the same spot (fig. 19.2). Represented in

Figure 19.1. Charles-Melchior Descourtis after Jean-Frédéric Schall, "The Death of Virginia," scene five in set of six prints based on Bernardin de Saint-Pierre's *Paul et Virginie* (1795). Engraving and color aquatint. Courtesy of Ackland Art Museum, the University of North Carolina at Chapel Hill, the William A. Whitaker Foundation Art Fund.

the medallion of his patron saint and imago held in the father figure's outstretched hand and then kneeling in prayer on her grave, Paul is situated as the principal mourner. However, the black slave Domingue figures prominently in each of the scenes of death. Published in 1795, a year after the abolition of slavery by the Revolutionary Convention, the Schall-Descourtis series reconceived *Paul et Virginie* amid renewed debate over slave labor.[36] In plate five Domingue, clothed in the bleu, blanc, rouge, stands at the apex of the composition with back turned and hands clasped. The clasped hands might call to mind Josiah Wedgwood's widely reproduced medallion "Am I not a man and a brother?" (1788) in which the supplicating slave is holding out his hands bound together by chains; the image became the official seal of the London Committee of the Society for the Abolition of the Slave Trade established in 1787 and the enduring symbol of the antislavery movement into the nineteenth century (fig. 19.3).[37] However, the sixth tableau directly reproduces the pose only in reverse. The loin cloth barely covering the slave's body in the antislavery cameo is replaced by full trousers, vest, and white linen.

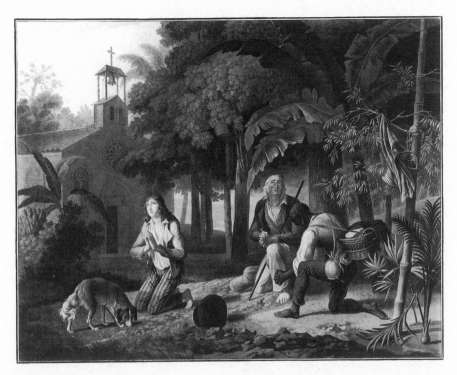

Figure 19.2. Charles-Melchior Descourtis after Jean-Frédéric Schall, "Virginia's Grave," scene six in set of six prints based on Bernardin de Saint-Pierre's *Paul et Virginie* (1795). Engraving and color aquatint. Courtesy of Ackland Art Museum, the University of North Carolina at Chapel Hill, the William A. Whitaker Foundation Art Fund.

As in plate five, the chains are notable by their absence. And though Domingue kneels under a weight, his burdens take the form of a large basket of provisions and a jug of liquid.

However dematerialized, the chains reappear in a different guise—bonds of sentiment solidified through death, loss, and the promise of renewal. Whereas in plate five the slave turns away from the father-figure's outstretched hand and the scene of the dead white woman, in plate six he dutifully kneels with head lowered under the supposedly benignly paternal staff of the white father. The whipping stick, raised violently over the head of the prostrate Maroon by the plantation owner in the first scene of the sequence (fig. 19.4), here becomes a staff that extends from over Domingue's head across the lap of the white father into the earth of Virginie's grave. The scene orchestrates the interment of the dead white woman as a social and botanical landscape, under the benevolent rule of a father figure, that renews the plantation with which the series begins. Rather than just a grave in the last scene, the dry, barren earth and broken, dead branch

Figure 19.3. Josiah Wedgwood, "Am I not a man and a brother?" (1788). Engraved cameo, in Erasmus Darwin, *The Botanic Garden* (London, 1795). Courtesy of the Rare Book Collection, the University of North Carolina at Chapel Hill.

in the foreground of the view of the plantation are transformed into freshly overturned earth at foreground right, a large bamboo tree festooned with a blue and red scarf, and, down at the very corner, the green fronds of a plant whose large red bulb is depicted above the ground in full view. Signs of phallic potency and fertility familiar from the erotic pictures commonly associated with Schall work here to transfer the sentimental and libidinal from bodies to plants in a kind of compositional circuit representing a cycle of death and life that replenishes the ground of the colonial system through a paternal authority at once leveled by and reinstated over the site of loss.

The landscape scene of the white French father figure, transplanted to the tropical island colony as custodian of the buried dead, refigures the ground of the colonial system. The father as agent of inhumation re-envisions the terms of relation between colony and metropole, particularly the metaphor of the bond between dependent child and parent borrowed from Roman law.[38] In *Paul et Virginie,* the father figure tends children, but they are not literally his. He is alienated from the metropolis and yet forms the conduit between France and l'Île de France as the one who inscribes the classical legacy into the landscape monuments erected by Paul and passes the account of the little society via the French traveler back to the metropole. Constituted not by the spawning of children but by transplanting, inhuming, and translating, paternal authority is represented as flexible, transportable, capable of reconciling in one space maternity and paternity, colony and metropole, under the guise of egalitarian friendship. After recounting the founding of the little society, how he cleared and partitioned the land, the father-narrator exclaims to the traveler: "Alas, there remains too much for my memory. Time that destroys so rapidly the monuments of empires seems to respect in this wilderness those of friendship to perpetuate my regret to the end of my life."[39]

Despite the devastation of its ending, the tale begins with the traces of the habitation established by the narrator for Mme de la Tour and Marguerite. These vestiges in the landscape ostensibly endure because of their basis in friendship, not empire. However, just as the landscape recycles like the tale itself, the remains that prepare the ground for new growth and new alliances, such as the friendship between the white French fa-

Figure 19.4. Charles-Melchior Descourtis after Jean-Frédéric Schall, "Paul and Virginia returning the maronne to her master," scene one in set of six prints based on Bernardin de Saint-Pierre's *Paul et Virginie* (1795). Engraving and aquatint. Courtesy of Ackland Art Museum, the University of North Carolina at Chapel Hill, the William A. Whitaker Foundation Art Fund.

ther figure and the traveler from France, suggest that systems may self-perpetuate if they can reinvent themselves. With the phrase "too much for my memory," the abundant materiality of the little society's habitation would seem to exceed the white French father's attempt to contain the colonial landscape in his account. The "trop," the "too much" in the exclamation, "Alas, there remains too much for my memory," gestures to a breaking out of the strictures of empire as paternal authority. However, the tropical island garden (this "wilderness") transforms the remains into funerary monuments to friendship that is lost and yet might be renewed through ritual mourning. Encouraging practices of perpetual and perpetuating regret or mourning, the island garden as grave nurses the colonial order. The tale's capacity to turn its readers and viewers into a virtual community of mournful participants at the site of empire's "enterrement" or interment sustains the colonial landscape with its black slave labor as a form of reluctant paternal empire given new life out of its legacy of tearful inhumation.

I have used the close analysis of this tale and related picture prints to develop a theoretical implication of Michel Foucault's lecture "Des Espaces Autres" (1967), which bears on how we understand the circuit of imagined and realized floating islands of empire. Foucault elaborates a way to think about history spatially and offers a means to theorize the problem of space in history. The spaces in which we go about our daily lives, he argues, are shaped by those sites that would seem to be outside the topography of the quotidian and yet are linked to these everyday spaces by a logic of contradiction.[40] These "other spaces" take two forms: utopias or "no real places" and the real places that, nonetheless, re-present, contest, or invert everyday topography. For these other real spaces, Foucault devises the term "heterotopias." The garden, as a small space that amasses the various parts of the world into one place, represents one of the main functions of these other spaces, the ability to bring together in one space multiple and seemingly incompatible sites.[41] The very vehicle that makes possible the garden's heterotopic amalgamation, the boat that "goes as far as the colonies in search of the most precious treasures they conceal in their gardens," Foucault considers another kind of heterotopia.[42] However, Foucault removes the boat from the imperial history of its use as an instrument of commerce and transplantation and instead preserves it as a "reserve of the imagination" that makes possible dreams and adventure. The itineraries of landscape gardens and narrative fiction may operate as vehicles, which like the ships of imperial "exploration" and commerce, take us other places and give us spaces in which to dream, the heterotopias of island gardens. However, in inverting the imperial real, the heterotopias of imagined geography do not necessarily upset the structuring logic of imperial ideology.

Rather, the *antiempire* of the island garden functioned as a transformation of empire. Certain types of colonies, Foucault argues, served as a kind of compensation in their creation of another real space, one more perfect, more meticulously ordered than the space of the metropole.[43] One may question from what perspective colonies ever appear ideal. However, the more general claim that the role of the heterotopia may be to create another real space challenges us to rethink the role of narrative fiction and the relation between the imagined and materialized domains of empire. Foucault emphasizes the productive link between spaces. Thus, in the history of space and the spatializing of history, there is more than merely topos and heterotopos, metropole and colony. There are also the spaces in between. And these in-between spaces—the dislocated, imagined spaces, the island gardens of narrative fiction—worked not merely to represent the real spaces of empire, the metropole and the colonial sugar plantation and the relations between them. The "other spaces" of the island garden worked to create real spaces of their own, to realize empire as an other space, the colony as *antiempire* or imperial nursery, impressing and reproducing imperial subjects within a saving fiction of innocence, autarchic independence, and inhumation as renewal.

CHAPTER TWENTY

South Seas Trade and the Character of Captains

Anna Neill

In a scene from Lewis Milestone's 1962 film, *Mutiny on the Bounty,* William Bligh is reprimanded by members of the Admiralty for having dispensed unusually cruel punishments on board his ship. Justice, they remind him, is carried not in the articles of war but in "the heart of a captain."[1] Although this wholly fictitious scene takes considerable liberties with the facts of eighteenth-century naval discipline, it nonetheless offers an accurate depiction of the moral economy operating in later eighteenth-century voyages to the islands of the South Seas. The imperial ambitions of these lengthy journeys were inseparable from the principles of moral sympathy, since for the later eighteenth century, sympathy offered a theory of social order (the sublimation of aggressive and dangerous passions) that privileged commercial growth. From Cook's three voyages into the Pacific to Bligh's breadfruit expedition to Tahiti a decade later, passions are everywhere in the tensions among the crew and between sailors and their indigenous hosts, on board the ship and on shore. Both Cook and Bligh encounter South Seas "savagery" in the tempers and appetites of sailors as much as in the barbaric or licentious customs of Pacific peoples.

While they had to be the ambassadors of an apparently humanitarian state that promised to deliver Pacific peoples into a more prosperous, comfortable, and law-abiding way of life, captains also had to exercise firm but benevolent rule over their sailor "subjects" and to manage the often unpredictable and volatile exchanges between members of their crew and the island peoples. The first of these tasks was to be accomplished through plant exchange, "gifting" the botanical wisdom of enlightened states to nations that were supposedly in need of it and opening up new regions of the world for global trade, which promised prosperity to all. The second task was to correct the raw affections and impulses of natives and seamen, both of whom were inclined to act on their immediate desires rather than in the service of finer and greater social ends. Disciplining labor as well as socializing savage subjects required the "compassion" of a global commercial vision as well as the authority of command. At an enormous distance from "civilized" metropolitan England, however, the sometimes attenuated authority of the captain was not always sufficient to preserve peace between crew and natives or to prevent desertion or mutiny. At such moments, the responsibilities of beneficent instruction and sympathetic command—responsibilities that entailed the infusion of moral sentiment into commercial imperialism—were also compromised.

Sympathy, Commerce, and Character

By the time Cook sailed for the last time into the Pacific, plenty had been said about the relationship between social order, commerce, and the passions. In different ways, Shaftesbury and Hutcheson had argued that the acquisitive passions, where they are not moderated by reason or an internal moral sense, are dissociative. In Hume's *Treatise on Human Nature,* however, the passions are not so much tamed as directly channeled into social order through the vehicle of sympathy. "Rules of morality are not conclusions of our reason," Hume suggests, since reason is "perfectly inert" and cannot adapt itself to the "heedless and impetuous movement" of the passions.[2] Instead the difference between virtue and vice must be *felt* rather than reasoned, and the mechanism for feeling justice is sympathy: competitive differences are effaced at the moment that we are able to enter into the feelings of others, converting their sentiments into our own. Commerce, which depends on peaceful relations within and between societies, relies on this conversion and the sociability and civility it makes possible.

However, because our feelings are naturally strongest for those closest to us, sympathy in itself is an undependable conduit of justice in a society of any considerable size. Moreover, because we are perpetually drawn to what is close, present, and immediately advantageous, there is no innate principle determining that we will look to our more distant advantage through the moderating institutions of law and government, rather than pursue the immediate gratification of our desires at the expense of others about whom we care little. Thus, says Hume, "the commerce of men [is] rendered dangerous and uncertain," and the desire for "great present advantage" might make us overlook

our more remote interests in preserving the peace of society and lead us instead to rebellion.[3] The solution offered by Adam Smith in *The Theory of Moral Sentiments* is for
us to sympathize with the happiness or grief of strangers through our respect for a man
of more extensive humanity than our own. Peace and commerce are secured, for Smith,
through the agency of someone whose "exquisite sensibility" and "self command"[4] enables him to suppress his own immediate passions in order to respond sympathetically
to the feelings of others. Such a man is a cut above his fellows and is likely to be able to
guide and manage the impulsive behavior of others. Sensibility of this finer kind is, according to Smith, determined by the degree to which a feeling agent is able to identify
with an "impartial spectator" who can judge with the moral strength of detached sympathy. This spectator adds "reason, principle and conscience" to the response he feels to
another's joy or suffering, and in so doing demonstrates "the propriety of generosity
and the deformity of injustice."[5] He represents, in fact, the general moral rules that un-
derpin any properly cohesive and commercial society. In order to belong to such a society, one must judge oneself with the eyes of others independently of one's own visceral response to an apparent injustice.

The action of sympathy, either as a passion communicated from one breast to another in Hume's formulation, or as the restraining power of moral spectatorhood in
Smith's, is therefore capable of harmonizing individual desires with public ends that
are at once commercial and philanthropic. Thomas Haskell has argued that humanitarian feeling is an offshoot of capitalism because the kind of calculating and forward-
thinking "cognitive style" that the market rewards is necessarily one that respects the
moral consequences of an act. At the same time, he argues, "capitalist thinking" recognizes how people far removed from one another in space and time might be differently
affected by a particular transaction.[6] "The very possibility of feeling obliged to go to the
aid of a suffering stranger," he suggests, "was enormously heightened by the emergence
of a form of life that made attention to the remote consequences of one's acts an emblem of civilization itself."[7] His account of the genesis of the modern promise-keeping
"man of principle" who combines the self-control that belongs to market discipline
with the expanded affection that arises out of remote interests also describes Smith's
impartial spectator. Even alongside his seemingly ruthless defense of the alienation of
labor, Smith reserves a place for the philosopher who, although he is as specialized as
any other laborer, is "often capable of combining together the powers of the most distant and dissimilar objects."[8] With this greater vision, he helps to invigorate workers
with generous, noble, and tender sentiments—sentiments that help them to appreciate, in Smith's words, "the great and extensive interests of [their] country."[9]

The South Seas voyage narratives that I examine here recognize the captain as a
moral spectator of the kind that Smith proposed. In the confined space of a ship sail-

ing enormous distances from home, captains had to be more than mere disciplinarians. In some respects its own floating society-in-miniature, the ship housed passions that were potentially quite volatile given the conditions in which seamen worked and, in the language of eighteenth-century geography, their distance from the "civilized" world. The humanity and self-command of captains, just as much as their direct authority, would ensure that they would be able to manage such passions, whether these arose among crewmembers or in the sometimes violent interactions between sailors and their indigenous hosts. Captains were therefore required to be exemplary moral subjects whose own conduct and capacity to recognize the distant consequences of an action was directed by a restraining "inner judge." Yet, at the same time, they also had to act as flesh-and-blood moral spectator-arbitrators, correcting the self-serving passions of their ignorant, violent, and greedy inferiors (whether seamen or natives) with their own humanitarian foresight. In this respect, they also represented the cosmopolitan vision of commerce over the nearsightedness, jealousy, and self-isolation of unenlightened nations.

Captaincy and Humanity

John Beaglehole has described Cook as a man of exemplary restraint whose professionalism was manifest in his "controlled imagination"—a characteristic of Smith's spectator.[10] In his own time, Cook was generally depicted as a man of extraordinary compassion and as the benefactor of "backward" nations whose economies he helped to diversify and to whom he introduced modern technologies of crop and animal cultivation. Anna Seward remembers him as the steward of an allegorical "Humanity" who "unite[s] the savage hearts and hostile hands" and "strew[s] her soft comforts over the barren plain" and a national hero furthering the power and glory of Britannia who in turn commemorates his "virtues just."[11] The dedicatory preface to a collection of cloth specimens gathered during Cook's voyages describes a heart expansive enough to spread happiness into every corner of the globe, declaring, presumably of Cook, that there was "no one more ready to feed the hungry and clothe the naked."[12] A surgeon on the companion vessel *Discovery*, David Samwell commemorated him through the figure of the "grateful Indian," who "in time to come, pointing to the herds grazing his fertile plains, will relate to his children how the first stock of them was introduced into the country; and the name of Cook will be remembered among those benign spirits, whom they worship as the source of every good, and the fountain of every blessing."[13] Such compassion was also, reputedly, extended to his crew. James King, who commanded the expedition following the deaths of Cook and of Charles Clerke, the captain of the *Discovery*, says it is impossible to describe the sincere loss felt by those who "had so long found their general security in his skill and conduct and every consolation under their hardships in his tenderness and humanity."[14]

In Cook's own journals, such "humanitarian" concern takes the form, first and foremost, of farsighted practical measures to manage the passions and appetites of his crew and to prevent conflict between sailors and their indigenous hosts. Drawing on instructions from the Admiralty that he should show every civility to the native peoples, he gave explicit orders that no violence was to be offered against any native unless absolutely necessary. In an effort to control the spread of syphilis, he prohibited infected sailors from going on shore and forbade any of the crew members from bringing native women on board the ship. He also gave his crew detailed directions about how trade was to be conducted with the natives in order to stabilize the value of the goods exchanged: only the officer appointed to trade with the natives for provisions could do so; any arms or working tools lost by any of the crew were to be charged against their pay; and iron and cloth were to be traded for provisions, not curiosities. "I thought it very necessary," he comments in the journal, "that some order should be observed in trafficking with the natives: that such merchandize as we had on board for that purpose might continue to bear a proper value, and not leave it to every one's own particular fancy which could not fail to bring on confusion and quarrels between us and the natives, and would infallibly lessen the value of such articles as we had to traffic with."[15] The danger of conducting trade according to "particular fancies" is especially acute in a new market where supply and demand can fluctuate with the very unstable conditions of contact. George Forster, the younger of the father-and-son team of naturalists who accompanied Cook on his second expedition, commented on the danger of allowing sailors to trade for curiosities, observing that there was no anticipating what a given commodity (like nails, or the red feathers that members of the ship's company acquired in Tonga) would fetch on another island or in a different region.[16] The price of provisions could be raised to such an unreasonable height that the market in curiosities and sex stifled trade for provisions altogether. The protection of "proper value" is thus an important labor of command designed to control the diversity of needs and desires that arise in a virtually unregulated marketplace.

There was more than the microeconomy of the ship at stake in such interventions because, according to what Europeans thought they had observed of Pacific peoples, the free expression of passions stifled productivity and commercial enterprise. A sailor who, as Forster puts it, "rushes headlong after the pleasures of the present moment" (*A Voyage*, 2:112) is not so different from a Tahitian who "spend[s] his life in the most sluggish inactivity and without one benefit to society" (*A Voyage*, 1:296). Cook also took pains to recognize where cultures managed to transcend present pleasures and how they flourished as a consequence. Emphasizing their difference from the Tahitians, he praised the islanders in the Tongan group for cultivating their soil so well and observed that it must have been divided as private property since industry is ordinarily stimulated by interest. He further observed that not only was theft severely punished on Tonga-tabu but also that the people were of a mild and benevolent character (*Voyages,* 2:270). On the eastern coast of Australia, on the other hand, a poor, nomadic people "move from place to place like wild beasts in search of food" (*Voyages,* 1:396).

In addition to overseeing the behavior of his crew, the captain's charge was to act as a detached and morally informed (rather than enthralled or horrified) spectator of such customs. In Tahiti, he observed that the regular practice of infanticide is "a custom . . . inhuman and contrary to the first principals of human nature" (*Voyages,* 1:128). His remark is uncannily anticipated by Adam Smith, who in *The Theory of Moral Sentiments* said of infanticide that "our disgust at a particular custom should never pervert our sentiments with regard to the general style and character of conduct and behavior." "No society," he added, "could subsist a moment in which the usual strain of men's conduct and behavior was of a piece with [that] horrible practice" (211). This is a lesson that Cook seems to put into practice in his record of events in the South Island of New Zealand when, during the second voyage, he first became convinced of the existence of cannibalism among the Maori. In Queen Charlotte Sound he asked that a piece of human flesh from a body that had been brought on board the ship be cooked and offered to his Maori visitors. Suppressing his own visceral horror at the spectacle of cannibalism, he offers a calm diagnosis of the cultural shortcomings that provoke such appallingly violent acts in a people who are to some degree civilized: "the New Zealanders are certainly in a state of civilization, their behaviour to us has been manly and mild, shewing always a readiness to oblige us . . . This custom of eating their enemies slain in battle . . . has undoubtedly been handed down to them from the earliest times . . . [A]s they become more united they will of consequence have fewer enemies and become more civilized and then and not till then this custom may be forgot" (*Voyages,* 2:294). Finding that commercial isolation and a lack of settled life and government is responsible for the persistence of savage customs like cannibalism, he observes that this primitive condition itself prevents these societies from allowing the proper mechanism of sociability—the exercise of normative moral judgment—to evolve. "At present," he goes on to say, "they seem to have but little idea of treating other men as they themselves would wish to be treated, but treat them as they think they should be treated under the same circumstances" (2:294). Without an impartial moral spectator, they are guided only by their own powerful passions of fear and vengeance. In the absence of any such judging figure within their own communities, Cook stands in as moderator and compassionate observer of their actions. His own suppression, in this instance, of what Smith calls "the insolence and brutality of anger"[17] in favor of a kind of reasonable distaste as he responds thoughtfully and "historically" to the spectacle of canni-balism, distinguishes him as much from the ship's crew as from the Maori themselves. The former were, as Forster describes them, extremely affected "beholders," some of whom were so heartlessly amused as to consider joining the feast, while others were in-spired with such disgust they were ready to murder the cannibals for a crime "they had no right to condemn" (*A Voyage*, 1:512).

In the same historicizing vein as Cook, Forster also commented of cannibalism that "the action of eating human flesh, whatever our education may teach us to the contrary, is certainly neither unnatural nor criminal in itself. It can only become dangerous in as far as it steels the mind against that compassionate fellow feeling which is the great ba-sis of civil society; and for this reason we find it naturally banished from every people as soon as civilization has made any progress among them" (*A Voyage*, 1:517). Yet Forster is frequently less than confident about the firm distinctions between savage and civi-lized upon which such observations depend. He cites Las Casas on the brutality of Span-ish colonialism in America and reflects that however brutal cannibalism might seem, Europeans continue to "cut one another's throats by the thousands" (1:516). Moreover, he complains of the "mercenary principles that commerce inspires" (2:190) and sug-gests that it would be better for both discoverers and discovered "that the South Seas had still remained unknown to Europe and its restless inhabitants" (1:386). At the end of the second volume, he tells the story of Mrs. Milton, whose son was one of the party from the *Adventure* who was killed and eaten in New Zealand, reflecting that "no heart [could] refuse a sympathetic tribute" to her grief and lament the enterprising spirit that had caused it (2:586).

This spirit of regret, a kind of expansive sympathy gone awry, is also visible in Cook's journals. For nearly every instance of moral arbitration in which Cook engages, he offers a less confident reflection on the impact of European arrival on the native peo-ples of the South Seas. Even in Queen Charlotte's Sound, he regrets that the prostitu-tion of Maori women is clearly the consequence "of a commerce with Europeans and what is still more to our shame, civilized Christians" (*Voyages*, 2:175). The natives of Aus-tralia, he suggests, are happier without the desire for riches that plagues Europeans, and "live in a tranquility that is not disturb'd by the inequality of condition" (1:399), and the Tahitians, New Zealanders, and Hawaiians, he regrets, have probably been infected with venereal diseases by European sailors. The effect of such reflections is to compromise the authority of the impartial spectator. Cook's superior feeling and the capacity for command that it lends him are immobilized by his recognition of the part he has played in the corruption of a formerly innocent people. Suddenly, his observations do not en-act the general moral rules that make society and commerce possible; instead they bring him to a moral impasse. He becomes an affected eyewitness, frozen, like Forster, com-

pelled to pay tribute to those who have directly suffered as a result of European inter-
vention and ambition.[18]

The other challenge to the theory of commerce's benevolent influence comes from
on board the ship itself. In his account of the voyage on the *Resolution,* midshipman Elliott praises Cook for his bravery, his calm, and his humanity, and insists that "no man
was better calculated to gain the confidence of savages."[19] Yet, commenting later on
Cook's decision in the New Hebrides to flog a sentry who shot a native dead, Elliott remarks that "I must think that here . . . he lost sight of both justice and humanity."[20] This
incident brings Cook's role as humanitarian statesman into conflict with his task as captain: he is appalled by the "inhumanity of the act" of killing a man who was merely
showing the visitors that he was armed, while members of the crew in turn accuse Cook
of excessive discipline (*Voyages,* 2:498). A similar conflict arises in accounts of the decision to sail the *Resolution* back south of New Zealand in 1774. Cook reports the readiness of the crew to make the expedition, praising their obedience and alertness and insisting that they were "so far from wishing the voyage at an end that they rejoiced at the
prospect of its being prolonged another year" (2:328). This directly contradicts Forster,
who reports with a very different emphasis that "the only thoughts which could make
them amends [for this voyage south] was the certainty of passing another season among
the happy islands in the torrid zone" (*A Voyage,* 1:526). "The hope of meeting with new
lands," he recalls, "was vanished, the topics of common conversation were exhausted,
the cruise to the south could not present anything new but appeared in all its chilling
horrors before us, and the absence of our consort doubled every danger" (1:524).

It is tempting to link this horror of the icy south and the resulting evacuation of social spirit from the ship to the incidents of "depravity" among the sailors who, in their
associations with native women, Forster reports, "disclaimed all acquaintance with
modesty" (*A Voyage,* 1:577). His father, Johann, having praised the entire expedition into
the Pacific as motivated by "principles of humanity,"[21] then went on to complain of the
"boasted civilization [and] parade of humanity and social virtues"[22] that characterize
European sensibilities, contrasting them with the natural tenderness of a Tahitian man
who wept when he saw the Maori men eating human flesh in Queen Charlotte Sound.
What he identifies as hypocrisy, however, seems more like a process of social breakdown
and growing disaffection among members of Cook's crew as the captain's acts of moral
judgment cease to appear uniformly humane. The consequences seem trivial: members
of the crew thought increasingly of their own discomforts and longed for the pleasures
of the torrid zone. Yet such "unsociable" inclinations, provoked, at least in part, by the
faltering moral authority of the captain, could be enormously troubling for British
commerce, as a later expedition into the South Seas was to show.

Mutiny on the *Bounty*

Tensions on Cook's ships never achieved crisis proportions in the way that they did aboard the *Bounty* in 1789. Bligh's expedition, however, faced much the same problems as Cook's—in particular, the enormous distance that had to be traveled and the need to carefully manage trade between European sailors and their island hosts. Bligh's task was to collect a large number of breadfruit plants in Tahiti, half of which were to be delivered to the King's botanical gardens at St. Vincent, and the other half to Jamaica, where the fruit would provide cheap food for plantation slaves. The *Bounty* reached Tahiti on 26 October 1788, where it remained for twenty-three weeks while the breadfruit was collected. A short way into the return voyage, on 28 April 1789, Fletcher Christian led the crew to mutiny, and Bligh and seventeen others were set adrift in an open boat in which they managed to traverse over three and a half thousand miles before finally reaching Timor. Bligh then traveled on through the East Indies to Batavia in a schooner, during which voyage he nearly faced another mutiny, and finally returned to England as a passenger in a Dutch vessel. Two years later he returned to the South Pacific on a second breadfruit expedition. Fletcher Christian's mutineers returned to Tahiti briefly and then sailed on to Pitcairn Island, where they settled and where most, including Christian, died in a conflict with the Tahitians who had accompanied them. Several of the mutineers who had remained in Tahiti were captured and brought back to England for court martial.

Beaglehole has pointed out that, while Cook was revered as the great humanitarian and mourned as a loss to the entire world, and while Bligh was and is remembered as a bully and a failure, there was not much to distinguish professionally between the two of them. Both were strict disciplinarians, and both, in Beaglehole's words, "were exceedingly humane men, careful of the lives of those who served under them."[23] Like Cook, Bligh was scrupulous about his seamen's general health, but also like Cook, he was known to lose himself from time to time in violent fits of temper. Bligh, who had sailed on the final voyage of the *Resolution*, to a large extent modeled his management skills on those of Cook, strictly regulating trade by determining who among the crew could conduct it and which goods were to be exchanged, and relying on the power of chiefs to capture and return deserters. However, in his log entries prior to the mutiny, Bligh actually expresses more interest in the diet, exercise, and cleanliness of his crew than in their behavior in Tahiti, and he is less concerned about how they are affected by the unfamiliar customs they witness than either Cook or Forster was about the impact of such observations on the crew of the *Resolution*. It is only when he later comes to reflect on how the experience of a lengthy stay in Tahiti might have precipitated the mutiny that he observes how tempting the ease of a life on this island must have appeared to men who were so far away from the comforts of home.

In Bligh's reconstruction of events, the sailors lose their ability to maintain a reflective distance on Tahitian customs and give in to their passions. This surrender to the pleasures of the moment explains why they reject his more farsighted authority. In his "Dispatch to the Admiralty," Bligh describes in detail the tattoos that several members of the mutinous party—Christian, Morrison, Peter Heywood, and Thomas Ellison—had pierced on their bodies in Tahiti, implicitly identifying these gestures of "going native" as proof of the guilt of the men who had made them. He suggests that these men are more likely to be "led away" because they are "void of connections."[24] They become like the protagonists of Defoe's travel fictions—unattached to family, home, or country and therefore easily seduced into a life of crime. In his 1792 *Voyage to the South Seas,* Bligh revises his account of an incident in Tahiti when the ship was cut adrift. In the logbook he assumes this was an act of native mischief; in the *Voyage* he reflects that "this was probably the act of some of our own people, whose purpose of remaining at Taheite might have been effectually answered, without danger, if the ship had been driven on shore."[25] Yet, at the time, he observes, he had no suspicion that the crew had "so strong an attachment to these islands . . . as to induce them to abandon every prospect of returning to their native country" (*Voyage,* 72). Also in the later narrative but missing from the logbook is the concerned observation that within a short time such an intimacy grew between the crewmembers and the natives that "there was scarce a man in the ship who did not have his *tyo* or friend" (38). Similarly, in the published narrative he expresses much more concern about the spread of venereal disease among his crew than he does in the logbook.

If Bligh is concerned to show, looking back, how vulnerable the members of his crew were to the charms of the South Seas, he is also anxious to demonstrate that he could not have anticipated the violent measures to which their fancies would lead them. In the *Voyage* he elaborates on the remark in his log that "the secrecy of this mutiny [was] beyond all conception,"[26] maintaining that while a commander might, at the utmost, have been prepared for a few desertions, he could not be expected to guard against anything as radical as mutiny unless he were to "sleep locked up and when awake be girded with pistols" (*Voyage,* 94). The mutiny was not, he insists here, the result of any lack of foresight or reasonable preparation on his part. In fact, he points out in his 1792 account of the voyage of the launch how careful he was to prepare against unforeseeable events. During this voyage, he recalls, he was "constantly assailed with the melancholy demands of my people for an increase of allowance which it grieved me to refuse" (*Voyage,* 134). He did so, however, knowing that a rigid economy was their best hope of survival, and congratulates himself that on their arrival at Timor they still had provisions for eleven days, which would have enabled them to sail on to Java, had they missed the Dutch settlement at Timor. He also reflects on the "caprice of ignorant people" (134) who, without his guidance, would have gone on shore as soon as they reached the island of Timor before they reached a European settlement. Here he is taking pains to counter any inference that he might lack the foresight and vision of a commander like Cook. It is not surprising then, to find him explaining the failure of the expedition to Joseph Banks and the Admiralty by insisting that in his careful preparations for the voyage home he "must have been more than a human being to have foreseen what has happened."[27]

Indeed, as he looks back on events in Tahiti in an effort to clear himself of any charge of incompetence, Bligh comments more broadly on the nature of a society in which present passions determine the way people act toward one another more powerfully than they do in a more "advanced" culture. Even in the logbook, he notes how unrestrained the passions of the islanders tend to be. He wonders, for instance, at how "in so prolific a country as this" the men are led into "deviant" practices like homosexuality and oral sex, or at how an expression of great sorrow and distress can change to laughter in an instant (*Log*, 2:17). In the *Voyage* he revises some of his descriptions of his exchanges with Chief Tinah to show that the latter is governed by passions and ambitions very remote from the humanitarian calculations that motivate British interest in South Seas' societies. In both the log and the narrative, Bligh records Tinah's account of how neighboring tribes killed and ate the cattle and sheep that Cook left on Tahiti to breed. Bligh responds to this news by telling the chief that King George will be very angry to learn of it, and in the log Tinah is reported to be "much pleased and satisfied" to hear so (*Log*, 1:379). In *A Voyage to the South Seas*, however, Bligh reports that Tinah's satisfaction had nothing to do with the loss of the cattle, "about which he appeared unconcerned and indifferent" (41), but that he is pleased to think that the English will take vengeance on the people who have robbed him. His desire for vengeance, Bligh also suggests in the *Voyage*, is only matched by his hunger for European commodities, which are highly valued by high-ranking Tahitians for their status rather than their usefulness. In this later version of events, then, Bligh supplements his account of how skillfully he has managed to establish and maintain important friendships with remarks intended to illustrate the difference between Tahitian passions and English prudence. In so doing he highlights the perspicacity of his many efforts to plant foreign seeds on the islands and to secure the remaining livestock. In their contributions as editors of the *Voyage*, Joseph Banks and James Burney enlarged the scope of Bligh's compassionate calculations by adding (as though in his words) a lengthy proposal to transport natives from Tahiti (where infanticide appeared to function as a means of controlling population growth) to underpopulated New Holland, thus "forwarding the purposes of humanity by bringing a people without land to a land without people" (*Voyage*, 46).

Bligh's efforts to present himself as a forward-thinking humanitarian in the style of Cook also become a means of defending himself directly against the charges of excessive discipline. In the log, he comments briefly on an incident of flogging a seaman who had struck an Indian, observing that he reduced the number of lashes at the request of Chief Tynah (*Log*, 2:27). In the *Voyage*, this episode is reported rather differently, and the reaction of the chief carries no political weight next to the more extensive view of the captain, who insists that the severity of the offense is such that he cannot afford to reduce the punishment, whatever intercession the chiefs might make (*Voyage*, 68). Like his item-by-item defense of the nutritional reasons why certain foods were given to the sailors in place of others, this justification for the flogging is calculated to represent him as a humanitarian in his strict discipline. It shows him as able to recognize where the violation of an order might precipitate serious conflict and so compromise the objectives of the voyage, while the chiefs are capable only of a softer and more immediate sympathy for the suffering seaman.

In this way, Bligh credits himself with the greater vision of a captain as he prepares the reader of the *Voyage* for the account of the mutiny. He presents himself as a thwarted humanitarian whose service to a commercial enterprise that promised so much prosperity to all the nations involved was to be reversed by a conspiracy "render[ing] all our past labour productive only of extreme misery and distress" (87). His insistence on the nearsighted, passion-driven behavior of his crew is challenged, however, by James Morrison, boatswain's mate on the *Bounty*. Morrison's journal argues that the mutiny was provoked by Bligh's brutal treatment of his crew rather than, as the latter represented it, by a rebellious longing for the pleasures of Tahiti. The Tahiti that Christian and his crew return to, Morrison shows, is not a world that romantically defies the moral calculations of British imperial culture—a world where the pursuit of pleasure is the first principle of social life—but rather an unhappy island of exiles onto which the mutinous sailors have been forced by desperate circumstances. Whereas Bligh reconstructs events in *A Voyage* to show that the sailors intended to remain in Tahiti, Morrison remarks that on the voyage out "everyone seemed in high spirits and began to talk of home . . . and one would readily have imagined that we had just left Jamaica instead of Tahiti, so far onward did their flattering fancies waft them."[28] Describing the life the mutineers tried to make for themselves once they returned to Tahiti, he also complains that the natives are backward in their agricultural methods and reflects on how the experiments in planting begun in Cook's time have been thwarted by the islanders' passions for new and curious commodities. These passions, he observes, have brought all

Cook's humanitarian intentions to nothing, for although "when he first thought of stocking these islands with cattle, poultry and the fruits and roots of Europe, [he] intended it for the good of mankind . . . these people knew not the value of them and for want of Europeans to take care of them they were soon destroyed."[29] The irony here is that such observations correspond closely to Bligh's comments about Tahitian neglectfulness. "All our fond hopes," the latter observes, "[and] the trouble Captain Cook [took] to introduce so many valuable things among them, [and that] would . . . have been found to be productive of every good, are entirely blasted" (*Log*, 1:318).

Morrison's journal offers a defiant response to Bligh's equation between South Seas indolence and the recalcitrance of seamen, in many ways presenting a stronger case against the captain's "humanitarianism" than the accusations about his excessive discipline provide. Yet Bligh's version of events, unsurprisingly, was the one to prevail, and he was given command of a second breadfruit voyage to Tahiti. It was, of course, easier for Bligh to demonstrate that he had exercised moral strength of character in the face of the uncontainable passions of his crew than for Morrison to argue that men who had willfully severed all ties to home were attuned to the kind of economic prudence characteristic of a civilized and settled people. This perhaps explains why Christian, when Bligh last spoke to him, declared that he was in hell. Bligh, on the other hand, as he looked back on the experience of the open boat voyage, observed that even with scarcely enough food and water to survive the journey ahead, he felt "wonderfully supported" and sure that he would "one day be able to account to [his] king and country for the misfortune."[30] For despite the costly failure of the expedition, he could be confident that the state would find evidence, first in his logbook and later in his published narratives, for the justice and humanity in his heart. His restored favor in the eyes of the Admiralty was testimony to the latter's faith in Bligh's character. Like Cook, he appeared to be a man of sympathy who had done his best to manage the raw passions of his crewmembers—passions that sought free expression in the "uncivilized" South Pacific. His captain's heart was indeed, his superiors recognized, capable of exercising the kind of justice necessary to preserve social order on board ship and to expand the commercial world. The challenges that he, like Cook, faced from seamen who objected to the brutal conditions of their employment thus had to be identified and dismissed as the impulsive actions of narrow-minded men who had unfortunately forgotten that social happiness demands respect and obedience to one of greater feeling and foresight.

CHAPTER TWENTY-ONE

Voyaging the Past, Present, and Future

Historical Reenactments on HM Bark *Endeavour* and the
Voyaging Canoe *Hokule'a* in the Sea of Islands

Greg Dening

At the end of the old and the beginning of the new millennium, there are two icons of
cross-cultural research sailing the Pacific—*Endeavour,* the replica of James Cook's discovery vessel, and *Hokule'a,* the living model of a Polynesian voyaging canoe.

The vastness of the Pacific makes a sublime and intriguing stage for the theater of human achievement these two vessels play. There is not one of the Pacific's thousands of islands, not even the most isolated, that has not been visited or settled by native wayfinders
through the past two thousand years. It was Francis Drake's, or perhaps his ship's secretary Francis Fletcher's triumphant phrase, "The World Encompassed," that expressed
what it meant for those who "came from across the horizon" to voyage across the Pacific.[1]
"The Discovery of the Sea," J. H. Parry called it in another famous phrase, the discovery
that the world's oceans were one and that they could be sailed globally.[2] It was left to
James Cook, though, to encompass Oceania—to put the islands of the Pacific within the
points of the great triangle of Hawai'i, Rapa Nui (Easter Island), and Aotearoa (New
Zealand) into the European mind and all its systems of mapping and knowledge.

There needs to be some social memory of these things—of course there does. All
peoples' identities turn on stories of their origins and achievements. Social memory is
as much about the present as the past. Social memory enlarges the continuities between
past and present. Social memory is, in Aristotle's theatrical term, *catharthis,* getting the

plot, seeing the meaning of things.[3] Seeing the meanings of things is the function of the theater of reenactment.

There needs to be historical understanding, as well. Truth and fiction weave a double helix into identity and living. The past has to be gazed upon with a sharp, true, unhallucinated eye. In the theater of reenactments of the performative kind, the people of the past can be made to seem to have been just like us, but in funny clothes. Yet the past in its totality—in its postures, its tones and accents, its evils and goods—is different, as different as another culture, "a foreign country," David Lowenthal has written.[4] The historical gaze is always cross-cultural, but difference is the hardest thing to see. To see difference we have to give a little—old to young, young to old; male to female, female to male; white to black, black to white.

That being said, let us make some historical reenactments of our own.

I first saw the *Endeavour* replica in 1998 in a place where the original *Endeavour* had never been, my own hometown port of Melbourne, Australia. I first saw *Hokule'a* in 1975. It was undergoing sea-trials in Kaneohe Bay on the north side of the Hawaiian island Oahu.

There was a lump in my throat when I first saw the *Endeavour* replica. Much of my work has been concerned with the poetics of space on an eighteenth-century naval vessel: the rituals of the quarterdeck that were the theater of command for captains like William Bligh and James Cook in the British navy, and David Porter in the American.[5] I have written how important the divisions of private and public space were for ordinary seamen, and how dangerous it was to blur their boundaries.

A sailing vessel, for me, is a thing of language. I get lost for hours in dictionaries like William Falconer's *Marine Dictionary;* everyday words and phrases derived from the sea are a delight to my land-locked soul.[6] Joseph Conrad called the language of the sea "a flawless thing for its purpose."[7] The *Endeavour* replica was the wooden world in which this language was materialized for me: cheats, bowlines, chewlines, bustlines, reeflines, brails, gaskets, halliards, staysails, shrouds.

I do not want to deceive anyone. I do all my sailing in the library. I do all my reading in ships' logs with a plan of rigging beside me. When Bligh or Cook write in their journals that a "severe gale" abated into a "mere storm," I reach anachronistically for my Beaufort Wind Scales to understand what that might mean and what are the signs in the sea to determine it. My heroes among writers of ships are those who write to their experience—Herman Melville, Richard Dana, Charles Nordhoff, Alan Villiers.[8]

The most magical moment for me on the *Endeavour* replica was when I first saw the Great Cabin. It did not seem possible that so much could come out of so cramped a space. It would have been a clutter of charts, drawings, specimens, paintings, and "artificial curiosities." Joseph Banks had spent £10,000—a fortune and more than the whole expedition cost the Admiralty—on every instrument of collection, observation, and preservation. The *Endeavour* was a traveling museum, laboratory, library, and study. From 8:00 A.M. to 2:00 P.M. each day, Banks and his scientific assistants, Daniel Solander and Herman Spöring, and his painters, Alexander Buchan and Sydney Parkinson, sat studying in the Great Cabin directing the draughtsmen and entering descriptions in their journals. At 4:00 P.M., "when the smell of cooking had vanished" after dinner, they began again, working till it was too dark.[9]

And the quarter deck! Here the midshipmen, commissioned and petty officers would "Get a *heiva* from the old boy." Midshipman John Trevenen explains: "*Heiva*, the name of the dance of the Southern Islanders, which bore so great a resemblance to the violent motions and stamping on the Deck of Captain Cooke in the paroxysms of passion, into which he threw himself on the slightest occasion that they were universally known by the same name, and it was a common saying among both officers and people: 'the old boy is tipping a *heiva* to such and such a one.'"[10]

Hokule'a in its sea-trials was as beautiful a sight as the *Endeavour* replica. Forty-five years ago I had begun a lifetime's passion, writing double-visioned history of the encounter between the native island peoples of Oceania and the intruding Euro-American outsiders. Our cross-cultural research at that time was characterized by a sort of intellectual innocence. Our excitement, too, was sparked as much as anything by a famous reenactment—Thor Heyerdahl's *Kontiki* raft voyages from the Peruvian coast to the great thousand-mile arc of atolls northeast of Tahiti, the Tuamotus. The Pacific peoples, specifically the Polynesians, came from the Americas, Heyerdahl had argued. We scoured everything botanical, linguistic, genetic, material, mythological, historical, anthropological, and archaeological to prove him wrong. It was a wonderful intellectual odyssey for us. Knowledge knew no boundaries. I have thanked Heyerdahl ever since. I am sure his writing of *American Indians in the Pacific*, his general theory, and *Aku Aku*, its Rapa Nui (Easter Island) expression of it, was as liberating an experience for him.[11]

We locked horns too with another famous but more curmudgeonly scholar of the day (1956–58)—Andrew Sharp. His *Ancient Voyagers in the Pacific* scoffed at the notion of Pacific Vikings freely wandering vast ocean spaces. They were blown hither and yon, he wrote. Traditions to the contrary were just myths. We younger scholars did not sense at the time how devastating and political a conclusion that was. It struck heavily at the island peoples' idea of their cultural identity.[12]

However, my first academic publication was a review essay of *Ancient Voyagers in the Pacific*. Essentially, it was a denial of Sharp's central thesis. I still have Sharp's stinging rebuke in my files. The faded blue aerogramme is a sort of scout's badge of adversarial academia. I proudly keep it because I knew I was right.[13]

Let me tell you how I knew I was right—it is, after all, reenactments that we are talk-ing about. One day I was reading in the glow of a lamp in the gloom of the Great Read-ing Room of the State Library of Victoria. The Great Reading Room was built in the time of gold-rush wealth in imitation of the great domed reading room of the British Library, but this was in the 1950s and the State Library was in poor repair. On the green leather desk at which I sat was carved the message that "Foo" had been there. Behind me was a bucket into which rain water dripped from a great height. Beside me was a smelly, sleeping drunk. I used to wear a clerical collar in those days, and half the home-less men in Melbourne used to sit beside me in the library because they thought that they would not be thrown out if they did. On this particular day, I read Harold Gatty's survival pamphlet for crashed airmen during the Second World War. It was full of the lore Gatty had learned from islanders about all the signposts to be found at sea—ocean swells and the shadows islands made in them, clouds and the color of the lagoons re-flected in them, birds migrating or returning to land to roost, orienting stars.[14] It was an enlightening moment for me in cross-cultural history. It was a moment of solidar-ity with experiences I had never had, a moment of trust and imagination. Anyone en-gaged in cross-cultural research will know that it is not the mountains of texts of the encounter between indigenous peoples and intruding strangers that are the problem. It is the depth of the silences. I thought that as a historian, my best chance of hearing what those silences hid was to learn a bit of anthropology. Yet I knew as well that puri-tanical intellectualism would never uncover the whole truth of anything. There had to be imagination, not a few leaps of trust, and an occasional gamble.

Two other scholars were making their very first contribution to Pacific cross-cultural research in those years: Marshall Sahlins and Ben Finney. I felt jealous of them both, I have to confess. Sahlins wrote "Esoteric Efflorescence on Easter Island" in the *American Anthropologist.* It was part of his library-oriented doctoral dissertation, "Social Strati-fication of Polynesia." His fieldwork in Fiji came later. I was jealous because he was read-ing everything that I was reading but reading it differently and more creatively—wrongly, but more creatively! I decided that anthropology helped him do it. So I went off to do anthropology to get those reading skills.[15]

However, it is Finney I want to talk about. He had just completed his graduate work on ancient surfboard riding in Hawai'i. I thought that surfboard research was a pretty good lure to get you out of the library and onto the beach. But for him it was the be-ginning of a career in which he has wedded theoretical knowledge with practical skill. He calls it "experimental archaeology" these days.[16]

Finney was about to reconstruct a Hawaiian double canoe, a replica of King Kame-hameha III's royal canoe. There was a precise plan of it in a French explorer's publications. Finney's purpose was modest: to test whether shallow rounded hulls would give resistance to leeway and whether the inverted triangular "crab-claw" sail would drive the canoe into the wind. It was skepticism on these two points that drove, among other things, Sharp's arguments about the possibilities of Polynesian deliberate voyaging.

When Finney brought the canoe to Hawai'i from California, where he had done his tests, Mary Pakena Pukui, one of Hawai'i's traditional scholars, called the canoe *Nahelia*, "The Skilled Ones"—for the way in which the hulls gracefully rode the swells and into the wind. Already the project was getting larger than itself. The admiration caught in the name *Nahelia* was a sign of deeper cultural and political forces beginning to be focused in the question of how the Hawaiians, Tahitians, Maori, and Samoans encompassed Oceania, "The Sea of Islands."[17]

In Oceania, the silences in cross-cultural research have been deep: the silences of victims, the silence of powerlessness, the silences of banal evil, the silences of what cannot be seen in any encounter with otherness. The voicelessness of an indigenous past and an indigenous present has been almost a presumption in Oceanic studies. "The Fatal Impact" was Alan Moorhead's famous metaphor for it.[18]

Yet all around the world, not just in the Pacific, there has been some resurrection found amid so much death. Histories now are of resistance. Not just of the open resistance that was crushed mercilessly by empires, but of that hidden resistance that preserved native identities in a new cultural idiom. "Reinvented tradition" has been the phrase used to describe it, but that has been spurned by indigenous peoples as suggesting political opportunism and insincerity. I have not a phrase that would satisfy them yet. In my own mind I see it as creative aboriginality: the ability to see, despite all the transformations, the continuities that connect an indigenous past with an indigenous present.[19] Gayatri Spivak and Homi Bhabha in their subaltern studies have shown how it is done.[20] It is done by imagination, not fantasy. The imagination of those many silence-breakers—poets, novelists, painters, carvers, dancers, filmmakers . . . I wish I had my time again. I can see my own dyslexia. My reading skills have to be enlarged.

Finney in 1975, now supported by and eventually relieved of his leading role by native-born Hawaiians, turned to the construction of an oceangoing canoe, *Hokule'a*. *Hokule'a* means "Star of Joy"—Arcturus, the zenith star, the homing star in Hawai'i's celestial latitude. The overriding ambition of all *Hokule'a*'s great voyages was to perform them as much as possible in the way in which they were performed a thousand years ago. *Hokule'a* has voyaged to nearly all parts of the central Polynesian Pacific: Hawai'i—Tahiti—Hawai'i; Tahiti—Rarotonga—Aotearoa; Samoa—Aitutaki—Tahiti.

These voyages have been an extraordinary achievement. There is no point in being romantic about them. The thirty years of this odyssey have had their pain and conflict, their tragedies and failures, their political machinations, their greed, their absurdities. Yet they also have been courageous overall triumphs, tapping wellsprings of cultural pride in a sense of continuity with a voyaging tradition. This has not just been in Hawai'i, but in Tahiti, Samoa, and Aotearoa as well. Everywhere she has gone it has been the same. The landfall has been a theater of who island peoples are, who they have been.[21]

The *Endeavour* replica's keel was laid in January 1988, the bicentennial of the arrival of the First Convict Fleet at Botany Bay and Sydney. Six years later she was launched in Fremantle, Western Australia—with speeches, of course. They quoted Charles Darwin saying that "Cook had added a hemisphere to the civilised world." This perfect *Endeavour* replica, built at a cost of five million dollars, was a living creature, they said, imbued with the spirit of Cook. Cook was "the most moderate, humane, gentle circumnavigator who went upon discovery." The *Endeavour* replica was a symbol of tenacity, skills, endurance, and leadership and of the Australian credo of "Have a go!" It didn't seem to matter that the man who had contributed most of the five million dollars was still in jail for fraud.[22]

James Cook (1728–79). Yorkshire villager and apprentice grocer; North Sea collier seamen; Royal Navy Master at the battle of Quebec; Pacific explorer; Fellow of the Royal Society.[23] Cook is a man of myth. Cook is a man of antimyth. Myth and antimyth are always true. Myth and antimyth are never true. Off the New South Wales coast where there were aboriginal first people to see the *Endeavour* replica, in the Bay of Islands and Poverty Bay, Aotearoa, where there were Maori eyes to see it, the *Endeavour* replica is not an icon of humanistic empire and science. The theater of reenactment there is the violence that Cook did in Tonga, Hawai'i, Aotearoa, and wherever he put foot on land. The theater is about the resistance that indigenous ancestors would have made if they had known the history that was to follow.[24]

The theater of the myth and antimyth is much the same. The abstraction is "us"—the resistance fighters with a sense of history, Australians with a sense of "having a go"—in the funny clothes of the past.

Deep in the mythic consciousness of the peoples of the Sea of Islands is a series of crossing metaphors that have served their understanding of themselves—rainbows, feathers, canoes. Each metaphor, embodied in story or artifact or ritual, described some bridging process—between sky and earth, human and suprahuman, sea and land. The voyaging canoe embodied something more. It embodied the people of the place. Owned in its parts by individuals and families, the canoe was a map of the whole temple congregation or political unit. In its name was a heroic ancestry. Its voyaging was always epic—from or to Tahiti ("A Distant Place"), to or from Havai'iki ("A Sacred Home"). Its launchings and arrivals were always larger than ordinary, always in places of power and significance, always occasions of memory and rite.

Hokule'a was launched with ceremony in March 1975 at Kualoa on the north side of Oahu, a beach full of *kapu* for the People of Old of Hawai'i. Signifying actions, out of season as it were, divorced from their times and those who see the meaning of the signs immediately and directly, can sometimes seem awkward, striving too hard. They cease to be sacramental, or effective of what they are signifying in the signifying, and become merely symbolic. Ritual and theater lose their cathartic effect if the ritual becomes ritualistic, succumbs to formalistic repetition, and the theater becomes too theatrical, overplaying the words, gestures, and signs. At *Hokule'a*'s launching, the *kahuna*, the master of old knowledge, sang the chants and blessings that had been rescued from oblivion a hundred and fifty years ago when the Hawaiian People of Old embraced the literacy that was the single greatest import of the strangers. All the proper garlands and proprietary parcels of sacrifices were used. *Kapu* were conscientiously and overtly obeyed. The moment was as inventive of solemnity and full of distractions as is every cultural act. The thousands of spectators on the beach gave *Hokule'a* their own blessing with their cheers.[25]

The *catharthis* of the launch was more long-coming than in those minutes on the beach at Kualoa, however. The politics of dispossession were strong in Oceania in those years. Bikini and Muroroa and their mushroom clouds still shadowed the islands. The *kamaiana, maohi, enata*—the native islanders of the Pacific—were asking what a "world encompassed" really meant for them. Hawaiians, Tahitians, and Maori were asking what joined them together in the Sea of Islands.[26] Moana, the Great Ocean, had been called names—*South Seas, Pacific*—that did not speak to their spirits or their hopes. *Sea of Islands,* or *Oceania* said more. When *Hokule'a* arrived in Tahiti at the end of her first successful thirty-four-day voyage, the peoples of the Sea of Islands were joined by their ancient mastery of the ocean and their cultural memory of it. The launching ceremonies of *Hokule'a* lasted from March 1975 at Kualoa, where thousands saw her take to the water, and June 1976 at Papeete, where thousands welcomed her after a voyage that they believed reenacted the voyages of their ancestors.

All history writing is a reenactment, of course, but it is never a replay. There is no time machine in reality. The past is gone forever and only returns transformed into word or picture. That being said, there are few historians who do not strive to meet the past as it left itself, on millions of one-off pieces of paper, some stained with tears, even blood, all marked with the transience of the present moment in which they were written. "Primary sources," the historian calls them. It is the privilege of a historian to work with "primary sources."

For a voyage as famous as the *Endeavour*'s, all these pieces of paper written within minutes or hours or days of the events they describe have long been transcribed and published. They can be owned by thousands of readers and put on library shelves. To read them in their original state, however, it is usually necessary to make a pilgrimage. To see James Cook's own handwritten account of what he called "Remarkable Occurrences on Board his Majesty's Bark *Endeavour*," with its elisions, errors, second thoughts, and self-censures, you will have to make a pilgrimage to the National Library of Australia in Canberra. "MS1 Cook, J. Holograph Journal" is in number and sentiment the library's foundation document. For the centenary of the National Library in 2001— the Australian nation had its beginnings in federation in 1901—I was honored to be invited to write a historical reenactment of the journal itself and the national treasure it has become. I am well practiced in the rules and customs of rare books and manuscript rooms, but it was a special moment for me to put on the white gloves and handle MS1 when it was brought to me from the strongroom. Here is the beginning of my efforts.

Remarkable Occurrences

"On Sunday the 7th I joined the Ship, discharged the Pilot & next Day sail'd for Plymouth,"[27] he writes. He won't often write "I." More often it is an impersonal "hoisted the Pendant & took charge of the Ship or we were constantly employed in fitting the Ship." But that moment on the Downs was special. The *Endeavour* was now his in ways it hadn't been till then. On this August Sunday in 1769, he sits at his writing desk at the head of his "cot" in his Captain's Cabin. The smell of paint and tar, flax and hemp, canvas and rope is heavy on the air, and is homely. Outside his door, the Great Cabin is empty. Sir Joseph Banks and his retinue will more than fill it for three years, however. Banks will join the ship in Plymouth. His servants and his baggage are already aboard. The captain's servant, sixteen-year-old William Howson, is there for his needs, and so is his clerk, Dick Orton, who will transcribe all his official documents except this one. Orton at this stage has his two ears intact. By the end of the voyage he'll have a slice taken out of both of them. Being a captain's clerk and assistant purser could be dangerous.

Now Cook opens a ninety-two-page folio journal book. It won't be large enough for this voyage. He'll add another 651 loose folded folio pages before he is finished. He writes across the first page with his spelling idiosyncrasies and clear hand, though not as even a hand as one would expect from so exact a mapmaker as he—"Remarkable Occurrences on Board his Majesty's Bark Endeavour—River Thames." "Remarkable," worthy of note. It is a modest word in this context with no great sense of extravagance. He will be troubled at times at who is doing the remarking—he, James Cook, laborer's son, little educated; he, Lieutenant James Cook, King's commissioned officer; he, James Cook, discoverer, cabin-companion of "experimental gentlemen." He will be troubled, too, about what should be remarked upon—native lubricity? officer's drunkenness? the "people's" immorality? his own imprudence?

Right now there is actually not much to remark upon at all, just that from 25 May to 29 July they lay in the Basin at Deptford, fitting and provisioning, then had moved to Gallion's Reach. He didn't say, because it didn't seem remarkable, that they had lain beside a sheer hulk, a sort of river crane, where the *Endeavour* crew themselves masted and rigged the ship, coiled the cables, stowed the ballast and anchors and stores of all kinds. He didn't say, but he would have been glad that his men built up all the working makings of the ship they would sail. Their lives would depend on their knowledge of every inch of the *Endeavour* and their ease in the use of every rope and sail. Gallion's Reach was where they loaded her six four-pounder carriage cannons (four more would come aboard at Plymouth), twelve swivel guns, and all the powder and shot. Samuel Wallis had just returned from Tahiti in the *Dolphin* and told of the disastrous beginnings to their encounter with the Tahitians. They had killed they didn't know how many. Cook doesn't know what he might have to do to follow his instructions to observe the transit of Venus at Tahiti.

At Plymouth, a sergeant, a corporal, a drummer, and nine private marines come aboard. So does the shipwright to make adjustments to Banks's cabin and the quarterdeck so that the gentlemen could promenade a little more easily. Two days before they expect to sail, he reads them the Articles of War, his power of life and death over them, and sees that the people get two months' advanced pay of £2.10s, a show of "fathering" that he also needs to make. The "I" returns. "I also told them that they are not to expect any additional pay for their performance of our intended voyage. They were well satisfied & express'd great chearfulness and readyness to prosecute the voyage." The sight of an extra 604 gallons of rum coming aboard also would have cheered them up.

They didn't sail, as it happened, till Friday 26 August, four days later than he expected. "At 2PM got under sail and put to sea having on board 94 persons including Officers Seamen Gentlemen & their servants, near 18 months provisions, 10 Carriage guns 12 swivels with good store of Ammunition & stores of all kind."

A sailing vessel is a machine energized by natural forces and human vigor. Power so harnessed gives every part of a ship a trembling, beating life that transmits itself to the bodies of the sailors and all their senses. Sailors feel the rhythm, hear it, smell it, see it, have the language to describe it. Their watches might be their hours of vigilance, but they are always awake to the signs of life in their machine. When life is so dependent on skill and knowledge and the choreography of their movements, true authority is divorced from power. True authority on a ship comes only from experience, not by birth or gift or wealth or Admiralty appointment. A seaman who has gone where others have not been—beyond that point, beyond that cape, beyond that sea—had knowledge into which all the others had to be initiated. To be "baptized" was the sailors' phrase for this initiation. Cook might have sailed these cat-built broad-beamed colliers out of Whitby, but he had to be "baptized" as he crossed the line for the first time by those who had been there before him.

For more than a third of the *Endeavour*'s company, this would be the voyage of a lifetime. Twenty-five of them would be dead before the *Endeavour* returned. The first died just three weeks out, at Madeira. "In heaving the Anchor out of the Boat Mr Weir Masters mate was carried over board by the Buoy-rope." There was no delay in replacing Alexander Weir. A John Thurman was impressed from a New York–bound sloop. He would never get home. He died of "flux" in Batavia. An accidental drowning, an impressment, then a flogging rounded off a naval sequence at Madeira. Henry Stephens and Thomas Dunster were punished with twelve lashes each—for "Mutiny," recorded John Gore, the third lieutenant. "For refusing to take their allowance of fresh beef," their captain wrote. He had scurvy in mind still just three weeks out.

The twenty-five who died would leave their bodies at Madeira, Tierra del Fuego, Tahiti, Botany Bay, Batavia—and in the sea. Off Tahiti, William Greenslade, a twenty-year-old marine, had been caught stealing a piece of sealskin for a money pouch. Within half an hour of having done it, he had thrown himself overboard. He could not face the shame of punishment in such a tightly knit group.

James Cook began the debate on the "Polynesian Problem." How was it, he asked himself, that every island he "discovered" in the vast Pacific was already peopled by natives whose physical appearance was similar and who seemed to speak the same language in dialect? He carefully watched their sailing techniques, asked what other islands they knew, admired their oceangoing canoes when they scooted past the *Resolution* in a good breeze. He even let one of them, Tupaia, a Tahitian priest-navigator, guide him over three hundred miles of unknown seas to a new "discovery." He was impressed that in the East, the Tahitians, and in the West, the Tongans, could name hundreds of islands in a great arc around them. He wanted to believe otherwise but in the end—probably persuaded by the "experimental gentlemen" around him—concluded that the dispersal of the Pacific peoples must have been largely by the accident of seafarers lost in storms.

James Cook began the debate, but he certainly did not end it. Andrew Sharp tried to

in 1956 with his *Ancient Voyagers in the Pacific.* Sharp's skepticism prompted the arm-
chair research, including my own, on how far the Polynesians could deliberately sail and
what would motivate them to such dangerous enterprises. But two brilliant books,
Thomas Gladwin's *East Is a Big Bird* (1970) and David Lewis's *We, the Navigators* (1972),
sent the debate in a different direction.[28] They described the extraordinary achievements of island navigators reading the swells in the sea and the stars in the sky. Gladwin, especially, showed the ways in which such complex knowledge might be transmitted through generations and be systematized on different principles to the global
navigation principles of the Europeans.

Computer simulations of Pacific voyaging came early into the debate, but hundreds
of thousands of deliberate and accidental voyages simulated in the computer did not
resolve the matter, or rather left scholars with the remarkable conclusion that not one
of the accidental simulations reached the three outer points of the Polynesian triangle—Hawai'i, Rapa Nui, Aotearoa.[29]

Before we attempt a reenactment flowing out of Ben Finney's "experimental archaeology," let us report an insight of a New Zealand archaeologist, Geoffrey Irwin.[30]
His is also a sailor's insight. Puzzling over the fact that most of the expansion eastward
into the Pacific was against prevailing weather conditions, he suggests that the chief
worry for a sailor was getting home. Prevailing and contrary weather conditions are not
a disincentive for exploration. They are an incentive for it. Prevailing and contrary
weather conditions will get a sailor home. He further suggests that the big jumps, east,
north, and south in the Pacific seemed to occur after about five hundred years local-
ization in a region. Five hundred years is a long time to create a knowledge bank of homing signs for a wayfinder.

For our reenactment, let me pick up the homecoming voyage of *Hokule'a* from Tahiti
to Hawai'i in June 1980. It begins in Matavai Bay, Tahiti, and ends thirty-two days later
on the big island of Hawai'i. Nainoa (Nainoa Thompson), a young man of Hawaiian
birth, twenty-five years old, was the wayfinder.[31]

Nainoa had apprenticed himself to Mau Piailug, the Micronesian navigator who had
taken *Hokule'a* to Tahiti in 1976. Mau had given David Lewis much of his navigator's
lore, too. Nainoa had no Hawaiian tradition of navigation to call upon. That was gone,
or rather, was too deeply imbedded in mythology and the language of the environment
to be of much use. Nainoa had virtually to invent his own system. He does not do it by
learning western celestial navigation. He avoids that. But he has the Bishop Museum
Planetarium in Honolulu to set in his mind the night skies. He can simulate the rising
and setting of the stars for all seasons in Hawai'i and for different latitudes. He creates
for himself a star compass and sets it in his mind as in all systems of oral memory, with

a metaphor. His metaphor for *Hokule'a* is *manu,* a bird with outstretched wings. He has not only a star compass in his mind—different from the ones we know of in Micronesia—but also a directional compass of thirty-two settings, or "houses" as he calls them, more regular than the traditional settings. He sets himself to remember the rising and setting of stars, sun, and moon in these houses. He also sets himself to calibrate his hand to the two great determinants of his Hawaiian latitudes, the North Star and the Southern Cross. When he is not in the planetarium, he is in the seas around Hawai'i, experiencing the swells made by the dominant weather patterns and their seasons, the seas created by the changing winds and the movements made by the backlash of the sea against island shores and in the island shadows. His latitudinal navigational lines, north and south in his system, are relatively easy. But his movements east and west along a longitudinal line are far more complex, involving dead reckoning of miles sailed and the relativizing of theorizing and settings in his star compass. That will be the greatest anxiety of his navigation. He has to make landfall upwind of his destination, northeast of Tahiti, southeast of Hawai'i. Downwind, if he ends up there, will require tacking.

Let's join him on the voyage from Tahiti to Hawai'i, from May to June 1980. They had to wait for wind to take them from Tahiti, in Nainoa's house of Na Leo (from the southwest). "The Southern Cross is now high in the sky behind us. Each night for the next three or four weeks we'll see it slightly lower, and by the time we reach Hawai'i it will be at the horizon. It will be ten days yet before we'll see the North Star."

They leave from Matavai, the bay forever held in the European mind by the paintings of Sydney Parkinson and John Webber on Cook's voyages. The crew of *Hokule'a* knew that there were more significant places for the Tahitian mythic spirit for them to have arrived at and departed from. In the years after 1980, they will sail through the sacred passage in the reef off Taputapuatea ("Sacrifices from Abroad"), a temple that is a mythic beach between the sea and land in Tahiti. But as they leave Tahiti, they know they are bonded to the *maohi* of the island nonetheless.

Nainoa has 2,000 miles of an arcing northwest sail to Hawai'i. In this vast open sea, huge forces are at work, especially in the clockwise systems of winds and currents of the northern hemisphere and the anticlockwise systems in the southern, and the in-between doldrums. Nainoa's knowledge can't be just local. It must be global and of the great regulators of time and direction—sun, moon, stars.

Each dawn is a precious time. The sun in its rising sets up a relationship with the swells of the ocean and its low shadows help the sight of this relationship. Mau, Nainoa's mentor, has thousands of dawns in his mind. The moon in its crescent carries the sun's shadow vertically near the equator, the more angled as they move north.

1 June 1980. They are within six days of a Hawaiian landfall. "Dawn. The first rays of dawn hurt my eyes to maintain the sailing course. I have an uneasy feeling this morn-

ing for I know that the thin sheet-like layer of cirrus cloud that moved in last night means a change of weather—a change from the regular trades that can make navigating difficult." He had difficulties in the night, too, identifying the stars in the breaks of the cloud.

Nainoa is tired. He is nearly sleepless. He is never, in fact, asleep on the inside. *Hokule'a*—*manu*—is no migratory bird. She has to be sailed off the wind and across the swells. Otherwise they will end up downwind of their Hawaiian destination, which would be disastrous. They are coming to the critical passage of their journey. Nainoa is tense with his responsibilities, and he is thinking of what he has been given by Mau and what it means. "[Mau] is a man of priceless gifts. A man who took our hands, as if we were children, and walked us through it all upon the wake of our ancestors."

They are in home skies by this time, but there are uncertainties. They are anxious whether they should trust their calculations, and whether they should turn westward for Hawai'i. They see white landbirds, but they are not easy to see amid the white crests of the waves. Are they fishing or are they flying home?

Nainoa will find, when the voyage ends, what errors he made each night and morning in his placing of *Hokule'a*. He will find his actual course weaves a line east and west over his presumed course. He will find, too, that his errors are random. This is an important point to make. When Andrew Sharp made his argument, it seemed incontrovertible that having lost a course in a storm or because clouds hid the stars, the error would have been irreversible. Nainoa discovers that his errors correct themselves in the long haul, and he knows that the wayfinder's true skill lies in reading the signs of a landfall. That doesn't calm his nerves, however.

He tells of a moment in which he was close to losing confidence. The night was black, the winds strong, the waves twelve feet high. "You keep the record of what you have done in your mind all the time. It is your history. If you forget it, you are lost. Keeping thirty days in the mind is difficult . . . We had two choices—to sail or to drop the sail and go nowhere . . . I gave up . . . I just gave up forcing myself to find answers . . . When I relaxed and gave up, somehow I knew. Then there was a break in the clouds and the moon showed—exactly as I thought it was supposed to be. Even when I saw it I was surprised. That's my most valued moment, that one."

He is anxious. He sleeps hardly at all at night and not more than an hour at a time in the day. For ten days, high clouds have obscured the stars. He has steered mainly with the sun and the moon. The moon in its crescent carries the sun's shadow vertically near the equator, then more angled as they move north. The full moon on the horizon gives them a steering target. Dawn is the most important time, not just for the compass point of the sun's rising but because the angle of the sun makes it easier to read swells and seas and the weather of the day to come. Mau, the Micronesian navigator, had thousands of dawns at sea in his mind. The Southern Cross as it moved lower and to the west brought him the judgment on that third to last day that they were 550 miles southeast of Hawai'i. But they saw a land dove during the day. How could it have flown that distance between dawn and dusk?

They have passed through the equatorial doldrums. They have passed through that part of the ocean where the northwest swell of the northern hemisphere passed over the southeast swell of the southern and gave the distinctive pitch and roll movement of the canoe. Nainoa learned to feel these different motions of the canoe from Mau Piaulug— by lying prone on the decking. Now they are at the most anxious time of their voyage, wondering whether they should trust their calculations and turn westward in the Hawaiian latitudes. In wayfinding—the term they prefer to *navigation*—each day and night is a new calculation, a new assessment. It is important to note that again. What seemed undeniable in Sharp's argument was that errors were cumulative and once committed drove canoes into oblivion. Yet the discovery over all of *Hokule'a*'s voyaging was that errors were random and tended to counter one another. Nevertheless, that did not relieve the tension at moments of critical commitment.

Tropic birds are plentiful, but these are no sure sign of the direction of land. But there are *manu ku,* land doves, too. The wayfinders know land is near. They catch the angle of the North Star against the horizon and get a clear sighting of the Southern Cross. These convince them that their latitude calculations are right. On the second to last day, Nainoa says they are 210 miles from the big island of Hawai'i but nervously changes his calculations to 300 miles.

All day on the last day, the clouds on the horizon seem stationary. Clouds at sea move. Clouds over land stay still. There is something different about the setting sun. They couldn't say what, its coloring perhaps, as it catches the air around and above Hawai'i. They alter their course a little in its direction. It is in the right house of Nainoa's compass for land.

Then a stationary white cloud opens up and reveals the long gentle slope of Mauna Kea on Hawai'i. Nainoa says to himself: "The wayfinding at this moment seems to be out of my hands and beyond my control. I'm the one given the opportunity of feeling the emotions of wayfinding, not yet ready to have a complete understanding of what is happening. It is a moment of self-perspective, of one person in a vast ocean given an opportunity of looking through a window into my heritage."

I think he is correct. All over Polynesia, island peoples saw themselves in their canoes— in the canoe's making, in its parts, in its launching, in its voyaging. The canoe was an icon of all sorts of continuities of identity, an icon of a conjoining past and present. I don't have difficulty in believing that island peoples can recognize themselves in *Hokule'a* and embroider that recognition with all sorts of rebirths of traditional arts and crafts, with dance, poetry, and song. Whatever the transformations of modernity that masquerade as discontinuities—religion, science, politics—the theater of *Hokule'a*'s reenactment is directed to that recognition.

Early in 1995, the theater of reenactment of voyaging canoes came to a climax. Seven voyaging canoes of the Sea of Islands collected at the sacred island of Ra'iatea in the Tahitian group in preparation for an epic sail from Tahiti to Te Fenua Enata (Marquesas) and then to Hawai'i. Three of the canoes were from Hawai'i—*Hokule'a, Hawai'iloa,* and *Makali'i;* one from Tahiti—*Tahiti Nui;* one from Aotearoa—*Te Aurere;* two from Rarotonga—*Takitumu* and *Te Au o Tonga.* Tradition, archaeology, linguistics, and anthrohistory suggest that Te Fenua Enata (Marquesas), a thousand kilometers northeast of Tahiti, were peopled first in the far Pacific, perhaps from Tonga. From there the settlement pattern was to Hawai'i, Tahiti, and Aotearoa.[32]

By 1995 the voyages of the canoes from north to south, south to north, east to west, west to east had long outlived their function as simply an argument against Andrew Sharp's denial of their possibility. They had become signs of the living vitality of a long cultural past. They had become empowering metaphors of identity, and that identity was a conjoined one—not just a sense of the legitimacy of their continuities within their individual island cultures but an identity of a shared nativeness to the Sea of Islands.

Taputapuatea on Ra'iatea was an ideal space to play out the conjoined identity. It was always a space larger than itself, always reaching out as well as receiving. It was the ritual ground of "The Friendly Alliance" of islands. The mythic chants that were sung there were anthems of union and treaty. The themes of these chants were recognizable as far away as Aotearoa, Tonga, and Hawai'i. It was Hava'iki (Sacred Home) to many Tahiti (Distant Places). Taputapuatea bred other Taputapuatea by establishment in shared foundation stones. 'Oro, its god, was a power over distance.

Catharthis, it seems to me, is not a piecemeal thing. It is whole and one. It is the reduction of complexity to simplicity in a blink. Rituals, on the other hand, can be piecemeal, blaring, empty, contradictory, driven by many forces. So the ritual at Taputapuatea to welcome and send the voyaging canoes from all over the Sea of Islands was uncomfortable, hot, boring to many there. The French powers-that-be, especially in Polynesia, are inclined to speak of such rituals as "folkloric" and bend to the politics in them with some cynicism, born of the belief that they are at least a boost to tourism. At Taputapuatea, antinuclear protest songs competed electronically with ancient chants, and fundamentalist Christians expressed dismay at modern libertarians. The experiences of the thousands were kaleidoscopic. But the *catharthis* was not. As the thousands took their leave, the social memory of it was one. They had looked into the past and seen the future. They were confident that a living culture was a metaphoric thing and that they had seen the metaphor at work in their Sea of Islands.

Notes

Introduction

1. Mary Louise Pratt, *Imperial Eyes: Travel Writing and Transculturation* (London: Routledge, 1992), 5, 38.

2. Anthony Pagden, "The Effacement of Difference: Colonialism and the Origins of Nationalism in Diderot and Herder," in *After Colonialism: Imperial Histories and Postcolonial Displacements,* ed. Gyan Prakash (Princeton: Princeton University Press, 1995), 129–52.

3. Charles W. J. Withers and David N. Livingstone, "Introduction: On Geography and Enlightenment," in *Geography and Enlightenment,* ed. David Livingstone and Charles W. J. Withers (Chicago: University of Chicago Press, 1999), 4.

4. For an exemplary essay, see Seteney Khalid Shami, "Prehistories of Globalization: Circassian Identity in Motion," *Public Culture* 12, no. 1 (2000), 177–204. "Prehistory" of the diasporic Circassians in this chapter, however, largely means the nineteenth century and after. The term is also employed by James Clifford, *Routes: Travel and Translation in the Late Twentieth Century* (Cambridge: Harvard University Press, 1997), and Frederick Buell, "Nationalist Postnationalism: Globalist Discourse in Contemporary American Culture," *American Quarterly* 50, no. 3 (1998): 548–91.

5. Jerry Brotton, *Trading Territories: Mapping the Early Modern World* (Ithaca: Cornell University Press, 1998), 34.

6. Ali Bedhad, "Globalism, Again!" manuscript. My thanks to the author for allowing me to consult this work.

7. Janet Abu-Lughod, *Before European Hegemony: The World System, A.D. 1250–1350* (New York: Oxford University Press, 1989).

8. Immanuel Wallerstein, *The Modern World-System,* vol. 3, *The Second Era of Great Expansion of the Capitalist World-Economy, 1730–1840s* (London: Academic Press, 1989).

9. Saskia Sassen, *Losing Control? Sovereignty in an Age of Globalization* (New York: Columbia University Press, 1996).

10. Manuel Castells, in *The Information Age: Economy, Society and Culture,* vol. 1, *The Rise of the Network Society* (Cambridge, Mass.: Blackwell Publishers, 1996), writes that in a globalized economy, "The *dominant segments and firms, the strategic cores* of all economies are deeply connected to the world market, and their fate is a function of their performance in such a market," 95.

11. Walter D. Mignolo, *Local Histories / Global Designs: Coloniality, Subaltern Knowledges, and Border Thinking* (Princeton: Princeton University Press, 2000), 43; and He'le' Be'ji, *A New Oceania: Rediscovering Our Sea of Islands,* ed. Eric Waddell, Vijay Naidu, and Epeli Hau'ofa (Suva, Fiji: University of the South Pacific, 1993).

12. Enrique Dussel, "Beyond Eurocentricism: The World-System and the Limits of Modernity," in *The Cultures of Globalization,* ed. Fredric Jameson and Masao Miyoshi (Durham: Duke University Press, 1998), 4.

13. See, for example, Kathleen Wilson, "Pacific Modernity: Theatre, Englishness and the Arts of Discovery 1760–1800," in *The Age of Cultural Revolution: Britain and France,* ed. Colin Jones and Dror Wahrman (Berkeley: University of California Press, 2002), 62–93.

14. Edward Said, *Orientalism* (New York: Random House, 1979); and Ranajit Guha, *Dominance without Hegemony: History and Power in Colonial India* (Cambridge: Harvard University Press, 1997).

15. Castells, *The Information Age,* 66.

16. Arjun Appadurai, *Modernity at Large: Cultural Dimensions of Globalization* (Minneapolis: University of Minnesota Press, 1996).

17. John Agnew, in "We Have Always Been Global" (paper delivered at "Envisioning Globalization," University of Chicago, May 2001), writes, "What is relatively new is the relative pace at which these transactions now take place." I am grateful to the author for permission to cite this paper.

18. On Britain, see, for example, *The New Imperial History: Culture, Identity, and Modernity, 1660–1836,* ed. Kathleen Wilson (Cambridge: Cambridge University Press, forthcoming); and David Armitage, *The Ideological Origins of the British Empire* (Cambridge: Cambridge University Press, 2000).

19. Edward W. Said, *Culture and Imperialism* (New York: Alfred P. Knopf, 1993), 68, 89.

20. David Brion Davis, "Slavery—White, Black, Muslim, Christian," in *The New York Review of Books,* 5 July 2001, 51–55, review of Peter Linebaugh and Marcus Rediker, *The Many-Headed Hydra: Sailors, Slaves, Commoners, and the Hidden History of the Revolutionary Atlantic* (Beacon Press, 2001); and Lamin Sanneh, *Abolitionists Abroad: American Blacks and the Making of Modern West Africa* (Cambridge: Harvard University Press, 2001), 51.

21. P. J. Marshall, "The British in Asia: Trade to Dominion," in *The Oxford History of the British Empire* (Oxford: Oxford University Press, 1998), 493.

22. Dipesh Chakrabarty, *Provincializing Europe* (Princeton: Princeton University Press, 2000), following Enrique Dussel, argues that modernity is often made synonymous with universalism and with the secularization of European Enlightenment thought. He proposes instead "translating" other histories in order to rethink Europe's self-created myth about itself as superior, civilized, and justified in its emancipatory violence against others. See also Enrique Dussel, "Eurocentrism and Modernity (Introduction to the Frankfurt Lectures)," *boundary 2* 20, no. 3 (1993): 65–76.

23. See especially the special issue on "Indigenous Knowledge," *Humanities Research* 1 (2000), guest editor Paul Turnbull, published by the Humanities Research Centre, Canberra, Australia.

24. Castells, *The Information Age,* 8.

25. Arjun Appadurai, "Grassroots Globalization and the Research Imagination," *Public Culture* 12, no. 1 (2000): 4.

26. Homi K. Bhabha, "In a Spirit of Calm Violence," in *After Colonialism: Imperial Histories and Postcolonial Displacements,* ed. Gyan Prakash (Princeton: Princeton University Press), 326–43.

27. Mignolo, *Local Histories / Global Designs: Coloniality, Subaltern Knowledges, and Border Thinking,* 69; and Ann Thomson, *Barbary and Enlightenment: European Attitudes toward the Magreb in the Eighteenth Century* (Leiden: E. J. Brill, 1987), 102.

28. See, for example, Robert Eric Livingston, "Glocal Knowledges: Agency and Place in Literary Studies," special issue "Globalizing Literary Studies," *PMLA* 20 (January 2001): 147; and Saskia Sassen, *Losing Control? Sovereignty in an Age of Globalization.*

29. Lisbet Koerner, *Linnaeus: Nature and Nation* (Cambridge: Harvard University Press, 1999), 187.

30. Anne Salmond, *Two Worlds: First Meetings between Maori and Europeans 1642–1772* (Auckland and London: Viking, 1991), defines New Zealand's early cultural encounters as dynamic events in which *both* sides were engaged as active agents. Similarly, Nicholas Thomas, in *Entangled Objects: Exchange, Material Culture, and Colonialism in the Pacific* (Cambridge: Harvard University Press, 1991) and *In Oceania: Visions, Artifact, Histories* (Durham: Duke University Press, 1997), has traced cultural interchange in the South Pacific to reveal the indigenous appropriation of European things as well as the European appropriation of indigenous culture and artifacts.

31. Antonio Benítez-Rojo employs the term in *The Repeating Island: The Caribbean and the Postmodern Perspective,* trans. James Maraniss (Durham: Duke University Press, 1996).

32. Be'ji, *A New Oceania.*

33. Vinay Lal, "Unanchoring Islands: An Introduction to the Special Issue on 'Islands: Waterways, Flowways, Folkways,'" *Emergences* 10, no. 2 (2000): 229–40.

o n e : Mapping an Exotic World: The Global Project of Dutch Geography, circa 1700

The research for this essay began with the support of an Ahmanson-Getty Fellowship in 1999–2000. Many thanks to Peter Reill for making my stay in Los Angeles so productive and pleasant. A version of this chapter was also presented at the Simpson Center for the Humanities (University of Washington), and I would like to acknowledge the helpful comments of my colleagues, especially those of Marshall Brown.

1. John Dryden, *Amboyna: A Tragedy* (London, 1673), for which see *The Works of John Dryden,* vol. 12, ed. Vinton A. Dearing (Berkeley: University of California Press, 1994). There is some debate on the precise dating of the play, though most evidence and scholarly consensus point to the spring of 1673, shortly after the Anglo-Dutch War broke out; see *Works of John Dryden,* 12:257–58. The play's successful performance is announced by the author in his dedication to Lord Clifford (ibid., 5).

2. *Works of John Dryden,* 12:7. See also Robert Markley, "Violence and Profits on the Restoration Stage: Trade, Nationalism, and Insecurity in Dryden's *Amboyna,*" *Eighteenth-Century Life* 22 (1998): 2–17, which also provides further bibliography. On Anglo-Dutch rivalries, see Charles Wilson, *Profit and Power: A Study of England and the Dutch Wars,* 2d ed. (The Hague: M. Nijhoff, 1978).

3. Dryden notes in the prologue the formidable abilities of Dutch printers and publicists to propagate their views: "Their Pictures and Inscriptions well we know; / We may be bold one medal sure to show" (*Works of John Dryden,* 12:7). He later invokes specifically the Dutch commerce in geography—"you traffick for all the rarities of the World, and dare use none of 'em your selves" (ibid., 31)—showing a keen understanding, too, of the Republic's role as merchant rather than consumer of exoticism.

4. Cited in John Seller, *The English Pilot, The Fourth Book,* ed. Coolie Verner (Amsterdam: Theatrum Orbis Terrarum, 1967), v.

5. See Michel Foucault, *The Order of Things: An Archeology of the Human Sciences* (New York:

Pantheon, 1970); and *Power/Knowledge: Selected Interviews and Other Writings,* ed. Colin Gordon, trans. Colin Gordon et al. (New York: Pantheon, 1980). The project of Dutch geography ca. 1700 also complicates the classic (and reflexively invoked) thesis of Edward Said's *Orientalism* (New York: Pantheon, 1978) by suggesting that the Dutch described the colonial world not so much to control it as to market it—albeit to others with a vested imperial interest. Said, it is worth adding, derives his source material mostly from the later eighteenth and nineteenth centuries—a period that follows, by half a century at least, the geographic moment described in this essay. See further David N. Livingstone and Charles W. J. Withers, eds., *Geography and Enlightenment* (Chicago: University of Chicago Press, 1999); and G. S. Rousseau and Roy Porter, eds., *Exoticism in the Enlightenment* (Manchester: Manchester University Press, 1990).

6. On the East, see Femme S. Gaastra, *De geschiedenis van de VOC* (Zutphen: Walburg, 1991); and Jaap R. Bruijn and Femme S. Gaastra, "The Dutch East India Company's Shipping, 1602–1795," in a Comparative Perspective," in *Ships, Sailors and Spices: East India Companies and their Shipping in the Sixteenth, Seventeenth, and Eighteenth Century,* ed. Jaap R. Bruijn and Femme S. Gaastra, NEHA–Series III, no. 20 (Amsterdam: NEHA, 1993), 177–208, which makes a persuasive case for the relative decline, from the late seventeenth century, of the Dutch in Asia. On the West, see Henk den Heijer, *De geschiedenis van de WIC* (Zutphen: Walburg, 1994); and Pieter Emmer and Wim Klooster, "The Dutch Atlantic, 1600–1800: Expansion without Empire," *Itinerario* 23, no. 2 (1999): 48–69, which dates the republic's Atlantic decline quite precisely to the final decades of the seventeenth century. The Atlantic slave trade is surveyed in Johannes Menna Postma, *The Dutch in the Atlantic Slave Trade, 1600–1815* (Cambridge: Cambridge University Press, 1990); and see more generally Pieter Emmer, *The Dutch in the Atlantic Economy: Trade, Slavery and Emancipation* (Aldershot: Ashgate, 1998).

7. *Works of John Dryden,* 12:71. For Dutch geography and the New World, see Benjamin Schmidt, "Exotic Allies: The Dutch-Chilean Encounter and the (Failed) Conquest of America," *The Renaissance Quarterly* 52 (1999): 440–73; and "Tyranny Abroad: The Dutch Revolt and the Invention of America," *De Zeventiende Eeuw* 11 (1995): 161–74, which also discusses the publication of Las Casas.

8. Benedict Anderson, *Imagined Communities: Reflections on the Origin and Spread of Nationalism,* rev. ed. (London: Verso, 1991), 4.

9. The classic bibliographies of Dutch geography—P. A. Tiele, *Nederlandsche bibliographie van land- en volkenkunde* (Amsterdam: Frederik Muller, 1884); and *Mémoire bibliographique sur les journaux des navigateurs Néerlandais réimprimés dans les collections de De Bry et de Hulsius, et dans les collections hollandaises du XVIIe siècle* (Amsterdam: Frederick Muller, 1867)—adopt a far less generous view of the range of "geography" than does this essay and offer, accordingly, only moderate guidance. For printed work with any relevance to the Dutch experience in Asia, see John Landwehr, *VOC: A Bibliography of Publications Relating to the Dutch East India Company, 1602–1800* (Utrecht: HES, 1991); and, for books that make mention of the Americas—which applies to the geographies of Cluverius, Varenius, and Hornius, and to many of the Dutch "books of wonders"—see John Alden and Dennis Landis, eds., *European Americana: A Chronological Guide to Works Printed in Europe Relating to the Americas, 1493–1750,* 6 vols. (New York: Readex Books, 1980–97). Also useful is John Landwehr, *Studies in Dutch Books with Coloured Plates Published 1662–1875: Natural History, Topography and Travel Costumes and Uniforms* (The Hague: Junk, 1976).

10. Dutch-produced atlases are excellently catalogued in Cornelis Koeman, *Atlantes Neer-*

landici: Bibliography of Terrestrial, Maritime and Celestial Atlases and Pilot Books, Published in the Netherlands up to 1880, 6 vols. (Amsterdam: Theatrum Orvis Terrarum, 1967–85) (see also the revised edition of this work edited by P. C. J. van der Krogt ['t Goy-Houten: HES, 1997–]); for globes, see P. C. J. van der Krogt, *Globi Neerlandici: The Production of Globes in the Low Countries* (Utrecht: HES, 1993). On Dutch cartographic materials more generally, see Kees Zandvliet, *De groote waereld in 't kleen geschildert: Nederlandse kartografie tussen de middeleeuwen en de industriële revolutie* (Alphen aan den Rijn: Canaletto, 1985); and, on the exotic world more particularly, his *Mapping for Money: Maps, Plans and Topographic Paintings and their Role in Dutch Overseas Expansion during the Sixteenth and Seventeenth Centuries* (Amsterdam: Batavian Lion International, 1998).

The Brazil map reproduced here, published in Blaeu's celebrated and widely circulated "major" atlas, derives from a still larger wall map that illustrated the entire extent of the former Dutch colony in Brazil. That original printed, and generally hand-colored, map, of which two of the three extant copies come from the king of England's and the elector of Brandenburg's collections, is covered with scenes of Brazilian life and tropical nature and surrounded by columns of descriptive text, demonstrating inter alia how cartographic sources could effectively offer mini-geographies of a region.

11. The literature on painted exotica is uneven. For Post, see Joaquim de Sousa-Leão, *Frans Post, 1612–1680* (Amsterdam: A. L. van Gendt, 1973); and P. J. P. Whitehead and M. Boeseman, *A Portrait of Dutch Seventeenth-Century Brazil: Animals, Plants and People by the Artists of John Maurits of Nassau*, Royal Dutch Academy of Sciences, Natural History Monographs, 2d ser., vol. 87 (Amsterdam: North Holland, 1989), which thoroughly studies Brazilian iconography and details the oeuvre of Albert Eckhout, Post's South American colleague specializing in exotic still lifes and portraits. Valkenburg, Beeckman, Nooms, and van Edema still lack biographers and cataloguers—though see the brief treatment of Valkenburg in C. P. van Eeghen, "Dirk Valkenburg: Boekhouder-schrijver-kunstschilder voor Jonas Witsen," *Oud Holland* 61 (1946): 58–69. On exotic themes in the visual arts more broadly, see Hugh Honour, *The European Vision of America* (Cleveland, Ohio: Cleveland Museum of Art, 1975).

12. David Freedberg, "Science, Commerce, and Art: Neglected Topics at the Junction of History and Art History," in *Art in History / History in Art: Studies in Seventeenth-Century Dutch Culture*, ed. David Freedberg and Jan de Vries (Santa Monica, Calif.: Getty Center, 1991), 376–428, which also discusses Dutch natural history more generally.

13. Patterns of Dutch collecting are surveyed in Ellinoor Bergvelt et al., *De wereld binnen handbereik: Nederlandse kunst- en rariteitenverzamelingen, 1585–1735*, 2 vols. (Zwolle: Waanders, 1992). On still lifes, see the exhibition catalogue, Alan Chong and Wouter Kloek, eds., *Still-Life Painting from the Netherlands 1550–1720* (Zwolle: Waanders, 1999).

Van Kessel's *Americque* belonged to a series of Continents, which represented the four "parts" of the globe. The other paintings—of Asia, Africa, and Europe—might likewise be cited as prime examples of the exoticizing tendencies of Dutch geography. Note that each of the allegories was surrounded by sixteen smaller panels containing vignettes of "local" fauna—including, in the case of *Americque*, elephants, tigers, and unicorns.

14. See Whitehead and Boeseman, *Seventeenth-Century Brazil*, 90–94, which offers a superb reading of the paintings' naturalia; cf. the armadillo-riding "America" in Cesare Ripa, *Iconologia* (p. 605 in the 1644 Amsterdam edition of this standard text, which first appeared with the American allegory in 1603 [Rome] and then in countless editions throughout the century). Note that

while van Kessel, technically speaking, was not a "Dutch" painter—his workshop was based in Antwerp—the painting *Americque* very clearly derives from Dutch iconographic sources, as is meticulously detailed by Whitehead and Boeseman.

15. Willem Piso et al., *Historia naturalis Brasiliae* (Leiden and Amsterdam, 1648); and cf. *De Indiae utriusque re naturali et medica libri quatuordecim* (Amsterdam, 1658).

16. Johan Nieuhof, *Gedenkweerdige Brasiliaense zee- en lantreize door de voornaemste landschappen van West en OostIndien,* 2 pts. (Amsterdam, 1682). Nieuhof's volume contained dozens of similarly engraved illustrations of exotic "races," which endeavored to show the reader not only the look of local inhabitants but also the "mores" and "habits" of the region. It was not uncommon for these plates to be confused in the process of printing—misnumbered, misplaced, mislabeled—especially in non-Dutch language editions of the book.

17. P. de Lange, *Wonderen des werelds* (Amsterdam, 1671), "Aen de Leser," sig. A2 (on exotic "morsels" and "admirabilia mundi"); Simon de Vries, *D'edelste tijdkortingh der weet-geerige verstanden: of De groote historische rariteit-kamer,* 3 vols. (Amsterdam, 1682); *Wonderen soo aen als in, en wonder-gevallen soo op als ontrent de zeeën, rivieren, meiren, poelen en fonteynen* (Amsterdam, 1687), 266 (on lack of Spanish curiosity); cf. *Curieuse aenmerckingen der bysonderste Oosten West Indische verwonderens-waerdige dingen,* 4 pts. (Utrecht, 1682); and *Historisch magazijn* (Amsterdam, 1686).

18. Engelbert Kaempfer, *Amoenitatum exoticarum politico-physico-medicarum fasciculi V, quibus continentur variae relationes, observationes & descriptiones rerum Persicarum & Ulterioris Asiae* (Lemgo, 1712).

19. Petrus Nylandt, *Het schouw-toneel der aertsche schepselen, afbeeldende allerhande menschen, beesten, vogelen, visschen, &c.* (Amsterdam, 1672).

TWO: Tupaia: Polynesian Warrior, Navigator, High Priest—and Artist

1. It is well summarized in David Turnbull, "Cook and Tupaia, a Tale of Cartographic *Méconnaissance?*" in *Science and Exploration in the Pacific: European Voyages to the Southern Oceans in the Eighteenth Century,* ed. Margarette Lincoln (London: Boydell Press, 1998), 117–31.

2. *The Journals of Captain James Cook,* vol. 1, *The Voyage of the Endeavour 1768–1771,* ed. J. C. Beaglehole (Cambridge: Cambridge University Press, 1955), 117.

3. *The Endeavour Journal of Joseph Banks, 1768–1771,* vol. 1, ed. J. C. Beaglehole (Sydney: Trustees of the Public Library of New South Wales, 1962), 312–13.

4. *Journals of Captain James Cook,* 1:564.

5. Ibid., 1:288.

6. Ibid., 1:240.

7. *The Endeavour Journal of Joseph Banks,* 1:435.

8. Johann Reinhold Forster, *Observations Made during a Voyage Round the World,* ed. Nicholas Thomas et al. (Honolulu: University of Hawai'i Press, 1996), 310–11. For some of the problems of interpretation of the chart, see Gordon R. Lewthwaite, "The Puzzle of Tupaia's Map," *New Zealand Geographer* 26 (1970): 1–19; see also Ben Finney's analysis in David Woodward and G. Malcolm Lewis, eds., *The History of Cartography,* vol. 2, book 3, *Cartography in the Traditional African, American, Arctic, Australian, and Pacific Societies* (Chicago: University of Chicago Press, 1998), 446–51.

9. Sydney Parkinson, *A Journal of a Voyage to the South Sea* (London, 1773), 182.

10. *Journals of Captain James Cook,* 1:141.

11. Or so J. R. Forster reported in *Observations*, 319n.

12. [John Marra?], *Journal of the Resolution's Voyage* . . . (London, 1775), 219.

13. George Forster, *A Voyage Round the World*, vol. 1, ed. Nicholas Thomas and Oliver Berghof (Honolulu: University of Hawai'i Press, 2000), 389.

14. *Journals of Captain James Cook*, 1:442.

15. *The* Endeavour *Journal of Joseph Banks*, 1:329.

16. Ibid., 1:402.

17. Ibid., 1:376.

18. Ibid., 1:334.

19. *Journals of Captain James Cook*, 1:291.

20. See Rüdiger Joppien and Bernard Smith, *The Art of Captain Cook's Voyages*, vol. 1, *The Voyage of the* Endeavour *1768–1771* (New Haven: Yale University Press, 1985), 60, 73, 108, 126. The drawings in question are reproduced in Joppien and Smith's volume as figures 1.41, 1.42, 1.50, 1.51 (a), 1.51 (b), 1.66, 1.87, 1.172; see also plates 50 [a], 50 [b], 51.

21. Harold B. Carter, "Note on the Drawings by an Unknown Artist from the Voyage of HMS *Endeavour*," in Lincoln, ed., *Science and Exploration*, 133–34.

22. *The* Endeavour *Journal of Joseph Banks*, 1:422.

23. I am following here Greg Dening's helpful suggestion during a discussion after the presentation of an earlier version of this chapter on 6 November 1999 at the William Andrews Clark Memorial Library, Los Angeles.

24. See Douglas L. Oliver, *Ancient Tahitian Society* (Honolulu: University of Hawai'i Press, 1974), 92. For the 1777 ceremony, see *The Journals of Captain James Cook*, vol. 3, *The Voyage of the Resolution and Discovery*, ed. J. C. Beaglehole (Cambridge: Cambridge University Press, 1961), 200, 204n, 982.

25. Quoted in Oliver, *Ancient Tahitian Society*, 1269.

26. [Marra?], *Journal*, 218–19.

27. See *Journal of the Polynesian Society* 74 (1965): 128.

28. *Journals of Captain James Cook*, 1:293–94.

29. *The Journals of Captain James Cook*, vol. 2, *The Voyage of the Resolution and Adventure 1772–1775*, ed. J. C. Beaglehole (Cambridge: Cambridge University Press, 1963), 407.

30. [Marra?], *Journal*, 29.

31. See Joppien and Smith, *Art of Cook's Voyages*, figures 1.48, 1.83, 1.158 for these drawings.

32. See ibid., figure 1.42; it should be noted that the two drawings of a *marae* are not reproduced in this article.

33. See W. Kaye Lamb, ed., *The Voyage of George Vancouver 1791–1795*, vol. 1 (London, 1984), 307, 307n.–308n.

34. Ian Donaldson and Tamsin Donaldson, *Seeing the First Australians* (Sydney: G. Allen and Unwin, 1985), 15.

35. Turnbull, "Cook and Tupaia," 128.

36. *The* Endeavour *Journal of Joseph Banks*, 2:34.

37. *Journals of Captain James Cook*, 2:157n., 167, 168, 171.

38. Forster, *Journal*, 2:615.

39. Ibid., 393–94.

40. *Journals of Captain James Cook*, 2:172.

41. *Journals of Captain James Cook*, 3:73.

42. Joel Polack, *New Zealand: Being a Narrative of Travels and Adventures* (London, 1838),

2:135. I was alerted to this reference by Anne Salmond in *Two Worlds: First Meetings Between Maori and Europeans 1642–1772* (Auckland: Viking, 1991), 176, 181. The particular drawings no longer exist in recognizable form. See Pamela Bain, "A Reappraisal of the Maori Rock Drawings at Cook's Cove, Tolaga Bay," *New Zealand Archaeological Association Newsletter* 29 (1986): 167–75.

THREE: The Caribbean Islands in Atlantic Context, circa 1500–1800

1. Sidney W. Mintz, "The Caribbean Region," in *Slavery, Colonialism, and Racism*, ed. Sidney W. Mintz (New York: W. W. Norton, 1974), 46; David Eltis, *The Rise of African Slavery in the Americas* (Cambridge: Cambridge University Press, 2000), 198; G. T. Raynal, as cited in Michael Duffy, *Soldiers, Sugar, and Seapower: The British Expeditions to the West Indies and the War against Revolutionary France* (Oxford: Clarendon Press, 1987), 6.

2. Bonham C. Richardson, *The Caribbean in the Wider World, 1492–1992: A Regional Geography* (Cambridge: Cambridge University Press, 1992); Sidney W. Mintz, *Caribbean Transformations* (Chicago: Aldine, 1974), 33.

3. B. W. Higman, *Writing West Indian Histories* (London: Macmillan, 1999), 46–147.

4. Peter J. Wilson, *Crab Antics: The Social Anthropology of English-Speaking Negro Societies of the Caribbean* (New Haven, Conn.: Yale University Press, 1973); Roger D. Abrahams, *The Man-of-Words in the West Indies: Performance and the Emergence of Creole Culture* (Baltimore: Johns Hopkins University Press, 1983).

5. Irving Rouse, *The Tainos: Rise and Decline of the People who Greeted Columbus* (New Haven, Conn.: Yale University Press, 1992).

6. For modifications of Rouse, see William F. Keegan, *The People Who Discovered Columbus: The Prehistory of the Bahamas* (Gainesville: University Press of Florida, 1992); Samuel M. Wilson, ed., *The Indigenous People of the Caribbean* (Gainesville: University Press of Florida, 1997).

7. Rouse, *The Tainos*, 43–45; Cornelis N. Dubelaar, *The Petroglyphs of the Lesser Antilles, the Virgin Islands and Trinidad* (Amsterdam: Foundation for Scientific Research in the Caribbean Region, 1995); Ricardo E. Alegria, *Ball Courts and Ceremonial Plazas in the West Indies* (New Haven, Conn.: Yale University Press, 1983); Elaine Breslaw, *Reluctant Witch of Salem: Devilish Indians and Puritan Fantasies* (New York: New York University Press, 1996).

8. Rouse, *The Tainos*, 21–23, 25, 130–33; Louis Allaire, "On the Historicity of Carib Migrations in the Lesser Antilles," *American Antiquity* 45 (1980): 238–45; and Dave D. Davis and R. Christopher Goodwin, "Island Carib Origins: Evidence and Nonevidence," *American Antiquity* 55 (1990): 37–48; Douglas Taylor, *Languages of the West Indies* (Baltimore: Johns Hopkins University Press, 1977).

9. Peter Hulme, "Making Sense of the Native Caribbean," *Nieuwe West-Indische Gids* 67 (1993): 189–220; Ricardo E. Alegria, "The Use of Noxious Gas as a Weapon of War by the Tainan and Carib Indians of the Antilles," in *Proceedings of the Sixth International Congress for the Study of Pre-Columbian Cultures of the Lesser Antilles* (Pointe-à-Pitre, Guadeloupe, 1975), 82–90; Robert A. Myers, "Island Carib Cannibalism," *Nieuwe West-Indische Gids* 58 (1984): 147–84; Neil Lancelot Whitehead, "The Snake Warriors—Sons of the Tiger's Teeth: A Descriptive Analysis of Carib Warfare, ca. 1500–1820," in *The Anthropology of War*, ed. Jonathan Haas (New York: Cambridge University Press, 1990), 146–70.

10. David Watts, *The West Indies: Patterns of Development, Culture, and Environmental Change since 1492* (New York: Cambridge University Press, 1988), 53–65; Carl O. Sauer, *The Early Spanish Main* (Berkeley: University of California Press, 1966), 51–62; Elizabeth S. Wing and Elizabeth J.

Reitz, "Prehistoric Fishing Communities of the Caribbean," *Journal of New World Archaeology* 5 (1982): 13–32; Marshall B. McKusick, *The Aboriginal Canoes of the West Indies* (New Haven, Conn.: Yale University Press, 1960).

11. Watts, *The West Indies,* xviii–xix, 41, 3, 40, 118, 383; J. H. Galloway, *The Sugar Cane Industry: An Historical Geography from Its Origins to 1914* (Cambridge: Cambridge University Press, 1989), 113; B. W. Higman, *Jamaica Surveyed: Plantation Maps and Plans of the Eighteenth and Nineteenth Centuries* (Kingston: Institute of Jamaica, 1988); David Buisseret, ed., *Rural Images: Estate Maps in the Old and New Worlds* (Chicago: University of Chicago Press, 1996).

12. Richard H. Grove, *Green Imperialism: Colonial Expansion, Tropical Island Edens, and the Origins of Environmentalism, 1600–1800* (New York: Cambridge University Press, 1995), esp. 7, 9; David Quammen, *The Song of the Dodo: Island Biogeography in an Age of Extinctions* (New York: Scribner, 1996).

13. Noble David Cook, *Born to Die: Disease and New World Conquest, 1492–1650* (Cambridge: Cambridge University Press, 1998), 15–59; John R. McNeill, "The Ecological Basis of Warfare in the Caribbean, 1700–1804," in *Adapting to Conditions: War and Society in the Eighteenth Century,* ed. Martin Utlee (Tuscaloosa: University of Alabama Press, 1986), 26–42.

14. Watts, *The West Indies,* 37–40; Quammen, *The Song of the Dodo,* 18, 158, 193.

15. Watts, *The West Indies,* 104–5, 220–21, 428, 440–42; J. H. Parry, "Plantation and Provision Ground: An Historical Sketch of the Introduction of Food Crops into Jamaica," *Revista de Historia de America* 39 (1955): 1–20.

16. Michel-Rolph Trouillot, "Motion in the System: Coffee, Color, and Slavery in Eighteenth-Century Saint-Domingue," *Review* 5 (1982): 331–88; Verene Shepherd, "Livestock and Sugar: Aspects of Jamaica's Agricultural Development from the Late Seventeenth to the Early Nineteenth Century," *Historical Journal* 34 (1991): 627–43; Jerome S. Handler, "The History of Arrowroot and the Origin of Peasantries in the British West Indies," *Journal of Caribbean History* 2 (1971): 46–93; Peggy K. Liss and Franklin W. Knight, eds., *Atlantic Port Cities: Economy, Culture, and Society in the Atlantic World, 1650–1850* (Knoxville: University of Tennessee Press, 1991).

17. Grove, *Green Imperialism;* Richard Drayton, "A l'École des Français: Les Sciences et le deuxième empire Britannique (1783–1830)," *Revue Français d'Histoire d'Outre-Mer* 86 (1999): 91–118.

18. Barbara L. Solow, "Slavery and Colonization," in *Slavery and the Rise of the Atlantic System,* ed. Barbara L. Solow (New York: Cambridge University Press, 1991), 31; David Eltis, "The Volume and Structure of the Transatlantic Slave Trade: A Reassessment," *William and Mary Quarterly* 58 (2001): Table III; Stanley L. Engerman, "A Population History of the Caribbean," in *A Population History of North America,* ed. Michael R. Haines and Richard H. Steckel (New York: Cambridge University Press, 2000), 483–528.

19. David Eltis et al., eds., *The Trans-Atlantic Slave Trade: A Database on CD-ROM* (Cambridge: Cambridge University Press, 1999).

20. Philip D. Morgan, "The Cultural Implications of the Atlantic Slave Trade: African Regional Origins, American Destinations, and New World Developments," *Slavery and Abolition* 18 (1997): 123.

21. Eltis et al., *The Trans-Atlantic Slave Trade: A Database* (my calculations for Barbados); for Jamaica compare David Eltis, "The Volume and Structure of the Transatlantic Slave Trade," *William and Mary Quarterly* 58 (2001): 40; and Trevor Burnard, "E Pluribus Plures: African Ethnicities in Seventeenth- and Eighteenth-Century Jamaica," *Jamaican Historical Review* 21 (2002): 8–22.

22. Eltis, *Rise of African Slavery,* 85–113; G. Ugo Nwokeji, "African Conceptions of Gender and the Slave Traffic," *William and Mary Quarterly* 58 (2001): 47–68; David Geggus, "The French Slave Trade: An Overview," ibid., 127.

23. Morgan, "The Cultural Implications of the Atlantic Slave Trade," 133–34; Eltis, "The Volume and Structure of the Transatlantic Slave Trade," 35–37.

24. Trevor Burnard and Kenneth Morgan, "The Dynamics of the Slave Market and Slave Purchasing Patterns in Jamaica, 1655–1788," *William and Mary Quarterly* 58 (2001): 205–28.

25. John Thornton, *Africa and Africans in the Making of the Atlantic World, 1400–1800* (New York: Cambridge University Press, 1998), 195–97; cf. David Northrup, "Igbo and Myth Igbo: Culture and Ethnicity in the Atlantic World, 1600–1800," *Slavery and Abolition* 21 (2000): 1–20.

26. Morgan, "The Cultural Implications of the Atlantic Slave Trade," 136–42.

27. Eric Hobsbawm, review in *New York Review of Books,* 22 February 1973, 8, as cited in Sidney W. Mintz, "Enduring Substances, Trying Theories: The Caribbean Region as *Oikoumene,*" *Journal of Royal Anthropological Institute* (N.S.) 2 (1994): 304.

28. Sidney W. Mintz, *Sweetness and Power: The Place of Sugar in Modern History* (New York: Penguin, 1985), 48–52; B. W. Higman, "The Sugar Revolution," *Economic History Review* 53 (2000): 213–36.

29. Orlando Patterson, *The Sociology of Slavery: An Analysis of the Origins, Development, and Structure of Negro Slave Society in Jamaica* (Rutherford, N.J.: Fairleigh Dickinson University Press, 1969), 9; Richard S. Dunn, *Sugar and Slaves: The Rise of the Planter Class in the English West Indies 1624–1713* (Chapel Hill: University of North Carolina Press, 1972), 340; V. S. Naipaul, *The Overcrowded Barracoon* (New York: Knopf, 1973), 254; Mintz, "Enduring Substances, Trying Theories," 289–311; Edward K. Brathwaite, *The Development of Creole Society in Jamaica 1770–1820* (Oxford: Clarendon Press, 1971); David Buisseret and Steven G. Reinhardt, eds., *Creolization in the Americas* (College Station: Texas A&M University Press, 2000).

F O U R : Bringing India to Hand: Mapping an Empire, Denying Space

1. William Alingham, *A Short Account of the Nature and Use of Maps* (London: Benj. Barke, 1703), v.

2. James Rennell, *Memoir of a Map of Hindoostan; or the Mogul's Empire* (London, 1783), i. On Rennell's surveys in and maps of India, see Matthew H. Edney, *Mapping an Empire: The Geographic Construction of British India, 1765–1843* (Chicago: University of Chicago Press, 1997; reprint, New Delhi: Oxford University Press, 1999), 9–18, 98–104, and 134–36.

3. The phrase is Michael Warner's: *The Letters of the Republic: Publication and the Public Sphere in Eighteenth-Century America* (Cambridge: Harvard University Press, 1990).

4. Rennell, *Memoir (1783),* i (quotation), xii; Edney, *Mapping an Empire,* 13–15.

5. Reginald H. Phillimore, *Historical Records of the Survey of India,* 5 vols. (Dehra Dun: Survey of India, 1945–68), 1:213.

6. Edney, *Mapping an Empire,* 3–16.

7. Matthew H. Edney, "Cartography without 'Progress': Reinterpreting the Nature and Historical Development of Mapmaking," *Cartographica* 30, nos. 2 and 3 (1993): 54–68, provides a preliminary statement of cartographic modes.

8. [James Salmond], "Memorandum respecting a General Survey of India," ca. August 1827, Pw Jf 2744/3, marginal note, Portland Papers, University of Nottingham.

9. There is no comprehensive cartobibliography of maps of India printed in the eighteenth

century. Susan Gole, *India within the Ganges* (New Delhi: Jayaprints, 1983), is unfortunately incomplete. Because the East India Company archives in London and India contain relatively few early printed maps, their catalogues are not helpful in this regard.

10. S. Harrington, *A New Introduction to the Knowledge and Use of Maps; Rendered Easy and Familiar to any Capacity,* 4th ed. (London: S. Crowder and J. Walter, 1775), ix–x.

11. Bruno Latour, "Drawing Things Together," in *Representation in Scientific Practice,* ed. Michael Lynch and Steve Woolgar (Cambridge: MIT Press, 1990), 19–68, esp. 19 and 54 (quotations); more generally, refer to Latour's *Science in Action: How to Follow Scientists and Engineers through Society* (Cambridge: Harvard University Press, 1987).

12. Latour, "Drawing Things Together," 33 and 45 (original emphasis).

13. Famously, Latour, in *Science in Action,* 215–57, and in several later essays, uses a 1787 exchange of geographical information between the comte de Lapérouse and native inhabitants of Sakhalin to exemplify how Europeans treated maps, and so knowledge of the world, differently from non-Europeans.

14. For example, Jonathan Crary, *Techniques of the Observer: On Vision and Modernity in the Nineteenth Century* (Cambridge: MIT Press, 1990).

15. James Welsh, *Military Reminiscences* (London, 1830), 243 (original emphasis).

16. Latour, "Drawing Things Together," 30–31, 37, 48.

17. Michel Foucault, *Discipline and Punish: The Birth of the Prison,* trans. Alan Sheridan (New York: Random House, 1977). For caveats regarding the map as panopticon, see Edney, *Mapping an Empire,* 25, and Michael Charlesworth, "Mapping, the Body, and Desire: Christopher Packe's Chorography of Kent," in *Mappings,* ed. Denis Cosgrove (London: Reaktion Books, 1999), 109–24, esp. 284, n.16.

18. For such an instance, see Matthew H. Edney, "Cartographic Culture and Nationalism in the Early United States: Benjamin Vaughan and the Choice for a Prime Meridian, 1811," *Journal of Historical Geography* 20, no. 4 (1994): 384–95.

19. [Braddock Mead {John Green}], *The Construction of Maps and Globes* (London: T. Horne et al., 1717), 6.

20. Edney, *Mapping an Empire,* 46–53, 96–104. Refer to Michel Foucault, *The Order of Things: An Archaeology of the Human Science* (New York: Random House, 1970).

21. Edney, *Mapping an Empire,* 97.

22. Matthew H. Edney, "Reconsidering Enlightenment Geography and Map Making: Reconnaissance, Mapping, Archive," in *Geography and Enlightenment,* ed. David N. Livingstone and Charles W. J. Withers (Chicago: University of Chicago Press, 1999), 165–98.

23. Robert Dodsley, *The Preceptor: Containing a General Course of Education, Wherein the First Principles of Polite Learning are Laid Down* (London: R. and J. Dodsley, 1748), xi–xx.

24. Asoka SinhaRaja Tammita Delgoda, "'Nabob, Historian, and Orientalist.' Robert Orme: The Life and Career of an East India Company Servant (1728–1801)," *Journal of the Royal Asiatic Society* 3rd ser., no. 2 (1992): 363–76.

25. Adam Smith, "The History of Astronomy," in *Essays on Philosophical Subjects* (London, 1795) (reprinted in a critical edition by W. P. D. Wightmann, J. C. Bryce, and I. S. Ross, in *Adam Smith,* edited by D. D. Raphael and A. S. Skinner [Oxford: Clarendon Press, 1980], 3:33–105), §III.2–3.

26. Edney, *Mapping an Empire,* 313–16.

27. Denis Wood exposed this pernicious habit of thought in "Maps and Mapmaking," *Cartographica* 30, no. 1 (1993): 1–9.

28. James Rennell, *Memoir of a Map of Hindoostan; or the Mogul Empire,* 2d ed. (London, 1792), 224; Susan Gole reproduced and discussed Sudanando's map in *Indian Maps and Plans From Earliest Times to the Advent of European Surveys* (Bombay: Manohar, 1989), 113; Edney, *Mapping an Empire,* 79–85.

29. William Morison, Minute 15, June 1839, &10, India Military Consultations 30 September 1839 §261, F/4/1872 79616, India Office Records, British Library, 26–41.

30. Francis Buchanan, quoted by Robert Montgomery Martin, *The History, Antiquities, Topography, and Statistics of Eastern India,* 3 vols. (London: Wm. H. Allen, 1838), 2:591–92.

31. Rennell, *Memoir (1783),* ii.

32. Colin Mackenzie to George Strachey, 1 June 1817, &5, Madras Military Consultations 19 June 1817, F/4/636 17424, India Office Records, British Library, 239–49.

33. Edney, *Mapping an Empire,* 16–25, 224–35, and 261–340.

FIVE: Concealing the Bounds: Imagining the British Nation through China

Many thanks to John Brewer, Sari Gilbert, Felicity Nussbaum, and Haun Saussy for commenting on earlier versions of this paper and to the Huntington Library for helping to sponsor the research.

1. Anthony Ashley, 3rd Earl of Shaftesbury, "Plastics," in *Second Characters or the Language of Forms,* ed. Benjamin Rand (Cambridge: Cambridge University Press, 1914): 105.

2. Recent studies include Andre Gunder Frank, *ReOrient: Global Economy in the Asian Age* (Berkeley: University of California Press, 1998), esp. 108–17, 165–225; Timothy Brook, *The Confusions of Pleasure: Commerce and Culture in Ming China* (Berkeley: University of California Press, 1998); Craig Clunas, *Pictures and Visuality in Early Modern China* (Princeton: Princeton University Press, 1997); Robert Batchelor, "The European Aristocratic Imaginary and the Eastern Paradise: Europe, Islam, and China, 1100–1780" (Ph.D. diss., University of California, Los Angeles, 1999), 515–648.

3. Elaborating upon Benjamin Anderson, *Imagined Communities* (London: Verso, 1992).

4. Fernando Ortiz coined the term *transculturation* in 1940 in his *Cuban Counterpoint: Tobacco and Sugar,* trans. Harriet de Onís (Durham: Duke University Press, 1995), in opposition to Melville Herskovits's term *acculturation.*

5. For some writers, this has been a way to open up the question of translation and the boundaries of language. For other writers, the "image" of the other defines a closed paradigm. This extensive literature is somewhat influenced by Michel Foucault's *Les Mots et les choses* (Paris: Editions Gallimard, 1966) and typified by David Porter's *Ideographia: The Chinese Cipher in Early Modern Europe* (Stanford: Stanford University Press, 2001), which considers "China as a construct of the Western imagination," depictions of which "reflected the collective longings and fantasies of the societies that produced and consumed them" (15). He contrasts as inverted tropes of a unified discourse the desire of seventeenth-century Jesuits to "know" China by using inherited frameworks about order, linguistic stability, and lineage descent, with the "projected fantasies" of "unremitting exoticism of total illegibility" described by aesthetes like Shaftesbury and commercial commentators like Daniel Defoe (134–35).

6. Donald Lach and Edwin van Kley, *Asia in the Making of Europe,* vol. 3, *A Century of Advance,* book 4, *East Asia* (Chicago: University of Chicago Press, 1993), 1890–1904; and Frank, *ReOrient.*

7. English sources from the 1730s, which will be the primary concern of this paper, include

translations of Jesuit works in Jean-Baptiste Du Halde's *Description géographique* (Paris: P. G. Lemercier, 1735; The Hague: H. Scheurleer, 1736; London: E. Cave, 1738–41; London: J. Watts, 1736, 1741), and Louis Le Comte's (1655–1728) *Nouveaux mémoires* (Paris: J. Anisson, 1696, 1697; Amsterdam: de Lorme, 1697; London: B. Tooke, 1697, 1698, 1699; London: J. Hughes, 1737).

8. Lydia Liu, "Robinson Crusoe's Earthenware Pot," *Critical Inquiry* 25, no. 4 (Summer 1999): 728–57; Porter, *Ideographia*, 192–240; Elizabeth Kowaleski-Wallace, *Consuming Subjects: Women, Shopping, and Business in the Eighteenth Century* (New York: Columbia University Press, 1997); and Bruce Lenman, "The English and Dutch East India Companies and the Birth of Consumerism in the Augustan World," *Eighteenth-Century Life* 1 (February 1990): 47–65.

9. J. G. A. Pocock, "The Varieties of Whiggism from Exclusion to Reform," in *Virtue, Commerce, and History* (Cambridge: Cambridge University Press, 1985), 231–32.

10. Henry St. John, Viscount Bolingbroke, "The Idea of a Patriot King," in David Armitage, ed., *Bolingbroke: Political Writings* (Cambridge: Cambridge University Press, 1997), 219–20.

11. See Bolingbroke's "On the Spirit of Patriotism" (1736), with its emphasis on "they who engross almost the whole reason of the species, who are born to instruct, to guide, and to preserve; who are designed to be the tutors and the guardians of human kind" (Armitage, *Bolingbroke*, 193).

12. See Carlo Ginzburg, "Killing a Chinese Mandarin: The Moral Implications of Distance," *Critical Inquiry* 21, no. 1 (Autumn 1994): 46–61; and Luc Boltanski, *Distant Suffering: Morality, Media and Politics,* trans. Graham Burchell (Cambridge: Cambridge University Press, 1999), 7.

13. Andrew Fletcher, "Speeches by a member of Parliament," in *Andrew Fletcher: Political Works,* ed. John Robertson (Cambridge: Cambridge University Press, 1997), 164. Fletcher cites Temple's "Of Heroick Virtue" in the speech. The question here is one of the independence of the Scottish parliament rather than the English gentry. The reference to "kingdoms" is based upon the confusion arising from some Jesuit texts that various Chinese provinces had been separate kingdoms in antiquity and that governors of provinces were often referred to in travel accounts as "vice-roys."

14. Quentin Skinner, "The Principles and Practice of Opposition: The Case of Bolingbroke versus Walpole," in *Historical Perspectives: Studies in English Thought and Society in Honour of J. H. Plumb,* ed. Neil McKendrick (London: Europa Publications, 1974); Christine Gerrard, *The Patriot Opposition to Walpole: Politics, Poetry, and National Myth 1725–1742* (Oxford: Clarendon Press, 1994); Robert Harris, *A Patriot Press: National Politics and the London Press in the 1740s* (Oxford: Clarendon Press, 1993).

15. Letter from Sir Thomas Robinson to Lord Carlisle, 23 December 1734, in *The Manuscripts of The Earl of Carlisle, Historical Manuscripts Commission,* 15th rpt., app. pt VI (London: HM Stationery Office, 1897), 143–44.

16. The possible exception here is Sir Thomas Pelham-Holles, 1st Duke of Newcastle.

17. For a more elaborate description, see Robert Batchelor, "The European Aristocratic Imaginary and the Eastern Paradise," 925–1122.

18. For the other "customs," which thrived on taxation boundaries, internal circulation patterns, and networks of collection, see John Brewer, *Sinews of Power: War, Money and the English State 1688–1783* (New York: Alfred A. Knopf, 1989).

19. Sir William Temple, "Upon the Gardens of Epicurus," *Miscellanea: The Second Part* (London: R. Simpson, 1690), 58.

20. Qian Zhongshu, "China in the English Literature of the 17th Century," *Quarterly Bulletin of Chinese Bibliography,* n.s. 1, no. 4 (December 1940): 376; Patrick Conner, "China and the Landscape Garden: Reports, Engravings and Misconceptions," *Art History* 2, no. 4 (December 1979): 430.

21. John Locke, *Essay Concerning Human Understanding,* book II, chap. 22, sec. 2–7.

22. Temple, "Upon the Gardens of Epicurus," 56.

23. Temple, "Upon the Gardens of Epicurus," 56.

24. Sir William Temple, "Of Heroic Virtue," *Miscellanea: The Second Part,* 37.

25. Temple, "Of Heroic Virtue," 28.

26. Anonymous, "Lord Cobhams Gardens 1738," folder 53, Box 8, Stowe Temple Manorial Papers, Huntington Library.

27. Samuel Boyse, "The Triumphs of Nature: A Poem, on the Magnificent Gardens at Stowe in Buckinghamshire," *Gentleman's Magazine* (July 1742): 382, ll. 283, 287.

28. *World,* vol. 1, no. 12 (22 March 1753), 60.

29. *World,* vol 3, no. 118 (3 April 1755), 76–77. David Porter's *Ideographia* misses the complex intertextuality of these articles, seeing them as simply discursive attacks on "Chinese taste" rather than interventions in a very particular historical struggle over defining the limits and achievements of "British" print culture in relation to both Europe and the global trade in images that emerges from the initial patriotic use of Chinese gardens in the 1730s. He does not cite any of the extensive writings on gardens that form the counterpoint to chinoiserie taste in the *World,* jumping in his own discussion from Temple's 1685 essay to Sir William Chambers's famous 1757 *Designs of Chinese Buildings.*

30. Linda Colley sees British patriotism as ultimately conservative, a tool for promoting "stable government by a virtuous, able and authentically British elite" (*Britons: Forging the Nation 1707–1837* [New Haven, Conn.: Yale University Press, 1992], 145), while Hugh Cunningham finds patriotism used as a language to critique that very elite ("The Language of Patriotism," in *Patriotism: The Making and Unmaking of British National Identity,* vol. 1, *History and Politics,* ed. Raphael Samuel [London: Routledge, 1989], 57–89).

SIX: The Global Parasol: Accessorizing the Four Corners of the World

1. Katherine S. Van Eerde, *John Ogilby and the Taste of His Times* (Folkestone, Kent: Wm Dawson & Sons, 1976), 23, 74–75.

2. See Joseph Roach, "The Enchanted Island: Vicarious Tourism in Restoration Adaptations of *The Tempest,*" in *"The Tempest" and Its Travels,* ed. Peter Hulme and William H. Sherman (London: Reaktion Books, 2000), 60–70, and "The Artificial Eye: Augustan Theatre and the Empire of the Visible," in *The Performance of Power: Theatrical Discourse and Politics,* ed. Sue-Ellen Case and Janelle Reinelt (Iowa City: University of Iowa Press, 1991), 131–45.

3. Van Eerde, *John Ogilby,* 103.

4. Laura Brown, *Fables of Modernity: Literature and Culture in the English Eighteenth Century* (Ithaca: Cornell University Press, 2001), esp. chap. 5, 177–220; Mita Choudhury, *Interculturalism and Resistance in the London Theatre, 1660–1800: Identity, Performance, Empire* (Lewisburg, Pa.: Bucknell University Press, 2000); Bridget Orr, *Empire on the English Stage, 1660–1714* (Cambridge: Cambridge University Press, 2001); and Felicity Nussbaum, *The Limits of the Human: Fictions of Anomaly, Race, and Gender in the Long Eighteenth Century* (Cambridge: Cambridge University Press, 2003).

5. Arjun Appadurai, "Disjunction and Difference in the Global Cultural Economy," *Public Culture* 2, no. 2 (1990): 1–24.

6. Philip H. Highfill Jr., Kalman A. Burnim, and Edward A. Langhans, eds., *A Biographical*

Dictionary of Actors, Actresses, Musicians, Dancers, Managers, and Other Stage Personnel in London, 1660–1800, 16 vols. (Carbondale: Southern Illinois University Press, 1973–93), s.v. "Betterton, Thomas."

7. See "The Performance," in *The Cambridge Companion to English Restoration Theatre,* ed. Deborah Payne Fiske (Cambridge: Cambridge University Press, 2000), 24.

8. Quoted in *My Head Is a Map: Essays and Memoirs in Honour of R. V. Tooley* (London: Carta Press, 1973), xiv.

9. *The Tatler,* 3 vols., ed. Donald F. Bond (Oxford: Clarendon Press, 1987), 2:421. Subsequent references will be given in the text.

10. See Erin Mackie, *Market à la Mode: Fashion, Commodity, and Gender in the* Tatler *and the* Spectator (Baltimore: Johns Hopkins University Press, 1997).

11. See Jessica Munns and Penny Richards, eds., *The Clothes That Wear Us: Essays on Dressing and Transgressing in Eighteenth-Century Culture* (Newark: University of Delaware Press, 1999).

12. John Greenhill (1644–76), chalk drawing of Betterton as Solyman in Davenant's *The Siege of Rhodes,* at Kingston Lacy, Winborne Minster.

13. In an oft-cited passage, the narrator of Aphra Behn's *Oroonoko* claims to have returned from Surinam with a feathered vestment worn by Native Americans—"glorious Wreaths for their Heads, Necks, and Arms, whose Tinctures are unconceivable"—as a gift to the wardrobe department of the King's Theatre, where it was used to dress the eponymous character in Dryden and Howard's *The Indian Queen:* Aphra Behn, *Oroonoko; or, The Royal Slave* (London, 1688), 2.

14. Linda Colley, *Britons: Forging the Nation 1707–1837* (New Haven, Conn.: Yale University Press, 1992), 33–35.

15. Brown, *Fables of Modernity,* 199.

16. John Ogilby, preface to *Africa* (London: Printed by Tho. Johnson for the Author, 1670). The full title bespeaks the scope of this volume and its companions: *Africa: Being an Accurate Description of the Regions of Aegypt, Barbary, Lybia, and Belledulgerid, The Land of the Negroes, Guinea, Aethiopia, and the Abyssines, With all the Adjacent Islands, either in the Mediterranean, Atlantick, Southern, or Oriental Sea, belonging thereunto, With several Demonstrations of their Coasts, Harbors, Creeks, Rivers, Lakes, Cities, Towns, Castles, and Villages, Their Customs, Modes, and Manners, Languages, Religions, and Inexhaustible Treasure; with their Governments and Policy, variety of Trade and Barter, and also their Wonderful Plants, Beasts, Birds, and Serpents. Collected and Translated from the most Authentic Authors, and Augmented with later Observations; Illustrated by Notes, and Adorn'd with Peculiar Maps, and proper Sculptures.*

17. *Pinacotheca Bettertonaeana: or, a Catalogue of the Books, Prints, Drawings, and Paintings of Mr Thomas Betterton, that Celebrated Comedian, lately Deceased* (London, 1710).

18. Richard Ligon, *A True & Exact History of the Island of Barbados* (London, 1657), commendatory verse by George Walshe. Ligon's account of Afro-Caribbean music is more open-minded than Steele's: "So strangely they vary their time, as 'tis a pleasure to the most curious eares, and it was to me one of the strangest noyses that ever I heard made of one tone; and if they had the variety of tune, which gives greater scope in musick, as they have in time, they would do wonders in that Art."

19. *The Royal Commentaries of Peru, in Two Parts, translated by Sir Paul Rycaut from Garicolaso de la Vega* (London, 1688).

20. *Pinacotheca Bettertonaeana,* 2.

21. *Pinacotheca Bettertonaeana,* 17–19.

22. *America: Being the Latest and most accurate description of the New World, containing The Original Inhabitants, and the Remarkable Voyages thither* (London, 1671), frontispiece, 214.

23. *Asia, the First Part: Being an Accurate Description of Persia, and the Several Provinces thereof. The Vast Empire of the Great Mogul, and other Parts of India* (London, 1673), 173.

24. *Atlas Chinensis: Being the Second Part of a Relation of Remarkable Passages in two Embassies from the East India of the United Provinces* (London: Printed by Thomas Johnson for the Author, 1671), 422.

25. *Biographical Dictionary,* s.v. "Bracegirdle, Anne."

26. Marga Weber, *Baldachine und Statuenschreine* (Rome: Giorgio Bretschneider, 1990), 85–105.

27. Donald F. Bond, ed., *The Spectator,* 5 vols. (Oxford: Clarendon Press, 1965), 2:178.

28. For the social semiotics of this particular intersection of women, children, and feathers, see Joseph Roach, *Cities of the Dead: Circum-Atlantic Performance* (New York: Columbia University Press, 1996), 123–31.

29. George C. D. Odell, *Shakespeare from Betterton to Irving,* 2 vols. (1920; reprint, New York: Dover, 1966), 1:207.

30. Ogilby, quoting Dryden, in *America,* 15.

S E V E N : Oceans and Floods: Fables of Global Perspective

1. Samuel Johnson, *The Vanity of Human Wishes,* in *The Yale Edition of the Works of Samuel Johnson,* vol. 6, *Poems,* ed. E. L. McAdam Jr., with George Milne (New Haven, Conn.: Yale University Press, 1964), ll. 1–2, 5–6, and 345–46. Subsequent references to the poem are to this edition.

2. *The Poetical Works of Edward Young,* vol. 2 (London: Bell and Daldy, 1866), 165. Subsequent references to Young's poetry will be to this edition.

3. George Rudé, *Hanoverian London 1714–1808* (Berkeley: University of California Press, 1971), 20–33.

4. Jonathan Swift, *Gulliver's Travels,* in *Gulliver's Travels and Other Writings,* ed. Louis A. Landa (Boston: Houghton Mifflin, 1960), 5.

5. John Denham, *Cooper's Hill,* in *The Poetical Works of Sir John Denham,* ed. Theodore Howard Banks Jr. (New Haven, Conn.: Yale University Press, 1928), ll. 159–64. Subsequent references to this poem are to this edition.

6. John Dryden, "An Account of the Ensuing Poem, in a Letter to the Honorable, Sir Robert Howard," preface to *Annus Mirabilis. The Year of Wonders, 1666,* in *The Poems and Fables of John Dryden,* ed. James Kinsley (Oxford: Oxford University Press, 1958), 45. Subsequent references to Dryden's poems are to this edition.

7. Michael McKeon documents the poem's adoption of the contemporary modes and assumptions of eschatological prophecy (chap. 5) in a way that emphasizes the cultural codependency of metaphysics and nationalist apologia that I am seeking to trace from this poem through to *The Vanity of Human Wishes.* See *Politics and Poetry in Restoration England: The Case of Dryden's* Annus Mirabilis (Cambridge: Harvard University Press, 1975), chaps. 1 and 3.

8. Steven N. Zwicker provides a close reading of the "technique of denial and misrepresentation" that for him defines Dryden's poetic form as well as his characterization of the Stuart monarchy in these works. See *Politics and Language in Dryden's Poetry: The Arts of Disguise* (Princeton:

Princeton University Press, 1984), esp. 39–43. For a more extended reading of such contradictory structures in Dryden's poetry, see Laura Brown, "The Ideology of Restoration Poetic Form: John Dryden," *PMLA* 97 (1982): 395–407.

9. Joseph Roach sees this as a recurrent trope "in the circum-Atlantic literature and orature of imperial surrogation, whereby the past and present must be reinvented to serve the needs of a hallucinatory future." See *Cities of the Dead: Circum-Atlantic Performance* (New York: Columbia University Press, 1996).

10. For other contemporary references to Peru in a similar context, see the note to this line in *The Poems of Samuel Johnson*, 2d ed., ed. David Nichol Smith and Edward L. McAdam (Oxford: Clarendon Press, 1974).

11. Daniel Defoe, *Review* (3 February 1713), in *Defoe's Review, Reproduced from the Original Editions*, intro. by Arthur Wellesley Secord (New York: Columbia University Press, 1938).

EIGHT: Proxies of Power: Woman in the Colonial Archive

1. Madeleine Albright, "Charting Further Gains in the Status and Rights of Women," remarks delivered at Center for National Policy Breakfast, Washington, D.C., 2 August 1995, in *UN Fourth-World Conference on Women Press Kit* (Washington: U.S. Dept of State, 1995).

2. Gayatri Chakravorty Spivak, *A Critique of Postcolonial Reason: Towards a History of the Vanishing Present* (Cambridge: Harvard University Press, 1999), 91.

3. Liu Kang, "Is There an Alternative to (Capitalist) Globalization? The Debate about Modernity in China," in *The Cultures of Globalization*, ed. Fredric Jameson and Masao Miyoshi (Durham: Duke University Press, 1998), 167.

4. Spivak, *A Critique of Postcolonial Reason*, 239. For a more thorough discussion of the "experiment" in Bengal, see Ranajit Guha, *A Rule of Property for Bengal: An Essay on the Idea of Permanent Settlement* (Durham: Duke University Press, 1996).

5. "Representation to the Nabob, Governor General, and the Gentlemen of the Council," *Eleventh Report from the Select Committee on the Administration of Justice in India*, in *Reports from Committees of the House of Commons, 1775–1801*, First Series, VI, 1803.741–42. Further references to material included in this report are cited in the text as *ER*, followed by page numbers.

6. For an account of the zamindar's imperial functions under the Mughals and the transformation of these under the English, see John R. McClane, *Land and Local Kingship in Eighteenth-Century Bengal* (Cambridge: Cambridge University Press, 1993), 8–15. This work proved to be an invaluable source for the family history of the Burdwan Raj.

7. For a concise account of the trial and its main players, see David Musselwhite, "The Trial of Warren Hastings," in *Literature, Politics, and Theory: Papers from the Essex Conference*, ed. Francis Barker et al. (London: Methuen, 1986), 77–103.

8. Extract of Revenue Consultations, *Eleventh Report*, 733.

9. John Shore, Minute of 18 June 1789, in *The Fifth Report from the Select Committee of the House of Commons on the Affairs of the East India Company, 1812*, 3 vols., ed. Walter Firminger (New York: Augustus M. Kelley, 1917), 71–81.

10. In 1776, Francis went on to draft a minute that outlined the guidelines under which the company would play ward for the three categories of incapable zamindars, but at this point, he is extremely sympathetic to the Rani and rallies to her cause. See extracted discussion of Philip Francis's Minute in *The Fifth Report*, 74.

11. "The Burdwan Ranny's Petition Dissected and Answered by Mr. Graham," *Eleventh Report*, 737–40.

12. I have not seen the format of Graham's original letter and am not aware if it exists, but the *Bengal Revenue Consultations,* 6 January to 15 February 1775 (Shelfmark 1OR/Z/P/662 1775) in the India Office Library has transcribed the letter in this format. All five council members have signed underneath the text of the letter thereby attesting to its status as a true copy and permitting it to be forwarded to the Court of Directors in London.

13. Nancy Armstrong, *Desire and Domestic Fiction: A Political History of the Novel* (New York: Oxford University Press, 1987), 111–13.

14. Letter from Graham to the Council, 6 January 1775, *Eleventh Report,* 735.

15. *Eleventh Report,* 737.

16. The coexistence of two timelines is itself a sign of the epistemic upheaval. In usual proceedings, company servants use the Bengali calendar to record local revenues and transactions with the natives but use the Christian calendar for all their general communications with each other.

17. See P. J. Marshall, *The Impeachment of Warren Hastings* (Oxford: Oxford University Press, 1965), 5–7.

18. Letter from the Rani of Burdwan to the Council, 10 March 1775, *Eleventh Report,* 746.

19. *Eleventh Report,* 751.

20. For an excellent comprehensive account of this phenomenon and the various cultural sites where such comparisons were staged, see Felicity Nussbaum's *Torrid Zones: Maternity, Sexuality, and Empire in Eighteenth-Century English Narratives* (Baltimore: Johns Hopkins University Press, 1995).

21. For a genealogy of this term see Perry Anderson, *Lineages of the Absolutist State* (London: NLB, 1974); and Guha, *Rule of Property,* 13–25. Althusser's reading of Montesquieu as the initiator of the new method of universalist history is also worth noting for this particular blind spot: "[N]ever before had anyone had the daring to reflect on *all the customs and laws of all the nations of the world.*" See Louis Althusser, *Montesquieu, Rousseau, Marx: Politics and History* (London: Verso, 1982), 19. Althusser argues that the real object of Montesquieu's work is law and that "despotism" is misrecognized as Eurocentrism for it is merely an "oriental myth" that allowed Montesquieu to posit what could happen to monarchy gone wrong in *Europe:* "It is the limit government, and already the limit of government. It is easy to guess that the example of real countries is only providing Montesquieu with a pretext" (75). This is a puzzling deflection of colonialism in what is otherwise a brilliant reading of Montesquieu's abdication of politics itself.

22. Ranajit Guha, "The Prose of Counter-Insurgency," in *Selected Subaltern Studies,* ed. Ranajit Guha and Gayatri Chakravorty Spivak (New York: Oxford University Press, 1988), 47.

23. Harry Verelst, *A View of the Rise, Progress, and Present State of the English Government in Bengal* (London: J. Nourse, 1772).

24. See Samuel Davis's letter to the president and members of the Board of Revenue of 31 January 1794, about Tejchand's imprisonment as a "defaulter to government," in *West Bengal District Records (New Series): Burdwan Letters Issued, 1788–1800,* ed. Ranajit Guha and A. Mitra (Calcutta: Sree Saraswaty Press, 1955), 98–99.

25. See chap. 5 in Betty Joseph, *Reading the East India Company, 1720–1840: Colonial Currencies of Gender* (Chicago: University of Chicago Press, 2003).

26. See Guha, *Rule of Property,* 55.

27. Jean-François Lyotard, *The Differend: Phrases of Dispute,* trans. Georges Van Den Abbeele (Minneapolis: University of Minnesota Press, 1988), 9.

N I N E : The Narrative of Elizabeth Marsh: Barbary, Sex, and Power

1. I have used the copy in the British Library, London, which contains manuscript notes. *The Female Captive* was published by Charles Bathurst of Fleet Street, London, sold for five shillings, and was printed by subscription. Twenty-six of the eighty-three subscribers were women. For James Crisp's account of the capture, see *Public Record Office,* London (henceforward PRO), SP 71/20, fol. 67.

2. Elizabeth Marsh, "Narrative of Her Captivity in Barbary," Item 170/604, unpaginated (hereafter *Female Captive MS*), Charles E. Young Research Library, University of California, Los Angeles. I am grateful to Felicity Nussbaum for referring me to this manuscript.

3. Joe Snader, "The Oriental Captivity Narrative and Early English Fiction," *Eighteenth-Century Fiction* 9 (1997), 267–98.

4. See my *Captives: Britain, Empire, and the World 1600–1850* (London: Jonathan Cape, 2002), 43–72.

5. For what appears to be the sole extant example, see *L'Annotation ponctuelle de la description de voyage étonnante et de la captivité remarquable et triste durant douze ans de moi Maria ter Meetelen* (Paris: Institut des hautes-études marocaines, 1956), a translation of the 1748 Dutch original.

6. John Dunton, *A True Journall of the Sally Fleet* (London, 1637), appendix.

7. *A Relation of the Whole Proceedings concerning the Redemption of the Captives in Argier and Tunis* (London, 1647), 17 seq.; PRO, SP 71/3, fol.182.

8. *Female Captive,* 1:18.

9. For European-wide patterns of female Barbary captivity, see Bartolomé Bennassar and Lucile Bennassar, *Les chrétiens d'Allah: L'histoire extraordinaire des renégats XVIe et XVIIe siècles* (Paris: Perrin, 1989), 289–307.

10. Calculations based on *Relation of the Whole Proceedings.*

11. For Shea, see *A Description of the Nature of Slavery among the Moors* (London, 1721), 18–19; John Braithwaite, *The History of the Revolutions in the Empire of Morocco* (London, 1729), 191 and 282.

12. PRO, SP 71/20, fols. 65 and 115.

13. *Female Captive MS,* 137. For valuable discussions of Wortley Montagu's writings, see Billie Melman, *Women's Orients: English Women and the Middle East, 1718–1918* (London: Macmillan, 1992); and Ruth B. Yeazell, *Harems of the Mind: Passages of Western Art and Literature* (New Haven, Conn.: Yale University Press, 2000).

14. *Female Captive,* 1:12–13, 42.

15. Ibid., 2:18–94.

16. "The Oriental Captivity Narrative," 268. I have found Snader's analysis of the evolution of Barbary captivity narratives in Britain most useful. It is his apparent assumption that the Orientalist motifs certainly present in some of these were necessarily linked with an imperial intent that I am questioning.

17. K. N. Chaudhuri, "From the Barbarian and the Civilised to the Dialectics of Colour: An Archaeology of Self-Identities," in *Society and Ideology: Essays in South Asian History,* ed. Peter Robb (Delhi: Oxford University Press, 1994), 4, 22–48.

18. Kenan Malik, *The Meaning of Race: Race, History and Culture in Western Society* (Basingstoke: Macmillan, 1996), 231.

19. English-language novels of the time that do refer to female captives usually stress their continental European rather than their British origins. See, for instance, Penelope Aubin, *The Noble Slaves: or, the Lives and Adventures of Two Lords and Two Ladies* (London: E. Bell et al., 1722).

20. Maija Jansson, ed., *Proceedings in Parliament, 1614* (Philadelphia: American Philosophical Society, 1988), 200; "To the Right Honourable the Commons," Guildhall Library, London, Broadside 12.12.

21. *A Relation of Seven Years Slavery under the Turks* (London, 1640), 50; C. R. Pennell, ed., *Piracy and Diplomacy in Seventeenth Century North Africa: The Journal of Thomas Baker* (London: Associated University Presses, 1989), 62.

22. *Robert Boyle*, 34; *The Present State of the Ottoman Empire* (London, 1668), 81.

23. See, for instance, Joseph Morgan's parallel between the reputed prevalence of sodomy in North Africa and the supposed English appetite for corporal punishment of young boys (*A Compleat History of the Piratical States of Barbary* [London, 1750], 98).

24. For the argument that sodomy accusations against the Barbary and Ottoman worlds were about "othering," see Nabil Matar, *Turks, Moors, and Englishmen in the Age of Discovery* (New York: Columbia University Press, 1999), 109–27.

25. For an interesting parallel, see the modern captivity narrative of Brian Keenan, an Irishman held in Beirut. Of his Muslim captors there, he writes: "For our captors homosexuality was a vice exclusive to the West . . . Our captors' obsession with God and sex were not about religion or morality. They were ciphers for their own powerlessness" (*An Evil Cradling* [London: Hutchinson, 1992], 201–2).

26. Useful guides to current revisionism on the Ottoman empire include Donald Quataert, *The Ottoman Empire, 1700–1922* (Cambridge: Cambridge University Press, 2000); Virginia H. Aksan, "Locating the Ottomans among Early Modern Empires," *Journal of Early Modern History* 3 (1999): 103–34; and Halil Inalcik and Donald Quataert, eds., *An Economic and Social History of the Ottoman Empire 1300–1914* (Cambridge: Cambridge University Press, 1994).

27. Rawlinson c.145, fol. 21, Bodleian Library, Oxford.

28. By the same token, whereas British elite males had occasionally chosen to be painted in "Turkish" dress before 1760, thereafter this was almost exclusively a female style of masquerade. See Aileen Ribeiro, *The Dress Worn at Masquerades in England, 1730 to 1790, and Its Relation to Fancy Dress in Portraiture* (London: Garland, 1984), 220–42.

29. *Female Captive MS.*

30. See Daniel Defoe, *Roxana: The Fortunate Mistress*, ed. Jane Jack (London: Oxford University Press, 1964), 173–74.

31. *Monthly Review* XLI (1769), 156; see also *Critical Review* 28 (1769), 212–17.

32. For Milbourne Marsh's will, see PRO, PROB 11/1053.

33. For Sidi Muhammad's own account of this incident, see PRO, ADM 1/383, fols. 514–15.

34. For a full development of these points, see my *Captives*.

35. Thus the British government refused to accede to international pressure to convert its naval bombardment of Algiers in 1816 into a full-blown land invasion and territorial conquest.

TEN: The Lama and the Scotsman: George Bogle in Bhutan and Tibet, 1774–1775

I would like to thank Linda Colley, Matthew Edney, Nigel Leask, Peter Marshall, and John Mullan for their helpful comments on this piece.

1. Tzvetan Todorov, *La Conquête de L'Amérique* (Paris: Seuil, 1982), 138.

2. George Bogle to Warren Hastings, 27 April 1775, MSS Eur E 226/23, Oriental and India Office Collections [OIOC], British Library.

3. L. Petech, "The Missions of Bogle and Turner according to the Tibetan Texts," *T'oung Pao* 39 (1949–50): 330–46.

4. John Riddy, "Warren Hastings: Scotland's Benefactor?" in *The Impeachment of Warren Hastings: Papers from a Bicentenary Commemoration,* ed. Geoffrey Carnall and Colin Nicholson (Edinburgh: Edinburgh University Press, 1989), 35.

5. See T. M. Devine, *The Tobacco Lords: A Study of the Tobacco Merchants of Glasgow and Their Trading Activities, 1740–90* (Edinburgh: John Donald, 1975; reprint, Edinburgh University Press, 1990); Andrew Hook and Richard B. Sher, eds., *The Glasgow Enlightenment* (East Linton: Tuckwell Press, 1995).

6. Carolyn Marie Peters, "Glasgow's Tobacco Lords: An Examination of Wealth Creators in the Eighteenth Century" (Ph.D. diss., Glasgow University, 1990), 257.

7. Ibid., 80.

8. Ibid., 216; Hook and Sher, *The Glasgow Enlightenment,* 87.

9. "Account sales of the following Effects belonging to the Estate of the late George Bogle," 26 October 1781, Bogle Collection, Mitchell Library [ML], Glasgow.

10. Jane Rendall, *The Origins of the Scottish Enlightenment* (London: Macmillan, 1978), 14.

11. Robert Crawford, *Devolving English Literature* (Oxford: Oxford University Press, 1992), 17.

12. See J. L. Brockington, "Warren Hastings and Orientalism," in Carnall and Nicholson, *Bicentenary Commemoration,* 91–108.

13. Charles Wilkins, *The Bhagvat Geeta* (London: C. Norce, 1785), 13.

14. "Private Commissions to Mr Bogle," MSS Eur E 226/6, OIOC.

15. Warren Hastings to George Bogle, 8 September 1774, Additional MS 29.117: 63v, British Library.

16. MSS Eur E 226/76, OIOC, British Library.

17. George Bogle to Robin, 15 February 1777, ML.

18. Clements R. Markham, *Narratives of the Mission of George Bogle to Tibet and of the Journey of Thomas Manning to Lhasa* (London: Trübner, 1876), cli.

19. MSS Eur E 226/14, OIOC, British Library.

20. George Bogle to David Anderson, 20 June 1774, Additional MS 45.421: 30v, British Library.

21. Letterbook June 1774–May 1775, MSS Eur E 226/77 (c), OIOC.

22. Adam Ferguson, *An Essay on the History of Civil Society,* ed. Fania Os-Salzberger (Cambridge: Cambridge University Press, 1995), 75–76, 94, 194–95.

23. Ibid., 100.

24. Ibid., 103.

25. Letterbook November 1774–March 1775, MSS Eur E 226/80, OIOC, British Library.

26. Ibid.

27. George Bogle to Robin, 20 January 1776, ML.

28. See my article, "The Sentimental Ambassador: the Letters of George Bogle from Bengal,

Bhutan and Tibet, 1770–1781," in *Epistolary Selves: Letters and Letter-Writers, 1600–1945,* ed. Rebecca Earle (Aldershot: Ashgate, 1999), 79–94.

29. Letterbook November 1774–March 1775, MSS Eur E 226/80, OIOC, British Library.

30. See Jean-Jacques Rousseau, *A Discourse on Inequality,* trans. Maurice Cranston (Harmondsworth: Penguin, 1984), 152.

31. Peter France, "Primitivism and Enlightenment: Rousseau and the Scots," *The Yearbook of English Studies* 15 (1985): 65.

32. George Bogle to Bess, 5 March 1775, MSS Eur E 226/25, OIOC, British Library.

33. See Peter Bishop, *The Myth of Shangri-La: Tibet, Travel Writing, and the Western Creation of Sacred Landscape* (London: Athlone Press, 1989), 35.

34. MSS Eur E 226/13, OIOC, British Library.

35. France, "Primitivism and Enlightenment," 64. Laurie Hovell McMillan has argued that the contradictions evident here reflect the "uneasiness of the alliance between mercantilism and humanism." See her "Enlightenment Travels: The Making of Epiphany in Tibet," in *Writes of Passage: Reading Travel Writing,* ed. James Duncan and Derek Gregory (London: Routledge, 1999), 53.

36. John Bell, *Travels from St. Petersburg in Russia to Diverse Parts of Asia* (Glasgow: Robert and Andrew Foulis, 1763), 1:284, 255.

37. George Bogle to George Bogle (Sr.), 8 January 1775, MSS Eur E 226/ 77 (i), OIOC, British Library.

38. Ibid.

39. Ferguson, *Civil Society,* 149.

40. Markham, *Narratives,* 110.

41. MSS Eur E 226/65, OIOC, British Library.

42. Ibid.

43. Ibid.

44. Markham, *Narratives,* 88; George Bogle to Mrs Brown, 8 March 1775, MSS Eur E 226/77 (k), OIOC, British Library.

45. Michael Aris, *Views of Medieval Bhutan* (London: Serendia, 1982), 20.

46. George Bogle to Mrs Brown, 3 November 1774, MSS Eur E 226/80, OIOC, British Library.

47. George Bogle to William Richardson, MSS Eur E 226/80, OIOC, British Library.

48. MSS Eur E 226/18, OIOC, British Library.

49. Markham, *Narratives,* 168.

50. Ibid., 6.

51. Mary Louise Pratt, *Imperial Eyes: Travel Writing and Transculturation* (London: Routledge, 1992), 84.

ELEVEN: The English Garden Conversation Piece in India

1. Ronald Paulson, *Emblem and Expression: Meaning in English Art of the Eighteenth Century* (Cambridge: Harvard University Press, 1975), 123.

2. See Marcia Pointon, *Hanging the Head: Portraiture and Social Formation in Eighteenth-Century England* (London: Yale University Press, 1993); Ellen G. D'Oench, *The Conversation Piece: Arthur Devis and His Contemporaries* (New Haven, Conn.: Yale Center for British Art, 1980); and Shearer West, "The Public Nature of Private Life: The Conversation Piece and the Fragmented Family," *British Journal for Eighteenth-Century Studies* 18 (1995): 153–72.

3. Paulson, *Emblem and Expression*, 123.

4. John Harris, *The Artist and the Country House: A History of Country House and Garden View Painting 1540–1840* (London: Sotheby's, 1985), 165. See also Mary Spivy, Ellen D'Oench, and Joy Breslauer, *Country Houses in Great Britain* (New Haven, Conn.: Yale Center for British Art, 1979).

5. Nigel Everett, *The Tory View of Landscape* (New Haven, Conn.: Yale University Press, 1994).

6. E. P. Thompson, "The Moral Economy of the English Crowd in the Eighteenth Century," *Past and Present* 50 (1971): 76–136.

7. Ann Bermingham, *Landscape and Ideology: The English Rustic Tradition, 1740–1860* (Berkeley: University of California Press, 1986), 31.

8. See Howard Newby, *Country Life: A Social History of Rural England* (Totowa, N.J.: Barnes and Noble, 1987).

9. For a fuller discussion of these issues, see Nigel Everett, "The Whig Idea of Landscape and Its Critics," in *Tory View;* and Denis E. Cosgrove, "England: Prospects, Palladianism, and Paternal Landscapes," in *Social Formation and Symbolic Landscape* (1984; reprint, Madison: University of Wisconsin Press, 1998).

10. For an overview of British artists and their work in India, see Mildred Archer, *India and British Portraiture, 1770–1825* (London: Sotheby Parke Bernet, 1979).

11. See Everett, *Tory View*, 95. For returning company employees, see P. J. Marshall, *East Indian Fortunes: The British in Bengal in the Eighteenth Century* (Oxford: Clarendon Press, 1976); Percival Spear, *The Nabobs: A Study of the Social Life of the English in Eighteenth-Century India* (1932; London: Oxford University Press, 1963); and Kate Teltscher, *India Inscribed: European and British Writing on India, 1600–1800* (Delhi: Oxford University Press, 1995).

12. See P. J. Marshall, chap. 4 of *The New Cambridge History of India*, vol. 2, *Bengal: The British Bridgehead: Eastern India 1740–1828* (Cambridge: Cambridge University Press, 1987).

13. Edmund Burke, "Articles of Impeachment," in *The Writings and Speeches of Edmund Burke*, vol. 6, *India: The Launching of the Hastings Impeachment, 1786–1788*, ed. P. J. Marshall (Oxford: Clarendon Press, 1991), 147. Subsequent references follow quotations in parentheses.

14. David Musselwhite, "The Trial of Warren Hastings," in *Literature, Politics, and Theory*, ed. Francis Barker et al. (London: Methuen, 1986), 77–103.

15. Ranajit Guha, *A Rule of Property for Bengal: An Essay on the Idea of Permanent Settlement* (Paris: Mouton, 1963), 16–17.

16. Guha, *A Rule of Property for Bengal*, 17.

17. Musselwhite, "The Trial of Warren Hastings," 84.

18. See Stephen Daniels, "The Political Iconography of Woodland in Later Georgian England," in *The Iconography of Landscape*, ed. Denis Cosgrove and Stephen Daniels (Cambridge: Cambridge University Press, 1988), 43–82.

19. Paulson, *Emblem and Expression*, 154–55.

20. See Bermingham's discussion of the Andrews portrait in *Landscape and Ideology*, 29–33. See also John Berger, *Ways of Seeing* (London: Penguin, 1972).

21. Mildred Archer, *India and British Portraiture, 1770–1825*, 139.

22. See P. J. Marshall, "The Private Fortune of Marian Hastings" and "The Personal Fortune of Warren Hastings," in *Trade and Conquest: Studies on the Rise of British Dominance in India* (Aldershot, England: Variorum [Ashgate Publishing Company], 1993).

23. Adam Smith, *The Wealth of Nations* (1776; reprint, New York: Penguin, 1986), 519.

24. David McNally, *Political Economy and the Rise of Capitalism: A Reinterpretation* (Berkeley: University of California Press, 1988), 263.

25. Thomas Gisborne, *Enquiry into the Duties of Men in the Higher and Middle Classes* (London, 1794), 398.

26. Hastings, *The Present State of the East Indies* (1786), quoted by Everett in *Tory View,* 67.

27. An exception is Arthur Devis's *Robert Gwillym and his Family,* in which a servant carries a message from the house to the family in the garden.

28. For the connection between women and the consumption of exotic commodities, see Suvir Kaul, "Why Selima Drowns: Thomas Gray and the Domestication of the Imperial Ideal," *PMLA* 105 (1990): 223–32, and Laura Brown, *Ends of Empire: Women and Ideology in Early Eighteenth-Century English Literature* (Ithaca: Cornell University Press, 1993). For the association of black servants with exotic commodities, see David Dabydeen, *Hogarth's Blacks: Images of Blacks in Eighteenth Century English Art* (Athens: University of Georgia Press, 1982).

29. Richard Leppert, "Music, Domestic Life, and Cultural Chauvinism: Images of British Subjects at Home in India," in *Music and Society: The Politics of Composition, Performance and Reception,* ed. Richard Leppert and Susan McClary (Cambridge: Cambridge University Press, 1987), 96, 106, 97. See also Teltscher, *India Inscribed,* 146–50, on British anxieties about servants.

30. Everett, *Tory View,* chap. 2.

31. John Barrell, *The Darkside of the Landscape: The Rural Poor in English Painting 1730–1840* (Cambridge: Cambridge University Press, 1980), and Michael Rosenthal, *British Landscape Painting* (Ithaca: Cornell University Press, 1982).

32. See Mildred Archer's *India and British Portraiture,* 166–67, 256–58 for these images.

33. For this "contradictory pursuit of revenue and order," see Nicholas B. Dirks, "From Little King to Landlord: Colonial Discourse and Colonial Rule," 175–208, in *Colonialism and Culture,* ed. Nicholas B. Dirks (Ann Arbor: University of Michigan Press, 1992), 199.

34. Marshall, *Bengal,* 125.

T W E L V E : Black, Yellow, and White on St. Vincent: Moreau de Jonnès's Carib Ethnography

Epigraph: Fernando Ortiz, *Etnia y Sociedad,* ed. Isaac Barreal (La Habana: Editorial de Ciencias Sociales, 1993), 135. Spoken during a 1934 homage to Jose Martí, the words translate, roughly, as "We are all, without exception, the mixed result of countless crossings."

1. Leslie Marmon Silko, *Almanac of the Dead* (New York: Penguin Books, 1992), 410–11.

2. See Stuart B. Schwartz and Frank Salomon, "New Peoples and New Kinds of People: Adaptation, Readjustment, and Ethnogenesis in South American Indigenous Societies (Colonial Era)," in *The Cambridge History of the Native Peoples of the Americas,* vol. 3, *South America,* part 2, ed. Frank Salomon and Stuart B. Schwartz (New York: Columbia University Press, 1999), 443–501. The standard study of "red-black" peoples is Jack D. Forbes, *Africans and Native Americans: The Language of Race and the Evolution of Red-Black Peoples,* 2d ed. (Urbana: University of Illinois Press, 1993); other examples include the Seminoles, the Miskitos, and the Lumbees.

3. Salman Rushdie, *Imaginary Homelands: Essays and Criticism, 1981–1991* (London: Granta Books, 1992), 394.

4. See James Clifford, *The Predicament of Culture: Twentieth-Century Ethnography, Literature, and Art* (Cambridge: Harvard University Press, 1988).

5. See Fatima Bercht et al., eds., *Taíno: Pre-Columbian Art and Culture from the Caribbean* (New York: Monacelli Press, 1998).

6. On transculturation, see Fernando Ortiz, *Cuban Counterpoint: Tobacco and Sugar,* trans. Harriet de Onís (Durham: Duke University Press, 1995).

7. J. W. Fortescue, *A History of the British Army,* vol. 4 (London: Macmillan, 1906), 325.

8. Around 50,000 British soldiers may have died in the Caribbean between 1793 and 1798 (David P. Geggus, *Slavery, War, and Revolution: The British Occupation of Saint Domingue 1793–98* [Oxford: Clarendon Press, 1982], 463, n.50).

9. J. Holland Rose, "The Conflict with Revolutionary France, 1793–1802," in *The Cambridge History of the British Empire,* vol. 2, *The Growth of the New Empire 1783–1870* (Cambridge: Cambridge University Press, 1940), 36–82, at 64. The best contemporary study is Michael Duffy, *Soldiers, Sugar, and Seapower: The British Expeditions to the West Indies and the War against Revolutionary France* (Oxford: Clarendon Press, 1987); see also Roger N. Buckley, *Slaves in Red Coats: The British West India Regiments, 1795–1815* (New Haven, Conn.: Yale University Press, 1979), and Michael Craton, *Testing the Chains: Resistance to Slavery in the British West Indies* (Ithaca: Cornell University Press, 1982).

10. Bernard Marshall, "The Black Caribs—Native Resistance to British Penetration into the Windward Side of St. Vincent 1763–1773," *Caribbean Quarterly* 19, no. 4 (1973): 4–19, at 8; referencing C.O. 101/11 (Sir William Young's propositions for Surveying and Selling the Carib lands on the Windward side of St. Vincent, 11 April 1767).

11. William Young, *An Account of the Black Charaibs in the Island of St Vincent's* [1795] (London: Frank Cass, 1971), 3. Apart from Young's *Account,* the main sources pertaining to Vincentian Carib history in the late eighteenth century are William Young, *A Tour through the Several Islands of Barbadoes, St Vincent, Antigua, Tobago, and Grenada, in the Years 1791, and 1792,* published as the third volume of Bryan Edwards, *History of the British Colonies in the West Indies* (London: John Stockdale, 1801), 260–301; Charles Shephard, *An Historical Account of the Island of Saint Vincent* [1831] (London: Frank Cass, 1971); F. W. N. Bayley, *Four Years' Residence in the West Indies during the years 1826, 7, 8, and 9 by the Son of a Military Officer* (London: Kidd, 1830); Thomas Coke, *Some Account of the Late Missionaries to the West Indies in Two Letters from the Rev. Dr. Coke, to the Rev. J. Wesley* (London: n.p., 1789); George Davidson, "The Copy of a Letter . . . containing a short History of the Caribbs" [24 July 1787], in *The Case of the Caribbs in St. Vincent's,* ed. Thomas Coke (Dublin?: n.p., 1788), 5–19; and Alexander Anderson, *Geography and History of St Vincent,* ed. and transcribed by Richard A. and Elizabeth S. Howard (Cambridge, Mass.: Arnold Arboretum, 1983). The best modern account of the Vincentian Caribs is Nancie L. Gonzalez, *Sojourners of the Caribbean: Ethnogenesis and Ethnohistory of the Garifuna* (Urbana: University of Illinois Press, 1988); see also C. J. M. R. Gullick, *Myths of a Minority: Changing Traditions of the Vincentian Caribs* (Assen: Van Gorcum, 1985); Michael Craton, "From Caribs to Black Caribs: The Amerindian Roots of Servile Resistance in the Caribbean," in *In Resistance: Studies in African, Caribbean, and Afro-American History,* ed. Gary Y. Okihiro (Amherst: University of Massachusetts Press, 1986), 96–116; and Michael Craton, "The Black Caribs of St. Vincent: A Reevaluation," in *The Lesser Antilles in the Age of European Expansion,* ed. Robert L. Paquette and Stanley L. Engerman (Gainesville: University Press of Florida, 1996), 71–85.

12. Young, *An Account,* 5.

13. See Peter Hulme, *Colonial Encounters: Europe and the Native Caribbean, 1492–1797* (London: Methuen, 1986), 45–87.

14. Quoted in Marshall, "The Black Caribs," 12, referring to C.O. 101/16 (Governor Leyborne to Hillsborough, no. 26, 30 July 1772). The 1773 peace treaty speaks simply of "Charaibs" (Young, *An Account,* 89).

15. Young, *An Account*, 5.

16. Shephard, *An Historical Account*, 22.

17. Craton, "The Black Caribs," 81. On the colonial tendency to stress African background over Native American, see Forbes, *Africans and Native Americans*, 85–86.

18. Young, *An Account*, 30.

19. Douglas Taylor, *The Black Carib of British Honduras*, Viking Fund Publications in Anthropology 17 (New York: Wenner-Gren Foundation, 1951), 28.

20. Alexandre Moreau de Jonnès, *Aventures de guerre au temps de la république et du consulat*, 2 vols. (Paris: Pagnerre, 1858), 1:312. Translations are mine.

21. "D'observations et de témoignages oculaires," Moreau de Jonnès, *Aventures de guerre*, 2:271. The Caribs had played an important role in Rousseau's *Discourse on the Origins of Inequality*.

22. Moreau de Jonnès, *Aventures de guerre*, 2:271–72.

23. Joseph-Marie Degérando, *The Observation of Savage Peoples*, trans. and ed. F. C. T. Moore (1800; reprint, Berkeley: University of California Press, 1969); and see Miranda J. Hughes, "Philosophical Travellers at the Ends of the Earth: Baudin, Péron and the Tasmanians," in *Australian Science in the Making*, ed. R. W. Home (Cambridge: Cambridge University Press, 1988), 23–44.

24. Alexander Anderson believed the Vincentian planters had provoked the Carib rebellion by their improvident attempts to deforest St Vincent (*Geography and History*, 37). On the hostile view of colonists towards woodland, see Richard H. Grove, *Green Imperialism: Colonial Expansion, Tropical Island Edens and the Origins of Environmentalism, 1600–1800* (Cambridge: Cambridge University Press, 1995), 273.

25. Moreau de Jonnès, *Aventures de guerre*, 1:288–89.

26. Ibid., 2:286.

27. Ibid., 2:276.

28. Ibid., 1:242–43.

29. Ibid., 1:246.

30. Pierre Larousse, ed., *Grand Dictionnaire Universel du XIXe siècle* (Paris: Larousse, 1866), 1:42 (Abyssinien).

31. See Julius S. Scott, "Crisscrossing Empire: Ships, Sailors, and Resistance in the Lesser Antilles in the Eighteenth Century," in *The Lesser Antilles in the Age of European Expansion*, ed. Robert L. Paquette and Stanley L. Engerman (Gainesville: University Press of Florida, 1996), 128–43.

32. Mary Louise Pratt, *Imperial Eyes: Travel Writing and Transculturation* (London: Routledge, 1992), 15–37.

33. See Joan Dayan, *History, Haiti, and the Gods* (Berkeley: University of California Press, 1995), 219–37.

34. Moreau de Jonnès from L. Maurellus, "Brun comme un Maure," *Le Gran Robert de la Langue Française*, 2d ed. (Paris: Le Robert, 1985), 6:575.

35. Johann Friedrich Blumenbach, *The Anthropological Treatises*, trans. and ed. Thomas Bendyshe (London: Longman, Green, Longman, Roberts, & Green, 1865), 156. For more details, see Peter Hulme, *Remnants of Conquest: The Island Caribs and Their Visitors, 1877–1998* (Oxford: Oxford University Press, 2000), 17–18.

36. Contradictions also discussed by Nancie L. Gonzalez in a valuable revisionary paper, which I draw on here: *Próspero, Calibán, and Black Sambo: Colonial Views of the Other in the Caribbean*, 1992 Lecture Series, *Working Papers* no. 11, Department of Spanish and Portuguese (College Park: University of Maryland, 1991).

37. Young, *An Account,* 99.

38. [Jean-Jacques Dauxion-Lavaysse], *A statistical, commercial, and political description of Venezuela, Trinidad, Margarita, and Tobago from the French of M. Lavaysse: with an introduction and explanatory notes, by the editor* [Voyage aux îles de Trinidad, de Tabago, de la Marguerite, et dans diverses parties de Venezuela] (London: G. and W. B. Whittaker, 1820), 435.

39. Schwartz and Salomon, "New Peoples," 490.

40. Moreau de Jonnès, *Aventures de guerre,* 1:337.

41. Ibid., 1:344.

42. Ibid., 1:363–64.

43. Gonzalez, *Sojourners,* 23.

44. Rebecca Bateman, "Africans and Indians: A Comparative Study of the Black Carib and Black Seminole," *Ethnohistory* 37, no. 1 (1990): 1–24, at 7.

THIRTEEN: Marketing Mulatresses in the Paintings and Prints of Agostino Brunias

My sincere thanks to the many people who invited me to present versions of this paper at the Clark Library, the Northeast American Society for Eighteenth Century Studies, Brown University's Pembroke Center, Yale University's Department of Art History, and the Huntington Library. I would also like to thank my research assistant, Jessica Dandona, and the following for their helpful comments: Roxann Wheeler, Timothy Barringer, Joseph Roach, Claire Buck, Lara Kriegel, Dietrich Neumann, Evelyn Lincoln, and Felicity Nussbaum.

1. Brunias returned to Britain in 1773, exhibiting three West Indian scenes at the Royal Academy in the late 1770s; in 1779 he published a series of six West Indian prints. Shortly thereafter, Brunias returned to Dominica, where he appears to have lived until his death in 1796. Biographical information for Brunias is sparse. I rely here on Hans Huth, "Agostino Brunias, Romano," *Connoisseur* 151 (December 1962): 264–69; and a chronology that appears in the clippings file on the artist at the Yale Center for British Art, compiled for or by the Aquarela Galleries in Port of Spain.

2. Patrick Baker, *Centering the Periphery: Chaos, Order and the Ethnohistory of Dominica* (Montreal: McGill-Queen's University Press, 1994), 57.

3. Beth Fowkes Tobin has written the only substantive analysis of Brunias's West Indian paintings to date in *Picturing Imperial Power: Colonial Subjects in Eighteenth-Century British Painting* (Durham: Duke University Press, 1999).

4. David Brion Davis, *The Problem of Slavery in the Age of Revolution, 1770–1823* (Ithaca: Cornell University Press, 1975), 469–501.

5. The quote is from William Young the Second, *Observations Respecting the Conduct, the Accounts and the Claims of the Late Sir William Young, Bart . . .* (London: W. Bulmer, 1793), 20.

6. Most of Brunias's works are undated but were produced in the 1770s and 1780s. They were also either untitled or their original titles were lost; the descriptive titles they now bear were assigned posthumously.

7. Janet Schaw, *Journal of a Lady of Quality,* ed. Evangeline Walker Andrews (New Haven, Conn.: Yale University Press, 1934), 112.

8. Edward Long, *The History of Jamaica,* 3 vols. (London: T. Lownes, 1774), 2:335; Bryan Edwards, *History, Civil and Commercial, of the British Colonies in the West Indies,* 3d ed., 3 vols. (London: John Stockdale, 1801), 2:25–26; [J. Stewart], *An Account of Jamaica and Its Inhabitants* (Lon-

don: Longman, 1808), 303; Médéric-Louise-Elie Moreau de St. Méry, *Description topographique, physique, civil, politique et historique de la partie française de l'Isle Saint-Domingue* (1797–98; reprint, Paris: Société de L'Histoire des Colonies Français, 1958).

9. William Young the Second, *An Historical Statistical and Descriptive Account of the Island of Tobago,* 1809, Stowe MS 922, f. 59, British Library.

10. Werner Sollers, *Neither Black, nor White, but Both: Thematic Exploration of Interracial Literature* (New York: Oxford University Press, 1997), 127.

11. Sylvana Tomaselli, "The Enlightenment Debate on Women," *History Workshop Journal* 20 (Autumn 1984): 101–24.

12. William Alexander, *The History of Women from the Earliest Antiquity, to the Present Time,* 3d ed. (London, 1782), 1:151, cited in Tomaselli, "The Enlightenment Debate," 114.

13. Felicity Nussbaum, *Torrid Zones: Maternity, Sexuality, and Empire in Eighteenth-Century English Narratives* (Baltimore: Johns Hopkins University Press, 1995), 11.

14. Peter Hulme, *Colonial Encounters* (London: Methuen, 1986), 242–47.

15. Peter Hulme has convincingly argued that the distinction between "yellow" and "black" Caribs had more to do with colonial politics than biological difference. See chapter 12 in this volume.

16. Nussbaum, *Torrid Zones,* 73–94.

17. Joseph Senhouse, entry for 20 June 1776, "The Diary of Joseph Senhouse," in *Wild Majesty: Encounters with Caribs from Columbus to the Present Day,* ed. Peter Hulme and Neil Whitehead (Oxford: Oxford University Press, 1992), 185.

18. Marietta Morrissey, *Slave Women in the New World: Gender Stratification in the Caribbean* (Lawrence: University Press of Kansas, 1989), 62–80; Hilary Beckles, *Natural Rebels: A Social History of Enslaved Black Women in Barbados* (London: Zed Books, 1989), 31–40.

19. James Forrester, *The Polite Philosopher,* 2d ed. (London, 1736), 49–50, cited in David Solkin, *Painting for Money: The Visual Arts and the Public Sphere in Eighteenth-Century England* (New Haven, Conn.: Yale University Press, 1993), 71.

20. Solkin, *Painting for Money,* 85.

21. Thomas Atwood, *The History of the Island of Dominica* (London, 1791), 209–10.

22. A. C. Carmichael, *Domestic Manners and Social Condition of the White, Coloured, and Negro Population of the West Indies,* 2 vols. (London: Whittaker, Treacher, and Co., 1833), 1:39 and 1:77; Schaw, *Journal of a Lady of Quality,* 80; Edwards, *History,* 2:13; Stewart, *An Account of Jamaica,* 190.

23. Long, *History of Jamaica,* 2:279.

24. In 1773 Wickstead traveled to Jamaica, where he apparently produced portraits of the plantocracy. None of his works appear to have survived in Jamaica, and those in British collections are difficult to date securely to his Jamaican sojourn. Frank Cundall, "Philip Wickstead of Jamaica," *Connoisseur* 94 (1934): 174–75.

25. Many thanks to Ellen Rooney, whose questioning of my use of this phrase stimulated this particular line of argument.

26. Campbell Dalrymple, letter to the Earl of Bute, 27 February 1763, Add. MS 38200, f. 263, British Library.

27. Kalpana Seshadri-Crooks, *Desiring Whiteness: A Lacanian Analysis of Race* (London: Routledge, 2000).

28. On West Indian markets, see Sidney Mintz, "Caribbean Marketplaces and Caribbean History," *Radical History Review* 27 (1983): 110–20, and *Peasant Market Places and Economic Devel-*

opment in Latin America (Nashville: Vanderbilt University Graduate Center for Latin American Studies, 1964).

29. James Aytoun, *Memoirs of a Redcoat in the Caribbean* (reprinted 1982), quoted in Lennox Honychurch, *The Dominica Story: A History of the Island* (London: Macmillan, 1995), 64–65.

30. Joseph Roach, *Cities of the Dead: Circum-Atlantic Performance* (New York: Columbia University Press, 1996), 2–3.

31. Elsa Goveia, *Slave Society in the British Leeward Islands at the End of the Eighteenth Century* (New Haven, Conn.: Yale University Press, 1965), 221.

32. Barry Higman, *Slave Population and Economy in Jamaica, 1807–1834* (Cambridge: Cambridge University Press, 1976), 176.

33. Thanks to Maryann O'Donnell for bringing to my attention this particular relationship among markets, value, and meaning.

FOURTEEN: Archipelagic Encounters: War, Race, and Labor in American-Caribbean Waters

1. Public Record Office, London (hereafter, PRO) Adm 1/2007 (Knowles), f. 150.

2. PRO, Adm 1/2100 (Wm Montague), 14 August 1745.

3. PRO, Adm 1/2100 (Wm Montague), 14 August 1745.

4. *Authentic papers concerning a late remarkable transaction* (London, 1746).

5. PRO, Adm 1/2100 (Wm Montague), 14 August 1745.

6. PRO, Adm 1/2100 (Wm Montague), 26 November 1745.

7. PRO, Adm 36/2008. The muster book of the *Mercury* has not survived for 1744. This number is derived from the muster of September 1745, when the *Mercury* had returned from the Caribbean.

8. PRO, Adm 1/2652 (John Williams), 19 January 1740.

9. Edward Vernon, *Original Letters to an Honest Sailor* (London, 1746), 4.

10. Cyril Hartmann, *The Angry Admiral* (London: Heinemann, 1953), 124–25. These are the figures offered for the sixth regiment from Cork under Lt. Col. Haldane. Hughes thinks the overall figure may have reached nearly 90 percent. See also John Robert McNeill, *The Atlantic Empires of France and Spain* (Chapel Hill: University of North Carolina Press, 1985), 102–3.

11. Duncan Crewe, *Yellow Jack and the Worm: British Naval Administration in the West Indies, 1739–48* (Liverpool: Liverpool University Press, 1993), 73–74, 78, tables 5–6.

12. Tobias Smollett, *The Adventures of Roderick Random*, ed. Paul-Gabriel Boucé (Oxford: Oxford University Press, 1979), 149.

13. For requests for supernumaries in 1739, see PRO, Adm 1/232/172–3. For a similar request in 1756, see PRO, Adm 1/234/590–1.

14. Crewe, *Yellow Jack*, 123. Richard Pares, "The Manning of the Navy in the West Indies, 1702–63," *Trans. Royal Historical Society*, 4th series, 20 (1937): 42. For examples of impressment from the logbooks, see PRO, Adm 51/691, part V, entries for 24 and 27 March 1741 on HMS *Princess Louisa*, and PRO, Adm 51/232, part II, entries for 29 February, 31 August, 5 September 1744, 1 January 1745 on HMS *Deal Castle*.

15. PRO, Adm 1/233/5/30.

16. Gareth Rees, "Copper Sheathing: An Example of Technological Diffusion in the English Merchant Fleet," *Journal of Transport History* 2 (1972): 85–94.

17. Crewe, *Yellow Jack,* 73–74, 83, tables 5 and 8. See also PRO, Adm 36/1730, the muster book of HMS *Lenox,* which registered a 21.8 percent desertion rate from 1744 to 1748, far higher than that recorded by Crewe for the period January to December 1747. For home desertions, see N. A. M. Rodger, *The Wooden World* (London: Wm. Collins, 1986), 144.

18. PRO, Adm 1/2007 (Knowles) 16 Aug 1744. See also PRO, Adm 1/5285, the trial of Thomas Kavanagh for desertion of HMS *Suffolk.*

19. PRO, Adm 1/233/4/159.

20. PRO, Adm 1/232, 5 September 1742, cited in Pares, "Manning of the Navy," 39.

21. PRO, CO 137/57/1/198, 210, 249–69.

22. PRO, Adm 1/2007 (Knowles), 15 October 1744.

23. PRO, Adm 1/1829 (Samuel Goddard), 1 October, 15 November 1743.

24. The statute is 6 Anne, c. 37.

25. John Lax and William Pencak, "The Knowles Riot and the Crisis of the 1740s in Massachusetts," *Perspectives in American History* 10 (1976): 161–214.

26. Pares, "Manning of the Navy," 48–49.

27. The statute is 19 Geo II c. 30. The act only applied to the West Indies.

28. The lack of provisions in wartime likely resulted from the propensity of American colonists to smuggle goods to Britain's enemies than from their reluctance to encounter British men-of-war. As Richard Pares noticed, the dislocation of North American–Caribbean commerce in wartime was modest. See Richard Pares, *Yankees and Creoles* (London: Longmans, 1956), 19.

29. PRO, CO 137/57/58–61.

30. Contemporaries exaggerated the ratio of blacks to white but not outrageously. One pamphleteer thought it 15:1, while modern scholars calculate it at 11:1 or 12:1. See *The Importance of Jamaica to Great Britain consider'd* (London, 1741), 15; David Watts, *The West Indies: Patterns of Development, Culture and Environmental Change since 1492* (Cambridge: Cambridge University Press, 1987), 311.

31. Peter H. Wood, *Black Majority* (New York: Knopf, 1974), chap. 12. The Spanish also created a company of black grenadiers, including runaways, to fight the British. See *Berrow's Worcester Journal* (3–10 December 1742).

32. PRO, CO 152/44/155, 1 July 1740; Michael Craton, *Testing the Chains* (Ithaca: Cornell University Press, 1982), 120–24.

33. Craton, *Testing the Chains,* 92.

34. PRO, CO 137/57/2/106.

35. On the use of black auxiliaries, see Hartmann, *The Angry Admiral,* 99; PRO, CO 137/57/1/101. The slaves were to be offered their freedom for participating in the expedition, although whether this promise was observed was unclear. Black slaves were also considered for General Wentworth's projected Panama expedition in 1742, although the Jamaicans were not happy about this, largely because they thought the sacrifice not worth the effort after the failure of the Cuban expedition. See PRO, CO 137/57/1/129, 146.

36. PRO, CO 137/57/2/210–11.

37. PRO, Adm 1/3817, Edward Trelawny to Thomas Corbett, 21 December 1743.

38. PRO, Adm 1/233/4/168–69.

39. W. Jeffrey Bolster, *Black Jacks* (Cambridge: Harvard University Press, 1997), 18.

40. PRO, Adm 1/3817, Trelawny to Corbet, 21 December 1743.

41. Charles Roberts, *Observations on the Windward Passage, or the Passage between Jamaica and St. Domingo* (London, 1795), 4–5.

42. CO 137/57/2/274. For contemporary recognitions of good pilots in the Bahamas, see Adm 1/237/42. In 1762, the second best was reckoned to be "Johnno, a Free Negro Man."

43. Clarence J. Munford, *The Black Ordeal of Slavery and Slave Trading in the French West Indies 1625–1715*, 3 vols. (Lewiston: E. Mellen, 1991), 3:753.

44. Richard Pares, *War and Trade in the West Indies, 1739–1763* (Oxford: Clarendon Press, 1936), 254.

45. Philip D. Morgan, *Slave Counterpoint* (Chapel Hill: University of North Carolina Press, 1998), 238. In 1784, concerned that an increasing number of slaves worked the rivers and tidewater, the Virginia legislature enacted that only a third of a crew should consist of slaves (240). For the fear that runaway slaves would seek berths in wartime, see Billy G. Smith and Richard Wojtowicz, eds., *Blacks Who Stole Themselves* (Philadelphia: University of Pennsylvania Press, 1989), Advertisements 7, 18, 19, 21, 27, 32, 41, 51.

46. PRO, CO 137/57/2/139v. For further evidence of blacks on privateers, see PRO, Adm 1/232/270.

47. Elsa V. Goveia, *Slave Society in the British Leeward Islands at the End of the Eighteenth Century* (Westport, Conn.: Greenwood, 1965), 256.

48. PRO, Adm 1/2007 (Knowles), 12 June 1744.

49. PRO, Adm 1/231/253, 7 October 1740. On the price of adult male slaves, see David Richardson, "The Slave Trade, Sugar, and British Economic Growth, 1748–1776," in *British Capitalism and Caribbean Slavery*, ed. Stanley Engerman (Cambridge: Cambridge University Press, 1987), 108.

50. On privateers taking slaves, see Howard M. Chapin, *Privateering in King George's War 1739–1748* (Providence, R.I.: E. A. Johnson, 1928), 125, 127, 132–33, 147, 154, 200, 216, 229, 238.

51. Olaudah Equiano, *The Interesting Narrative and Other Writings*, ed. Vincent Carretta (London: Penguin, 1995), 79–94.

52. Muster book for HMS *Plymouth*, 1747. PRO, Adm 36/2775.

53. PRO, Adm 36/466 and Adm 36/1730.

54. On the possibility of blacks being enslaved for vagrancy in Antigua, see J. Luffman, *A brief account of the island of Antigua* (London, 1789), 130–31.

55. PRO, Adm 1/2006, 21 September 1740.

56. Mavis Campbell, *The Maroons of Jamaica 1655–1796* (Granby, Mass.: Bergin and Garvey, 1988), 151.

57. PRO, Adm 51/232, part II, entry for 17 January 1744.

58. PRO, Adm 1/234/96; PRO, Adm 1/2041 (Lisle), 23 November 1743.

59. *An essay concerning slavery, and the danger Jamaica is expos'd to from too great number of slaves* (London, 1746).

60. For those in Jamaica, see PRO, Adm 1/233/4/166–7. By a 1745 act, the fine was £50 for carrying off sailors or soldiers. An earlier act, in 1725, had levied fines of £200, and £100 for hiding deserters or runaway servants.

61. PRO, Adm 1/233/5/233–4, 240–1.

62. PRO, Adm 1/233/5/256–7.

63. Jane Landers, *Black Society in Spanish Florida* (Urbana: University of Illinois Press, 1999), 41–45.

64. For an example of this, see the entry for 2 November 1746 in the muster book of HMS *Lenox*, PRO, Adm 36/1730. For an instance of a privateer handing over recalcitrant seamen to a man-of-war, see the case of the *Stephen and Elizabeth* in Chapin, *Privateering*, 132.

65. PRO, Adm 1/2007/141–8.

66. PRO, Adm 1/5283, court martial of Lieut. Joseph Willis, 14 March 1743; PRO, Adm 1/5284/507–48.

67. PRO, Adm 1/5285, court martial of Edward Stow, quartermaster of HMS *Eltham,* 7 November 1745.

68. PRO, Adm 1/5285, court martial of Humphrey Lion and William Hillman of HMS *Dorsetshire,* 9 December 1745.

69. Rodger, *Wooden World,* 128–29; Carl E. Swanson, *Predators and Prizes* (Columbia: University of South Carolina Press, 1991), 216–19.

70. Swanson, *Predators,* 219.

71. PRO, Adm 1/3818/311–13A. For Bermudan privateering raiding the coast of Hispaniola for slaves, see Chapin, *Privateering,* 125.

72. Swanson, *Predators,* 118.

73. Edward Long, *The History of Jamaica,* 3 vols. (London, 1774), 1:331.

74. PRO, CO 137/57/1/179.

75. Nathaniel Uring, *A History of the Voyages and Travels of Capt. Nathaniel Uring* (London, 1726), 355.

76. PRO, Adm 36/2775, entries for December 1743–February 1744.

77. PRO, CO 137/57/2/236.

78. PRO, CO 137/57/2/275v.

79. PRO, Adm 1/306 (Henry Osborn), 4 August, 15 December 1748.

80. PRO, Adm 1/3818/424–25.

81. PRO, CO 152/45/136–38. On Norman's as a rendezvous for contraband goods, see PRO, Adm 1/578, letter of Thomas Frankland, 28 April 1757.

82. PRO, Adm 1/2041 (Lisle), 24 Oct 1743. Among the trials was that of the crew of the *Old Noll* privateer, which had mutinied off Baltimore in Ireland in October 1747. Ten sailors received 300 lashes each; eight were hanged. *London Evening Post,* 3–6 September 1748.

83. *General Evening Post,* 3–5 November 1748. See also Nicholas Rogers, "Confronting the Crime Wave: The Debate over Social Reform and Regulation, 1749–1753," in *Stilling the Grumbling Hive: The Response to Social and Economic Problems in England, 1689–1750,* ed. Lee Davison et al. (New York: St. Martin's Press, 1992), 77–98.

84. John Brown, *An Estimate of the Manners and Principles of the Times,* 5th ed. (London, 1757), 88–89.

85. Peter Linebaugh and Marcus Rediker, *The Many-Headed Hydra: Sailors, Slaves, Commoners, and the Hidden History of the Revolutionary Atlantic* (Boston: Beacon Press, 2000).

86. PRO, Adm 1/2007/150, 162.

87. PRO, SP 36/52/137–39; John Lax and William Pencak, "The Knowles Riot and the Crisis of the 1740s in Massachusetts," *Perspectives in American History* 10 (1976): 165, although Lax and Pencak make the further point that the riot "was indeed actively supported by all of Boston."

88. Daniel Horsmanden, *The New York Conspiracy,* ed. Thomas J. Davis (Boston: Beacon Press, 1971), 117, 151, 159, 177–87, 260–61.

89. Thomas J. Davis, *A Rumor of Revolt: The "Great Negro Plot" in Colonial New York* (New York: Free Press, 1985), 5–6, 60, 131–37; Horsmanden, *The New York Conspiracy,* 13–16, 48, 73, 446–48, 450.

90. Daniel Defoe, *A General History of the Pyrates,* ed. Manuel Schonhorn (London: J. M. Dent, 1972), 222–28, 280, 513, 517, 528, 533–38, 688; PRO, CO 137/57/2/157; see also 50n.

91. Dorothy Porter, ed., *Early Negro Writing 1760–1837* (Boston: Beacon Press, 1971), 524; Vincent Carretta, ed., *Unchained Voices* (Lexington: University Press of Kentucky, 1996), 22.

92. Linebaugh and Rediker, *The Many-Headed Hydra;* see also "The Many-Headed Hydra: Sailors, Slaves, and the Atlantic Working Class in the Eighteenth Century," *Journal of Historical Sociology* 3 (September 1990): 225–51.

93. Bernard Bailyn, *The Peopling of North America* (New York: Knopf, 1986), 112–21.

94. Philip D. Morgan, "Encounters between British and 'Indigenous' Peoples, c. 1500–c. 1800," in *Empire and Others: British Encounters with Indigenous Peoples, 1600–1850,* ed. Martin Daunton and Rick Halpern (London: University College London Press, 1999), 62. See also Peter Way, "The Cutting Edge of Culture: British Soldiers Encounter Native Americans in the French and Indian War," in ibid., 123–48.

95. See *London Daily Post,* 17 March 1740.

FIFTEEN: Questioning the Identity of Olaudah Equiano, or Gustavus Vassa, the African

An earlier version of this essay appeared in the journal *Slavery and Abolition* 20, no. 3 (1999): 96–105. I am very grateful to the editors for giving me permission to publish a revised version here.

1. All quotations taken from Vincent Carretta, ed., *The Interesting Narrative and Other Writings* (New York: Penguin, 1995) are cited henceforth by page number parenthetically within the text.

2. My biographical findings have obvious implications for the issues raised by the Nigerian critic S. E. Ogude about the assumed veracity of Equiano and his reliability as a historical source on African life. In "Facts into Fiction: Equiano's Narrative Reconsidered," *Research in African Literatures* 13 (1982): 30–43, Ogude argues that because an eleven-year-old was very unlikely to have the almost total recall Equiano claims, "Equiano relied less on the memory of his experience and more on other sources" (32) in his account of Africa. In "No Roots Here: On the Igbo Roots of Olaudah Equiano," *Review of English and Literary Studies* 5 (1989): 1–16, Ogude denies that linguistic evidence supports Equiano's account. Arguments for Equiano's memory of Africa have been made by Catherine Obianju Acholonu, "The Home of Olaudah Equiano—a Linguistic and Anthropological Search," *Journal of Commonwealth Literature* 22 (1987): 5–16; and Paul Edwards and Rosalind Shaw, "The Invisible Chi in Equiano's Interesting Narrative," *Journal of Religion in Africa* 19 (1989): 146–56. Despite Ogude's skepticism about Equiano's veracity, however, he does not question Vassa/Equiano's fundamental identity as an African. The question remains of what details about Africa were available to him. As my essay demonstrates, the surviving documentary evidence shows that Equiano's astounding ability to remember details from his early life, at least from the time he met Michael Henry Pascal on, is indisputable, but that if and when he left Africa he was much younger than eleven years old.

3. J. Oliver, "William Borlase's Contribution to Eighteenth-Century Meteorology and Climatology," *Annals of Science* 25 (1969): 275–317, 309. I thank Joanna Mattingly, assistant curator at the Cornwall Maritime Museum, for bringing Oliver's article to my attention.

4. I am deeply indebted to David Richardson for sharing with me information from the Du Bois Institute data set of slave-trade statistics (PRO CO 28/30 dd 61–dd 76) that enabled me to identify the *Ogden* as the most probable vessel bearing Equiano from the Bight of Biafra to Barbados by comparing the Du Bois data with that found in Walter Minchinton, Celia King, and Pe-

ter Waite, eds., *Virginia Slave-Trade Statistics 1698–1775* (Richmond: Virginia State Library, 1984), 155, and with the information Equiano gives us about his arrival in Virginia. The sloop *Nancy,* built in Virginia in 1753, which most likely brought him to Virginia from Barbados, was not the same slave-trading sloop *Nancy,* built in Massachusetts Bay in 1762, on which Vassa, then owned by Robert King, sailed under the command of Thomas Farmer in 1766; see Elizabeth Donnan, *Documents Illustrative of the History of the Slave Trade to America,* 4 vols. (Washington, D.C.: Carnegie Institution, 1930–35), 4:620. I gained access to some of the relevant PRO records through the Virginia Colonial Records Project Database at the Library of Virginia.

5. Unfortunately, records of regular admissions and releases from St. George's Hospital during this period do not exist. I am very grateful to Terry Gould, archivist at the St. George's Hospital Library and Archive, for checking the available records for me.

6. Although the muster books do not identify crew members by ethnicity, even if we did not know that Jonathan Syfax was born in Madagascar we could deduce from his name that he was a person of African descent and probably a former slave. Slave owners frequently ironically named their slaves after important classical or modern European figures—e.g., Pompey, Soubise, or Gustavus Vassa—to emphasize their own power over them. Syphax was a Numidian hero who fought the Carthaginians, though Vassa's shipmate may have been named after the Numidian soldier in Joseph Addison's tragedy *Cato* (1713).

7. Michael A. Gomez, *Exchanging Our Country Marks: The Transformation of African Identities in the Colonial and Antebellum South* (Chapel Hill: University of North Carolina Press, 1998), 114–22, calculates that in the period 1733–1807 only about 2 percent of South Carolina's Africans originated from the Bight of Biafra, as contrasted with Virginia, which imported more than 40 percent of its slaves from that region during the same period.

8. Philip D. Morgan, *Slave Counterpoint: Black Culture in the Eighteenth-Century Chesapeake and Lowcountry* (Chapel Hill: University of North Carolina Press, 1998), 465.

9. A surviving copy of the subscription proposal for the first edition of *The Interesting Narrative,* to which Josiah Wedgwood subscribed, includes a holograph note to Wedgwood signed "Gustavus Vassa—The African." Dr. Mark Jones recently found the proposal among the Wedgwood papers at Keele University Library (74/12632) and kindly sent me a photocopy of it.

10. I am grateful to John Barrell for bringing to my attention one such example, in William Gifford's footnote to line 263 of his *The Baviad, A Paraphrastic Imitation of the First Satire of Persius* (London, 1791), a satire on the fashion for silly love poetry exemplified by Robert Merry (1755–98), who wrote under the pseudonym "Della Crusca":

> What the ladies may say to such a swain, I know not; but certainly [Merry] is prone to run wild, die, &c. &c. Such indeed is the combustible nature of this gentleman, that he takes fire at every female signature in the papers: and I remember that when Olaudo Equiano (who, for a black, is not ill-featured) tried his hand at a soft sonnet, and by mistake subscribed it Olauda, Mr. Merry fell so desperately in love with him, and "yelled out such syllables of dolour" in consequence of it, that "the pitiful-hearted" negro was frightened at the mischief he had done, and transmitted in all haste the following correction to the editor—"For Olauda, please to read Olaudo, the black MAN."

SIXTEEN: The Point Venus "Scene," Tahiti, 14 May 1769

1. For a fuller account of events at Tahiti, see my *Far-Fetched Facts: The Literature of Travel and the Idea of the South Seas* (Oxford: Oxford University Press, 1995).

2. *The Journals of Captain James Cook on His Voyages of Discovery,* rev. ed., vol. 1, *The Voyage of the* Endeavour *1768–1771,* ed. J. C. Beaglehole (Cambridge: Cambridge University Press, 1968), 119.

3. *The* Endeavour *Journal of Joseph Banks,* 2 vols., ed. J. C. Beaglehole (Sydney: Sydney University Press, 1962), 1:277.

4. Ibid.

5. *The Voyage of the* Endeavour, 93–94. The passage is not significantly different in the Admiralty manuscript of Cook's journal with which Hawkesworth presumably worked (Public Record Office, Adm 55/40).

6. *The Early Diary of Frances Burney, 1768–1778,* 2 vols., ed. A. R. Ellis (London, 1889; reprint, Bell, 1907), 1:133–34. For a fuller account of Hawkesworth's *Voyages,* see Philip Edwards, *The Story of the Voyage: Sea-Narratives in Eighteenth-Century England* (Cambridge: Cambridge University Press, 1994), 80.

7. James Boswell, *The Life of Samuel Johnson,* 6 vols., ed. G. B. Hill, rev. L. F. Powell (Oxford: Clarendon Press, 1934–50), 2:248.

8. Ibid.

9. Ibid., 247.

10. Cook, quoted in *Journals of Captain James Cook,* 1:cxciii, cxciv. Cook's literary ability is assessed in J. C. Beaglehole, *Cook the Writer* (Sydney: Sydney University Press, 1970).

11. Hawkesworth to Sandwich, 19 November 1771, quoted in J. L. Abbott, *John Hawkesworth, Eighteenth-Century Man of Letters* (Madison: University of Wisconsin Press, 1982), 145.

12. John Hawkesworth, *An Account of the Voyages undertaken by the order of his present Majesty for making Discoveries in the Southern Hemisphere, and successively performed by Commodore Byron, Captain Wallis, Captain Carteret, and Captain Cook, in the Dolphin, the Swallow, and the Endeavour: drawn up from the Journals which were kept by the several Commanders, and from the Papers of Joseph Banks, Esq.,* 3 vols. (London, 1773), 1:iv.

13. Ibid., v.

14. Ibid.

15. *Journals of Captain James Cook,* vol. 2, *The Voyage of the* Resolution *and* Adventure *1772–1775,* ed. J. C. Beaglehole (Cambridge: Cambridge University Press, 1961), 661.

16. Hawkesworth, *Voyages,* 2:124, chapter heading.

17. Ibid., 128.

18. It is worth noting that Hawkesworth may have been influenced by Bougainville's depiction of a Tahitian cult of Venus in his *Voyage autour du monde* (Paris, 1771), translated into English by J. R. Forster as *A Voyage Round the World* (London, 1772).

19. Mrs. Hayes's invitation, quoted in *Nocturnal Revels: or, The History of King's Place, and other Modern Nunneries,* 2 vols. (London, 1779), 2:21–22.

20. *Covent-Garden Magazine; or, Amorous Repository* 2 (June 1773): 203, 204.

21. "A Christian," "To Dr. Hawkesworth," *Public Advertiser,* 3 July 1773.

22. John Wesley, 17 December 1773, *The Journal of the Rev. John Wesley,* 8 vols., ed. Nehemiah Curnock (London, 1909–16; reprint, Epworth Press, 1938), 4:7.

23. Ibid.

24. Elizabeth Montagu to her sister, in Mrs. Montagu, *"Queen of the Blues": Her Letters and Friendships from 1762 to 1800,* 2 vols., ed. Reginald Blunt (Boston: Houghton Mifflin [1923?]), 1:279.

25. Elizabeth Carter to Mrs Montagu, 14 August 1773, in Elizabeth Carter, *Letters from Mrs. Elizabeth Carter to Mrs. Montagu between the years 1755 and 1800,* 3 vols., ed. Montagu Pennington (London, 1817), 2:209.

26. *The Early Diary of Frances Burney,* 1:255.

27. "Remnant of an Old Letter to Mr. Crisp," in *The Early Diary of Frances Burney,* 1:262–63.

28. [John Scott?], *An Epistle from Oberea, Queen of Otaheite, to Joseph Banks, Esq.* (London, 1774 [1773?]), 5.

29. Ibid., 11–12.

30. [J. Courtenay?], *An Epistle (Moral and Philosophical) from an Officer at Otaheite to Lady Gr*s**n*r* (London, 1774), 2, 3, 4.

31. Ibid., 8, 10.

32. Ibid., 11–12.

33. Voltaire to Jean Baptiste Nicolas de Lisle, 11 June 1774, *Correspondence,* 51 vols., ed. Theodore Besterman (Geneva: Institut et Musée Voltaire, 1968–77), 41:17, translation mine.

34. Voltaire, "Les Oreilles du comte de Chesterfield et le chapelain Goudman," in *Romans et contes,* ed. F. Deloffre and J. van den Heuvel (Paris: Pléiade edn., 1979), 577, translation mine.

35. James Boswell, *Boswell: The Ominous Years 1774–1776,* ed. C. Ryskamp and F. A. Pottle (New York: McGraw-Hill, 1963), 308.

36. Ibid.

37. Ibid., 309.

38. Ibid.

39. Boswell, *The Life of Samuel Johnson,* 3:7.

40. Ibid.

41. Ibid.

42. Ibid., 8.

43. Boswell, *The Ominous Years,* 341.

44. Ibid.

45. Ibid.

46. Ibid.

47. See James Boswell, *Private Papers of James Boswell from Malahide Castle,* 18 vols., ed. Geoffrey Scott and F. A. Pottle (Mt. Vernon, N.Y.: W. E. Rudge, 1928–34), 11:262.

48. "Mutiny on board the Bounty Armed Ship," *General Evening Post,* 16–18 March 1790.

49. *An Account of the Mutinous Seizure of the Bounty: with the succeeding Hardships of the Crew: to which are added Secret Anecdotes of the Otaheitean Females* (London, 1792), 43.

50. UTA French airline advertisement, *The Far Eastern Economic Review* (25 March 1972), facing 45.

51. See Denis Diderot, *Supplément au voyage de Bougainville,* ed. G. Chinard (Paris: E. Droz, 1935).

52. *The Journal of James Morrison Boatswain's Mate of the 'Bounty',* ed. O. Rutter (London: Golden Cockerel Press, 1935), 237, 235, 236.

53. For an account of the Arioi, see, for example, J. A. Moerenhout, *Voyages aux îles du Grand Océan,* 2 vols. (Paris, 1837), 1:484–503; 2:129–36.

54. Cook, *The Voyage of the* Endeavour, 128. Cook is copying Banks's journal here (or perhaps vice versa) but that does not invalidate what he says (cf. *The* Endeavour *Journal,* 1:351–52).

55. Bengt Danielsson, *Love in the South Seas,* trans. F. H. Lyon (New York: Reynal, 1956), 180.

56. Douglas Oliver, *Ancient Tahitian Society,* 3 vols. (Honolulu: University of Hawai'i Press, n.d.), 1:363; Danielsson, *Love in the South Seas,* 64.

57. William Wales, *Remarks on Mr. Forster's Account of Captain Cook's last Voyage round the World, in the Years 1772, 1773, 1774, and 1775* (London, 1778), 52n.

S E V E N T E E N : Island Transactions: Encounter and Disease in the South Pacific

1. Richard Wrigley and George Revill, eds., *Pathologies of Travel* (Amsterdam and Atlanta, Ga.: Rodopi, 2000), 10.

2. Alan Bewell, *Romanticism and Colonial Disease* (Baltimore: Johns Hopkins University Press, 1999), 30.

3. Debbie Lee, "Yellow Fever and the Slave Trade: Coleridge's 'The Rime of the Ancient Mariner,'" *ELH* 65 (1998): 675.

4. Johann Reinhold Forster, *Observations Made during a Voyage Round the World*, ed. Nicholas Thomas, Harriet Guest, and Michael Dettelbach (Honolulu: University of Hawai'i Press, 1996), 221.

5. See Harriet Guest, "The Great Distinction: Figures of the Exotic in the Work of William Hodges," *Oxford Art Journal* 12, no. 2 (1989); also Bernard Smith, *Imagining the Pacific: In the Wake of the Cook Voyages* (New Haven, Conn.: Yale University Press, 1992), chap. 5. Hodges's painting is in the National Maritime Museum, London.

6. Nicholas Thomas, *Entangled Objects: Exchange, Material Culture, and Colonialism in the Pacific* (Cambridge: Harvard University Press, 1991), chaps. 3 and 4.

7. *The* Endeavour *Journal of Joseph Banks, 1768–1771*, 2 vols., ed. J. C. Beaglehole (Sydney: Angus & Robertson/Public Library of New South Wales, 1962), 1:373.

8. Louis-Antoine de Bougainville, *A Voyage Round the World*, trans. J. R. Forster (London, 1772), 248.

9. Francis Wilkinson, *Journal*, ADM 51/4547/149–50, Public Records Office, entries for 14 April, 19 June 1769.

10. *The Journals of Captain Cook on His Voyages of Discovery*, 3 vols., ed. J. C. Beaglehole (New York: Hakluyt Society/Kraus Reprint, 1988), 1:cxlvi.

11. Nicholas Thomas, "Liberty and Licence: New Zealand Societies in Cook Voyage Anthropology," in *In Oceania: Visions, Artifacts, Histories* (Durham: Duke University Press, 1997).

12. *Journals of Captain Cook*, 2:117.

13. *The* Resolution *Journal of Johann Reinhold Forster, 1772–1775*, 4 vols., ed. Michael E. Hoare (London: Hakluyt Society, 1982), 2:248.

14. *Journals of Captain Cook*, 2:780.

15. *Journals of Captain Cook*, 2:136–37.

16. J. R. Forster, Resolution *Journal*, 2:247.

17. J. R. Forster, *Observations*, 194.

18. J. R. Forster, Resolution *Journal*, 2:302.

19. J. R. Forster, *Observations*, 194–95.

20. This painting is in the National Maritime Museum, London.

21. J. R. Forster, Resolution *Journal*, 2:307–8.

22. *Journals of Captain Cook*, 2:175.

23. J. R. Forster, Resolution *Journal*, 2:348; *Journals of Captain Cook*, 2:232.

24. George Forster, *A Voyage Round the World*, 2 vols., ed. Nicholas Thomas and Oliver Berghof (Honolulu: University of Hawai'i Press, 2000), 1:201–2.

25. Sir James Watt, "Medical Aspects and Consequences of Cook's Voyages," in *Captain James Cook and his Times*, ed. Robin Fisher and Hugh Johnston (London: Croom Helm, 1979), 151.

26. J. R. Forster, Resolution *Journal*, 3:380.

27. Ibid., 3:413–15.

28. J. R. Forster, *Observations*, 297.

29. Bougainville, *Voyage*, 286.

30. Ibid., 290–91.

31. J. R. Forster, Resolution *Journal*, 4:622; *Journals of Captain Cook*, 2:462.

32. J. R. Forster, *Observations*, 298–99.

33. Sir James Watt, "Medical Aspects and Consequences of Cook's Voyages," *Captain James Cook and his Times;* John Miles, *Infectious Diseases: Colonising the Pacific* (Dunedin: University of Otago Press, 1997); Howard M. Smith, "The Introduction of Venereal Disease into Tahiti: A Re-examination," *Journal of Pacific History* 10 (1975): 38–45.

34. J. R. Forster, *Observations*, 193.

35. George Forster, *A Voyage Round the World*, 2:593–94.

36. Ibid., 1:240.

37. *Journals of Captain Cook*, 2:322.

38. George Forster, *A Voyage Round the World*, 1:297.

39. Ibid., 2:617.

40. Ibid., 1:284.

41. Jonathan Lamb, "'The Rime of the Ancient Mariner': A Ballad of the Scurvy," in *Pathologies of Travel*, ed. Wrigley and Revill, 164.

42. Ibid., 172.

43. Bewell, *Romanticism and Colonial Disease*, 4.

EIGHTEEN: George Berkeley the Islander: Some Reflections on Utopia, Race, and Tar-Water

1. See William Butler Yeats, "Blood and the Moon," ll. 26–28, from *The Winding Stair and Other Poems*, in *The Collected Poems of W. B. Yeats*, ed. Richard J. Finneran, rev. 2d ed. (New York: Scribner, 1983; 1996), 328; and *Explorations* (London: Macmillan, 1962), 333. For more recent discussions of Berkeley within a specifically Irish context, see Richard Kearney, *Postnationalist Ireland: Politics, Culture, Philosophy* (New York: Routledge, 1997), 145–56; and David Berman, "The Irish Counter-Enlightenment," in *The Irish Mind: Exploring Intellectual Traditions*, ed. Richard Kearney (Dublin: Wolfhound Press, 1985), 119–40.

2. See A. A. Luce, *The Life of George Berkeley, Bishop of Cloyne* (Edinburgh: Thomas Nelson and Sons, 1949).

3. *The Works of George Berkeley, Bishop of Cloyne*, ed. A. A. Luce and T. E. Jessop, 9 vols. (Edinburgh: Thomas Nelson and Sons, 1948–57), 8:106. Hereafter cited as *Works* in the body of the text.

4. See Pope, *Windsor-Forest*, in *Pastoral Poetry and An Essay on Criticism*, ed. E. Audra and Aubrey Williams (New Haven, Conn.: Yale University Press, 1961; 1969), 148–94.

5. *The Correspondence of Jonathan Swift*, ed. Harold Williams, 5 vols. (Oxford: Clarendon Press, 1963–65), 3:82.

6. J. H. Lefroy, *Memorials of the Discovery and Early Settlement of the Bermudas or Somers Islands, 1515–1685*, 2 vols., The Bermuda Historical Society and Trust (Toronto: University of Toronto Press, 1981), 1:16. Hereafter cited as *Memorials* in the body of the text.

7. *The Poems and Letters of Andrew Marvell*, ed. H. M. Margoliouth, 2 vols. (1927; Oxford: Clarendon Press, 1952), 1:17; and *The Poems of Edmund Waller*, ed. G. Thorn Drury, 2. vols. (London: George Routledge and Sons [The Muses' Library], 1893), 1:66.

8. See the introductory and supplemental materials to *The Tempest*, ed. Frank Kermode, 6th ed. (London: Methuen, 1983); and *The Tempest*, ed. Stephen Orgel (New York: Oxford University Press, 1987). Hallett Smith argues for the ambiguity of the island's location in *The Riverside Shakespeare*, ed. Harry Levin et al. (Boston: Houghton Mifflin, 1974), 1606. Quotations from *The Tempest* are taken from this edition. For a more extensive discussion of the role of the Americas in *The Tempest*, see Peter Hulme, *Colonial Encounters: Europe and the Native Caribbean, 1492–1797* (1986; London: Routledge, 1992), 89–134.

9. Hugh Thomas, *The Slave Trade: The Story of the Atlantic Slave Trade, 1440–1870* (New York: Simon & Schuster, 1997), 270.

10. Edwin S. Gaustad, *George Berkeley in America* (New Haven, Conn.: Yale University Press, 1979), 94.

11. Virginia Bernhard, *Slaves and Slaveholders in Bermuda, 1616–1782* (Columbia: University of Missouri Press, 1999), 215.

12. *The Historical Works of Giraldus Cambrensis*, ed. Thomas Wright, trans. Thomas Forester (London: G. Bohn, 1863), 134–35.

13. Sir Richard Cox, "An Apparatus: Or Introductory Discourse to the History of Ireland," in *Hibernia Anglicana: or, The History of Ireland from the Conquest to this Present Time, Pt. I* (London, 1689), n.p.

14. *The Prose Works of Jonathan Swift*, 14 vols., ed. Herbert Davis (Oxford: Basil Blackwell, 1939–1968), 10:31.

15. Theodore W. Allen, *The Invention of the White Race*, 2 vols. (London: Verso, 1994; 1998). The sections most relevant to this discussion are chaps. 2 and 3 of vol. 1.

16. Quoted in David Berman, *George Berkeley: Idealism and the Man* (Oxford: Clarendon Press, 1994), 115.

17. Quoted in Gaustad, *George Berkeley in America*, 204.

18. From the Bancroft Archives of the University of California, Berkeley; cited in Gaustad, *George Berkeley in America*, 200–201.

19. Details of McSparran's mission and of the proselytizing efforts of the Episcopal Church in this area more generally may be found in Wilkins Updike, *A History of the Episcopal Church in Narragansett, Rhode Island*, 3 vols. (Boston: Merrymount, 1907).

20. Whether Berkeley did in fact learn about tar-water from the Indians during his stay in Rhode Island cannot be definitively answered. Luce assumes this to have been the case (*Life*, 122), while Berman more generally states that "it was either in or from America that he heard of [tar-water's] use as a medicine" (*Berkeley*, 177). Gaustad argues that the first therapeutic use of tar-water did not occur until 1739, in South Carolina, and that Berkeley learned of it "not through direct observation but from the pages of a learned journal" (174)—a view earlier advanced by Ian Tipton, in "Two Questions on Bishop Berkeley's Panacea," *Journal of the History of Ideas* 30, no. 2 (1969): 203–24. Whatever the exact circumstances in this regard, it seems almost certain that the medicinal use of tar-water was connected to practices first known to have occurred on the American continent, as Berkeley himself asserts (*Works*, 5:32, 37). It is likely that these practices were then transmitted to other parts of the world by seamen who learned about them on their travels (a number of examples of the medicinal liquid being used aboard ship, especially as an antidote for smallpox, appear in *Siris*).

21. Cited in Luce, *Life*, 201.

22. Berman, *Berkeley*, 176.

23. Luce, *Life*, 201.

24. Berkeley was instrumental in setting up a spinning school for the children of Cloyne (supervised by his wife) and encouraged work projects and practical training for the poor as part of a broader program of economic self-sufficiency for Ireland which he promoted in works such as *The Querist*.

25. Fredric Jameson's discussion of utopia and class consciousness is relevant to my argument here. See *The Political Unconscious: Narrative as a Socially Symbolic Act* (1981; Ithaca: Cornell University Press, 1986), 281–99.

26. See Raymond W. Houghton, David Berman, and Maureen T. Lapan, *Images of Berkeley* (Dublin: The National Gallery of Ireland and Wolfhound Press, 1986), 55.

NINETEEN: Inhuming Empire: Islands as Colonial Nurseries and Graves

1. Richard Walter and Benjamin Robins, *A Voyage round the World in the Years MDCCXL, I, II, III, IV by George Anson* (London: Oxford University Press, 1974), 115–18. A French translation of the memoir was published as *Voyage autour du monde, fait dans les années MDCCXL, I, II, III, IV* (Amsterdam and Leipzig, 1749).

2. Jean-Jacques Rousseau, *Émile ou de l'éducation* (Paris: Éditions Garnier Frères, 1964), 90: "[J]e laboure pour lui la terre; il en prend possession en y plantant une fève; et sûrement cette possession est plus sacrée et plus respectable que celle que prenait Nuñes Balboa de l'Amérique méridionale au nom du roi d'Espagne, en plantant son étendard sur les côtes de la mer du Sud." All translations are my own unless otherwise noted.

3. In Mary Louise Pratt's important analysis of how travel writing works to narrate colonization such that possession is secured in terms that would signify its opposed double, she encapsulates this rhetorical strategy with the designation "anti-conquest." See Pratt, *Imperial Eyes: Travel Writing and Transculturation* (New York: Routledge, 1992).

4. Geographer Richard Grove demonstrates the influence of the island myth as imagined and popularized by Defoe, Rousseau, and Bernardin de Saint-Pierre on the "conservationist" policy developed by Pierre Poivre on the Île de France (Mauritius) in the context of a larger historical argument about the development in the eighteenth century of a colonial discourse of environmental protectionism. See Grove, "Protecting the Climate of Paradise: Pierre Poivre and the Conservation of Mauritius under the Ancien Régime," in *Green Imperialism: Colonial Expansion, Tropical Island Edens, and the Origins of Environmentalism, 1600–1860* (Cambridge: Cambridge University Press, 1996), 168–263.

5. Jean-Jacques Rousseau, *Émile ou de l'éducation* (Paris: Éditions Garnier, 1965), 210–11: "Quel est donc ce merveilleux livre? Est-ce Aristote? est-ce Pline? est-ce Buffon?"

6. The eighteenth-century accounts include: William Dampier, "Rescue of a 'Moskito Indian' Marooned over Three Years on Juan Fernandez Island," in *A New Voyage round the World . . .*, 5th ed. (London, 1703), 84–88; Edward Cooke, "Rescue of Selkirk from Juan Fernandez Island," in *A Voyage to the South Sea, and around the World* (London, 1712), 36–37; and Woodes Rogers, "Account of Alexander Selkirk's Solitary Life on Juan Fernandez Island for Four Years and Four Months," in *A Cruising Voyage round the World* (London, 1712), 121–31.

7. See J. Paul Hunter, "The 'Occasion' of *Robinson Crusoe*," in Daniel Defoe, *Robinson Crusoe*, Norton Critical Edition, ed. Michael Shinagel (New York: W. W. Norton, 1975), 366.

8. John Donovan, introduction to *Paul and Virginia*, by Jacques-Henri Bernardin de Saint-Pierre, trans. John Donovan (London: Peter Owen, 1982), 11.

9. On the complexities and contradictions inherent in the injunction, particularly post-Holo-

caust, "never to forget," see Yosef H. Yerushalmi et al., *Usages de l'oubli* (Paris: Éditions du Seuil, 1988).

10. Jacques-Henri-Bernardin de Saint-Pierre, *Paul et Virginie,* ed. Édouard Guitton (Paris: Lettres françaises, Collection de l'Imprimerie Nationale, 1984), 233.

11. For engagement with Bernardin de Saint-Pierre's use of landscape as a means to envision a model society, see Diana M. Moore, "Colonial Arcadias: Symbolic Landscapes in the Works of Bernardin de Saint-Pierre" (Ph.D. diss., New York University, 1998). For a reading of the novel's "narrative landscapes" as an unresolved effort to imagine a republican social space that ultimately leaves "old values," including colonial ones, in place, see Doris Y. Kadish, "Exiled in Exotic Lands: *Paul et Virginie* and *Atala*," in *The Literature of Images: Narrative Landscape from Julie to Jane Eyre* (New Brunswick, N.J.: Rutgers University Press, 1987), 53–70.

12. See Auguste Toussaint, *A History of the Indian Ocean,* trans. June Guicharnaud (Chicago: University of Chicago Press, 1966); *A History of Mauritius,* trans. W. E. F. Ward (London: Macmillan, 1977); *Le mirage des îles: le négoce français aux mascareignes au XVIIIe siècle* (Aix-en-Provence: Édisud, 1977); *L'Océan Indien au XVIIIe siècle* (Paris: Flammarion, 1974), and *La Route des Îles: contribution à l'histoire maritime des Mascareignes* (Paris: S.E.V.P.E.N., 1967).

13. Bernardin de Saint-Pierre, *Paul et Virginie,* 77: "J'ai tâché d'y peindre un sol et des végétaux différents de ceux de l'Europe."

14. Auguste Toussaint, "Entreprises Agricoles" in *Le Mirage des îles,* 101–28.

15. Jacques-Henri-Bernardin de Saint-Pierre, *Voyage à l'Isle de France,* ed. Robert Chaudenson (Ile Maurice: Éditions de l'Océan Indien, 1986), 181: "Le gouvernement a fait apporter la plupart des plantes, des arbres & des animaux que je vais décrire. Quelques habitants y ont contribué, entre autres MM. de Cossigni, Poivre, Hermans, & le Juge." The spelling of *l'Île de France* varies in both historical and contemporary usage. Bernardin de Saint-Pierre's account of his travels was first published by Merlin in 1773, and the editions are not consistent in their orthography. None of the current editions of Bernardin de Saint-Pierre's travel narrative resolve the question of how to handle variations in orthography in the same way. While the Chaudenson edition uses "l'Isle de France," the 1996 publication edited by L'abbé Ducrocq employs "l'île de France," and the 1983 edition introduced by Yves Bénot chooses to modernize the orthography by utilizing "l'Ile de France" with and without a circumflex over the "I." See Jacques-Henri-Bernardin de Saint-Pierre, *Voyage à l'Île de France, Un officier du roi à l'île Maurice, 1768–1770,* ed. Yves Bénot (Paris: La Découverte/Maspero, 1983) and Jacques-Henri-Bernardin de Saint-Pierre, *Voyage à l'île de France* in Bernardin de Saint-Pierre, Thomi Pitot, et L'abbé Ducrocq, *Ile de France: Voyage et Controverses* (Ile Maurice: Éditions AlmA, 1996). The page numbers in the footnotes to this chapter refer to the Chaudenson edition, and I have, therefore, retained that volume's spelling of the title *Voyage à l'Isle de France* in my citations to that edition of the text. As "l'Île de France" is one of the more commonly used spellings in current scholarship on eighteenth-century French colonial empire, on the works of Bernardin de Saint-Pierre, and on the history of Île Maurice or Mauritius, I make use of that spelling throughout the analysis and discussion that form the body of the chapter.

16. Bernardin de Saint-Pierre, *Voyage à l'Isle de France,* 188–89.

17. Bernardin de Saint-Pierre, *Paul et Virginie,* 126: "Le pain du méchant remplit la bouche de gravier."

18. Ibid., 182.

19. Homi Bhabha, "Signs Taken for Wonders: Questions of Ambivalence and Authority under a Tree outside Delhi, May 1817," in *The Location of Culture* (London: Routledge, 1994), 102–22.

20. Bernardin de Saint-Pierre, *Voyage à l'Isle de France,* 138.

21. Bernardin de Saint-Pierre, *Paul et Virginie,* 139.

22. Bernardin de Saint-Pierre, *Paul et Virginie,* 142: "Chaque site recevait de son végétal sa parure naturelle."

23. For Bernardin de Saint-Pierre's characterization of Africans as an inherently inferior race, see his *Études de nature* (Paris, 1792), 487–92. On climate theories of difference, see, for example, Henry Vyverberg, *Human Nature, Cultural Diversity, and the French Enlightenment* (New York: Oxford University Press, 1989), 64–87.

24. For a discussion of the imagined garden of Paul and Virginie in the context of metropolitan European landscaping, see Ingrid Kisliuk, "Le symbolisme du jardin et l'imagination créatrice chez Rousseau, Bernardin de Saint-Pierre et Chateaubriand," *Studies on Voltaire and the Eighteenth Century* 185 (1980): 297–418.

25. Bernardin de Saint-Pierre, *Paul et Virginie,* 144: "Que si cette inscription est de quelque nation ancienne qui ne subsiste plus, elle étend notre âme dans les champs de l'infini, et lui donne le sentiment de son immortalité, en lui montrant qu'une pensée a survécu à la ruine même d'un empire."

26. Ibid., 221.

27. See Janine Baudry, "Un Aspect mauricien de l'oeuvre de Bernardin de Saint-Pierre: La Flore locale," *Revue d'Histoire Littéraire de la France* 89 (1989): 782–90. On Bernardin de Saint-Pierre's use of the discourses of botany, see also Jean-Jacques Simon, *Bernardin de Saint-Pierre ou le triomphe de flore* (Paris: Éditions A.-G. Nizet, 1967).

28. Bernardin de Saint-Pierre, *Paul et Virginie,* 222: "Ô arbre dont la postérité existe encore dans nos bois, je vous ai vu moi-même avec plus d'intérêt et de vénération que les arcs de triomphe des Romains! Puisse la nature, qui détruit chaque jour les monuments de l'ambition des rois, multiplier dans nos forêt ceux de la bienfaisance d'une jeune et pauvre fille."

29. Bernardin de Saint-Pierre, *Voyage à l'Isle de France,* 354.

30. Jacques-Henri Bernardin de Saint-Pierre, *Études de nature,* 377: "Certainement si j'avais quelque souhait a faire pour perpetuer mon nom, j'aimerais mieux le voir porté par un fruit en France que par une île en Amérique."

31. For the history of French colonial botanical enterprise in the Mascareignes, see Madeleine Ly-Tio-Fane, *Mauritius and the Spice Trade: The Odyssey of Pierre Poivre* (Port Louis, Mauritius: Esclapon Limited, 1958) and *Mauritius and the Spice Trade: The Triumph of Jean Nicolas Céré and His Isle Bourbon Collaborators* (Paris: Mouton & Co and École Pratique des Hautes Études, 1970).

32. Bernardin de Saint-Pierre, *Paul et Virginie,* 255: "les pâles violettes de la mort" and "les roses de la pudeur."

33. Ibid, 271: "a subi le sort réservé à la naissance, à la beauté, et aux empires mêmes."

34. Ibid., 46: "Comme deux bourgeons qui restent sur deux arbres de la même espèce, dont la tempête a brisé toutes les branches, viennent à produire des fruits plus doux, si chacun d'eux, détaché du tronc maternel, est greffé sur le tronc voisin; ainsi ces deux petits enfants, privés de tous leurs parents, se remplissaient de sentiments plus tendres que ceux de fils et de fille, de frère et de soeur, quand ils venaient à être changés de mamelles par les deux amies qui leur avaient donné le jour."

35. On the diffusion of the story of *Paul et Virginie* in print and visual culture, see Paul Toinet, *Paul et Virginie: Répertoire bibliographique et iconographique* (Paris: G.-P. Maisonneuve et Larose, 1963). For information relating to Schall, consult André Girodie, *Jean-Frédéric Schall, Strasbourg 1752–Paris 1825* (Strasbourg: Compagnie Alsacienne des Arts Photomécaniques, 1927), 30, 59.

36. On the uses of antislavery rhetoric in discourses that ultimately worked in support of the French colonial system, see Michèle Duchet, *Anthropologie et histoire au siècle des lumières* (Paris: Flammarion, 1977) and Louis Sala-Molins, *Les misères des lumières: sous la raison, l'outrage* (Paris: Éditions Robert Laffont, 1992).

37. See Marcus Wood, *Blind Memory: Visual Representation of Slavery in England and America 1780–1865* (New York: Routledge, 2000), 22–23, and Albert Boime, *Art in an Age of Revolution, 1750–1800* (Chicago: University of Chicago Press, 1987), 212, 307.

38. See Anthony Pagden, *Lords of All the World: Ideologies of Empire in Spain, Britain, and France, c. 1500–c. 1800* (New Haven, Conn.: Yale University Press, 1995), 145, and Pierre Pluchon, *Histoire de la colonisation française: le premier empire colonial des origines à la Restauration*, vol. 1 (Paris: Fayard, 1991), 900.

39. Bernardin de Saint-Pierre, *Paul et Virginie*, 109: "Hélas! il n'en reste encore que trop pour mon souvenir! Le temps, qui détruit si rapidement les monuments des empires, semble respecter dans ces déserts ceux de l'amitié, pour perpétuer mes regrets jusqu'à la fin de ma vie."

40. Michel Foucault, "Of Other Spaces," trans. Jay Miskowiec, in *The Visual Culture Reader*, ed. Nicholas Mirzoeff (London: Routledge, 1998), 237–44. First published in English as "Of Other Spaces," trans. Jay Miskowiec, *Diacritics* 16, no. 1 (1986): 22–27. Originally published as "Des Espaces Autres," *Architecture, mouvement et continuité*, no. 5 (Octobre 1984).

41. Foucault, "Of Other Spaces," 242.

42. Ibid., 244.

43. Ibid., 243.

T W E N T Y : South Seas Trade and the Character of Captains

1. *Mutiny on the Bounty* (Lewis Milestone, Metro-Goldwyn-Mayer, U.S., 1962).

2. David Hume, *Treatise of Human Nature*, ed. L. A. Selby-Bigge (Oxford: Clarendon Press, 1928), 457–58.

3. Ibid., 534.

4. Adam Smith, *The Theory of Moral Sentiments*, eds. D. D. Raphael and A.L. MacFie (Oxford: Clarendon Press, 1976), 152.

5. Ibid., 137.

6. Thomas L. Haskell, "Capitalism and the Origins of the Humanitarian Sensibility," *American Historical Review* 90, no. 2 (April 1985): 339–61, and no. 3 (June 1985): 547–66.

7. Ibid., 562.

8. Edwin Cannan, ed., *The Wealth of Nations*, 2 vols. (Chicago: University of Chicago Press, 1976), 1:14.

9. Ibid., 2:782.

10. J. C. Beaglehole, *The Life of Captain James Cook* (Stanford: Stanford University Press, 1974), 698.

11. Anna Seward, *Elegy on Captain Cook* (London, 1781), ll. 35, 41, 43, 267.

12. *A Catalogue of the different specimens of cloth collected in the three voyages of Captain Cook to the Southern Hemisphere* (London, 1787), [1].

13. David Samwell, *A Narrative of the Death of Captain James Cook* (London, 1786), 27.

14. James King, *The Death of James Cook* (Book Club of California, 1940), [6].

15. *The Journals of Captain James Cook on his Voyages of Discovery*, 4 vols., ed. J. C. Beaglehole (Cambridge: Cambridge University Press, 1955), 1:75. Hereafter referred to in the text as *Voyages*.

16. George Forster, *A Voyage Round the World in His Britannic Majesty's Sloop, Resolution,* 2 vols. (London, 1777), 2:71. Hereafter referred to in the text as *A Voyage.*

17. Smith, *Theory of Moral Sentiments,* 24.

18. Jonathan Lamb has argued that, in such moments, the European observer is the subject not of enlightened knowledge but of an unregulated free-floating intensity. See Lamb, "Minute Particulars and the Representation of South Pacific Discovery," *Eighteenth-Century Studies* 28, no. 3 (1995): 281–94.

19. Christine Holmes, ed., *Captain Cook's Second Voyage: The Journals of Lieutenants Elliott and Pickersgill* (London: Caliban Books, 1984), 17.

20. Ibid., 34.

21. Johann Forster, *The Resolution Journal of Johann Reinhold Forster, 1772–1775,* 4 vols., ed. Michael E. Hoare (London: Hakluyt Society, 1982), 2:314.

22. Ibid., 3:427.

23. J. C. Beaglehole, *Captain Cook and Captain Bligh: The W. E. Collins Lecture* (Wellington: Victoria University, 1967), 3.

24. William Bligh, *A Narrative of the Mutiny on Board His Majesty's Ship Bounty* (London, 1790), 9.

25. William Bligh, *A Voyage to the South Seas* (Adelaide: Griffin Press, 1975), 74. All subsequent references cited in the text.

26. William Bligh, *The Log of the Bounty,* 2 vols., ed. Owen Rutter (London: Golden Cockerel Press, 1936–37), 2:223. All subsequent references cited in the text.

27. "Letter to Sir Joseph Banks" (Safe 1/37), Mitchell Library, Sydney, Australia, quoted in Gavin Kennedy, *Captain Bligh: The Man and his Mutinies* (London: Duckworth, 1989), 182.

28. *The Journals of James Morrison* (London: Golden Cockerel Press, 1935), 35–36.

29. Ibid., 238.

30. Bligh, *A Narrative,* 9.

TWENTY-ONE: Voyaging the Past, Present, and Future: Historical Reenactments on HM Bark *Endeavour* and the Voyaging Canoe *Hokule'a* in the Sea of Islands

1. Sir Francis Drake, *The World Encompassed* (London: Nicholas Bourne, 1628).

2. J. H. Parry, *The Discovery of the Sea* (London: Weidenfeld and Nicolson, 1974).

3. Stephen Halliwell, *Aristotle's Poetics* (Chapel Hill: University of North Carolina Press, 1986), 23–25; Greg Dening, "The Theatricality of History-Making and the Paradoxes of Acting," *Cultural Anthropology* 8 (1993): 73–95; Stuart B. Schwarz, ed., *Implicit Understandings* (Cambridge: Cambridge University Press, 1994), 451–83.

4. David Lowenthal, *The Past is a Foreign Country* (Cambridge: Cambridge University Press, 1985). For the anthropological debate on historical reenactment, see Richard Handler and William Saxton, "Dyssimulation: Reflexivity, Narrative, and the Quest for Authenticity in 'Living History,'" *Cultural Anthropology* 3 (1988): 242–60.

5. Greg Dening, *Mr Bligh's Bad Language: Passion, Power and Theatre on the Bounty* (New York: Cambridge University Press, 1992); *The Death of William Gooch: A History's Anthropology* (Honolulu: University of Hawai'i Press, 1995); "The Battle of Valparaiso, 1814," in *Performances* (Chicago: University of Chicago Press, 1996), 79–88; "The Theatricalities of Derring-Do" in *Readings/Writings* (Melbourne: Melbourne University Press, 1998).

6. See William Falconer, *Falconer's Celebrated Marine Dictionary: The Wooden Walls*, ed. Claude S. Gill (London: W. and G. Foyle, 1930); Peter D. Jeans, *Ship to Shore* (Santa Barbara, Calif.: ABC-Clio, 1993).

7. Joseph Conrad quoted J. H. Parry, "Sailors' English," *Cambridge Journal* 2 (1948–49): 660–70.

8. Herman Melville, *White Jacket or The World in a Man-of-War* (1850; reprint, Oxford: Oxford University Press, 1966); R. H. Dana, *Two Years Before the Mast or A Sailor's Life at Sea* (1840; reprint, London: Arrow, 1964); Charles Nordhoff, *Man-of-War Life: A Boy's Experience in the United States Navy, During a Voyage Around the World in a Ship-of-the-Line* (1855; reprint, Annapolis: Naval Institute Press, 1985); Alan Villiers, *Captain Cook, The Seamen's Seaman: A Study of the Great Discoverer* (Harmondsworth: Penguin, 1967).

9. Ray Parkin, *HM Bark* Endeavour: *Her Place in Australian History* (Melbourne: Melbourne University Press, 1997), presents the most complete physical description of the *Endeavour* and embroiders it with exquisite drawings. These days, however, one can move through the *Endeavour* and read the journals at the same time on CD-ROM (*Captain Cook's Journal 1768–71* Endeavour, National Library of Australia, 1999: ISBN0642 106924); Peter Petroff, *Sailing* Endeavour (Fremantle: Maritime Heritage Press, 1994).

10. Trevenen's quote is to be found in *The Journals of Captain James Cook*, vol. 3, *The Voyage of the Resolution and Discovery*, ed. J. C. Beaglehole (Cambridge: Hakluyt Society, 1967), cliii.

11. Thor Heyerdahl, *The Kontiki Expedition* (London: Allen and Unwin, 1951); *The American Indians in the Pacific* (London: Allen and Unwin, 1952); *Aku Aku: The Secret of Easter Island* (London: Allen and Unwin, 1958).

12. Andrew Sharp, *Ancient Voyagers in the Pacific* (Wellington: Polynesian Society, 1956).

13. Greg Dening, "Ancient Voyagers in the Pacific," *Historical Studies* 10 (1960): 322–28.

14. Harold Gatty, *The Raft Book: The Lore of the Sea and Sky* (New York: Grady Press, 1943).

15. Marshall Sahlins, "Esoteric Efflorescence on Easter Island," *American Anthropologist* 57 (1955): 1045–52.

16. Ben R. Finney, "Surfing in Ancient Hawaii," *Journal of the Polynesian Society* 68 (1959): 327–47; Ben Finney and James B. Houston, *Surfing: A History of the Ancient Hawaiian Sport* (San Francisco: Pomegranate Artbooks, 1996).

17. Ben Finney, *Voyage of Discovery: A Cultural Odyssey through Polynesia* (Berkeley: University of California Press, 1994).

18. Alan Moorhead, *The Fatal Impact: An Account of the Invasion of the South Pacific 1767–1840* (New York: Harper and Row, 1966).

19. For the debate on these issues in the Pacific, see Roger M. Keesing, "Creating the Past: Custom and Identity in the Contemporary Pacific," *The Contemporary Pacific* 1 (1989): 19–42; Haunani-Kay Trask, "Natives and Anthropologists: The Colonial Struggle," *The Contemporary Pacific* 3 (1991): 159–69; Roger M. Keesing, "Reply to Trask," *The Contemporary Pacific* 3 (1991): 168–71.

20. Homi Bhabha, *The Location of Culture* (New York: Routledge, 1994); Gayatri Chakravorty Spivak, "Can the Subaltern Speak?" in *Marxism and the Interpretation of Culture*, ed. Cary Nelson and Lawrence Grossberg (Urbana: University of Illinois Press, 1988), 271–313.

21. Ben R. Finney, *Hokule'a: The Way to Tahiti* (New York: Dodd, Mead and Company, 1979); Will Kyselka, *An Ocean in Mind* (Honolulu: University of Hawai'i Press, 1987).

22. Mike Lefroy, *The Replica of H M Bark* Endeavour: *The Story So Far, 1987–1994* (Fremantle: Endeavour Bark Foundation, 1994).

23. J. C. Beaglehole, *The Life of Captain James Cook* (Stanford: Stanford University Press, 1974).

Cook's voyages of discovery—their records, their art, and their maps are described in the following works: *Journals of Captain Cook on his Voyages of Discovery*, 3 vols., ed. J. C. Beaglehole (Cambridge: Hakluyt Society, 1967–69); Rüdiger Joppien and Bernard Smith, *The Art of Captain Cook's Voyages*, 3 vols. (Melbourne: Oxford University Press, 1985–87); Andrew David, Rüdiger Joppien, and Bernard Smith, eds., *The Charts and Coastal Views of Captain Cook's Voyages*, 3 vols. (Oxford: Hakluyt Society, 1988–97).

24. See Chris Healy, *From the Ruins of Colonialism: History as Social Memory* (Cambridge: Cambridge University Press, 1997); Chris Healy, "Captain Cook between White and Black" and Paddy Fordham Warnburrunga, "Too Many Captain Cooks," in *The Oxford Companion to Aboriginal Art and Culture*, ed. Sylvia Kleinert and Margo Neale (Oxford: Oxford University Press, 2000), 92–96; Anne Salmond, *Two Worlds: First Meetings between Maori and Europeans 1642–1772* (Auckland: Viking, 1991).

25. See Finney, *Hokule'a*, 3–6; Kyselka, *An Ocean in Mind*, 14–16. For the sources of Hawaiian confidence in their rituals, see Mary Kawena Pukui, E. W. Hastings, and Catherine A. Lee, *Nana I Ke Kumu (Look to the Source)*, 2 vols. (Honolulu: Hui Hanai, 1972); Samuel Manaiakalani Kamakau, *Ka Po'e Kahiko (The People of Old)* (Honolulu: Bishop Museum, 1964); David Malo, *Moolelo Hawaii (Hawaiian Antiquities)* (Honolulu: Bishop Museum, 1951).

26. For the debate and discourse on the placing of Moana in the mind and imagination of the people of the islands, see Epeli Hau'ofa, *A New Oceania: Rediscovery of our Sea of Islands* (Suva: University of South Pacific, 1993); Epeli Hau'ofa, "Our Sea of Islands," *The Contemporary Pacific* 6 (1994): 147–61; "The Ocean in Us," *The Contemporary Pacific* 10 (1998): 391–410.

27. Quoted with permission of the National Library of Australia from Peter Cochrane, ed., *Remarkable Occurrences: The National Library of Australia's First Hundred Years, 1901–2001* (Canberra: National Library of Australia, 2001).

28. Thomas Gladwin, *East Is a Big Bird: Navigation and Logic on Puluwait Atoll* (Cambridge: Harvard University Press, 1970); David Lewis, *We, the Navigators: The Ancient Art of Landfalling in the Pacific* (Canberra: ANU Press, 1972); Greg Dening, "The Geographical Knowledge of the Polynesians and the Nature of Inter-Island Contact," in *Polynesian Navigation*, ed. Jack Golson (Wellington: Polynesian Society, 1962), 132–53.

29. Michael R. Levison, Gerard Ward, and John W. Webb, *The Settlement of Polynesia: A Computer Simulation* (Minneapolis: University of Minnesota Press, 1972).

30. Geoffrey Irwin, *The Prehistoric Exploration and Colonisation of the Pacific* (Cambridge: Cambridge University Press, 1992).

31. All that I tell of Nainoa here comes to me from Finney, *Voyage of Discovery*, and Kyselka, *An Ocean in Mind*. Kind permission has been given to me to quote from the transcripts of conversations with Nainoa in Kyselka, *An Ocean in Mind*.

32. For a full description of this occasion, its contradictions and its fuller meaning, see Ben Finney, "The Sin at Awarua," *The Contemporary Pacific* 11 (1999): 1–33.

About the Contributors

Robert Batchelor teaches history at Georgia Southern University. He is currently working on a book about China, London, and gardens in the seventeenth and eighteenth centuries. He has presented papers on the orangery, the tea table, and the coffeehouse and is the author of a forthcoming article on Leibniz.

Laura Brown is a member of the English Department at Cornell University. Her most recent book is *Fables of Modernity: Literature and Culture in the English Eighteenth Century* (Cornell University Press, 2001). Among her other writings are *Ends of Empire: Women and Ideology in Early Eighteenth-Century English Literature* (Cornell, 1993) and *Alexander Pope* (Blackwell, 1985).

Vincent Carretta, a professor of English at the University of Maryland, has published separate Penguin editions of the complete works of Olaudah Equiano (1995, revised and expanded 2003), Ignatius Sancho (1998), Quobna Ottobah Cugoano (1999), and Phillis Wheatley (2001). Among his other writings are *George III and the Satirists from Hogarth to Byron* (University of Georgia Press, 1990); and *Unchained Voices: An Anthology of Black Authors in the English-Speaking World of the Eighteenth Century* (University Press of Kentucky, 1996). Most recently he has co-edited, with Philip Gould, *Genius in Bondage: Literature of the Early Black Atlantic* (University Press of Kentucky, 2001).

Jill Casid is an assistant professor of Visual Culture Studies in the Department of Art History at the University of Wisconsin–Madison. Her chapter in this volume forms part of the larger book project, "Sowing Empire: Landscape and Colonization in the Eighteenth Century," to be published by the University of Minnesota Press. She is currently working on a book, "Necromancy of Observance: The Magic Lantern and Technologies of Projection, 1650–1850." Her interest in developing the transnational study of visual culture extends to the anthology she is planning for Routledge on "Visual Transculture."

Linda Colley is a Fellow of the British Academy and currently Leverhulme Research Professor and School Professor in History at the London School of Economics. In 2003 she becomes Shelby M. C. Davis 1958 Professor of History at Princeton University. She has published *In Defiance of Oligarchy: The Tory Party 1714–1760* (Cambridge University Press, 1982), *Britons: Forging the Nation 1707–1837* (Yale University Press, 1992), and *Captives: Britain, Empire, and the World 1600–1850* (Jonathan Cape, 2002).

Greg Dening has written some dozen books on "double-visioned" eighteenth-century histories of Oceania—historical ethnographies and ethnographic histories of both sides of Pacific island beaches. *Islands and Beaches* (Melbourne University Press, 1980), *Mr Bligh's Bad Language* (Cambridge University Press, 1992), *The Death of William Gooch* (University of Hawai'i, 1995), and *Performances* (University of Chicago Press, 1996) are samples of his work. In his retirement as an adjunct professor at the Centre for Cross-Cultural Research, Australian National University, he conducts postgraduate workshops called "Challenges to Perform."

Rod Edmond is Reader in Nineteenth Century and Postcolonial Studies at the University of Kent at Canterbury. His writing includes *Affairs of the Hearth: Victorian Poetry and Domestic Narrative* (1988) and *Representing the South Pacific: Colonial Discourse from Cook to Gauguin* (1997). He is co-editing a volume, *Islands: History, Theory, Writing* to be published by Routledge in 2003, and is currently writing a book on colonialism and disease, with particular reference to leprosy.

Matthew Edney is an associate professor of geography-anthropology and American and New England Studies, at the University of Southern Maine, Portland. He is the author of *Mapping an Empire: The Geographical Construction of British India, 1765–1843* (University of Chicago Press, 1997), and is co-editor of *Cartography in the European Enlightenment,* in preparation as volume 4 of *The History of Cartography,* a series edited by David Woodward for the University of Chicago Press.

Carole Fabricant teaches in the English Department at the University of California, Riverside. The author of *Swift's Landscape* (Johns Hopkins University Press, 1982; reissued by University of Notre Dame Press, 1995), she has published numerous essays on eighteenth-century, Irish, and postcolonial topics. She is currently editing *Jonathan Swift's Miscellaneous Prose* for Penguin Classics and *Swift's Irish Writings* for St. Martin's Press and is working on a book exploring the problems of colonial representation in eighteenth-century Ireland.

Peter Hulme is a professor in literature at the University of Essex. His most recent books are *Remnants of Conquest: The Island Caribs and their Visitors, 1877–1998* (Oxford University Press, 2000) and two co-edited projects: *"The Tempest" and Its Travels* (Reaktion Books, 2000) and the forthcoming *Cambridge Companion to Travel Writing* (Cambridge University Press). His chapter in this volume is part of a larger project on history and fiction in the Caribbean.

Betty Joseph is an associate professor of English at Rice University. The chapter in this volume is excerpted from a longer version in her book *The Imperial Patriarchive: Gender, History and Colonial Narratives, 1720–1840* (University of Chicago Press, 2003). Her work has appeared in *Genders, Criticism,* and *Tulsa Studies in Women and Literature,* among other journals. Her current book project is "Creolisms: Race and Hybridity in the Eighteenth Century."

Kay Dian Kriz is associate professor in the Department of History of Art and Architecture at Brown University. She is the author of *The Idea of the English Landscape Painter: Genius as Alibi in the Early Nineteenth Century* (Yale University Press, 1997) and is currently working on a book project, "Slavery, Sugar, and the Culture of Refinement," concerning visual culture and the British West Indies, 1700–1840.

Philip D. Morgan teaches history at the Johns Hopkins University and is a former editor of the *William and Mary Quarterly.* His book *Slave Counterpoint: Black Culture in the Eighteenth-Century Chesapeake and Low Country* (University of North Carolina Press, 1998) has won the American Historical Association's Albert J. Beveridge Award, the American Historical Association Wesley-Logan Prize, the Organization of American Historians Elliott Rudwick Prize, and the Bancroft Prize.

Anna Neill teaches English at the University of Kansas. She is the author of *British Discovery Literature and the Rise of Global Commerce* (Palgrave, 2002), which investigates science, state power, and mercantilism in discovery texts from the long eighteenth century. She has also published articles on travel literature and political philosophy in such journals as *Eighteenth-Century Studies, Women's Writing,* and *The Eighteenth Century: Theory and Interpretation.*

Felicity A. Nussbaum teaches at the University of California, Los Angeles. Her writing includes *The Autobiographical Subject* (Johns Hopkins University Press, 1989) and *Torrid Zones* (Johns Hopkins University Press, 1995) and *The New Eighteenth Century,* co-edited with Laura Brown (Methuen, 1987). Her most recent book, *The Limits of the Human: Fictions of Anomaly, Race, and Gender in the Long Eighteenth Century,* was published by Cambridge University Press in 2003.

Neil Rennie is a reader in English at University College London, the author of *Far-Fetched Facts: The Literature of Travel and the Idea of the South Seas* (Oxford University Press, 1995), and the editor of R. L. Stevenson's *In the South Seas* (Penguin Classics, 1998).

Joseph Roach, the Charles and Dorathea S. Dilley Professor of Theatre at Yale, has chaired the Department of Performance Studies at the Tisch School of the Arts at New York University and the interdisciplinary Ph.D. in Theatre at Northwestern University. He is the author of *The Player's Passion: Studies in the Science of Acting* (University of Delaware Press, 1993) and *Cities of the Dead: Circum-Atlantic Performance* (Columbia University Press, 1996), and co-editor, with Janelle Reinelt, of *Critical Theory and Performance* (University of Michigan Press, 1992).

Nicholas Rogers is a professor of history at York University, Toronto, and co-editor of the *Journal of British Studies* (2002–2007). He is the author of *Whigs and Cities: Popular Politics in the Age of Walpole and Pitt* (Oxford University Press, 1989), *Crowds, Culture and Politics in Georgian Britain* (Oxford University Press, 1998), and with Douglas Hay, *Eighteenth-Century English Society: Shuttles and Swords* (Oxford University Press, 1997). He is completing a book on naval impressment in the eighteenth century.

Benjamin Schmidt teaches early modern history at the University of Washington, Seattle. He has written widely on Europe's encounter with the non-European world in the sixteenth through the eighteenth centuries. His publications include *Innocence Abroad: The Dutch Imagination and the New World* (Cambridge University Press, 2001) and (as editor) Sir Walter Raleigh, *The Discoveries of the Large, Rich and Bewtiful Empyre of Guiana* (forthcoming from Bedford/St. Martin's). His current book project, "Inventing Exoticism," explores geography and globalism.

Kate Teltscher, a senior lecturer in the School of English and Modern Languages at the University of Surrey, Roehampton, is the author of *India Inscribed:*

European and British Writing on India: 1600–1800 (Oxford University Press, 1995). She undertook her doctoral research at Oxford University and has published widely on colonial discourse and travel writing. She is currently working on a biography of George Bogle.

Beth Fowkes Tobin, professor of English at Arizona State University, previously taught at the University of Hawai'i, Manoa. Her books include *Picturing Imperial Power: Colonial Subjects in Eighteenth-Century British Painting* (Duke University Press, 1999) and *Superintending the Poor: Charitable Ladies and Paternal Landlords in British Fiction, 1770–1860* (Yale University Press, 1993). The editor of Eliza Haywood's *Betsy Thoughtless* (Oxford University Press, 1997), she is currently working on the representation of the tropics in the late eighteenth century.

Glyndwr Williams, Emeritus Professor of History at Queen Mary, University of London, specializes in the history of exploration, especially of the Pacific and North America. Among his recent publications are *The Great South Sea: English Voyages and Encounters* (Yale University Press, 1997), *Captain Cook's Voyages 1768–1779* (Folio Society, 1997), *The Prize of All the Oceans: The Triumph and Tragedy of Anson's Voyage Round the World* (HarperCollins, 1999), and *Voyages of Delusion: The Northwest Passage in the Age of Reason* (HarperCollins, 2002).

Index

3m

DATE DUE

ILL: 56093631			9/7/09
GAYLORD			PRINTED IN U.S.A.